T0229513

BEST PRACTICES SERIES

Business Continuity Planning

Protecting Your Organization's Life

THE AUERBACH
BEST PRACTICES SERIES

Broadband Networking,
James Trulove, Editor,
ISBN: 0-8493-9821-5

Business Continuity Planning,
Ken Doughty, Editor,
ISBN: 0-8493-0907-7

Designing a Total Data Solution: Technology, Implementation, and Deployment,
Roxanne E. Burkey and
Charles V. Breakfield, Editors,
ISBN: 0-8493-0893-3

High Performance Web Databases: Design, Development, and Deployment,
Sanjiv Purba, Editor,
ISBN: 0-8493-0882-8

Electronic Messaging,
Nancy Cox, Editor,
ISBN: 0-8493-9825-8

Enterprise Systems Integration,
John Wyzalek, Editor,
ISBN: 0-8493-9837-1

Financial Services Information Systems, Jessica Keyes, Editor,
ISBN: 0-8493-9834-7

Healthcare Information Systems, Phillip L. Davidson, Editor,
ISBN: 0-8493-9963-7

Internet Management,
Jessica Keyes, Editor,
ISBN: 0-8493-9987-4

Multi-Operating System Networking: Living with UNIX, NetWare, and NT, Raj Rajagopal,
Editor, ISBN: 0-8493-9831-2

Network Design, Gilbert Held,
Editor, ISBN: 0-8493-0859-3

Network Manager's Handbook,
John Lusa, Editor,
ISBN: 0-8493-9841-X

Project Management,
Paul C. Tinnirello, Editor,
ISBN: 0-8493-9998-X

Server Management,
Gilbert Held, Editor,
ISBN: 0-8493-9823-1

Web-to-Host Connectivity,
Lisa Lindgren and Anura Guruge,
Editors, ISBN: 0-8493-0835-6

Winning the Outsourcing Game: Making the Best Deals and Making Them Work,
Janet Butler, Editor,
ISBN: 0-8493-0875-5

AUERBACH PUBLICATIONS

www.auerbach-publications.com
TO ORDER: Call: 1-800-272-7737 • Fax: 1-800-374-3401
E-mail: orders@crcpress.com

BEST PRACTICES SERIES

Business Continuity Planning

Protecting Your Organization's Life

Editor

KEN DOUGHTY

AUERBACH

Boca Raton   London   New York   Washington, D.C.

Chapter 2, "The Four Phases of Risk Realization," and Chapter 7, "Learning from a Crisis," ©Andrew Blades. Reprinted with permission.

Chapter 5, "Identifying a Crisis: A Critical Factor in Business Continuity Planning," ©Steve York. Reprinted with permission.

Chapter 8, "Plans to Rehearse the Crisis – Before the Crisis Tests the Organization," ©Steve York and Angus Graham. Reprinted with permission.

Chapter 10, "Trauma: The Forgotten Factor," ©Steve Watt and David Ball. Reprinted with permission.

Chapter 13, "Trials and Tribulations of Business Continuity Planning," ©Steve Watt and David Ball. Reprinted with permission.

Library of Congress Cataloging-in-Publication Data

Doughty, Ken
    Business continuity planning : protecting your organization's life / Ken Doughty.
      p. cm. -- (Best practices series)
    Includes bibliographical references and index.
    ISBN 0-8493-0907-7 (alk. paper)
      1. Crisis management. 2. Risk management. 3. Database management. I. Title. II. Best practices series (Boca Raton, Fla.)

HD49 .D688 2000
658.4'056--dc21

00-044202

© 2001 by CRC Press LLC
Auerbach is an imprint of CRC Press LLC

No claim to original U.S. Government works
International Standard Book Number 0-8493-0907-7
Library of Congress Card Number 00-044202
Printed in the United States of America   3 4 5 6 7 8 9 0
Printed on acid-free paper

Contributors

C. WARREN AXELROD, PH.D., *Senior Vice President, Corporate Information Systems, Carroll McEntee & McGinley, Inc., Great Neck, New York*

DAVID BALL, *Director, Finance and Administration, Intech Pacific Pty. Ltd., Mount Waverley, Australia*

ANDREW BLADES, *Lecturer, Security Science, Edith Cowan University, Perth, Australia*

JOANN BOZARTH, *Author and Principal, Menkus Associates, Manchester, Tennessee*

MICHAEL D. CANNON, CDRP, CISA, CIA, CCP, *Vice President and Manager of Corporate Contingency Planning, Boatmen's Bancshares, Inc., St. Louis, Missouri*

HOUSTON H. CARR, *Faculty Member, Department of Management, Auburn University, Auburn, Alabama*

STEVEN P. CRAIG, *Management Partner, Venture Resources Management Systems, Lake Forest, California*

MARK B. DESMAN, *Manager, Information Security, Micron Technology, Inc., Eagle, Idaho*

JOHN DORF, *Risk Management Consulting, Ernst & Young LLP, Chicago, Illinois*

KEN DOUGHTY, CISA, CBCP, *Manager, Disaster Recovery, Colonial, Sydney, Australia*

BRUCE EDWARDS, *Data Security Services Pty. Ltd., Willoughby, Australia*

FREDERICK GALLEGOS, CISA, CDE, CGFM, *Adjunct Professor, Computer Information Systems, California State Polytechnic University, Pomona, California*

ANGUS GRAHAM, *Business Risk Services Pty. Ltd., Sydney, Australia*

DOUGLAS B. HOYT, *Consultant and Writer, Hartsdale, New York*

CARL B. JACKSON, *Principal and National Service Leader, Business Continuity Planning, Ernst & Young LLP, Houston, Texas*

MERIDA L. JOHNS, PH.D., R.R.A., *Vice President, Education and Certification, American Health Information Management Association, Chicago, Illinois*

MARTY JOHNSON, *Information Systems Assurance & Advisory Systems, Ernst & Young, Chicago, Illinois*

JONATHAN R. KING, CDP, CISA, *ITAS Senior Associate, Coopers & Lybrand, Cleveland, Ohio*

DENISE JOHNSON MCMANUS, *Faculty Member, Department of Management, Auburn University, Auburn, Alabama*

Contents

Introduction   xi

SECTION I   THE NEED FOR BUSINESS CONTINUITY PLANNING . .   1

Chapter 1   Risk and the Need for Business Continuity Planning . . .   3
Denise Johnson McManus and Houston H. Carr

Chapter 2   The Four Phases of Risk Realization   11
Andrew Blades

Chapter 3   The Legal Issues of Business Continuity Planning   15
Tari Schreider

Chapter 4   Building a Culture for Business Continuity Planning . . .   21
Merida L. Johns

SECTION II   CRISIS MANAGEMENT   35

Chapter 5   Identifying a Crisis: A Critical Factor in Business
Continuity Planning   37
Steve York

Chapter 6   Crisis Management Planning   45
Mark B. Desman

Chapter 7   Learning from a Crisis   51
Andrew Blades

Chapter 8   Plan to Rehearse the Crisis — Before the Crisis Tests
the Organization.   57
Steve York and Angus Graham

Chapter 9   The Crisis Management Command Center   69
Mark B. Desman

Chapter 10   Trauma: The Forgotten Factor   73
Steve Watt and David Ball

Contents

SECTION III **BUSINESS CONTINUITY PLANNING**. 77

Chapter 11 Overview of Business Continuity Planning. 79
Sally Meglathery

Chapter 12 Corporate Contingency Planning. 97
Michael D. Cannon

Chapter 13 Business Continuity Planning: Trials
and Tribulations. 109
Steve Watts

Chapter 14 The Business Impact Assessment Process. 115
Carl B. Jackson

Chapter 15 Selecting the Right Business Continuity Planning
Strategies. 131
Ken Doughty

Chapter 16 Business Continuity in the Distributed
Environment 141
Steven P. Craig

Chapter 17 Details Overlooked in Contingency Plans. 161
Jonathan R. King

Chapter 18 Restoration Component of Business Continuity
Planning. 169
John Dorf and Marty Johnson

Chapter 19 Systems and Communications Security during
Recovery and Repair 183
C. Warren Axelrod

SECTION IV **BUSINESS CONTINUITY PLANNING
FOR COMMUNICATIONS** 193

Chapter 20 Network Business Continuity Planning. 195
Nathan J. Muller

Chapter 21 Business Recovery Planning for Communications 217
Leo A. Wrobel

Chapter 22 Documenting a Communications Recovery Plan. 227
Leo A. Wrobel

Chapter 23 Adding Communications Network Support
to Existing Business Continuity Plans. 235
Leo A. Wrobel

SECTION V **MAINTENANCE AND TESTING OF BUSINESS CONTINUITY PLANS** 243

Chapter 24 Strategies for Developing and Testing Business Continuity Plans 245
Kenneth A. Smith

Chapter 25 Maintenance and Update of Business Continuity Plans 263
Ken Doughty

Chapter 26 Testing Business Continuity Plans 273
Leo A. Wrobel

Chapter 27 Changes that Could Affect the IS Business Continuity Plan 281
JoAnn Bozarth and Belden Menkus

SECTION VI **BUSINESS CONTINUITY MANAGER'S TOOL KIT** 289

Chapter 28 Business Continuity Planning Tools and Management Options 291
Jon William Toigo

Chapter 29 Choosing a Hot-Site Vendor 303
Philip Jan Rothstein

Chapter 30 A Proactive Approach to Improving the IS Business Continuity Plan 317
Belden Menkus

Chapter 31 Reengineering the Business Continuity Planning Process 323
Carl B. Jackson

Chapter 32 Backup: The Forgotten Essential 341
Bruce Edwards

SECTION VII **AUDITOR'S PERSPECTIVE OF BUSINESS CONTINUITY PLANNING** 347

Chapter 33 Using Audit Resources in IT Business Continuity Planning 349
JoAnn Bozarth and Belden Menkus

Chapter 34 How IS Auditors Can Enhance Business Continuity Planning 359
Douglas B. Hoyt

Contents

Chapter 35   Auditing Contingency and Business Continuity
Planning. 373
Fred Gallegos and Karen Seketa

INDEX 385

Introduction

Business Continuity Planning: Protecting Your Organization's Life

Ken Doughty, CISA, CBCP

THE DEVELOPMENT AND IMPLEMENTATION OF BUSINESS CONTINUITY MANAGEMENT IS AN INTEGRAL PART OF RUNNING AN EFFECTIVE ORGANIZATION IN TODAY'S WORLD. Business Continuity Management is a term that broadly covers the following areas:

- Business Resumption Planning
- Disaster Recovery Planning
- Crisis Management
- Business Continuity Planning

The Disaster Recovery Journal provides a definition for the terms listed in Exhibit 1.

The business continuity management process must embrace risk, emergency, and recovery planning if an organization is going to be able to manage a crisis or disaster event and have any hope of returning to business-as-usual operations. Undertaking any of the above business continuity activities should form part of a wider planning structure and process and is not an end in itself, but rather a means to an end.

Business Resumption, Disaster Recovery, and Business Continuity Plans are being appreciated by those organizations that have suffered a disaster event, executed the plan, and survived.

Today, business continuity plans (BCP) are no longer a luxury, but an essential element of the organization's risk management program. For many organizations, the decision to invest in a BCP is being forced upon them, for example, via change in accountability either by legislation, by third parties,

Exhibit 1. Terms from *The Disaster Recovery Journal*

Business resumption planning	The operations piece of business continuity planning. *Also see* Disaster recovery planning.
Disaster recovery planning	The technological aspect of business continuity planning. The advance planning and preparations, which are necessary to minimize loss and ensure continuity of the critical business functions of an organization in the event of disaster. Similar terms: contingency planning; business resumption planning; corporate contingency planning; business interruption planning; disaster preparedness.
Crisis management	The overall coordination of an organization's response to a crisis, in an effective, timely manner, with the goal of avoiding or minimizing damage to the organization's profitability, reputation, or ability to operate.
Business continuity planning (BCP)	An all-encompassing, "umbrella" term covering both disaster recovery planning and business resumption planning.

or the occurrence of a disaster or near disaster. As an example, the U.S. Controller of Currency enacted legislation on January 1, 1989, requiring federally chartered financial institutions to have a demonstrable BCP.

The imposed change in accountability by legislation has made managers of corporations personally susceptible to action at law (e.g., from shareholders) for failing to carry out their fiduciary duties. For many organizations, however, senior executives have either ignored or deferred the investment in business continuity, believing that a disaster would not strike their organization.

Studies of organizations in the United States that have experienced a disaster have shown that over 40 percent of the organizations struck by a serious disaster never resume operations. Over 25 percent of those that do manage to open their doors again are so weakened that they close down permanently within three years.

Recent surveys have indicated that:

- 92 percent of Internet businesses are not prepared for a computer system disaster (*Source:* IBM survey of 226 business recovery corporate managers).
- 82 percent of companies are not prepared to handle a computer system disaster (*Source:* Comdisco 1997 Vulnerability Index Research Report).

DEVELOPING A BCP ENVIRONMENT

Developing a BCP environment or culture in any organization is a significant undertaking, particularly if the organization has traditionally seen

BCP as an information technology (IT) issue and not an organization-wide issue. IT is only one of many dependencies the organization has in the delivery of its products and services.

Many organizations fail to develop a BCP culture because there is a perception that it is a process that is too costly, time-consuming, and requires a large amount of resources that could otherwise be employed in the generation of revenue. Management must be assured that by investing in BCP, it is protecting the organization's life and it makes good business sense.

As stated previously, government legislation, insurance requirements, and the threat of litigation from third parties has forced executive management to recognize the need to take action to develop a BCP. However, this does not mean that the organization will develop and continue to support a BCP culture.

Management often needs to be "educated" that the aim of BCP is to keep the organization in business in the event of a disaster by maintaining its critical core processes in the delivery of products and services to its internal and external customers. It is important that once it has been recognized that BCP is a critical component of the organization's risk management program, that the organizational management continues this recognition.

The external operating environment has an influence on the development of a BCP culture. For example, if the organization is operating in a dynamic environment where the market is constantly changing through new products and IT services, then resourcing and commitment to BCP will suffer as management is focusing its energy on meeting the challenge of remaining competitive.

For many organizations today, growth is being achieved through acquisition rather than organic growth. Management must take into consideration the BCP issues of purchasing other companies. The recovery strategies that have been developed and implemented for the existing organizational critical business processes may not necessarily apply to the "acquired" part of the business.

It is unrealistic for management to expect requests for additional BCP resources (i.e., human and financial) to address the recovery issues of these additional business processes or changes to existing business processes due to organizational growth. It would be unfortunate for management to view the request as an additional cost of acquisition and thus reducing the potential cost-savings and future earnings of acquisition.

Management's failure to recognize that through acquisition the organization's exposure to a disaster event may significantly increase. Management needs to recognize that additional resources for BCP activities may be required to ensure that the increase in exposure is reduced to an acceptable level.

To develop and sustain a BCP culture will require commitment and funding from all levels of management throughout the organization to nurture and sustain this environment. The achievement of a proactive BCP environment can be facilitated through the continued support of a senior executive who will act as the BCP "champion." The development of tactical and strategic plans will also help to sustain a positive BCP culture. These plans may include:

- BCP as part of:
  — the organization's change management processes
  — system development life cycle
  — corporate planning cycle
- development of BCP awareness program for:
  — new employees
  — lower, middle, and executive management
  — third-party service providers

RESOURCING BCP

For many organizations, once the BCP has been developed, the organization's executive management believes that its responsibility has been discharged. This is incorrect. In the event of a disaster, the likelihood of a cost-effective recovery in a timely manner depends on continued executive management support for the maintenance and updating of the BCP.

Executive management's commitment and support for BCP extends beyond issuing a policy on BCP and funding its initial development. Management commitment and support must encompass development of the infrastructure for the implementation of the policy and ongoing maintenance of the plan, as well as the ongoing provision of critical resources (financial and human).

Maintenance of the BCP is often seen as an impost onto an already overloaded employee. Competition with the existing day-to-day duties of this employee is one of the main reasons why the BCP is not maintained up-to-date. It is imperative that the necessary lines of communication be open, so that all relevant organizational changes are communicated to allow maintenance and updating of the plan.

Investing in a BCP is a difficult decision for any organization. The questions to be answered include:

- Who should fund BCP?
- How much should be invested?

Funding Responsibility

There are two ways for an organization to fund a BCP: corporate and business unit.

Corporate Funding. For many organizations, the funding decision is very simple; as the BCP is viewed as an organizational responsibility and is part of the cost of being in business, funding is provided at the corporate level. The benefit of this strategy is that the BCP will have a strong and continuous commitment from executive management. Further, that the executive management of the organization has carried out its fiduciary duties and in the event of a disaster would be protected from any legal action.

Business Unit Funding. Many organizations view BCP funding as a business unit expense and therefore each business unit must fund the cost of its BCP. The disadvantage with this strategy is that business unit managers, who are often under pressure to control costs, will often target BCP as a candidate for cost-cutting. In particular, BCP is often eliminated as it is seen as an easy target.

This decision, which in the short term may be cost-effective (i.e., saves funds), can expose the organization's management to criticism from third parties (e.g., shareholders, external auditor, etc.) and, in the event of a disaster, can expose executive management to legal action for failing to perform its fiduciary duties.

BCP Investment

Determining the amount to invest in BCP is difficult; however, as a guide, research by the Gartner Group (Determinants of Business Continuity Expenditure — Research Note, March 21, 1996) found that "on average, data centers spend around 2 percent of their budget on disaster recovery."

Gartner further stated that the move away from centralized processing has meant "that the proportion of total IT expenditure dedicated to recovery-related matters is already below the reported average." This suggests that organizations have not recognized that there are still risks although they may not be so obvious as those of a centralized processing (i.e., mainframe) environment.

BCP METHODOLOGY

It is important that a recognized BCP methodology be utilized to ensure a structured approach is adopted and consistently applied throughout the development and implementation of a BCP. By adopting a best practice approach BCP methodology, organizational management gains such assurance.

There are two business continuity organizations that have BCP methodologies that have been developed on best practice:

- Disaster Recovery Institute (DRI), United States (www.dr.org)
- Business Continuity Institute (BCI), United Kingdom (www.survive.com)

While the methodologies differ slightly, the process and content are almost identical. The Disaster Recovery Institute's methodology includes:

1. project initiation phase (objectives and assumptions)
2. functional requirements phase (fact-gathering, alternatives, and decisions by management)
3. design and development phase (designing the plan)
4. implementation phase (creating the plan)
5. testing and exercising phase (post-implementation plan review)
6. maintenance and updating phase (updating the plan)
7. execution phase (declare disaster and execute recovery operations)

Both organizations have a certification program that supports the business continuity profession. Further, both organizations have a strong training program to assist personnel to gain training on developing, implementing, and testing BCPs.

There are a number of publications available to assist organizations in developing a BCP that uses a BCP methodology that complies with best practice. Two such publications that are recommended and have an information technology focus are:

- *Business Resumption Planning* (Devlin, Emerson, and Wrobel), Auerbach Publications
- *Call Center Continuity Planning* (Rowan and Rowan), Auerbach Publications

BCP STRATEGIES

If a business is to survive a disaster, it must select the "right" recovery strategies. If the "wrong" BCP strategy is selected, then the BCP plan will be developed upon an incorrect premise. In the event of a disaster, it may actually exacerbate the disaster.

Before selecting the BCP recovery strategies, a comprehensive risk evaluation and business impact analysis (known as BIA) should be performed to identify the organization's core business processes and their critical dependencies (e.g., IT, third-party service providers, etc.). The analysis will also identify the potential impact to the organization of a disaster event, both in the short-term (financial) and the long-term organizational "brand" damage.

The recovery strategies may be two tiered:

- *Technical:* Information technology (e.g., desktop, client/server, mid-range, mainframe computers, computers, data and voice networks)
- *Business:* Logistics, accounting, human resources, etc.

The organization's recovery strategy needs to be developed for the recovery of the core business processes. In the event of a disaster, it is *survival* and *not business* as usual.

The overall objective is to identify the BCP recovery strategies that are low risk and cost-effective. Too often there is a greater emphasis on cost without consideration given to the risks associated with the recovery strategy. To undertake this analysis, a risk methodology needs to be utilized, as this will provide assurance to management that a scientific approach was employed.

Backup Regimes

For the timely recovery of business applications and its associated data in the event of a disaster to be achieved, a strong backup regime must exist. There is a tendency by users to view backups as an information technology responsibility rather than their own. The organization's IT department has the responsibility to perform the backups; however, determining their frequency is the business system owner's responsibility.

Back-Up Frequency. Business system owners often fail to advise the organization's IT department to meet their operational requirements to perform backups. Backup frequency can vary, depending on the sensitivity and value of data and access requirements. It can also be determined by how much data the business system owners can afford to lose in the event of an incident or disaster (i.e., 1 hour, 4 hours, 1 day, 3 days, 1 week, etc.).

An example of a backup regime would be as follows:

1. A partial backup is performed daily of files that have had changes since the previous day.
2. A weekly backup, which is a full image of the data at that point in time supplements the daily backup.
3. The weekly backup is rotated on a four-weekly cycle to create a monthly backup.
4. The monthly backups are archived for up to 12 months before a yearly backup is created.
5. The yearly backup is created at financial year-end and archived off-site for a designated period meeting local taxation laws.

The frequency of backups and the volume to be backed up will also assist in determining the backup strategies. The frequency of backups and the strategies used to backup will have a significant impact on the timeliness of recovery.

Restoration Testing of Backups. Organizations often fail to perform regular full restoration testing of their backups to ensure that, in the event of an incident or disaster, all the data can be recovered completely and accurately from the backup media. There are cases where organizations have gone out of business because they have been unable to recover from their backups. Backup media can be compromised due to an unreported technical fault or damaged through carelessness by technical support staff.

Without a strong backup regime, there is no recovery!

Legacy Systems

Legacy systems are systems that often have not migrated to a new technology platform. Legacy system BCP strategies are often overlooked, as frequently there is an expectation that such systems will either be replaced or decommissioned in the near future. However, experience has shown this author that legacy systems are simply either overlooked, ignored, or put into the too-hard basket. If legacy systems are not considered, then it potentially exposes the organization to a "disaster" through its inability to recover these legacy systems.

BCP strategies for legacy systems are often high-cost, particularly if the hardware or software is either no longer supported or available. To gain support from management to support the development of a BCP for legacy systems, the information gained from the BIA will provide sufficient evidence on the dependency of the organization on these systems and the impact if a disaster was to strike the organization, rendering these systems inoperative.

From the information gained, management may be forced to not only address the BCP legacy system issues, but also take action to migrate these systems where they can be covered by an existing BCP.

Third-Party Service Providers

There is greater reliance on third-party service providers in today's business environment than in previous years. This has occurred as organizations have outsourced non-core business processes to third parties that have a greater capacity and specialization to deliver a quality service at a lower cost to the organization.

Management of many organizations believe that they have transferred any risks associated with these business processes to the third-party service provider. The reality is that although the risk has been transferred, management still "owns" the risk.

BCPs must address this critical component of the organization's business infrastructure. For many managers, ownership of risk becomes apparent when a crisis, near-disaster, or disaster event occurs through the non-provision of services or products by the third-party service provider. Therefore, management must extend its BCP responsibility to include its third-party service provider.

This responsibility includes:

- a contractual requirement for the third-party service provider to have a demonstrable BCP that includes services and products provided to the organization
- the authority (contract) to audit the third-party service provider's BCP on a periodic basis
- observe the third-party service provider testing its BCP

SUMMARY

Business continuity must be part of the organization's risk management program. Without business continuity planning, the organization's very life and survival are potentially under threat. Management will only realize the value of its investment in business continuity when a real disaster situation strikes the organization.

Section I
The Need for Business Continuity Planning

Chapter 1
Risk and the Need for Business Continuity Planning

Denise Johnson McManus
Houston H. Carr

ARTICLES ABOUND ABOUT THE RISK TO BUSINESS CONTINUITY THAT IS ALWAYS PRESENT DUE TO THE ERRATIC ACTIONS OF MOTHER NATURE. Risk is often equated with external forces (e.g., natural disasters such as floods, hurricanes, or earthquakes) that present the risk of power disruption, building destruction, or worse. Less obvious is the risk inherent in the adoption of a new computer-based system or the distribution of systems and data across a country or world via telecommunications networks. Risk may even be present in disruption due to labor disputes, labor shortages, a poorly run or missing training program, or a flu epidemic that takes out one-half of the personnel for a week.

This chapter discusses risk in its more generic or basic form — not its outcome as the result of a fire, flood, or earthquake. Risk is inherent in any organization, in any operation, in any situation where the goal is continuance. There are ways to assess and manage this risk; however, first an examination of the nature of risk is necessary. Then, the reaction to risk will be addressed.

THE NATURE OF RISK

According to *Webster's Dictionary,* **risk** is "the possibility of loss or injury; also, the degree of the probability of such loss." The four components of risk are threats, resources, modifying factors, and consequences. Threats are the broad range of forces capable of producing adverse consequences. Resources consist of the assets, people, or earnings potentially affected by threats. Modifying factors are the internal and external factors that influence the probability of a threat becoming a reality, or the severity of consequences when the threat materializes. Consequences have to do with the way the threat manifests its effects on the resources and the extent of those effects.[5]

Risk becomes loss when there is some adverse change in existing or expected circumstances. Change produces the uncertainty inherent in risk. No one can be sure if and when change will take place, nor can one be certain about the consequences of change. From an organizational standpoint, change may be internal or external. Because internal change is by definition controllable, an organization can respond to the risk associated with internal change in a proactive fashion. For example, the installation of a new management-ordered procedure invokes change. Part of the procedure-creating process should be a contingency plan in case some of the people or resources are temporarily not available.

External change, on the other hand, is uncontrollable by the organization, requiring responses that can be reactive. Such a situation would be a new tax law and the resultant financial consequences. To the degree that change can be anticipated, a proactive response is preferred. In any case, and for any risk environment, organizations should prepare for unforeseen incidents through risk assessment and management.

RISK ASSESSMENT AND MANAGEMENT

In the use of any technology, process, or procedure, someone should determine where unexpected or undesired consequences are likely to occur. Managers must think about objectives, the system, and procedures they have installed to achieve these objectives, and the weak points in the equipment, staffing, and procedures. By detecting and recognizing risks, the result of adverse consequences will be less catastrophic than ignoring them.

Risk assessment and analysis involves a methodological investigation of the organization, its resources, personnel, procedures, and objectives to determine points of weakness. Finding such points, managers overtly control the risk by passing it to someone else (insurance or outsourcing the task) or strengthening the weak points by changes or building redundancies.

Risk management is the science and art of recognizing the existence of threats, determining their consequences to resources, and applying modifying factors in a cost-effective manner to keep adverse consequences within bounds.[2]

Hurricanes Hugo and Andrew on the East Coast of the United States, the San Francisco earthquake on the West Coast, and the Chicago/Hinsdale, Illinois, central office fire are well-publicized, significant acts of nature or accidents. Just as significant but somewhat less expected are more common acts of nature and accidents. A severe storm in Florida left 500,000 people (homes and offices) without power. (If the organization or home used ISDN telephone service or cordless phones, it also will be without voice service because, unlike its analog counterpart, ISDN and cordless telephones in the home or office are not powered from the central office.) This storm was followed by a tornado with less widespread but more severe consequences.

A major snowstorm in the city of Birmingham, Alabama, in early March of 1993 brought more than 13 inches of snow to that southern city and business halted. The city planners had not prepared for the possibility of a blizzard of this magnitude. Risk assessment would have considered, for example, whether their telecommunications systems needed to function in spite of the snow. Equally important for review is the vulnerability of equipment to water damage from the runoff as the snow melted. Meanwhile, 12,000 miles and five years away, New Zealand suffered a countrywide power outage. Although the country "closes down for each weekend," lack of a recovery plan could have disastrous consequences.

A credit card processing company in Georgia was prepared for Hurricane Opal in 1995, except it failed to account for the lack of telephone service and thus could not call its employees back to work. In a different city and time, a college in Texas placed its academic mainframe computer in the basement of a low-lying building, just above the sanitary sewer level, and the rains came. A commercial timeshare firm knew the risk of low-lying areas for its mainframe in Chicago and placed it on the fifth floor of a ten-story building. Snow came as expected, crushed the roof, and flooded the computer despite its lofty positioning.

Several more examples to support the vital nature of business continuity planning are in order. In a major defense contractor's facility in Texas, the entire second shift operation was halted due to a (drunk) truck driver running into a utility pole that carried the primary power to the facility. The only light in the office complex was provided by the buttons on the telephone. In the college of business at a major southeastern university, an electrical storm — not a hurricane, just a storm — took out all power to the building and campus. Although this eventuality had been foreseen, the emergency generator did not come online because the battery that powered the starter motor was dead.

A less obvious problem to assess and manage is what to do when someone in an office goes on vacation, is sick, or goes on medical leave. Hopefully, provisions have been made for another person with like skills to take that person's place; that person has been properly trained; and adequate documentation is in place to do the job. What about a labor strike, the flu season, or a computer virus? Snowstorms, hurricanes, flu epidemics, and floods are acts of nature, but labor strikes, computer viruses, and ill-prepared training programs are not. These latter events are seemingly less consequential, but more likely to happen.

What about the everyday operations of a network and computers? Mainframe and desktop computers can be halted by a 100-millisecond flicker of the power when there is no uninterruptible power supply (UPS). Does the LAN file server have redundant components to avoid a single point of failure? Does it have a backup server for critical functions? Are there alternate lines from the PBX to the Telco's central office in case of an inadvertent line cut by a backhoe? One telecommunications-dependent firm has buried the telecommunications trunks on their premises in deep trenches and then poured concrete to protect against such digging. The authors have personal UPS devices on their desktop computers and surge protectors on the telephone lines.

Risk management is the analysis and subsequent actions taken to ensure that the organization can continue to operate under foreseeable adverse conditions, such as illness, labor strikes, hurricanes, earthquakes, fire, power outages, heavy rains, oppressive heat, or flu epidemics. The beginning of risk management is assessment, which leads to management on a continuous basis. A specific point is the creation of a business continuity plan in case of a catastrophic occurrence. The plan is based on procedures that occur every day that allow an organization to recover after a disaster and continue operations. It describes the place, procedures, and resources to provide for continued operations. Business continuity plans are often referred to as business continuity plans for good reason.

BUSINESS CONTINUITY

A business continuity plan is a series of procedures to restore normal operations following a disaster — with maximum speed and minimal impact on operations. A comprehensive plan will include essential information and materials for necessary emergency action.

Planned Procedures

Planned procedures are designed to eliminate unnecessary decision-making immediately following the disaster. Business continuity planning begins with preventive measures and tests to detect situations that might lead to significant problems. If this planning process is completed, the chance of experiencing a total disaster is lessened. The severity of a disaster determines the level of recovery measures. Disaster classifications are helpful in organizing procedures for a business continuity. Exhibit 1-1 shows such a classification. Regardless of the importance of the activity, there are nine essential steps for a successful implementation of disaster recovery planning, which are displayed in Exhibit 1-2. The first is commitment.

Exhibit 1-1. Buisiness continuity planning process.

- Mission-critical activity: interruption is unacceptable (e.g., power, telecommunications networks, bank teller terminal, files, DBMS, file cabinets)
- Business-critical activity: short duration, interruption acceptable
- Facilities support: (e.g., security force)
- Personnel support: (e.g., cafeteria)

Commitment

The key to beginning a successful business continuity plan is to gain commitment from top-level management and the organization. To obtain the required support, the CEO and top managers need to understand the business risk and personal liability if a business continuity plan is not developed and a disaster occurs. Although many companies have excuses for not developing a plan, a corporate policy should be mandated requiring business continuity planning. The corporate policy would assist in defining the charter for contingency planning, while encouraging cooperation with internal and external staff.

Furthermore, if the financial impact to the business does not warrant the financial support of the corporate executives, an analysis of The Foreign Corrupt Practices Act of 1977 should get the required attention and support of the officers. The Act deals with the fiduciary responsibilities, or "standard of care," of the officers, which may be judged legally. In the legal publication *Corpus Juris Secundum,* the "standard of care" is defined as follows: "A director or officer is liable for the loss of corporate assets through his negligence, fraud, or abuse of trust."[6]

However, the most convincing reason for having a business continuity plan is that it simply makes good business sense to have a company protected from a major disaster. Additional reasons to have a recovery plan include a potential for greater profits and reduced liabilities to the company

Exhibit 1-2. Business continuity planning process.

1. Obtaining top management commitment
2. Establishing a planning committee
3. Performing risk assessment and impact analysis
4. Prioritizing recovery needs
5. Selecting a recovery plan
6. Selecting a vendor and developing agreements
7. Developing and implementing the plan
8. Testing the plan
9. Continuing to test and evaluate the plan

and the employees. Thus, a risk assessment provides a powerful argument for recovery planning. The assessment of current operations tells where the organization is at risk, and helps determine the critical areas that require change to protect from the threats. Recovery from a major disaster will be expensive. However, the inability to recover quickly and support primary business functions would be significantly more costly and destructive to the company.

Computer resources are a specific area of concern. Rare would be the organization not utilizing a computer for daily operations. Many firms today rely fully on realtime processing, if only for credit checks. Statistics indicate that if a company's computers are down for more than five working days, 90 percent of those companies will be out of business in a year. Hubert Huschke, Executive Vice President of Union Bank of Switzerland, estimates that a complete breakdown of the company's network for two days could cause the failure of the bank. In this computer-intensive environment, several instances in financial services have been reported where collapses of services for only a few minutes have resulted in losses that could have financed the entire network several times over.[1]

However, these can be avoided or greatly lessened if a coherent disaster recovery plan is developed and implemented.[7] "The disaster recovery process generally is much longer than the duration of the disaster itself."[3] The company experiences immediate problems from the disaster and continues to experience difficulties for several months. Financial and functional losses increase rapidly after the onset of an outage. Corrective action must be initiated quickly, and business continuity methods should be functioning by the end of the first week, if not the first day, of an outage. Loss of revenues and additional costs rise rapidly and become substantial as the outage continues. The inability to communicate with customers and suppliers is devastating, and can prevent the company from staying in business. Therefore, an effective business continuity plan directly affects the bottom line — staying in business.

Costs

Costs are a major concern for business continuity plans. Some of the costs incurred for business continuity are costs of insurance, fees for hot-site backup, stockpiled equipment, supplies, forms, redundant facilities, cold sites, communications networks for recovery purposes, testing, and training and education. Business continuity planning costs are calculable and can be budgeted. Not only can they be allocated across many business units, but also can be amortized over many years. Many costs must be considered when developing the plan — not only the time invested by the team members, but also implementation costs must be considered when developing the budget.

Exhibit 1-3. Business continuity planning issues.

- Unanticipated interruption of routine operations
- Identify key risks and the exposure to risk
- Identify consequences if existing plan fails
- Identify recovery strategy
- Identify test and evaluation process

Planning

The process of developing a recovery plan involves management and staff members. Each member of the business continuity team has a specific role that is defined in the plan. Business continuity planning is a complex process; organizations must utilize a structured approach in determining the scope, collecting the data, performing analysis, developing assumptions, determining recovery tasks, and calculating milestones. The issues displayed in Exhibit 1-3 must be considered during the planning process. This highly interactive process requires information from throughout the organization. The plan requires continuous revision. It is out of date whenever a major change occurs in the organization.

The process of building a plan is extremely valuable to the company. The purpose of identifying problems and developing a recovery process not only forces the organization to examine the impact of a disaster on the company and the business, but questions the very mode of operation. Thus, the end result should be a plan that can be utilized for all levels of disasters and potentially a change in the way business is conducted. Recovery from a major disaster requires the efficient execution of numerous small plans that comprise the master plan. Recovery managers select the plan, assign responsibility, and coordinate resources to execute the plan.

CONCLUSION

Many disasters that have occurred in the United States in recent years have driven companies to recognize the importance of disaster assessment, management, and recovery planning. Business continuity plans appear to be a cost-effective but underutilized tool. Organizations that have prepared for an extended outage through insurance and a contingency plan reported significantly lower expected loss of revenues, additional costs, and loss of capabilities.[6] In the last ten years, a major disaster has been reported somewhere in the United States, on the average, every year. Meanwhile, standard problems occur each month somewhere in the United States, for example, tornadoes in Oklahoma or Texas, severe storms in Florida, heavy rains in California, or a flu epidemic across the eastern seaboard. The size of the disaster is not the determining factor of staying in business; it is the business continuity plan that will determine if the doors will stay open or be closed. "Smart companies make it their business to have a business continuity plan in place. If a disaster does strike, being prepared can make the difference between a smooth recovery and a slow terrifying struggle to survive."[3]

Therefore, it will be the organization that analyzes its operations and determines the *threats* to resources, the *modifying factors* in place, and the *consequences* of adding additional resources, procedures, or modifying factors on the ability of the organization to continue business in case of a disaster. The success of the assessment and business continuity plan will be determined by the extent to which planned procedures are in place to eliminate unnecessary decision-making immediately following the disaster.

Notes

1. Borsi, Robert S. Union Bank of Switzerland: Strategic Options When Outsourcing ATM Services, *Harvard Business School Case 9-397-013,* Oct 21, 1996, 1–16.
2. Carr, Houston and Charles A. Snyder. *The Management of Telecommunications,* Irwin, 1997, Boston, MA.
3. Howley, Peter A. Disaster Preparedness is Key to Any Telecommunications Plan. *Disaster Recovery Journal,* 7, April/May/June 1994, 26–32.
4. Lewis, Steven. Disaster Recovery Planning: Suggestions to Top Management and Information Systems Managers. *Journal of Systems Management,* 45, May 1994, 28–33.
5. McGaughey, Ronald E. Jr.; Charles A. Snyder; and Houston H. Carr. Implementing Information Technology for Competitive Advantage: Risk Management Issues, *Information & Management,* 26, 1994, 273–80.
6. Powell, Jeanne D. Justifying Contingency Plans, *Disaster Recovery Journal,* 8, October/November/ December 1995, 41–44.
7. Preston, Kathryn. Disaster Recovery Planning, *Industrial Distribution,* 83, December 1994, 65.
8. Seymour, Jim, Y2K v.2: Time for Triage, *PC Magazine,* June 30, 1998, 93–94.

Chapter 2
The Four Phases of Risk Realization

Andrew Blades

THE TERMS BUSINESS CONTINUITY PLANNING (BCP), DISASTER RECOVERY PLANNING (DRP), AND EMERGENCY MANAGEMENT ARE BANDIED ABOUT WITH ABANDON. The choice of terminology appears to depend on the industry involved, rather than on the appropriateness of the term for the activity being described. This chapter suggests that each of these terms is not interchangeable, but rather refers to specific elements of action taken when an incident causes a risk to be realized.

Risks and hazards surround people in both their personal and professional lives. All activities carry some form of risk and thereby require a decision to be made as to whether to conduct an activity based on weighing the risk against the benefit of the activity. Demands for greater and greater reductions in risk exposure can proceed beyond the point of overall benefit and be counterproductive. As risk cannot be totally removed from activities, all organizations must accept some degree of risk exposure.

PHASES OF RISK REALIZATION

There are four phases that an organization goes through when a risk is realized, based on Fink's (1986) approach to crisis management. BCP and DRP are the last two phases of the cycle. The aim of managing a risk that has been realized is to return to normal business operation as soon as possible. The most effective management of a risk incident will move from phase 1 to a return to normal business operations. The four phases of a crisis or incident are now considered.

Precondition Phase

Incidents rarely "just happen;" rather, there is a build-up of contributing factors or preconditions. These manifest themselves in a number of ways: poor training leads to technical errors, low staff morale leads to a bad attitude, a busy operations schedule may push maintenance limits. All of these are indicators of potential trouble or preconditions. Building a facility in a

0-8493-0907-7/00/$0.00+$.50

known earthquake area is a precondition to disaster. There is usually some sign that an incident may occur.

Incidents such as Piper Alpha and the Lockerbie disaster all had preconditions and early warnings that a problem might occur, but managers ignored them. During this phase, there is opportunity via risk assessment and analysis to identify problems and take appropriate action. This includes proper review and monitoring procedures to ensure risks are not permitted to accidentally escalate. This phase can be years in duration.

The Incident and Response Phase

An incident has occurred and some damage has been experienced; it is this stage that most people refer as crisis. The incident could be a fire, a bomb threat, industrial action, power cuts, loss of IT facilities, fraud, product tampering — the list is endless. Incidents and disasters are not limited to IT and natural disaster. Organizations need to consider the full range of incidents that might disrupt business. These threats to business operations should have been identified in the risk analysis program and the risk management plan. Careful post-incident analysis will usually demonstrate that somewhere in the organization a department or staff member knew of the potential risk that has just been realized. It should have been identified in the preconditions phase.

Once the incident has been experienced, the organization commences damage control; how much will depend on the organization and its ability to respond to the crisis. Actions during this phase can be categorized as emergency management and response procedures. The organization tries to limit its exposure to damage and risk. This phase is often characterized by the speed at which things move and may appear to be the longest phase, but that title usually belongs to phase 3.

The Business Continuity Phase

This phase is designed and implemented to continue operations and enable the organization to survive. It does not provide "business as usual," but rather continues operations, albeit in a degraded mode to allow the organization to stay in business. In a private company, this would mean to continue trading; while in a government organization, it would mean to continue to service client needs. Depending on the event, this may result in some service not being delivered due to degraded service levels.

The business continuity process can be seen as "first aid." It is designed to keep the organization alive until it receives more advanced treatment and begins recovery. However, if the organization is to return to its original state of capacity, then it must begin the recovery process. Stabilizing the patient is not enough — the patient must receive treatment so that recovery is possible.

The Business Recovery Phase

It is not enough to simply continue business. The organization must have a recovery strategy that will enable it to return to normal operations. During this phase, the organization aims to move from simply continuing operation to total recovery. This would include such tasks as returning to full operational capacity and service provision, moving into new buildings, and returning to business as normal, where possible.

CONCLUSION

There are four phases in reacting to risk realization. Organizations cannot afford to stagnate in any one phase. A comprehensive plan must address all of the above phases and allow the organization to fully recover. The risk management process should effectively address the issues in the preconditions phase. For this reason, the BCP and DRP should flow from the risk management plan, rather than being seen as a totally separate process.

BCP, it has been argued, forms part of a wider planning structure and process and is not an end in itself — but rather a means to an end. The continuity plan needs to be integrated with risk, emergency, and recovery planning if an organization is going to truly be able to manage risk realization and return to normal business operations.

For BCP to grow as a discipline, there needs to be strong constructive debate that serves to further enhance and refine our common body of knowledge.

References

Fink, S., *Crisis Management: Planning for the Inevitable*, Amacom, New York, 1986.

Chapter 3
The Legal Issues of Business Continuity Planning

Tari Schreider

THE LEGAL ISSUES INVOLVED IN CORPORATE CONTINGENCY PLANNING ARE SOME OF THE MOST MISUNDERSTOOD AND CONFUSING ASPECTS OF THE ENTIRE PROCESS OF CREATING A BUSINESS CONTINUITY PLAN. Data center managers often must assume the role of business continuity planners. And whereas they are not expected to be as knowledgeable as lawyers in this role, they are encumbered with the responsibility of understanding the minutiae of existing regulatory guidelines and the legal consequences of their companies' failure to implement an effective business continuity plan. No specific laws categorically state that an organization must have a business continuity plan (BCP), but there is a body of legal precedents that can be used to hold companies responsible to those affected by a company's inability to cope with or recover from a disaster. This chapter outlines those precedents and suggests precautions.

Despite the widespread reporting in the media of disasters and their effects, many companies and corporate directors and officers remain apathetic toward implementing a business continuity plan. Companies are generally unwilling to commit the finances and resources to implement a plan unless they are forced to do so. However, implementing a proper BCP is a strategic, moral, and legal obligation to one's company.

If the billions of dollars spent annually on technology to maintain a competitive edge is an indication of how reliant society is on technology, then failing to implement a BCP is an indication of corporate negligence. Standards of care and due diligence are required of all corporations — public or private. Not having a BCP violates that fiduciary standard of care.

The entire basis of law relating to the development of business continuity plans is found in civil statutes and an interpretation of applicability to business continuity planning. These legal precedents form the basis of this chapter.

One of the precedents that can be used against companies that fail to plan for a disaster is drawn from the case of FJS Electronics v. Fidelity Bank. In this 1981 case, FJS Electronics sued Fidelity Bank over a failure to stop payment on a check. Although the failure to stop payment of the check was more procedural in nature, the court ruled that Fidelity Bank assumed, and therefore was responsible for, the risk that the system would fail to stop a check. FJS was able to prove that safeguards should have been in place and therefore was awarded damages.

This case shows that the use of a computer system in business does not change or lessen an organization's duty of reasonable care in its daily operations. The court ruled that the bank's failure to install a more flexible, error-tolerant system inevitably led to problems. As a result, information technology professionals will be held to a standard of reasonable care. They can breach that duty to maintain reasonable care by not diligently pursuing the development of a business continuity plan.

CATEGORIES OF APPLICABLE STATUTES

To help make the data center manager aware of the areas in which business continuity planning and the law intersect, Contingency Planning Research, Inc., a White Plains, New York-based management consulting firm, has categorized the applicable statutes and illustrated each with an example. Each area is described; however, this discussion is not intended to present a comprehensive list.

Categories of statutes include, but are not limited to the following:

- *Contingency planning statutes.* These apply to the development of plans to ensure the recoverability of critical systems. An example is the Federal Financial Institutions Examination Council (FFIEC) guidelines.
- *Liability statutes.* These statutes establish levels of liability under the "Prudent Man Laws" for directors and officers of a corporation. An example is the Foreign Corrupt Practices Act (FCPA).
- *Life/safety statutes.* These set out specific ordinances for ensuring the protection of employees in the workplace. Examples include the National Fire Protection Association (NFPA) and the Occupational Safety & Health Administration (OSHA).
- *Risk-reduction statutes.* These stipulate areas of risk management required to reduce or mitigate (or both) the effects of a disaster.
- *Security statutes.* These cover areas of computer fraud, abuse, and misappropriation of computerized assets. An example is the Federal Computer Security Act.

- *Vital records management statutes.* These include specifications for the retention and disposition of corporate electronic and hardcopy (i.e., paper) records. An example is the body of IRS Records Retention requirements.

STATUTORY EXAMPLES

When the time comes for the data center manager to defend his or her company against a civil or criminal lawsuit resulting from damages caused by the company's failure to meet a standard of care, he or she needs more than an "act of God" defense. When no direct law or statute exists for a specific industry, the courts look instead to other industries for guidelines and legal precedents. The following three statutes represent the areas in which a court will most likely seek a legal precedent.

The Foreign Corrupt Practices Act (FCPA)

The Foreign Corrupt Practices Act (FCPA) of 1977 was originally designed to eliminate bribery and to make illegal the destruction of corporate documents to cover up a crime. To accomplish this, the FCPA requires corporations to "make and keep books, records, and accounts, which, in reasonable detail, accurately and fairly reflect the transactions and dispositions of the assets..." The section of this act that keeps it at the forefront of business continuity liability is the "standard of care" wording, whereby management can be judged on its mismanagement of corporate assets.

The FCPA is unique in that it holds corporate managers personally liable for protecting corporate assets. Failure to comply with the FCPA exposes individuals as well as companies to large financial penalties and prison terms up to five years.

The Federal Financial Institutions Examinations Council

The Comptroller of the Currency has issued various circulars dating back to 1983 (e.g., Banking Circular BC-177) regarding the need for financial institutions to implement business continuity plans. However, in 1989, a joint-agency circular was issued on behalf of the following agencies:

- The Board of Governors of the Federal Reserve System (FRB)
- The FDIC
- The National Credit Union Administration (NCUA)
- The Office of the Comptroller of the Currency (OCC)
- The Office of Thrift Supervision (OTS)

The circular states:

> The loss or extended interruption of business operations, including central computing processing, end-user computing, local-area networking,

and nationwide telecommunications, poses substantial risk of financial loss and could lead to failure of an institution. As a result, contingency planning now requires an institution-wide emphasis...

The Federal Financial Institutions Examinations Council guidelines relating to contingency planning are actually contained within ten technology-related Supervisory Policy Statements. These policies are revised every two years and can be acquired through any of the five agencies listed above.

The Consumer Credit Protection Act

On November 10, 1992, the 95th Congress, 2nd Session, amended Section 2001of the Consumer Credit Protection Act (15 U.S.C. 1601 *et seq.*) "TITLE IX-Electronic Funds Transfers." The purpose of this amendment was to remove any ambiguity the previous statute had in identifying the rights and liabilities and consumers, financial institutions, and intermediaries in "Electronic Funds Transfers." This Act covers a wide variety of industries, specifically those involved in electronic transactions originating from point-of-sale transfers, automated teller machines, direct deposits or withdrawals of funds, and fund transfers initiated by telephone. The Act further states that any company that facilitates electronic payment requests that ultimately result in a debit or credit to a consumer account must comply with the provisions of the Act.

Failure to comply with the provisions of this Act exposes a company and its employees to the following liabilities:

- any actual damage sustained by the consumer
- amounts of not less than $100 and not greater than $1,000 for each act
- amounts of $500,000 or greater in class-action suits
- all costs of the court action and reasonable attorneys' fees

Companies covered under this Act are subject to all the liabilities and all the resulting damages approximately caused by the failure to make an electronic funds transfer. The Act states that a company may not be liable under the Act if that company can demonstrate a certain set of circumstances. The company must show by a "preponderance of evidence" that its actions or failure to act were caused by "...an act of God or other circumstances beyond its control, that it expressed reasonable care to prevent such an occurrence, and that it expressed such diligence as the circumstances required..."

Standard of Care. Each of the three statutes mentioned in this section is based on the precept of standard of care, which is described by the legal publication entitled *Corpus Juris Secundum*, Volume 19, Section 491. The definition is that "... directors and officers owe a duty to the corporation to be vigilant and to exercise ordinary or reasonable care and diligence and the utmost good faith and fidelity to conserve the corporate property; and, if a loss or depletion of assets results from their willful or negligent failure to perform their duties, or to a willful or fraudulent abuse of their trust, they are liable, provided such losses were the natural and necessary consequences of omission on their part..."

DETERMINING LIABILITY

Courts determine liability by weighing the probability of the loss occurring compared to the magnitude of harm, balanced against the cost of protection. This baseline compels companies to implement a reasonable approach to business continuity in which the cost of implementation is in direct correlation to the expected loss. In other words, if a company stands to lose millions of dollars as a result of an interruption to its computerized processing, the courts would take a dim view of a recovery plan that lacked the capability to restore the computer systems in a timely manner.

Another precedent-setting case, referred to as the Hooper Doctrine, can be cited when courts are looking to determine a company's liability. This doctrine establishes that although many companies do not have a business continuity plan, there are "precautions so imperative that even their universal disregard does not excuse their omission." Simply put, a company cannot use, as a defense, the fact that there are no specific requirements to have a business continuity plan and that many other companies do not have one.

Liability is not just related to corporations but extends to individuals who develop business continuity plans as well. In 1989, in Diversified Graphics *v.* Ernst & Whinney, the United States Eighth Circuit Court of Appeals handed down a decision finding a computer specialist guilty of professional negligence. In this case, professional negligence was defined as a failure to act reasonably in light of special knowledge, skills, and abilities.

If the directors and officers of a corporation can be held accountable for not having a business continuity plan, then this case provides the precedent for individuals who are certified business continuity planners to be held personally accountable for their company's business continuity plan.

INSURANCE AS A DEFENSE

Directors and officers (D&O) of companies have a fiduciary responsibility to ensure that any and all reasonable efforts are made to protect their companies. D&O insurance does exist, but it only protects officers if they used good judgment and their decisions resulted in harm to their company or employees, or both. D&O insurance, however, does not cover a company officer who fails to exercise good judgment (e.g., by not implementing a business continuity plan).

Errors and omissions (E&O) insurance covers consequential damages that result from errors, omissions, or negligent acts committed in the course of business, or from all of these together. In a 1984 precedent-setting case heard in the District Court of Ohio, the court ruled, "Negligence is a failure to exercise the degree of care that a reasonably prudent person would exercise under the same circumstance." With regard to a trade, practice, or profession, the court added that "the degree of care and skill required is that skill and knowledge normally possessed by members of that profession in good standing in similar communities." Liability insurance does not prevent an organization from being brought to court, but it will pay toward the litigation and penalties incurred as a result.

Business continuity practitioners possess a unique expertise and subsequently could be held accountable for their actions and advice in the development of a business continuity plan. A word of caution here is that if data center managers pass themselves off as experts, they should expect to be held accountable as experts.

CONCLUSION

Courts assess liability by determining the probability of loss, multiplying it by the magnitude of the harm, and balancing them against the cost of prevention. Ostensibly, should the data center manager's company end up in court, the burden of proof would be on the company to prove that all reasonable measures had been taken to mitigate the harm caused by the disaster. There are clearly enough legal precedents for the courts to draw on in determining if a standard of care was taken or if due diligence was exercised in mitigating the effects of the disaster on the company's critical business operations. Every business is governed by laws that dictate how it must conduct itself in the normal course of business. By researching these laws and statutes, the data center manager will eventually find where penalties for nonperformance are stipulated. These penalties become the demarcation point for reverse engineering the business operations, thus finding the points of failure that could affect the company's ability to perform under the statutes that specifically govern the company's business.

Chapter 4
Building a Culture for Business Continuity Planning

Merida L. Johns

THE "TO DO" LIST IS AT LEAST ARM'S LENGTH — developing the repository, integrating the ancillary systems, updating the architecture, expanding the training program, bringing up the intranet, and implementing the document imaging system. An A+ for the information systems team as it adds up accomplishment after accomplishment! Until, that is, a disaster strikes, and accomplishments fall like a domino effect. Who remembers the accomplishments when the basket holding all the eggs falls apart? Or who cares about past accomplishments or who accomplished them when the effects of a disaster impair, impede, interrupt, or halt a company's ability to deliver its goods and services.

We plan for disasters in our everyday lives. A significant part of our personal disaster planning is taking preventative measures to minimize the likelihood that a disaster will befall us. We make sure that our automobile does not run out of fuel; we install smoke detectors in our homes; we pay our utility bills; and we do a host of other things that reduce the chance of a personal disaster.

We also put effort into developing an organized response if disaster does strike. We have candles and matches in the drawer and batteries in the flashlight should the electricity go off. We have a store of fuses in our closet should a fuse be blown. We have battery cables in our trunk should our battery die. We carry a spare tire in case we have a flat. Our lives are full of contingency plans should those "just-in-case" events occur.

In addition to preventing personal disasters and developing organized responses, we also ensure that we can carry out our response plans. We know how to replace fuses, we know how to operate the flashlight, and we know how to put on a spare tire. In other words, we are usually very good risk managers.

The proclivity for self-protection is powerful when it comes to ensuring our personal well-being. The propensity for protection is also powerful when it comes to public safety. Many of the measures in place today to reduce the likelihood of disasters in the workplace and community are the result of experience with the effects of disasters or because we recognize the potentially disastrous effects that may result from an untoward event. While we try to minimize the likelihood of disasters and develop contingencies should they occur in our personal lives and in the community, why is it that too few organizations have contingency plans for information systems? Among the reasons cited for not committing to disaster planning is the perception that it is a process which is too costly, time-consuming, and tedious. The terminology "disaster planning" itself has propagated, to a great degree, misunderstandings about the true nature of the process and its intended outcomes. "Disaster planning" has been interpreted by some as planning for an event that has a very low likelihood of occurring. Is it any wonder that, when approached from this viewpoint, cost-conscious executives put disaster planning on the back burner? Why allocate resources for an endeavor that is not believed to have a good return on investment?

THE PHILOSOPHY OF BUSINESS CONTINUITY PLANNING

It has been recognized that planning for a disaster is not an answer for ensuring that information systems, which support business processes, are not impaired, adversely impacted, halted, or interrupted by untoward events. The primary goal of any organization is to deliver its goods and services without interruption. Thus, the concept of planning for a disaster falls short of this intended goal. Instead, what is required is a broader view of keeping the organization in business by maintaining its processes so that goods and services can be delivered without interruption. Thus, the foundation for a successful business continuity planning (BCP) process is understanding that the primary goal and outcome is to save the business not the computer. A critical component of saving the business includes setting up procedures that prevent an organization "from being placed at-risk or in jeopardy, and, if such unavoidably occurs, to provide the organization with the flexibility and elasticity to be able to bounce back with minimal effect on operational continuity" (p. 5).[1] Thus, like the personal preparedness scenarios cited above, experts agree that BCP has at least four components.[2-3] These include:

1. identifying potential disasters and their effects
2. taking preventive measures to minimize the likelihood of disasters occurring
3. developing an organized response should a disaster strike
4. ensuring that business processes continue during the disaster recovery period

Essentially, then, BCP is based on the theory of managing risk as opposed to preparing for a disaster. As Levitt[1] notes,

> The approach, the underlying philosophy, and the operational activities and functions are based on the premise that the organization (1) faces a finite number of definable risks; (2) each of these risks can be measured in terms of likelihood of occurrence; (3) there are substantial opportunities to reduce these inherent levels of risk; (4) the impact of any of the risks, when occurring, on each business function can be determined or predicted before it occurs; and, (5) each risk, and its impact on any business function, can be managed in a manner consistent with the needs of the organization (p. 5).

While these steps appear fairly straightforward, organizations have had difficulty translating them into action. Various reasons have been cited for inaction. Some of these concern the cost of plan development, misunderstanding as to the nature of BCP, and the complexity of the process itself. In a study conducted by *Contingency Planning and Management* magazine and Ernst & Young LLP, 95 percent of companies surveyed report that they are either developing or have some type of BCP in place. On the face of it, this is a remarkable percentage. Further scrutiny, however, indicates that

> ... twenty-five percent of the respondents state this as currently developing which is of no help if a major disruption occurs in the meantime. Thirty-three percent say they have local plans in certain departments/divisions, yet to fully realize the value of a BCP, it must be implemented corporate wide. Therefore, it could be that only 38 percent who stated that they had corporate wide plans in effect are fully protecting their companies.[3]

ISSUES IN DEFINING DISASTER

What is a disaster? The term disaster is context-specific. For example, there are political disasters, business disasters, publicity disasters, and natural disasters. What may be a disaster in one context, may not be a disaster in another. In the business context, the term disaster has been applied to significant business losses, such as a loss in market share, loss of top executives, and loss in balance sheet figures. It has also been applied to low product acceptance or to poor product performance. In the information systems realm, the term disaster has been defined in many ways. A disaster can range from "a flood, fire or earthquake to labor unrest or erasure of an important file" (p. 569).[4]

Alternatively a disaster has been described as "an incident of such severity and magnitude that emergency steps are needed to stay in business" (p. 259).[5] From a business continuity perspective, the definition of disaster is probably best described as "when the organization is unable to continue to function in a predetermined manner, or is unable to recommence such functioning after the lapse of a predetermined, tolerable, time lapse" (p. 44).[1] What is of paramount importance in any BCP development is that the definition of disaster be established and used consistently throughout the enterprise.

While floods, hurricanes, fires, and power, communication, and technological failures might be included in anyone's list of top disaster causes, Rothstein notes that if a careful analysis of corporate disasters were conducted, it would be evident that there are numerous disaster causes or potential causes which are largely overlooked.[5] Examples include a seven-figure dollar loss because of a single database corrupted by a programmer who updated a production program without following production sign-off or turnover standards or procedures; the loss of a hospital pharmacy database when a disk crash led to the discovery that backup tapes had been made of the wrong files; sabotage of a data center by a former disgruntled employee; and when employees were prevented, due to flooding around corporate offices, from retrieving backup files stored on site so that they could be delivered to the off-site recovery area. Potential disasters lurk every day in our organizations. They may not be of the newspaper headline type, yet they will effectively produce the same results as an earthquake or a fire. As often as not, disasters "are compounded failures gradually escalating from seemingly innocuous, recoverable glitches to near-tragedies. In most cases, human error (whether proactive or reactive commission or omission) is the single greatest factor in growing a large headache into a small disaster."[6]

Businesses have indicated that the greatest cause for business interruption could be attributed to problems with their electrical power grid. In one survey of 560 respondents, 72 percent reported power outages, and 34 percent indicated lightning/storm-related interruptions. More than 46 percent reported telecommunications failure. In addition, 52 percent of these respondents reported hardware problems and 43 percent reported problems with software.[3]

What is apparent today is that "disaster" has a very broad meaning. No longer is disaster solely associated with headline events such as hurricanes, earthquakes, tornadoes, or floods. Indeed, as Jackson and Woodworth note,[7] even brief interruptions to information systems can mean the inability to deliver products and services to the customer, which then impacts revenue, productivity, and customer relations. No longer does it take the worst-case disaster scenario to adversely impact a company's business processes or bottom line.

DEVELOPMENT OF THE BUSINESS CONTINUITY PLAN

There are a variety of methodologies available for development of the business continuity plan. Some are more structured than others; some are more complex than others; some are proprietary and some are not. Whatever methodology is used, however, must be predicated on the underlying philosophy that BCP first and foremost concerns risk prevention and management and then concerns recovery and resumption. The emphasis must be on saving the company, as opposed to saving the computer system. Ultimately, the outcome of BCP is to ensure that if an untoward event does occur, irrespective of preventative measures that have been taken, it will not result in the collapse of the organization.

Fundamental Guidelines for Building a Culture of Business Continuity Planning

While abundant methodologies exist for development of the business continuity plan, some straightforward guidelines should be applied to any planning process. These are not listed in order of importance, but rather compose a set of considerations that should be incorporated into any plan development.

The process used to develop the plan must be manageable in nature and in cost. Too frequently organizations embark upon planning using complex methodologies that result in a high price tag in terms of time, resources, and personnel. Often this results in abandonment of the process entirely and the business continuity plan is never realized. The moral is to select a methodology that makes sense for the organization and is compatible with the culture of the enterprise. When the methodology used is out of sync with the company culture the result is more often than not unfavorable.

Another guiding principle is that BCP will only be successful when it has the full support of executive management. When the focus is on saving the company rather than saving the computer system, top management support is required to secure cooperation among the various stakeholders and to ensure that they understand that BCP is a high company priority. Executive management support is essential to support allocation of resources to the project. No matter how simple the chosen planning methodology is, the project will require time and resources — and this translates into cost. The "kiss of death" to any project is insufficient allocation of resources at the onset.

The goals of BCP must be clearly understood by all stakeholders. This means that every player understands that business continuity is first a process for management of risk and secondly a process of contingency planning and recovery. The goal is to keep the healthcare enterprise operational, not to save the computer system. Understanding this goal includes every functional manager as a stakeholder in the process. As stakeholders, managers are expected to assume responsibility for identifying and managing risk within their business process areas and for developing alternatives for operation should an untoward event occur.

Irrespective of the methodology used, the planning process must include an effective awareness and education program. Executive and functional managers must be made aware of specific incidents to which the organization is vulnerable. They must also understand that reducing the level of vulnerability is the top priority of a business continuity plan.

Specifically, as Myers[5] notes,

> Senior management must be made aware of the following facts: the business is exposed to sudden disaster. It makes good business sense to have at least a set of guidelines as a point of reference should a disaster actually happen.
>
> The Contingency Plan strategy is to protect market share, cash flow, and the ability to service customers during a disaster recovery period. The methodology to be used in plan development should specifically be designed to yield cost-effective solutions (p. 39).

An important component in any business continuity plan development is focus on business process areas. A vanilla plan that is "one size fits all" simply does not work. While many vulnerabilities are enterprisewide, some functional areas may be at higher risk for certain out-of-course events or have unique vulnerabilities. In addition, it is important to identify alternative contingency approaches for each functional area in order to coordinate and integrate operations in the event of a crisis. Thus, a systemic view must be taken to ensure that the alternative approaches used in one business area will meld with, integrate, or support those taken by another functional unit.

Any business continuity plan must be built upon a companywide definition of disaster. As previously noted, a disaster must be defined in terms of what constitutes an unacceptable interruption in normal business process and what constitutes a tolerable time lapse before normal functioning is resumed. A disaster should be defined in terms of the specific business environment. For example, what may be considered a disaster in a university medical center may not be a disaster for a small clinic. Additionally predictable events and those that cause minor inconveniences or that can be corrected in a short period of time should be addressed in standard operating and availability management procedures. A succinct definition of disaster should include type of incident (i.e., unplanned, local, regional) which results in disruption of normal operations for a specific period of time (i.e., 12 hours, 24 hours, 2 days, 3 days) and which has a significant impact (defined by specific criteria) on patient care, the bottom line, customer satisfaction, or cash flow.

Content of the BCP is also dependent upon the organization's size, processes, and amount of risk. The goal, however, should be toward simplicity and flexibility. The plan should be free of unnecessary detail, be easily updatable, and provide reasonable alternatives for continuing business processes. It should also include an organized response. Having alternatives is one thing; putting them into action is another. The plan should identify specific individuals who are responsible for decisions, actions, and issues during the response and recovery periods. Processes and procedures for recovery must be identified, along with a systematic plan for bringing up individual business process areas. Finally, any plan must include provisions for testing. Without a continuity exercise, an untested plan is unlikely to work during an actual disruption or, worse yet, could turn out to be even dangerous as a result of unverified processes or assumptions about integration.

Steps Toward Building a Culture of Business Continuity Planning

The strategy chosen for business continuity planning will determine how well a business continuity culture is developed within the organization. Regardless of what vendors or consultants may lead one to believe, there is no one right way to approach planning. The strategies used are highly dependent upon the existing culture and politics within the organization, its size, the past experience and background of its stakeholders, and the nature of its processes. Therefore, the successful strategy used in a teaching facility environment may be an abysmal failure in a 100-bed acute care facility. Therefore the steps discussed below must be viewed as a general outline for development of a strategy. The nuances in approach and dynamics and the content of each step will be different for each organization. Some organizations may wish to approach the process sequentially; others may do several steps simultaneously. Exhibit 4-1 shows the elements necessary for developing a company culture that supports the business continuity philosophy.

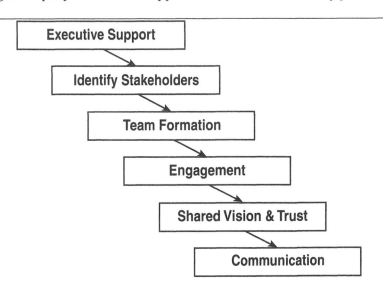

Exhibit 4-1. Elements of a successful business continuity plan.

Securing Executive Management Support. As noted previously, securing executive management support is essential to the success of any business continuity project. Top management must support not only undertaking the planning process but must also support the creation of the infrastructure to install, maintain, and implement the plan. Too frequently development of plans may be supported, but support for creation of the accompanying infrastructure to carry out the plan is not understood or negotiated from the beginning.

A critical question is how to secure top management support. First, management must understand that BCP is primarily concerned with risk management and keeping the company in business. Secondly management must be educated that BCP concerns cost, image, and getting product delivered. It is not exclusively confined to recovering operations in the worst case scenario but rather addresses minimizing the risk of even brief interruptions that can mean loss of revenue, productivity, or consumer goodwill. History from the individual organization can be compiled as well as innumerable examples published in the literature or on the Internet which detail adverse impact on revenue, costs, and customer service due to untoward events.

Management must also be convinced that the planning process will not turn into a "monster under the bed." A planning budget needs to be developed based upon "1) just how much plan you will need; 2) the net cost (planning expenditures less savings resultant from the plan); and 3) personnel time and costs that will be required in the planning, installation, and implementation activities" (p. 69).[1] To determine the planning budget, it is wise to initially secure funding for feasibility or needs assessment study. Findings of this review will not only provide a solid basis for determining budget but will also provide basic facts on the current condition of the company's exposure to risk.

Identifying the Stakeholders. No BCP process should be started without identification of the major stakeholders. Because BCP is about keeping the company in business every level of management must be considered a BCP stakeholder. Myers presents a tiered approached to garnering stakeholder participation.[5] The first tier is establishment of a steering committee composed of senior management staff. This group must be educated and committed to risk management and recognize the need to establish a plan that ensures an organized response should a disaster occur. The composition of the steering committee will depend upon the politics and culture of the organization. Normally this committee should be composed of representatives from finance, operations, auditing, information systems, and executive management. The steering committee should serve as an advisory group on plan development and methodology, recommend policy changes, and set an expectation that department managers will participate in plan development.

The second tier of stakeholders includes department managers. Because BCP involves risk management and maintaining operations in the event of unplanned disruption, every functional manager or head of a business process area must be considered a stakeholder. Like executive and senior management, this tier must be educated as to the purpose and outcomes of BCP. They are also the needed link to obtaining access to first-line supervisors in plan development. A major roll of this tier is to endorse the philosophy of BCP, participate in development of planning strategy, and to review and approve contingency plans and guidelines.

The third tier is composed of the first-line supervisors in each business process area. These are the individuals who are the most knowledgeable in current operations and who "know the business." It is the first-line supervisors who will examine alternatives to support operations should an untoward event and disruption occur.

Setting the Stage: the Education Program. The stakeholder education program is one of the most important steps to ensuring success of the BCP process. The education program must be deliberate. That is, like any education program, outcomes and instructional strategy must be identified and developed. This means more than conducting a one-hour meeting "telling" stakeholders about BCP. Rather it means engaging stakeholders in the process through active participation and learning. Lectures, handouts, and memoranda do very little to engage the interest of people. Rather the educational process needs to be placed in a discussion leadership context, where participants are presented with problems and scenarios and work as a group to develop solutions and outcomes.

Forming the Team. A several tiered and team approach to BCP is recommended. This tiered approach consists of executive, senior, and department managers and front-line supervisors. Each tier must recognize its own value and discipline as well as that of the others. A systematic view must be incorporated so that team members see how each other's work contributes to the success of the BCP process. An important element of team success is the exchange of information and communication. Communication must be open and solution-oriented. It must contain constructive feedback and above all trust must be cultivated among all team members. One of the most critical jobs of the business continuity planner and manager is to develop the team. With a good team all other elements of the planning process will easily fall into place. No amount of structure or methodology, however, can compensate for the lack of a functioning and healthy team.

Identifying the Risks. Because BCP is about risk management, an initial step in the process is to identify the exposure of the company. Once a functioning team is in place, risks to business operations that could result in the company's definition of a disaster need to be identified. Some of these vulnerabilities will cross departmental boundaries and be companywide; others may be unique to specific business process areas. While, in theory, any type of untoward event may occur, the emphasis should be placed on what events are likely to occur given the geographical location of the company, the processes that are performed, the physical facilities occupied, and the people who are present. Remember that the outcome of this step is to minimize risk. Therefore, events that have a higher probability of occurring within a specifically determined period of time should receive the attention for risk management. Those events that have been determined with a degree of acceptable certainty as unlikely to occur within a determined period of time should be dismissed. Thus, when risk assessment and subsequent management is approached in this manner planning costs are reduced and a less complex and less costly plan to implement and maintain is developed.

Identifying Impact. Identifying the impact of out-of-course events is often referred to as business impact analysis or BIA. Impact needs to be assessed for each business process area. Some business areas may be minimally impacted by an event while for others the event may have catastrophic consequences. Impact should be assessed from the standpoint of how the event affects patient care, customer service, product delivery, cash flow, revenue, and productivity within each functional area. Assessment also needs to be systematic and interdependencies among functional areas identified. For example, the impact of an out-of-course event may be minimal to the admitting function. However, there may be interdependencies between admitting and other functional areas such that lower productivity or loss of a business process for any length of time in admitting might catastrophically impact the other functional areas.

Determining which functions are more critical than others is also associated with impact analysis. In other words, what functions, if lost, would have the greatest adverse impact on patient care, product delivery, customer service, cash flow, revenue, and the like. For example, the most critical processes may not be the admitting functions but rather those in the clinical laboratory. Patient care, cash flow, and revenue may be hardest hit by disruption of clinical laboratory services. The primary reason for identification of the most critical processes is to develop a priority restoration schedule in order to return to normal productivity.

Identifying Interim Processes and Recovery Strategies. Alternatives to regular business processes should be cost-effective solutions. The BCP team must recognize that the goal in meeting the crisis is survival, not business as usual. Therefore, supervisors and managers must recognize that alternatives are developed to continue business processes but that they will not necessarily ensure the same efficiency. Any front-line supervisor or department manager who is asked how long he or she can function given an unplanned interruption, will likely say that it would be impossible to carry out business processes or deliver services for any length of time. This perception often results in implementing costly back-up solutions. Rather, front-line supervisors should be asked, "How could you survive given an event that impedes or interrupts your normal business process." The answer to this question takes on a whole different perspective. Options may include suspension of an activity or living with less efficient alternatives. Supervisors are therefore encouraged to think first about developing cost-effective solutions rather than resorting to costly and redundant alternatives.

As Levitt points out, contingency plans most frequently provide for: (1) hot, warm, or cold sites; (2) provision of additional hard copy-based information and/or magnetic-media-based data; (3) telecommunication paths via alternate routings, carriers, or mores; and (4) standby sources of electric power. However, "the importance of these provisions notwithstanding, organizations need to develop paper systems that will allow them to continue operating without the use of their computer systems" (p. 233).[1]

Alternative processes are only interim solutions. When a disaster is identified, recovery operations must go into effect immediately. These processes will be based upon a predetermined schedule of recovery actions. Depending upon the type of out-of-course event, restoration may include the relocation to a "cold" site, power generator activation, or retrieval of off-site stored media. Recovery also includes a schedule that identifies what processes come up first. This determination is often based on the criticality of the process, its interdependencies with other processes, and to what degree disruption will affect patient care, cash flow, revenue, and consumer satisfaction.

Developing the Organized Response. Alternative solutions and recovery schedules and processes are useless unless there is an organized process for their application. The organized response should include the immediate emergency response. This includes the plan for immediate situational assessment; criteria for determining and calling a disaster; notification of the emergency response team, vendors, and suppliers; and determination of what parts of the plan should go into effect and when. The BCP should outline the general emergency actions to be taken during an emergency response and who is responsible for each action. In addition for each business process area, system descriptions should be available, interdependencies noted, hardware and software used cataloged, and interim processing strategies and processes identified.

Compiling and Maintaining the Plan. The BCP must be a well-annotated, usable, and visible physical document. This does not mean that the document must be complex. On the contrary, the intent of the BCP is that it be a useful and functional tool. It should be developed in such a way as to avoid unnecessary detail — containing only the elements necessary to carry out an emergency response to events that may impede, interrupt, or halt business functions. The plan should be well organized and above all be a communication tool. It should be designed so that it can be easily updated. A plan that is too complex impedes communication as well as hinders timely and necessary review and update. A simple approach to contingency plan content is suggested by Myers.[5]

Essentially this includes policy and strategy statements; executive summary; description of maintenance and user continuing education and preparedness reviews; general actions and responsibilities in the emergency response; interim processing strategies for each business process area; and restoration strategies. The plan should also include appendices as necessary, such as the emergency response notification list; list of vendors and suppliers; and restoration priority list.

BUILDING THE BUSINESS CONTINUITY CULTURE: REVISITED

No program for business continuity can be totally successful without first considering the development of a company culture that supports the philosophy, goals, and outcomes of BCP. While executive management support is crucial to the success of the process, no plan can be accomplished without the engagement of managers, department heads, and first-line supervisors. Building a culture means developing a vision. It also means building a shared vision among all the stakeholders.

However, the culture cannot be realized until there is team learning and experience. Building the team, sharing the vision, and creating the culture will make all the difference in the world in the degree of success that is obtained from business continuity planning. Unfortunately, philosophies of organizational learning are rarely applied to endeavors that are considered on the "hard side," such as business continuity planning. Is it any wonder then that so many of these attempts fail and no one even understands why?

References

1. Levitt, A.M. 1997. *Disaster Planning and Recovery: A Guide for Facility Professionals,* New York: John Wiley & Sons.
2. Myers, K.N., *Total Contingency Planning for Disasters.* John Wiley & Sons, Inc., New York, 1993.
3. Levitt, A.M. and Ernst & Young LLP. Information Systems Assurance and Advisory Services — Business Continuity Planning. http://www.ey.com/aabs/isaas/bcp/bcm.asp.

4. Stair, R.M. 1996. *Principles of Information System: A Managerial Approach.* Danvers: Boyd and Fraser Publishing Company.
5. Myers, K.N. 1993. *Total Contingency Planning for Disasters.* New York: John Wiley & Sons.
6. Rothstein, P.J. 1996. "Almost disasters," *InfoSecurity News Magazine* January/February.
7. Jackson, J.A. and Woodworth, M. 1998. "Integrating disaster recovery into the high-availability agenda," *Contingency Planning and Management* June: 22–26.

Section II
Crisis Management

Chapter 5
Identifying a Crisis: A Critical Factor in Business Continuity Planning

Steve York

"a disaster can strike any organization, large or small"… whether the business recovers or not and whether it is still operating 12 months later depends on what advanced planning has taken place. This means action before and not after disaster strikes."

— British Home Office (1998)

UNDERSTANDING WHAT CONSTITUTES A "CRISIS" AND THE SITUATION THAT REQUIRES ACTIVATION OF ANY CRISIS MANAGEMENT PLAN OR EMERGENCY RESPONSE PROCEDURES IS ESSENTIAL TO DEALING WITH ANY SITUATION.

RISK AND RISK ASSESSMENT

An assessment of risk, made by humans, is open to individual subjective interpretation. This is outlined and expanded by Pidgeon et al. in the *Royal Society Report* (1992, p. 89–134). Hood and Jones also state that "Risk" can be said to comprise perceptions about the loss potential and probability associated with the interrelationship among humans and between humans and their natural (physical), biological, technological, behavioral and financial environments — a complex that may conveniently be termed (the) risk environment. (Hood and Jones [1996], and supported by the *Australian/New Zealand Standard,* AS/NZS 4360, 1995/99). This standard is the first generic risk management standard in the world.

With this understanding, a hazard, or potential threat, must be considered in the "current" environment and assessed against some agreed standard in the terms of likelihood of occurrence and the potential impact of the realization of the hazard or threat.

This risk assessment is often based on historical data of the occurrence of the hazards. Crossland et al. in the *Royal Society Report* (1983, p. 18) made the point that the assumption that there is dependable data may be doubtful. Further, the data that is available is in short supply; and as the realization of high-impact, low-probability hazards or threats is rare, it is sometimes dangerous to rely on the available data. Therefore, this assessment will rely heavily on the individual's perception and assessment of the risk using the information known to that person.

The base assessment of risk will impact the way the risk will be managed and have an effect on how a crisis is managed or a disaster is averted.

Risk Perception

Pidgeon et al., in the *Royal Society Report* (1992, p. 89) make the point, as stated above, that risk assessment is intertwined with individual beliefs, judgments, and feelings. Pidgeon further argued that it is not only the individual perceptions and assessment, but also "social and organizational factors such as the credibility and trustworthiness of risk management and regulatory institutions."

The community is now generally aware of risk — especially threats against the environment. The media may also be a catalyst in broadcasting developments in preventative measures in risk and any failures.

Wells makes the point in her article, citing Douglas, that complex issues surround the identification of risk, trouble people and corporations. There are also issues of trust, accountability, and personal responsibility in the way these risks are identified and addressed (Douglas, M. [1992], cited in Wells [1999]).

For example, the perception of the risk in participating in a sporting event, as in all other human activities, relies on the individual assessment of the environment. This risk maybe seen as voluntary, such as participants in ocean sailing races or car racing, who start and continue the event assessing their exposure to danger.

Starting a race or participating is based on the competitor's knowledge of the environment or potential risk environment. This would be also weighted as to their perceptions of their experience or ability in the activity. The risks perceived by the competitors may have been in the terms of heuristics described by Pidgeon, being simplifying judgmental strategies in order to reduce cognitive strain to understand the holistic risk environment.

Competitors may also take into account what they believe should be taken or instigated by the authorities or organizers in minimizing risks.

This is also true in the corporate world. The complexity of the interrelated issues and potential problems are often too worrying and outside normal workloads. This may result in individuals taking an overall decision to accept the risk, take the chance of "nothing happening," and deal with the situation as a media "beat up" and not implement any business continuity plans.

At this point in time, a decision to commit resources to the mitigation or business continuity strategies is based on an individual's risk assessment. What decision is right or wrong will be determined in less than six months' time.

Risk Management

Prevention is better than cure — a well-worn adage and relevant in considering human activity. As Norman R. Augustine stated in the *Harvard Business Review* (1995), "The first stage (of a crisis), not surprisingly, is prevention. Amazingly, it is usually skipped altogether, even though it is the least costly and simplest way to control a potential crisis."

The key to risk management is the assessment of the identified information of the threats, the vulnerabilities that may exist, and the systematic process of analysis and evaluation. The result would be a quantifiable determination, at a point in time, that is understood by another individual. Risk management is described by Hood and Jones, quoting Dunshire, as a process involving the three basic elements of any control system, namely:

- goal setting (whether explicit of implicit)
- information gathering and interpretation
- action to influence human behavior, modify physical structure, or both.

> (Dunshire [1978, p. 59–60], cited by Hood and Jones [1996, p. 6])

The *Australian and New Zealand Standard, Risk Management* (1995) argues that risk management is an integral part of good management practice and should become part of an organization's culture.

However, there seems to be an inference that risk management and crisis management are separate tasks rather than a complex interaction of understanding, assessment, and management response functions (Rosenthal and Pijnenburg, 1990).

Irwin (1995) points out several features that are relevant in risk management and what he describes as "citizen science." One of the features Irwin describes as the "second feature" is "the possibility that science is based upon sets of assumptions about the external world which are social in the origination" and that people will act rationally and predictably.

This is important in the arguments contained in this chapter that put forward the position that human action and response are often predicted as rational but are, in fact, unpredictable and many times irrational — especially in the times of crisis.

Risk management may then be mistaken for the total solution, rather than a step in the process of development of a culture of safety, risk reduction, and quick response to maintain business and personal continuity. A disaster may actually result from humans acting in ignorance or without fully understanding a situation because of a lack of training or knowledge, rather than a failure of the preventative risk management strategies.

Risk Communication

The term "public enquiry" usually follows closely on the heels of a disaster. Lawyers line up, and relatives of victims, affected corporations, government agencies, individuals, and stakeholders start to attribute blame (Wells, 1999).

The media, using emotive vision and words to highlight areas where people or organizations have failed to address the problems or respond appropriately, usually fuels the public enquiry "fire."

The communication of the risk reduction and management practices employed rarely gets the same media attention.

As Adams observes in his assessment of the guidelines for engineers confronting a disaster (published in 1992), the main message was, "that the professional engineer should ensure that when the music at the inquest stops, he is not left without a chair" (Adams, 1995, p. 187).

Professionals and scientists should not only be encouraged in the development of new technologies and products, but also for the "antidote" in the event that there is development of potential hazards. Beyond this, they must be encouraged to identify early warning signs and communicate the potential risk.

Crisis

Crisis has been defined as an emergency, as a condition or situation requiring urgent action or attention.

A crisis is defined by the *Macquarie Dictionary* (Australian) as:

> 1. A decisive or vitally important stage in the course of anything; a turning point; a critical time or occasion. ... 3. The point in the course of a disease at which a decisive change occurs, leading to either recovery or to death.

Fink describes a crisis as being:

> an unstable time or state of affairs in which a decisive change is impending — either with the distinct possibility of a highly undesirable outcome or one with a the distinct possibility of a highly desirable and extremely positive outcome (Fink, 1986, p. 15).

Fink proposes that a crisis situation can arise after an incident where there is a combination of a technical/equipment failure, procedural failure, and human error or ignorance (Kennedy Commission Report, quoted in Fink, 1986, p. 7; Silva and McGann, 1995, p. 7)

A crisis can also occur after an incident or natural event that is beyond the ability of the community to manage. The turning point can be difficult to define; as Adams states, some disasters are slow-moving affairs, such as famine or epidemics. A crisis is also where the response is, or appears to be unclear (Adams, 1996).

The common thread in all of these definitions is that a crisis is a turning point in a situation that can be positive or negative. The identification of this point in time in decision-making is an essential element in correctly dealing with the situation and averting a disaster.

The appropriate actions, determined by understanding the threats or hazards in their prodromal or anticipation risk assessment stage, may avert a disaster (Fink, 1986, p. 7). If successful, these actions can strengthen an individual or organization through learning or inoculation and implementing further preventative risk management measures. The crisis situation does not necessarily represent the failure of risk-management or a disaster. Rather, it can be attributed to the actions in dealing with the incident or crisis.

Disaster: Negative Outcome of a Crisis

> A disaster is a cultural construction of reality. A disaster is distinct from both emergencies and crises only in that physically it represents the product of the former.
>
> — Turner 1978

Disasters are situations that are irreversible and any actions following these situations are directed toward repair, blame, or directing public enquiry to determine how the situation was managed or could have been prevented.

Horlick-Jones (1995), describing a disaster, states that a disaster is the collapse of cultural precautions for dealing with socio-technical phenomena in some systematic way. Others also describe a disaster in the terms of the inability to deal with a situation, or in terms of cost or repair, severity in lives lost, or loss in dollar terms. However, is it clear that disasters are outcomes of events, which can be examined and measured.

Authors in this area have made the point that a storm beyond any experience in the world, raging in the Antarctic, does not represent a crisis; or even if there was massive damage, a disaster. It is where the storm threatens and encounters human activity that a crisis situation develops or results in a disaster. The resulting situation or outcome can be then examined to determine to what extent could the damage or vulnerability be attributed to the failure of risk-management activities or the appropriate response or crisis management.

Crisis Management

A crisis may develop or result from an incident where there is a combination of a technical/equipment failure, procedural failure, human error, or ignorance. The management of the resulting situation may prevent a disaster. This is the response part of the total risk management equation that is sometimes forgotten. (Kennedy Commission Report quoted in Fink, 1986, p. 7; Silva and McGann, 1995, p. 7).

Mitroff and Pearson state that to be comprehensive, crisis-risk assessments must include the analysis of management priorities, how real people interact with technology, and how reward systems will affect human response (Mitroff and Pearson, 1993, p. 12). The assumption that people, when confronted with a crisis, will act rationally is just as dangerous as the assumption that people managing the crisis will act rationally and without influence from outside forces or culture.

The need for the training of personnel in dealing with emergency situations and implementing contingency plans has been recognized the world over by government agencies.

The response phase to a crisis and the management of the situation can be equally contributory to the consequences as the measures taken in risk management phases.

Business Continuity: Organization Culture

The *Macquarie Management Papers* cite Hardy, who poposed that all events that occur to an individual or organization can be described in the terms of predictable/unpredictable and controllable/uncontrollable. Contingency planning is planning for all the events, including those that fall into the grid of unpredictable and uncontrollable. The events that fall into this category may be defined as a crisis or emergency (Hardy, 1992, p. 24, cited in *The Macquarie Management Papers*, 1998, p. 25).

However, it may be more efficient and effective to direct much of the effort into training people to manage the events and implementing contingency plans and risk management strategies.

Contingency planning has been broadly defined as "planning to address events that may happen at a later time and overwhelm existing levels of protection — planning to address residual risk." Contingency planning is now known as business continuity management.

It can be argued that the residual risk for events that are both unpredictable (potential loss, vulnerability, and likelihood) and uncontrollable, can only be addressed by developing strong management responses to divert resources and implement "work-around" strategies to minimize the impact.

CONCLUSION

Risk management has previously been described as a process involving the three basic elements of any control system, namely:

1. goal setting (whether explicit of implicit)
2. information gathering and interpretation
3. action to influence human behavior, modify physical structure, or both (Dunshire, 1978, p. 59–60; cited by Hood and Jones, 1996, p. 6).

This chapter sets out to challenge that risk management is the full equation for dealing with crisis situations. As in the above definition, risk management is generally seen as a preventative measure. This chapter contends that the response functions and the identification of crisis points and symptoms are equally as important as risk prevention strategies.

The chapter also sets out to identify the difference between crisis and disaster. Crisis situations are inevitable in a society that is increasingly complex and reliant on socio-technological systems.

The key to the prevention of disasters is the way crisis situations are handled and resultant impacts are minimized. Management-driven response strategies, defined as business continuity plans, encompassing risk management strategies are more relevant. Crisis situations can also be positive learning experiences — if handled effectively.

Disasters are by-products of crisis situations or emergencies that are outside the capacity of the community. Disasters may indeed represent the failure of risk management. However, the result must be examined with respect to the possible business continuity plans that were in place or could have been considered. This must be considered, together with the cost and the viability of those plans in the face of a massive incident, especially a natural event such as earthquake, storm, or volcanic activity.

Any resultant public inquiry would then focus on the management of the disaster. This is a clue to the argument. The effect of a disaster can be reduced in terms of life or monetary impact. This can be achieved through effective implementation of response strategies based on planning for the events Hardy defined as unpredictable and uncontrollable (Hardy, 1992, p. 4, cited in the *Macquarie Management Papers*, 1997).

The failure of addressing the training of the managers may also contribute to a disaster, as many risk management strategies and business continuity plans are based on the assumption of the rational actions of humans in extreme environments.

The culture that an individual or business must adopt to prevent a disaster is one of business continuity management, encompassing anticipation of all possible events, risk management and reduction strategies, and management of response actions. Approaching it with this cultural basis will encourage individuals and organizations to identify crisis situations at an early point, respond effectively, and grow stronger by the experience.

The action (or lack of) taken by management and management's approach to risk prevention strategies seem to be the focus of many public inquiries and Royal Commissions.

Notes

Musson, D. and Jordan, E., Business and Computer Contingency Planning in Australia, *The Macquarie Management Papers*, Macquarie University, Australia. 1997, 25.

British Home Office, How Resilient Is Your Business to Disaster?, http://www.homeoffice.gov.uk/epd/hrib.htm, 21 March 1998.

Hood, C. and Jones, D. K. C., *Accident and Design: Contemporary Debates in Risk Management*, University Press, London, 1996.

Mitroff, I., Pearson, C., and Harrington, L. K., *The Essential Guide to Managing Corporate Crises*, Oxford University Press, Oxford, 1996.

Wells, Celia, Inquiring into Disasters: Law, Politics and Blame, in *Risk Management: An International Journal*, 1(2), 8, 1999, Perpetuity Press.

Further Reading

O'Reilly, S., World Cup 2006? An Examination of the Policing of Risk in Context of Major Football Events, in *Risk Management: An International Journal*, 1(2), 29, 1999, Perpetuity Press.

Ross, B., Bombed, *Australian Sailing*, February 18–26, 1999.

Scarman Centre for the Study of Public Order. Notes. Module 1, 1999.

Toft, B. and Reynolds, S., *Learning from Disasters: A Management Approach*, Perpetuity Press, Leicester, 1997.

Chapter 6
Crisis Management Planning

Mark B. Desman

CRISIS MANAGEMENT PLANNING IS AN INTEGRAL PART OF THE BUSINESS RESUMPTION PLAN. For years, crisis management professionals have been differentiating between the concepts presented in business resumption planning and the concepts used in crisis management.

Crisis management planning involves a number of crises other than a physical disaster.

- It identifies a number of types of crises. Many of these threaten a company just as severely as a physical disaster.
- It shows how problems in the pre-crisis stage, which are not visible outside the company, are managed to ensure that they do not become an acute crisis.
- It also shows how the *crisis management team* should manage a crisis once it is in the acute-crisis stage.
- It suggests how the crisis management team should manage the crisis after it has moved to the post-crisis stage.
- It indicates how to select the crisis management team.

PERSPECTIVE

The business continuity plan, as shown in Exhibit 6-1, includes the controls, the procedures, and the policies designed to:

- prevent a disaster from occurring (prevention)
- respond to a disaster during and immediately after it has occurred (response)
- resume time-sensitive business operations quickly after a disaster has occurred (resumption)

The business resumption plan is designed to resume business operations quickly following a disaster. The BRP contains three main elements as shown in Exhibit 6-2:

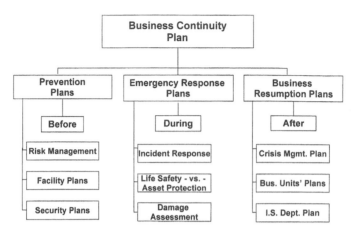

Exhibit 6-1. Business continuity plan diagram.

1. Crisis management plan
2. Business units' plans
3. IT plans

Differences Between Crisis Management and Business Resumption Planning

Crisis management planning is a term used to describe a methodology used by executives to respond to and manage a crisis. The objective is to gain control of the situation quickly so a company can manage the crisis

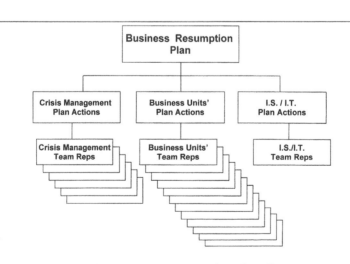

Exhibit 6-2. Business resumption plan diagram.

Exhibit 6-3. Differences between business resumption plans and crisis management plans.

Business Resumption Plan	Crisis Management Plan
1. The incident causes physical damage to company assets	1. The incident does not cause physical damage to company assets
2. Plan is based on worst-case scenarios	2. Plan does not address specific types of crises

efficiently and minimize its negative impacts. Crisis management planning is defined in the *American Heritage Dictionary* as "special measures taken to solve problems caused by a crisis."

In a crisis management plan, if a crisis strikes the company, the crisis management team will activate and manage the crisis until its conclusion.

The crisis management plan is also used in a disaster. The business resumption plan identifies how the business units affected by the disaster go about resuming business operations. During that time, the business units receive support from members of the executive management and crisis management teams.

In a business resumption plan, if a disaster struck a computer center, the crisis management team would activate and provide support to IT until the business operations are back to normal. This team's support is, in essence, crisis management support.

Difference in Scope

The business resumption plan deals with incidents that cause physical damage to assets of the company (see Exhibit 6-3). The crisis management plan deals with incidents that do not cause physical damage to assets of the company. This is one area of difference between the two planning concepts.

DIFFERENCE IN DEVELOPMENT SCENARIOS

Another difference is the use of scenarios. The concept used in crisis management planning is different than that used in business resumption planning. In business resumption planning, business units in a company build their resumption plans based on a *worst-case disaster scenario*. They do not build a plan to resume business from each type disaster that they could experience; i.e., fire, explosion, internal floods, damage from storms, etc.

In the mid-1970s, companies started building their disaster recovery plans with actions to respond to different scenarios. They were developed and documented as "what if" contingency plans: "What if" the computer equipment failed? "What if" the computer software failed? "What if" we lost power?

Companies carried that thinking over to their disaster recovery plans (DRP). They began developing a DRP for a fire, and another one for a flood, and a third for a storm.

Disaster recovery planners realized that most of the information used to resume business operations from one specific type of disaster was the same, or similar to, resuming business operations from an entirely different type of disaster. Whether it was a fire, or a flood, or a storm that struck their location, their plan called for them to:

- activate their alternate operating location
- retrieve their backup files from the off-premises storage location
- relocate key people to the alternate site to resume time-sensitive business operations

The same concepts would be used and the same recovery resources would be used, despite the fact that the cause of the disaster was different.

The planners realized that much of their plan contained redundant information. They decided that if the plan would work in "a worst-case disaster," that is the scenario that would be used. They recognized that the "worst-case disaster," as rare as it is, provided all the planning actions they would need. If the disaster that they needed to recover from was less damaging than a "worst-case disaster," the plan could still be used. Not all of the elements would need to be activated, only those elements applicable to the disaster situation at hand. Those elements that would be activated would be determined at the time of the disaster, based on an assessment of the damage. Therefore, they rebuilt their plans to resume operations from a "worst-case disaster."

The crisis management plan, on the other hand, does need to address specific types of crises. The reason is that the actions needed to manage one type of crisis could be quite different from the actions needed to manage a different type. For example, if the company is faced with a "sudden market shift" crisis, the company executives would manage the crisis entirely different than a "product safety" crisis. In a company that could realistically be faced with each of these crises, the company should pre-plan the actions and options they could take in each case to minimize the impact to the company.

What Is a "Crisis?"

A crisis is defined by:

- *Webster's New Collegiate Dictionary* as "a time of decision, an unstable or crucial time whose outcome will make a decisive difference for better or worse, an emotionally significant event or radical change of status in a person's life."

- Crisis management experts define a crisis as an unstable time for a company, with a distinct possibility for an undesirable outcome that could interfere with the normal operations of the business, or damage the bottom line, or jeopardize the positive public image, or result in close scrutiny from the media or government.

Types of Crises

A company can be faced with a number of different "types of crises." The list below contains some of the incidents that can evolve into a crisis. It is by no means all-inclusive. There are other incidents that are not identified here, but could be considered a crisis situation by your company.

Examples of incidents that can escalate into an acute crisis are:

- a product safety issue (where a product fails or is tampered with)
- a negative public perception of your company (appears your company doesn't care about the problem)
- a sudden market shift
- a financial problem
- an industrial relations problem (worker strike)

Other examples could be an adverse international event, a workplace violence incident, a lawsuit, and a regulatory fine.

Chapter 7

Learning from a Crisis

Andrew Blades

"WHAT CAN BE LEARNED FROM THE SUCCESSFUL MANAGEMENT OF A CRISIS?" This chapter discusses why studying successful management of a crisis is beneficial, as opposed to the study of any other crisis or desktop exercise, and why some organizations do not learn from past crises. The chapter also examines risk management's impact on managing a crisis and the principle points of developing a crisis plan.

Why should the study of successful crisis management enable us to learn more than the study of crisis management in general? While there is much to be learned from the management of any crisis or disaster, successful management of a crisis enables practitioners to consider what worked and why. Crisis situations that have turned into disasters enable a post-event analysis to determine what went wrong, but will not necessarily allow a proven alternative to be implemented. For the same reason, a successful crisis resolution provides better opportunities to develop successful crisis plans than do table-top exercises. For example, both a table-top exercise and a disaster may reveal that communications were ineffective; but post-incident analysis of a successfully managed crisis provides for identification of effective communication and allows it to be implemented in future crisis plans.

The opportunity to learn from the successful management of a crisis is greater than table-top exercises and unsuccessful crisis management for a number of reasons. Table-top exercises do not provide a real situation, and simulation can never completely replicate a true crisis. Human behavior will differ between an exercise and a real scenario, in part due to what is at stake in each situation. The successful management of a crisis provides a positive learning experience where people can be praised for their actions rather than being castigated for them, thus allowing more people to benefit from the experience. While unsuccessful management of the crisis will provide a real situation, it does not allow for a positive learning experience; and the post-event analysis will look for reasons why the situation was unsuccessfully managed. In doing so, personnel will be criticized. This may have the negative effect of lowering morale among crisis response staff.

Those events that an individual organization determines to constitute a crisis will vary and will, in part, be defined by that organization's risk management strategy. In theory, any event or realization of risk exposure should not result in a crisis. Risk management is supposed to ensure that the organization is not exposed to an unacceptable level of risk, or provide a (crisis) plan for dealing with situations that result from the realization of risk. From the above definitions, any act, event, or omission, that might result in a crisis should have been planned to limit and, where possible, extinguish the organization's risk exposure. However, the realization of a risk exposure will cause the organization to deal with a crisis situation. Particularly in complex systems, the risk exposure that leads to the crisis situation may have not been assessed, or it may have been incorrectly assessed.

Fink (1986), in his survey, discovered that of those organizations that had suffered a crisis in the past, only 42 percent now had a crisis plan in the event of another crisis. Fink (1986) has argued that a more vigilant attitude to crisis preparedness may have resulted in fewer headline-grabbing crises. The fact that more organizations do not have a crisis management plan indicates there is a feeling of denial. The culture of many organizations appears to be that of complacency — hoping it will not happen to them. For those organizations to which it already has happened, there appears to be an attitude of "lightning never strikes twice."

The passage of time results in new threats rising to the fore and humans tending to deal with the most recent event and forgetting those longer in the past. The significant point to note is that in many cases where organizations can learn from crisis management — successful or not — they do not and thus remain exposed to future crises. Although people can learn from a crisis or disaster, many will not because they no longer feel they are exposed to risk.

There are many reasons why an organization may not learn from its own crisis, or the crisis of another. These include economic, managerial, and denial of the organization's risk exposure, which if realized will result in a crisis. If an organization does not believe it is at risk, then it is unlikely to take the measures necessary to meet the threat. An organization's executive(s) must be held accountable for the organization's ability to meet crisis situations. However, as is the problem with risk communication, in many cases those who are responsible for crisis management do not have the understanding or knowledge to address the problem. Thus, there is a requirement for those who are charged with managing and planning for a crisis to be educated and trained to perform this function. One of the key reasons an organization does not learn from the mistakes of others is that many organizations lack the capability to conduct a post-event analysis. Equally important, many organizations do not wish to release information relating to their misfortune to more people than is essential. If an organization lacks the ability and expertise to plan for a crisis, it is unlikely to have staff trained to conduct a meaningful post-event analysis of its own or of other organizations.

The key to emergency planning is to have a plan — a set of detailed procedures and policies — that will take into account any reasonably foreseeable emergency or disaster; this is paramount to the successful management of a crisis. The plan should be in writing and describe, in as much detail as possible, the actions to be taken in a time of crisis. The process for developing an effective plan in most organizations will involve more than one person or component of an organization. Thus, the plan must be communicated to a diverse audience, all with different expectations and understandings of the plan and the crisis it is being designed to manage. There should be both expert and lay personnel providing input and assisting in actioning the plan.

Although each plan will differ in both its content and aim, it should provide for the following:

1. Designate authority to declare an emergency and order shutdown procedures and evacuation.
2. Establish an emergency chain of command.
3. Establish reporting responsibilities and chains.
4. Design emergency command and control points.
5. Establish and train emergency teams.
6. Establish asset protection and life-saving steps.
7. Designate equipment, facilities, and locations to be used in an emergency.
8. Communicate the plan to all involved.
9. Communicate with outside agencies.
10. Public relations and release of information.

Having briefly outlined how a crisis management plan should be developed and which points need consideration, it is appropriate to consider relevant theories on risk management and how they apply to managing a crisis.

In The Royal Society report, *Risk: Analysis, Perception and Management,* Hood et al. (1992) discuss the six rules in public risk management. These rules all contribute to the way risk is assessed. Although Hood deals specifically with public risk, this can be extrapolated to cover risk in other than public organizations. Most organizations would have similar constraints on their risk management methods. The rules are listed below:

1. *Boundary rules:* define who has access to the risk management process and who is involved in the process.
2. *Scope rules:* govern what comes within the province of risk management, and thus which factors risk managers may consider.
3. *Position rules:* identify at which point in the organization decisions relating to risk exposure are made.
4. *Information rules:* determine who has access to what information.
5. *Authority and procedural rules:* define the way in which decisions can be made.
6. *Preference-merging rules:* define ways decision-makers come together to make group decisions.

While these rules are for risk management, they have two impacts on crisis management: (1) they determine how the organization assesses risk, and (2) they can be superimposed over the organization's crisis management plan. Each one of these processes or rules is used in crisis management. In following the above outline, one can see how it is necessary to define who is involved in the management of the crisis; what they act on; who makes decisions and at which point in the management of the crisis; what information they will receive; how decisions will be made; and which decision-makers must come together to make decisions affecting the whole organization. Within the crisis management plan should be a crisis management team (CMT). The CMT will be responsible for managing both the crisis and resources committed to management of the crisis.

Risk management occurs at two stages. In the first instance, risk management processes will be utilized to determine risk exposure and thus where a crisis may occur. In the second instance, throughout the crisis, risk management will be used to determine which risks within the crisis need to be dealt with first. To this end, it is worth noting risk management issues that may impact the decision-making of the CMT and initial risk-management process.

The perceptions held by people will affect the decisions they make in relation to both risk and, by extension, crisis management. If the assessment of risk is subjective, then determinations are more likely to be governed by perception and not by facts. Biases and heuristics will influence many decisions. The impact of these factors is that decision-makers are affected by the situation they perceive, and not necessarily the situation as it exists. If their perception is wrong, then it is likely their decisions will be wrong; thus, any actions they choose may be misguided or incorrect. Perceptions that are incorrect or ill-informed, may lead to risk-blindness. Risk-blindness increases the likelihood of a crisis occurring, because the risk has not been considered. In a serious case, this could lead to disaster.

A second key issue is risk communication. One of the reasons behind communicating risk is to educate the lay people as to the level and impact of risk. If, as discussed above, people act on perception, then by educating personnel, their perception should closer represent reality.

How does this impact the management of a crisis? Incorrect perceptions can cause inappropriate actions and wasted resources. By definition, there is little time or place for wasted actions in a crisis situation. Risk communication between members of the CMT or, as is preferable, before a crisis can result in the CMT being better informed and taking more appropriate actions. Informed decisions will yield a better result than uninformed decisions. In a crisis situation, correct information is essential to the management of the crisis.

Having discussed some of the issues pertaining to crisis, the question of what can be learned from the successful management of a crisis can be answered. There is much that can be learned from any successfully managed crisis. As discussed, the amount learned is dependent on those conducting the post-event analysis and whether their training, knowledge, and experience allows them to capitalize on the learning opportunity.

Successful crisis management shows which procedures and practices worked and why. It allows a post-event analysis, which is not cathartic and as a result focuses on the constructive elements of the crisis management. Probably the most important lesson from successful management of a crisis is what works in a given situation. Although many lessons may be transportable between crisis situations, not all lessons and successful techniques will be transferable.

The question must be asked as to whether the difference between successful and unsuccessful crisis management is a matter of luck. Although good crisis management planning and sound training can lead to a successful outcome, a sudden change in circumstance can result in a disaster and no amount of learning from previous crises will prevent a sudden change in circumstances or nature. Successful management of a crisis allows an organization to validate its crisis management plan. Although not all lessons learned can be transferred from one situation to another, the underlying principles, such as the importance of good communication, can be transferred to future crisis plans. The validation of crisis plans is really only possible when the crisis is successfully managed, as only then can post-event analysis confirm what is successful and not only what is unsuccessful. Thus, the ultimate lesson learned from the successful management of any crisis is validation of the principles of crisis management and planning.

References

Fink, S., *Crisis Management: Planning for the Inevitable,* Amacom, New York, 1986.

Hood, C.C. et al., Risk Management, in: *The Royal Society, Risk: Analysis, Perception and Management,* The Royal Society, London, 1992.

Chapter 8

Plan to Rehearse the Crisis — Before the Crisis Tests the Organization

Steve York
Angus Graham

Most crisis management manuals do not explain how an organization can ascertain whether it has the capability of carrying out the recommended plans and procedures. Put differently, very few manuals specify the education, knowledge, and training required to implement an effective crisis management program.

— Mitroff, Pearson, and Harrington

A COMPREHENSIVE BUSINESS CONTINUITY PLAN (BCP) AND PROGRAM, WITH A DETAILED CRISIS MANAGEMENT PLAN IS VIRTUALLY USELESS WITHOUT A VALIDATION THROUGH AN EFFECTIVE REHEARSAL AND REVIEW PROCESS. The rehearsals must be with the people who are charged with the implementation of the plans at the time of a crisis. Independent persons with practical experience in dealing with real-life crisis situations, management, and integration of external agencies and regulatory authorities must be used to conduct these rehearsals.

THE RISKS

To make sense of a complex operational environment, it is argued that a somewhat heuristic approach to risk is necessary, made by people with experience in that particular business environment. This approach is necessary and appropriate, as a detailed assessment of all the factors that can go wrong may tend to prevent organizations from taking opportunities.

Friedal (1991) comments that there is some conflict between the role of senior management and that of the risk manager in this area. Senior management is charged with looking forward and identifying opportunities for growth, but this is based on short-term growth measurements. The risk manager's role is to look forward, identify the threats or dangers, and move cautiously to reduce risks. The combination of these two approaches is far more desirable. Rescher (1983) has stated that there are three cardinal rules in a rational approach to risk management and crisis management in an organization:

1. the maximization of expected values
2. the avoidance of catastrophe
3. the ignorance of remote possibilities

Rescher points out that the opportunities must be identified and maximized along with the process of minimizing risks, because the two are inseparable and form the essential elements of a successful organization.

Ritchie and Marshall (1993) propose that the methodology must start with the distinction between the internal and external risks. First, address the risks that are inherent in the organization, or the internal risks. These are likely to come from four main areas or sources:

1. assets and resources owned or under the control of the organization
2. the organization's current structure and culture
3. strategies that are being used
4. effectiveness of the management of the preceding three elements

The risks external to the organization are probably limitless. According to Ritchie and Marshall (1993), there are three main areas or sources of risk external to the organization:

1. opportunities and threats that relate to the organization
2. complexity
3. market/competitive forces

The interaction between these areas increases with the complexity of the task and the organizational structure. The ability to anticipate the risks is underpinned by the ability of management to understand the entire environment in which it operates.

CRISIS MANAGEMENT CONCEPTS

In today's increasingly sociotechnological and complex world, many organizations have been required to assume the position that it is not a question of if or whether they will experience a crisis, but rather, it is really a matter of what type of crisis will occur, what form it will take, or, more importantly, how and when it will happen. Traditionally, a crisis situation occurs at the worst possible time — Murphy's law. Seldom will the right people be readily available, resources plentiful, and communication lines accessible.

The critical factor in determining how well an organization will perform during a crisis is how well-prepared it is before the crisis occurs. For this reason, one cannot emphasize too strongly the importance of advance preparation.

One of the best ways to understand what you need to do before a crisis takes place is to understand what you need to do during a crisis. Exposing management personnel to a simulated operation allows a certain amount of "stress inoculation" and better understanding of the capabilities the organization should have in order to perform effectively. In other words, the best-formulated crisis plans, as well as the best abilities to "ad hoc it," will be useless if an organization does not have the capabilities required to handle a crisis.

Although plans and the ability to think and act quickly are certainly necessary and desirable qualities, neither is sufficient without the capability of the organization to carry it out.

WHAT IS A CRISIS?

There is no single, universally accepted definition of a crisis, although there is general agreement that a crisis is an event that can destroy or affect an entire organization. Accordingly, if something affects merely a part or one unit of an organization, it may or may not be or lead to a crisis.

Analysis of multiple crisis events clearly indicates that one cannot identify only one single point of failure — there are multiple factors that lead to a crisis.

A potential crisis event commences as an act of God or incident, coupled with design failure, procedural failure, and human failure — all these elements can lead to a crisis event. They are also points that, if identified and acted upon, can lead to crisis prevention. (Kennedy Report)

A crisis can affect the very existence of an organization, a major product line, a business unit, or other critical components. A crisis can also damage, perhaps severely, an organization's financial performance, and the health and well-being of consumers, employees, the surrounding community, and the environment. Finally, a crisis can destroy the public's basic trust or belief in an organization, its reputation, and its image.

CRISIS MYTHS

Many senior executives believe that during a time of crisis, it is "business as usual." It is not; it is "business survival." A fatal flaw is to believe that because one is constantly dealing with problems, that a crisis is just a bigger problem. An organization that does not identify (the earlier, the better) that it is now confronting a completely different environment, may become extinct. There is a two-edged responsibility in crisis management: maintaining unaffected business streams and a business-as-usual appearance while, at the same time, dealing with the crisis — using nonstandard procedures.

The myths surrounding crisis management can be summarized as follows.

1. The Crisis Must Be Someone's Fault

There are must be a combination of events, which culminate in a crisis incident (these include systems failure, procedure failure, and human failure). Certainly, human error causes or contributes to many such crises. However, other factors, including the natural environment and external influences over which one has no control, can play a greater role.

If one spends valuable time and intellectual energy focusing on a human mistake and directing a witch-hunt, this will not solve the actual problem at hand. It is an issue that can be adequately dealt with when the crisis has been eliminated. **WORK THE PROBLEM.**

2. An Organization in a Crisis Situation Indicates an Inability to Manage

Every crisis, whether common or unthinkable, comprises three components: those that one can directly control, those that one can only indirectly control, and those that defy control.

No organization voluntarily places itself into crisis mode. However, the organization should identify indicators that can assist in crisis prevention; the establishment of a Crisis Management Center facilitates that philosophy. Realistically, however, the elements outside one's control will have the greatest impact.

Once again, developing solutions and resolving the issue is a better indication of an ability to manage. Do not lose time defending — time will be short — **FIND THE ANSWERS.**

3. Crisis Always Destroys

The *Macquarie Dictionary* (Australian), defines crisis, from a medical perspective, as "the point in the course of a disease at which a decisive change occurs leading either to recovery or to death."

While a crisis might disrupt an organization, it does not have to destroy the organization. It will be a test of the strength of the organization — it can be an opportunity for management to focus on what really counts, to use innovative solutions to problems, and to capitalize on the positive aspects of the organization's culture.

This demands excellent leadership from the crisis management team. **BE PREPARED TO LEAD.**

4. Contingency Planning Equals Crisis Management

Most crisis management plans are supported by a series of contingency plans; some of these plans are little more than wishful thinking and others are extremely comprehensive, detailing minute procedures.

However, the flaw in most contingency plans is the mistaken belief that every crisis follows a predictable pattern. If a crisis is truly predictable, it is not a crisis.

Genuine crisis management allows one to deal with crisis wherever and however it occurs. It is an imaginary comfort zone to believe that a series of contingency plans will cater to every possible situation. **THERE WILL NEVER BE A CONTINGENCY PLAN FOR EVERY ISSUE.**

5. Lone Wolves Resolve Crises Best

The best crisis management involves team play. It works best when a motivated group addresses a challenge with focus, unity, and cooperation. Nothing damages organization crisis management more than the lone wolf — the solo player who has a tunnel vision or a biased objective.

The crisis management team is also supported by a number of vital "behind-the-scenes" people working within the crisis management center as well as all the field operatives. These people do the dirty work, painstakingly gathering the required information and identifying potential hazards for the crisis management team.

It a combination of efforts of all these players that can help resolve the situation intelligently and quickly. However, these efforts require crisis management leadership. **TEAMWORK WILL MAKE ALL WORK EASIER.**

THE ROLE OF CRISIS MANAGEMENT REHEARSALS

Simulations and training exercises are an essential part of the development of crisis management response. A good scenario tests every aspect of the crisis management process, including as many of the possible dynamics that might occur in a real event.

It is important for the simulation not to be so transparent that the decisions and actions of the crisis management team are obvious or reduced to a single choice. Instead, a good simulation contains generous amounts of uncertainty. This forces the members of the crisis management team to state their assumptions as clearly as they can, reach agreement where they can, tolerate disagreement where they cannot, and identify for every step:

- what they know
- what they do not know
- what they must do immediately
- what they must postpone
- what they must monitor and keep track of over time

The crisis management team must keep track of the details and the Big Picture. This is easier said than done. As leading managers, one is accustomed to making decisions within a controlled environment, with all the available data and sufficient time to reflection. However, during a crisis, that sense of control is diminished, all the facts are not readily available, and decisions are needed quickly.

Rehearsals will develop a systematic process whereby all these problems can be logically addressed.

CRISIS MANAGEMENT PLANS

The crisis management plan is a framework. It will not and cannot provide the answers to every possible situation. It is a guidebook to assist the crisis management team in developing the solutions.

There are some key points to keep in mind when developing a crisis management plan:

1. Avoid copying other plans. Seldom can one take a plan from one organization to another and it remain completely relevant. Further, due to international vagaries, it is difficult to take a plan from another country, and expect it to work, even if it is from the same company.
2. The plan must clearly define the roles and responsibilities of all people involved. This should include the lines of communication.
3. The plan must be continuously reviewed and updated. Any review must take into consideration current national and international trends.
4. The plan must incorporate the strategies of business continuity or business resumption. Remember that after the crisis, there is a future. Many of these efforts can be accomplished simultaneously.
5. The plan must also address occupational health and safety, and duty of care legislative requirements.
6. The plan must support other local management plans and act in symmetry with other emergency responses.
7. Where possible, simple and easy-to-use checklists, aide-memoirs, and the like should adjunct the plan.

THE CRISIS MANAGEMENT TEAM

Each organization has a unique approach to the formulation of its crisis management team. Some organizations, ensure that the CEO is a key member of the team, whereas other organizations keep the CEO separate from the team.

In general, the crisis management team has a guiding philosophy, that it uses to guide and direct its decision-making. Some of the basic principles may include:

- maximize the safety and security of all stakeholders
- protection of public image
- protection of profitability
- maintain occupational health and safety standards
- minimize legal consequences
- minimize the further degradation of equipment and services

For a crisis management team to be successful, the following ingredients must apply:

- small select team
- capable of making decisions
- representing all of the organization's key stakeholders
- has authority to take command
- will work and act as a team

HOW TO CONDUCT CRISIS MANAGEMENT REHEARSALS

Phase One

This preliminary stage should be regarded as an introduction phase. This would include:

- introduction to crisis management concepts
- principles of operations for crisis management centers
- initial rehearsal scenarios

These phases and rehearsals are based upon Australian Standard AS4360:1999 and Emergency Management Australia protocols. The outcomes from the preliminary stage include:

- creation of individual and team awareness of roles and responsibilities
- assessment of the capacity of the crisis management team
- assessment of the suitability of procedures and checklists
- review of resource allocations and CMC layout
- identification of key improvement areas

Phase Two

This stage should be regarded as a development phase. Following the initial rehearsal, a critical assessment of planning assumptions and identification of key improvement areas should occur, as well as a recommendation of the various teams that need to receive specific development training.

At this stage, the teams might include:

- primary crisis management team
- alternate crisis management team members
- support staff

During this phase, one anticipates that all relevant documentation will be validated, improved, and agreed upon by management.

The level of skills, knowledge, and understanding demonstrated during the Phase One Rehearsal will determine the style of training for this phase. However, workshop sessions should successfully cater to the individual team needs. These sessions would be designed to encourage discussions, understanding, and at the same time be instructive. The training emphasis would include:

- briefing and debriefing
- communication issues
- corporate policy and procedures
- corporate support for key personnel
- leadership
- media considerations
- problem identification and solving
- problem-solving
- team approach

Participants in the training phase will not only learn about crisis management and the issues that may occur, but they will also gain individual experience and knowledge. This should raise their level of competence and allow them to become comfortable with the planning arrangements.

Phase Three

This stage should be regarded as the thorough systems test. This will be achieved through a more detailed rehearsal of the key players, using a comprehensive crisis scenario(s). The design of the rehearsal will deliberately test all systems and further challenge the skills of the teams working within the crisis management center.

This exercise management plan will be based on feedback from Phase One and Phase Two, as well as further detailed consideration of specific identified risks relating to hazards. The exercise can occur over an extended period, which will allow a simulated shift change-over and multiple problem inputs.

Phase Four

This stage involves consistent monitoring and review. Should it be deemed necessary, additional training can be provided or supplementary rehearsals can be conducted at regular intervals to ensure that the plan is current and the team is "battle-ready."

COMMENT

Weir (1996) warns that a "system, however well conceived, for ordering and clarifying the administrative consequences of disaster, cannot itself prevent these events happening." The successful management of the consequences will also be based on the anticipatory approach of the organization and training of the management team. The amount of control that a management team can implement in the face of a crisis depends on how well the team has planned for the worst-case scenario.

Weir (1996) warns that the relationship between the internal and external factors can be complex, and control systems can be based on what should happen rather than what does happen. Weir says, "it seems to be normal for senior management to underestimate the nature of a crisis and overestimate its ability to manage it."

CONCLUSION

In the final analysis, all the preparation in the world for any crisis is fraught with uncertainties, as is life itself. But it does seem that many people cause themselves — and others — a great deal of unnecessary stress by being concerned about the inevitable unfairness of life, upset because they do not have a crystal ball. If ever overcome by such feelings, find solace in the knowledge that no one has a crystal ball. As Adams (1995) has said, "the future does not exist, except in the minds of those trying to predict future events."

During a crisis, it is no help to ask why this is happening to your organization? "Why?" is a luxury question. Instead, take the position that: now that this is happening to us, what are we going to do about it?

Effective decision-making is a technique. High-quality decision-making in the midst of crisis-induced stress is a process with mechanics to it. Crisis management is a process with mechanics to it.

With pratice and adequate preparation, one will be inoculating oneself against stress so that, during times of stress, during crises, during times of urgency, intensity, and enormous pressure, one is still going to go through the techniques that constitute vigilant decision-making. These techniques will provide the greatest likelihood of achievement, of attaining and maintaining selfconfidence in the face of uncertainty.

And, finally, one will be in the best position possible to be able to develop solutions, to resolve the multiple issues at hand, thereby allowing one's organization to provide the necessary support to staff and other critical stakeholders.

Crisis management is leadership and communicating with the right people to make the right decisions at the right time. Having a crisis management plan without practically exercising it with the people who would be involved in a real incident, is like writing a food critique from a menu.

References

Adams, J., *Risk*, UCL Press London 1995.

Fredel, W., A Changing World Inspires New Definitions of Risk, *Risk Management*, 38(10), 22–30, October 1991.

Rescher, N., *Risk: A Philosophical Introduction to the Theory of Risk Evaluation and Management*, University Press of America, 1983.

Ritchie, B. and Marshall, D., *Business Risk Management*, Chapman & Hall, London, 1993.

Weir, D. T. H., Risk and Disaster: Role of Communications Breakdown in Plane Crashes and Business Failure, in *Accident and Design, Contemporary Debates in Risk Management*, Hood, C. and Jones, D. K. C., Eds., University Press, London, 1996, 114–125.

Further Reading

Ansell, J. and Wharton, F., *Risk Analysis, Assessment and Management*, John Wiley & Sons, Chichester, 1992.

Australian and New Zealand Standard, Risk Management, AS/NZS: 1995/9, Standards Australia.

Craig, A., Risk Evaluation and Control: Practical Guidelines for Risk Assessment, in *The Definitive Handbook of Business Continuity Management*, Hiles, A. and Barnes, P., Eds., John Wiley & Sons, Chichester, 1999, 123–131.

Interviews with Dr. Michael Diamond and Murray Wright.

Douglas, M., in Wells 1999: 8, Inquiring into Disasters: Law, Politics and Blame, in *Risk Management: An International Journal*, 1(2), 8, 1999, Perpetuity Press.

Hardy (1992), cited in Musson, D. and Jordan, E., Business and Computer Contingency Planning in Australia, in *The Macquarie Management Papers*, Australia. Macquarie University, 25, 1997.

Heath, R., A Crisis Management Perspective of Business Continuity, in *The Definitive Handbook of Business Continuity Management*,Hiles, A. and Barnes, P., Eds., John Wiley & Sons, Chichester, 1999, 43–55.

Hiles, A. and Barnes, P., Eds., *The Definitive Handbook of Business Continuity Management*, John Wiley & Sons, Chichester, 1999.

Hood, C. and Jones, D. K. C., Eds., *Accident and Design: Contemporary Debates in Risk Management*, University Press, London, 1996.

Irwin, A., *Citizen Science: A study of people, expertise and sustainable development,* Routledge, London, 1995.

Musson, D. and Jordan, E., Business and Computer Contingency Planning in Australia, in: *The Macquarie Management Papers,* Macquarie University, Australia, 1997.

Toft, B. and Reynolds, S., *Learning from Disasters: A Management Approach*, Perpetuity Press, Leicester, 1997.

Wells, C., "Inquiring into Disasters: Law, Politics and Blame, in *Risk Management: An International Journal,* 1(2), 1999, Perpetuity Press.

Chapter 9
The Crisis Management Command Center

Mark B. Desman

THE LOCATION OF THE CRISIS MANAGEMENT COMMAND CENTER (CMCC) SHOULD BE PREPLANNED. It is too late to begin looking for a place to meet after the crisis has struck.

The first suggestion for the crisis management command center is a conference room or meeting room in the headquarters building. If these are unavailable during the crisis, a conference room or meeting room in another company building would be a good choice. Another alternative would be a hotel near the headquarters building.

If the location is not to be in a company-owned facility, some requirements in selecting the site include:

- it should be easy to find
- it should be near a main transportation route
- it should have sufficient parking space

OTHER CONSIDERATIONS FOR THE CRISIS MANAGEMENT COMMAND CENTER

There are other considerations that the crisis management team may want to address in planning for the location of the crisis management command center.

Some companies have chosen to have a single room available for the crisis management team members. Other companies have chosen to locate the crisis management team in multiple rooms in order to lessen the noise and emotional stress. In those cases, however, the rooms are on the same floor of the building. This allows for ease of communication between the various teams.

0-8493-0907-7/00/$0.00+$.50
© 2001 by CRC Press LLC

Some companies have planned a separate room in which the executive management team can meet with one another and discuss the latest updates in the crisis. This room can also be used for the executive management team to meet with particular members of the crisis management team for feedback and information regarding the crisis. In addition, the plan can include a "news briefing" room for meetings with media personnel.

Some companies have chosen to have their crisis management command center in a mobile trailer with key equipment already installed. This is similar to the command posts used in the public sector.

USING THE CRISIS MANAGEMENT COMMAND CENTER?

Members of the crisis management team will use the crisis management command center as a focal point during a crisis. During the acute-crisis stage, it should be entirely dedicated to the management of the crisis. It should be sealed off from the day-to-day activities of the company, because normal office settings are filled with distractions. Having such a facility will promote prompt and responsible reactions to the crisis.

One must recognize in setting up a crisis management command center that the location and resources will change depending on the stage of the crisis. The stage of the crisis will dictate the location and resources of the crisis management command center.

THE PRE-CRISIS STAGE

If the problem is in the *pre-crisis stage*, the executive management team will deal with it. The location of the CMCC will probably be the company's boardroom. During this stage, the CMCC should be used during pre-crisis for fact gathering, threat assessment, and action selection. The resources required will be limited.

THE ACUTE-CRISIS STAGE

If the problem is in the *acute-crisis stage*, the crisis management team will deal with the problem. The location of the command center will be the prepositioned crisis management command center. Team members will assemble there and could stay for the duration of the event.

The CMCC will be used for:
- fact gathering
- situation evaluation
- options assessment
- action selection
- issuance of instructions
- monitoring of progress

The resources needed could be extensive and should be prepositioned.

THE POST-CRISIS STAGE

When the crisis reaches the *post-crisis stage*, the executive management team will deal with the recovery. The location of the crisis management command center will again be the company's boardroom.

The CMCC will be used to deal with:

- recovery issues
- development of any new strategies

The resources that will be required will not be as extensive as those needed during the acute-crisis stage. If specific resources are needed, they can be brought to the boardroom from the CMCC.

RESOURCES OF THE CRISIS MANAGEMENT COMMAND CENTER

The particular stage of the crisis will dictate the resources of the crisis management command center. More resources will be needed during the acute crisis stage. As many resources as possible should be pre-positioned in the CMCC. The normal office furniture and supplies are needed in the crisis management command center, e.g., desks, chairs, clocks, paper, pencils and pens, envelopes, stamps, etc.

The following is a list of some of the resources that may be required in the executive management team's room or the crisis management command center.

- Computer equipment
  - Personal computers
  - Peripherals, servers, printers
- Power equipment
  - Power strips
  - Generator, backup power
- Telephones
  - Phones — how many will be needed?
  - How many will be accessed through the switchboard?
  - How many will be direct lines?
  - Cellular phones — check duration of batteries
- Televisions (cable hookup)
  - one for local; one for national
  - VCR recorders
  - Video camera/camcorder
  - Digital camera
- Dual-powered radios
- Copy machines
- Fax machines
- Tape recorders

- Transcribing units
- Status boards
  - Grease boards
  - Flip charts and masking tape
- Typical documentation
  - Prevention plans
  - Policies/procedures
  - Emergency response plans
  - Incident response plans
  - Evacuation plans
  - Business resumption plans

Some examples of additional resources that may be needed, especially during the acute-crisis stage, are diagrams of installations, pictures of key people, organization charts, and information on products and processes. Permanently on file at the crisis management command center should be all contingency plans, scenarios, and emergency procedure instructions that have been developed in advance. The addresses and telephone numbers of major players should be on hand, as well as information on outside resources.

The list is not all-inclusive. It is a compilation of suggested resources to respond to an assortment of crises. There could be additional resources that your company would want on the list. On the other hand, this list is not a requirement for all companies. A small- or medium-sized company may not be able to cost-justify the prepositioning of all the equipment.

PREPOSITIONING THE RESOURCES

Before obtaining all of the equipment listed above, you need to ask: does the company normally have these resources? Are they readily available? If not, how long will it take to get them? Could the time to acquire them result in a failure to control the crisis?

CONCLUSION

Crisis management planning is becoming a major element in business continuity plans throughout the country. In order to have an effective crisis management plan, a number of people have to be committed to the concepts in this chapter. This chapter will give those companies without a crisis management plan the basics to begin, and ultimately to implement, their own crisis management plan.

Chapter 10

Trauma:
The Forgotten Factor

Steve Watts
David Ball

ONE OF THE ESSENTIAL TASKS THAT THE BUSINESS CONTINUITY PLANNER FACES IS THE ORGANIZATION OF PERSONNEL. The business continuity plan (BCP) will feature recovery teams, created from the available personnel, brought together because of the skills they can offer under disruptive conditions to bring about the resolution of the situation.

It is a truism that an untested BCP can often be worse than having no BCP at all. This is being recognized in many quarters, and testing programs have been embarked upon. For those organizations that require recovery to be achieved within extremely short time scales — for example, those operating in the financial sector — recovery can become a very slick operation.

There are various suggested methodologies for testing plans. These are not be explored here: it is sufficient to say that, so far as BCP testing is concerned, each component of the BCP should initially be tested, followed by the testing of combinations of components, culminating in a comprehensive, real-life test.

The result of the test will be that, so far as the organization is concerned, a workable BCP is in place. But, so far as the personnel who are both prominent in the BCP and who are required to implement it, there is often very little in place.

TRAUMA CREATED BY DISRUPTION

It is difficult to realistically simulate the conditions and pressures that would be faced under real disruption conditions. Perhaps lessons can be learned from the United States. Until the well-publicized attack on the World Trade Center in New York occurred, BCPs were often compiled primarily to combat threats brought about by natural phenomena — earthquakes, hurricanes, tornadoes, etc. If such an occurrence did manifest itself, the

0-8493-0907-7/00/$0.00+$.50
© 2001 by CRC Press LLC

organization would be affected, together with the surrounding locality and community. The result would be that employees, their families, and their property could suffer the same fate as the organization. Specialist personnel are often specifically brought in to help deal with these situations.

It has often been stated that personnel are the most valuable asset of an organization, no more so than under disruption conditions. But they can only be expected to function correctly under adverse conditions if they can be assured that their families are being cared for, and that a bigger problem does not exist at home. Therefore, consideration must be given to the levels of stress and trauma created by a disruption.

It is all too easy to provide lists of actions and responsibilities in times of normal working. Under disaster conditions, human reactions have been demonstrated to be unpredictable. For example, following a terrorist attack on a public house in London, a survivor received prompt medical attention and was discharged the same evening. Twelve hours later, the Samaritans were doing their best to dissuade him from committing suicide.

BEHAVIOR OF PERSONNEL

The disruption is likely to be the first and only opportunity to evaluate the behavior of personnel under unique and stressful circumstances. A reason for the apparent lack of attention to this area concerns the status given to any topic that involves mental well-being. For example, a hospital treating physical ailments has a high profile, whereas those treating mental conditions are usually hidden from view, and little is known about them and their activities. Physical conditions have high status; mental conditions have low status.

- When disruption strikes, various reactions can be expected. A group of people will react in a certain way; individuals will display definite symptoms.
- What is the chain of reactions to be expected under times of stress brought about by disruption?

Initially, everyone will want to help to resolve the situation; a degree of loyalty can be expected in the face of adversity. The realization that the incident has occurred and that "it has happened to me and my organization" will then surface. As a result, personnel will attempt to seek refuge as close as possible to the seat of the incident. This will be followed by a sense of anger against both the organization, for allowing the disruption to occur, and also against the perpetrator(s) of the incident. Finally, demands as to what is to be done to resolve the situation will be made.

The individual faced with crisis can be expected to display symptoms of numbness, anger, fear, depression, elation, irritability, helplessness, aggression, and guilt. Such reactions will be worsened if the exposure to the crisis is prolonged; where there is a (perceived) threat to life; where multiple deaths have occurred; where the crisis is sudden and unexpected; where the crisis has a special significance, such as where the incident involves the death or injury of a close relative; where there is lack of proper support; and where, in addition to the immediate problem, there are additional life stresses to be dealt with, such as those mentioned in the United States example.

Clearly, to ensure that the negative aspects do not prevail, the business continuity planner should be aware of the above, and should incorporate controls and checks into the BCP.

ADDRESSING TRAUMA IN THE PLANNING PROCESS

A method of ensuring that stress and trauma is addressed is for a personnel response team to be established as part of the BCP recovery team. This team will play a supportive role to the recovery team to ensure that the victims of the disaster needs are addressed. The purpose of this team will be primarily to liaise with the organization's personnel and their relatives. The coordinator of the team, in addition to directing and managing it, should maintain an employee master register, containing details of all involved personnel and their activities over the disruption period, in order that assistance can be directly provided to them.

The coordinator might decide that professional help is needed and summon a crisis incident management unit to assist. Among the skills that the members of the unit can be expected to provide is post-trauma stress counseling. Under normal conditions, counseling is the fastest-growing welfare benefit. While it is a logical progression to take full advantage of it under disruption conditions, it is not an area that should be entered into in a hurry. Such help should not be forced on people; an adverse result could ensue, in that they could be led to believe that they are not feeling what is expected of them. Adverse situations must not be created, or made more complex than they already are.

The topic of stress is likely to become more prominent. For example, the tort of negligence states that a duty of care is owed. If that duty of care is breached, then an offense will have been committed, and the organization will be liable for injury or damage sustained as a direct result of the breach. It is possible that the infliction of stress upon an individual could equally be considered to be injurious or damaging.

CONCLUSION

Currently, there are liability issues being faced for the effects of asbestos, atmospheric and noise pollution, and visual display units with far-reaching implications. Could the effects of stress and trauma be the next areas for litigation?

The issue stress and trauma suffered by the "victims" of a disaster is not addressed by many organizations' business continuity plans. For many organizations, this issue will only be addressed when they are faced with litigation from the victims of the disaster.

Section III
Business Continuity Planning

Chapter 11
Overview of Business Continuity Planning
Sally Meglathery

CORPORATE BUSINESS CONTINUITY PLANNING SPECIFIES THE METHODOLOGY, STRUCTURE, DISCIPLINE, AND PROCEDURES NEEDED TO BACK UP AND RECOVER FUNCTIONAL UNITS STRUCK BY A CATASTROPHE. Therefore, every functional unit must accept responsibility for developing and implementing the business continuity plan, and the plan must have the total support of management.

Strategically, senior management must ensure the development of a policy stating that the company will recover from any type of outage. Such recovery requires high-level commitment to the policy from all levels of management. Tactically, however, middle management implements the policy and the plan and is responsible for the daily operation of the plan. For management and the functional units to participate, they must have a comprehensive methodology to guide them in their actions and activities. This chapter discusses methods of developing a corporate business continuity plan.

PROJECT PLANNING

There are numerous reasons for developing a total business continuity plan. Some of the most compelling are legal and regulatory requirements. Consideration must be given to the following when developing the plan:

- Are there any federal statutes or regulations applicable to the business which would apply to disasters relating to the business?
- Are there any state statutes or regulations applicable to the business which would apply to disasters relating to the business?
- What contract requirements (e.g., labor contracts, insurance agreements, mortgages, loans, or other financial documents) should be addressed by the plan?
- Are there any common-law considerations, such as claims against directors and officers raised by shareholders and others? Could there be negligence claims against the company for property damage or injuries to customers or business visitors?

Before beginning development of the business continuity plan, management should identify a business continuity project team. The project team is responsible for developing the business continuity plan and designing procedures and reporting techniques to support overall project management. In addition, the project team should identify individuals from senior management to review and approve the work performed by the project team.

Although the makeup of the project team will vary among companies, the following departments should be represented on the team:

- real estate and facilities
- security
- human resources
- information systems
- communications
- technology, planning, and development

Additional departments may also be represented. A business continuity manager should be delegated for the team.

DEVELOPING THE PLAN

The plan that is developed must ensure that any disaster will have a minimum impact on the company. The plan should address the company's reasons for establishing the plan, the functional area of the company's business that the plan will cover, and what staff or materials are in place or should be in place for the plan to function. The following sections discuss the requirements of the business continuity plan, the various elements of the plan, and the scope of the plan.

Plan Requirements

Although most plans address the need to continue system operations and to support critical operations during a crisis, most plans fail to consider loss of other functional units within the organization. Data processing generally initiates the need for business continuity planning; however, it is now recognized that recovering data centers alone cannot ensure the continuing health of the organization. Companies must address corporate division and department business continuity planning as well. In fact, planning should be done for all essential functional units of the organization.

The plan must be comprehensive; it must deal with the broadest range of disasters possible. There should be a basic plan with additional procedures for specific hazards (e.g., earthquakes, fires, or exposure to hazardous materials). The plan should preserve the integrity of the business, not individual items or goals.

The plan must contain sufficient detail so that its users will know what procedures to follow, how to perform these activities, and the resources that will be available. The plan should contain action steps that have been decided on and agreed to in advance. Both the response to the immediate disaster and the recovery and continuance of business operations and functions must be specified.

The plan must be owned by the organization. Key personnel must participate in identifying priorities, determining alternative strategies, negotiating agreements, and assembling necessary materials. The plan should be reviewed on a periodic basis or when circumstances change. It should be periodically tested with a defined testing program to ensure that it remains effective and up to date.

Plan Elements

The plan itself has five major elements:

1. Risk and business impact analysis
2. Alternative analysis
3. Response and recovery planning and plan documentation
4. Plan publication and testing
5. Training and implementation

These are discussed in the following sections

1. Risk and Business Impact Analysis. Before the plan is written, the hazards that may affect the company's facilities must be identified and their potential impact determined. It is also necessary to identify and rank the major business functions and operations. This helps determine the maximum allowable downtime for individual business functions and operations. From there, the minimum resource and personnel needs and time frames in which they will be needed can be identified. Finally, consideration of emergency operating procedures and strategies can begin.

2. Alternative Analysis. Using the risk and business impact analysis as a base, consideration is given to the internal and external alternatives available for continuation of each function within the necessary time frames. These alternatives should be chosen on the basis of their cost, benefits, and feasibility. The alternatives considered should include not only those that are currently available but those that can be developed.

3. Response and Recovery Planning and Plan Documentation. This involves the development and documentation of the procedures to be used to activate the plan (by declaration or event), move specific functions to the alternative or backup facility, maintain operations at that site while the primary site is being restored or a new permanent site prepared, and return operations to the primary site or another permanent location. The plan must identify ways to procure alternative resources to carry out business activities; determine responsibilities and notification procedures for the company, vendors, customers, and others; and detail recovery strategies and responsibilities.

4. Plan Publication and Testing. The plan must be reviewed and agreed to by senior management and all departments. It must then be documented and distributed to key personnel with additional copies secured off site. Individual sections of the plan should be distributed to those who will be involved with its activation and operation.

The plan should contain a schedule for periodic review and updating. The only way to assess the adequacy of the plan before a disaster occurs is with a program of periodic tests. The tests used will vary from conceptual walkthroughs to actual relocation of specific departments or business functions.

5. Training and Implementation. Employees should understand what is expected of them in a disaster and what their roles will be in the recovery process. This is achieved with a training and education program, which should be conducted before the plan is implemented.

The Scope of the Plan. All key personnel should be identified in the business continuity plan and given specific assignments. Common terminology should be defined in the plan document to avoid confusion at the time the plan is put into effect. In addition, the plan should interface with the IS business continuity plan. Budgets should be prepared for the initial costs of developing the plan and for the costs of maintaining the plan.

The scope of the business continuity plan should include the features discussed in the following sections.

A Vital Records Program. The plan should help establish an information valuation program to determine which records should be retained and for how long. In addition, there should be a methodology for ensuring that critical records are retained off site.

Security Requirements. The plan defines what security measures must be in place in the event of a disaster and what security measures are necessary for an off-site location. It also states who has access to each location.

Accounting Procedures. Procedures must be put in place to facilitate the acquisition of needed replacement parts and to properly account for the costs of recovery. This in turn facilitates the filing of insurance claims, among other benefits.

Insurance Requirements. The plan should define what insurance claims must be filed and give guidelines on working with risk managers to file a claim. One of the benefits of developing the business continuity plan is that insurance requirements are specifically defined.

Interdepartmental Interfaces. Interfaces between divisions and departments must be defined in the business continuity plan.

Backup, Recovery, and Restoration Strategies. All critical data, files, and documents should be backed up and stored off site. Recovery procedures should be documented in the business continuity plan, defining the steps necessary to recover the information that was lost. Restoration may require recreating the lost data, files, or documents rather than recovering with a backup. Procedures for such restoration must be documented.

Plan Maintenance and Testing. Once implemented, the plan must be tested regularly to ensure that it is up-to-date. The plan should include a maintenance and testing schedule as well as a methodology for testing the plan to ensure that it is operating as expected.

IDENTIFYING CRITICAL RESOURCES

Not all activities within an organization are critical at the time of a catastrophe. The management disaster decision team identifies those operations that it deems critical to the organization. This determination is based on several specific factors, including the time at which the disaster occurs, legal and regulatory requirements, the amount of time that availability is lost, the company's public image, loss of market share, loss of revenue, the type of service loss (e.g., administrative, executive, or financial), and deadline requirements.

In addition, the plan should account for the facilities, equipment, materials, and supplies needed to adequately perform required tasks. Voice and data communications are particularly critical and should be given proper consideration.

For example, personnel are vital to the success of the recovery, and their comfort and support should be given special attention. Supplies and forms should be maintained off site so that a supply is readily available in times of emergency. In addition, transportation can easily be disrupted in times of emergency, and transportation to an off-site location may not be readily available. Therefore, transportation to the main site or an off-site location must be planned if employees are to arrive at the designated stations in a timely manner.

Spare parts and units for power and environmental systems (e.g., air conditioners, fans, and heaters) should be available at the central business location. The engineering staff should have spare parts on hand for replacing broken parts. A backup unit should be available to replace the disabled units. When that is not possible or when the outage is outside the control of the company (e.g., the loss of a telephone company's central office or a power company's power station), the company must be prepared to move to its off-site location.

A vital record is any document that is necessary to ensure the survival of the business. To ensure the preservation and availability of vital records, all corporate documents should be classified as to their importance (e.g., essential, valuable, important, or nonessential). Corporate recordkeeping policies as well as retention requirements based on legal or regulatory requirements should be documented. The source document should be controlled and protected. In addition, there should be backup procedures for the documents, and a copy of them should be maintained at the off-site location.

Documentation, policies, procedures, and standards should be available in hard copy and should be accessible in both main and off-site locations. A business continuity plan has no value if the business continuity team cannot locate a copy of it.

ORGANIZING THE PROJECT

The business continuity plan should be prefaced with a mission statement or purpose. This can be incorporated into the introductory section of the plan. All departments and functions involved in the project must understand the need for the plan, agree to participate in its implementation, and be committed to enforcing the plan.

The departments and functions that participate in the project vary among companies. In most companies, however, senior management must be kept up-to-date and is responsible for making most key decisions. The audit department oversees the entire process, ensuring that controls are enforced. When a disaster strikes, the building and facilities staff determine any losses and necessary repairs, and the public relations and marketing staffs calm customers and reassure them that the company is all right. A legal staff helps protect the company from litigation, negotiates purchase contracts, and enforces contracts.

The human resources department is usually responsible for keeping all employees informed during and after a disaster, particularly in union shops. In addition, this staff often serves as the go-between for employees and management.

When it is necessary to replace equipment or parts, the purchasing department acquires the necessary components at the best possible price, and the financial or accounting department controls costs and purchases.

The engineering department ensures that the components are properly ordered and installed.

At some level, all disasters have an impact on information systems. Therefore, the IS department must be kept up-to-date and should participate in the recovery procedures. The operations department ensures that the company continues to run as smoothly as possible.

Depending on the company's business, the following departments might also be included in the business continuity planning process:

- manufacturing
- research and development
- warehouse and distribution
- customer service
- field support services

Representatives from these business areas can identify the functional, management, and support operations of the company in the initial phases of the project, while gathering information for the plan. As a result, critical divisions and departments that support the organization in times of catastrophe are identified.

In any company, the business continuity plan cannot be developed without the commitment and assistance of management and departmental staff. A considerable amount of coordination is also required, both within the company and between any external resources or consultants and company personnel. To facilitate this, it is recommended that different planning teams and functions be created. The size, number, and type of teams used are determined by the size of the company and by the computing environment. The following are various options, ranging from senior-level management teams on down:

- *The management decision-making team.* This team consists of senior management. It is responsible for making major decisions about the continuity plan and about whether or not to move off site after a disaster.
- *The business continuity steering committee.* This committee provides overall management of the project. It establishes and controls policies, standards, and procedures, and it defines the organization of the departments and other participants to ensure cohesive planning groups. This committee should include members of operations, IS, and finance. The actual composition of the team can be agreed on at the initiation of the project.
- *The business continuity planning coordinator.* This individual provides day-to-day coordination of the project and typically works with external resources or consultants. This person must be able to commit sufficient time to the project to ensure that it is completed within the agreed time frame.

- *The management operations team.* This team consists of line managers who are responsible for managing the day-to-day operations after a disaster occurs. They advise the management decision-making team and report decisions down through their respective areas.
- *Department coordinators.* These individuals are responsible for providing information on their department's operations, completing forms, and developing draft plans. Related departments can be grouped under one coordinator; other departments may have their own individual coordinators. The time required of these individuals increases with each phase of plan development.
- *The emergency operations team.* This team consists of those people who are responsible for ensuring that operations keep running in the off-site environment.
- *The damage assessment and post investigation team.* This team is responsible for evaluating damages to the facility and determining the cost to restore operations. It should consist of those people in charge of facilities and operations.
- *The reconstruction team.* This team consists primarily of facilities personnel. It is responsible for managing restoration activities.

It is recommended that at least a business continuity steering committee, a business continuity planning coordinator, and department coordinators be appointed.

It is important that departmental employees involved in developing the plan for their departments be aware of the reasons for developing the plan, the project organization, what is expected of them during the project, and the tools and information that will be provided to assist them in their work. This can be achieved by holding one or more group business continuity training meetings to discuss these points. During these meetings, any software that will be used should be demonstrated and all questionnaires and forms to be used in developing the plan should be explained in detail.

The following sections discuss the responsibilities of the various teams that may be involved in business continuity planning.

The Disaster Decision-Making Team

The disaster decision-making team is primarily responsible for notifying the board of directors, regulatory bodies, regional companies, local companies, international bodies, and the media as required. This team may make these notifications itself or delegate the work.

In addition, members of this team make the final business decisions regarding whether the plan should go into effect, whether to move operations to the off-site location or continue business at the main site, and even whether to continue conducting business at all. Should the plan be put into effect, the team is kept up to date through management operations teams, the business continuity coordinator, and those functional areas reporting to the team that are in charge of handling areas of the disaster.

All recovery activities are submitted to this team for review; however, all disaster containment activities are handled on site as the events take place. Steps taken to contain the disaster are reported back to this team through the management operations team, as they occur if possible or after the fact if not. All major decisions regarding expenditures of funds are made by this team.

The Business Continuity Steering Committee and Planning Coordinator

The business continuity steering committee is responsible for establishing and controlling policies, standards, and procedures and for defining the structure of the project to ensure that the departments and other participants work together cohesively. In addition, the committee reviews, approves, and coordinates the plans developed by the participating groups.

In the event of a disaster, this committee serves as a facilitator, responsible for providing transportation to the backup facilities, if required; notifying affected personnel and families of the status of the disaster; providing cash for needed travel or emergency items; securing the affected areas, the business resumption control center, and the backup site; escorting personnel, if necessary; and presenting a carefully formatted release to the media and affected personnel as to the status of operations and personnel. Several areas are represented on the business continuity steering committee during the disaster, to ensure that basic necessities are made available to support those individuals working to recover the business.

The size of the business continuity steering committee depends on the extent of the disaster and the recovery needs. The following departments should be consulted in forming the committee:

- Purchasing
- Human resources
- Communications
- Auditing
- Finance and accounting
- Transportation and amenities
- Facilities
- Security
- Public relations
- Risk management and insurance
- Administrative services

- Operations
- Information systems

The business continuity planning coordinator interfaces with the business continuity steering committee to ensure a smooth and successful transition to each phase of the plan. In addition, the coordinator acts as team manager for the management operations team, discussed in the following section.

The Management Operations Team

The management operations team is responsible for coordinating all emergency operations teams. When management decides that the business continuity plan is to be implemented, these team members (or their alternates) contact the emergency operations team members to advise them of the disaster declaration. They then report to the business resumption control center to begin damage assessment. Once at the disaster site, the management operations team monitors the emergency operations team's progress and acts as overall manager for all emergency operations teams activated by the operational group.

The management operations team forwards all requests for space, equipment, supplies, and additional human resources support to the department coordinator. The team members report daily on the status of all emergency operations to the business resumption coordinator for the management operations team.

The management operations team is primarily responsible for determining the extent of the disaster, relocating at the business resumption control center, and notifying emergency operations team managers and department coordinators. In addition, the team monitors recovery progress, and compliance with the business resumption plan during recovery and reports on recovery status to the business resumption coordinator, who in turn reports to the company president as required.

The Department Coordinators Team

The department coordinators team is composed of members from all functional areas. Each department coordinator acts as chairperson for his or her department's emergency operations team. In addition, the department coordinator manages the management disaster decision team and the business continuity steering committee. They communicate all of the department's needs and the department's status.

Department coordinators have access to the business resumption control center and attend strategic planning meetings. When a disaster occurs, they contact all emergency operations team managers and coordinate recovery efforts. Department coordinators submit written requests for equipment or supplies as soon as needs are made known to the business continuity steering committee.

Perhaps most important, the department coordinators monitor recovery operations. In this capacity, they receive and communicate status reports, receive daily reports from all emergency operations team managers, request additional human resources support as necessary, and maintain a log of the department's status and progress. In addition, the department coordinators communicate all decisions made by the management disaster decision team to affected managers within the department.

The Emergency Operations Team

The members of the emergency operations team are responsible for the smooth transition to the prearranged emergency backup center, continued operations, emergency procedures, notification of users, requisition of equipment and supplies, and a return to normal processing. Each member of the team should designate an alternate in case the primary team member is unavailable when a disaster occurs.

The size of the emergency operations team depends on the extent of the disaster and operating needs. The responsibilities of the team members include forwarding requests to the business continuity steering committee for transportation to the alternative facilities, if required, and for notification of key employees, affected families, and any employees who were off duty at the time of the disaster. In addition, the emergency operations team makes requests for first aid, supplies, mail or courier service, replacement software or equipment, temporary workers, additional security or communications measures, backup power, and documentation. Team members also work with the enterprise operations and communications departments.

Each emergency operations team has a team manager and a backup manager, who report to the department coordinator. The team manager is responsible for coordinating the recovery effort. The managers participate in the damage assessment meeting to determine the extent of the damage. The manager gives daily status reports regarding recovery and ongoing operations to the business resumption coordinator.

The Damage Assessment and Post Investigation Team

The damage assessment team reports directly to the management operations team and notifies it of the extent of damage. After damages have been assessed, this team functions as a post investigation team to determine the cause of the disaster. In some cases, the cause is obvious (e.g., an earthquake), but in many cases it is not. For example, in the case of a fire, the origin of the fire must be determined as well as how to prevent such a fire from happening again.

The Reconstruction Team

The reconstruction team is composed of those departments required to restore the damaged site. It should include all departments associated with building services as well as representatives from the damaged areas.

The reconstruction team's responsibilities include both temporary and long-term reconstruction efforts. From the initial damage assessment to final reconstruction of the damaged area, the reconstruction team directs and coordinates efforts to bring about a smooth, efficient reconstruction of the damaged areas.

PREPARING THE PLAN

In preparing the plan, members of the business continuity project team must assemble documentation about their specific functional area and operating environment. In addition, they must identify critical performance requirements and rank the tasks within their jobs according to priority.

Departments that rely heavily on systems must explain in detail how their operations interface with each other and are supported by them. The needed information can be gathered from:

- organizational charts
- job descriptions
- procedures manuals
- technical support requirements
- existing business continuity or business continuity plans
- risk analyses
- business impact analyses
- vulnerability assessments

Questionnaires can be used successfully to gather information that can provide a foundation for the strategies that must be developed in the planning process. Although questionnaires should be customized for individual projects, they should always provide the basic information presented in Exhibit 11-1.

Departments should be asked to complete the questionnaire after the initial training meeting. The completed form should be returned to the department coordinator and any external consultants for review. The department coordinator and external consultants should review the answers with the department manager and the employee who completed the form to clarify, amend, and confirm the information.

The completed questionnaires should be compared to determine the priority of departmental functions, the impact relative to specific time frames, and the minimum resources needed to maintain the company's

Exhibit 11-1. Checklist of basic information required on business continuity planning questionnaires.

- Description of departmental operations.
- Functions that support those operations.
- Peak operating times.
- Impact of department downtime.
- Recovery priorities and time frames for departmental functions.
- Staffing requirements under normal circumstances and in an emergency.
- Computer support for both departmental operations and individual functions. (This should cover both centralized and decentralized computer operations).
- Site requirements for both normal and emergency operations.
- Equipment needed (and the vendors of that equipment).
- Office and other supplies (and the vendors).
- Critical records needed and their backup and recovery requirements.
- Priority ranking of departmental functions.
- Name and address of alternative-site vendor.
- List of responsibilities and home telephone numbers of key personnel.
- Emergency telephone numbers (e.g., fire and police departments).
- Critical forms (number, names, and average use).
- Special equipment specifications.
- Area user list.
- Vendor backup contracts.
- Critical functions and assumptions (e.g., individuals might assume that they will have access to backup files).
- Minimum equipment and space requirements.

critical functions. This information is helpful when considering alternative or backup sites that will be needed.

All of the information obtained in these early phases of plan development is integrated into the business continuity plan. Plan development is designed to integrate or provide interfaces between sections of the IT plan and the corporate business continuity plan. In addition, the plan incorporates any emergency procedures and provides references to any applicable sections of existing data center and departmental standards and procedures manuals.

The prompt recovery of an organization's corporate and functional operations from a loss of capability depends on the availability of a broad spectrum of resources. The procedures necessary to restore operations — initially in temporary facilities and later in the original or another permanent location — are detailed in the plan.

Each of the functional units prepares its plan on the basis of the outline provided by the plan coordinators (see the sample outline provided in

Exhibit 11-2). The outline can be modified to suit the needs of the individual units. Although the plan discussed in this section addresses disaster backup and recovery from a worst-case scenario, less severe or even short-term interruptions can also be planned for by using subsets of the overall plan.

BUSINESS CONTINUITY PLANNING SOFTWARE

Several contingency planning and risk analysis software packages are currently on the market. It is not practical to list and evaluate them because that list is constantly changing. However, there are certain criteria that should be used during the software package selection process.

For example, ease of use and the number of installations or users are important when the company is selecting any software package, as are the frequency and availability of updates, the quality of documentation and vendor support, the reputation of the vendor, and the amount of training the vendor provides. The usability of output should also be considered. Specific to contingency planning, the software should be evaluated in terms of whether it provides total business continuity planning assistance or simply data center recovery.

RECOMMENDED COURSE OF ACTION

For each company, the business continuity plan should cover all types of disaster situations. Procedures should be focused on getting the system running again within an acceptable time frame. The cause of the downtime is not important except in cases of regional disasters (e.g., earthquakes) or such specific hazards as a toxic spill. Special procedures should be included in the plan for these types of disasters.

The recovery strategies and procedures should be organized according to business functions. Strategies and procedures should be sufficiently detailed to enable company personnel to understand what is expected of them and how they should complete their responsibilities. However, strategies and procedures should be sufficiently flexible to permit changes should circumstances warrant them. Procedures should cover the maintenance of critical functions in an emergency mode as well as restoration of the primary facility or relocation to another permanent location.

The plan must specify the priority of recovery activities. It is impractical to determine during an emergency the order in which recovery procedures are to be conducted.

Personnel from the departments covered by the plan should be involved in its development from the start. These departments will be the users of the plan and therefore should play an integral part in its development.

Exhibit 11-2. Sample outline of business continuity plan.

I. Introduction
    a. Executive overview or summary
    b. Organizational overview
    c. Minimum requirements
    d. General categories of disasters and contingencies

II. Responsibilities of the Disaster Decision-Making Team

III. Responsibilities of the Business Continuity Coordinator and the Business Continuity Steering Committee

IV. Responsibilities of the Management Operations Team

V. Responsibilities of the Department Coordinators Team

VI. Responsibilities of the Emergency Operations Team

VII. Responsibilities of the Damage Assessment and Post Investigation Team

VIII. Responsibilities of the Reconstruction Team

IX. General Issues
    a. Awareness of critical events
    b. Notification of relevant persons
    c. Diagnosis of the cause, severity, and expected duration of the event
    d. Coordnation of emergency response
    e. Communications
    f. Investigation and analysis of the event

X. The Corporate Recovery Plan (corporatewide outage)*
    a. Organization and staffing
    b. Arrangements with vendors, contractors, and other organizations
    c. Backup and recovery plans
        1. Information and communications systems
        2. Hardware
        3. Site
        4. Location of business resumption control center

XI. The Operational Area Recovery Plan (based on functional areas)
    a. Responsibilities of the backup operations team
    b. Responsibilities of the emergency operations team
    c. Responsibilities of the reconstructions team
    d. General issues
    e. Priority ranking of functions
    f. Name and address of alternative-site vendor
    g. List of responsibilities and home telephone numbers of key personnel
    h. Emergency telephone numbers (e.g., fire and police departments)
    i. Critical forms (number, names, and average use)
    j. Special equipment specifications
    k. Area user list (ranked according to priority)
    l. Copy of vendor backup contract
    m. Critical functions and assumptions (e.g., individuals may assume that they will have access to backup files)
    n. Minimum equipment and space requirements
    o. Appendixes (Same as Section XV)

Exhibit 11-2. Sample outline of business continuity plan. (continued)

XII. Emergency Notification
    a. General categories of disasters and contingencies
    b. Immediate evacuation
    c. Fire emergency procedures
    d. Telephone bomb threat procedures
        1. Bomb search procedures
        2. General alert for bomb threats
    e. Medical emergencies
    f. Civil disorder
    g. Severe weather or threat of a natural disaster
    h. Extortion and terrorist threats
    i. Building and equipment emergencies (e.g., loss of power)
    j. Notification
        1. Company closings for a disaster
        2. Activating the business resumption control center
        3. Access control procedures
    k. Company closings for early release of employees (e.g., because of an impending storm)
    l. Major milestones in the notification process
    m. Backup sites
XIII. Testing the Business Continuity Plan
    a. Methodology for testing the plan
    b. Determination of frequency of testing
XIV. Business Resumption Plan Maintenance
    a. Procedures for updating the plan
        1. Areas that require regular review
        2. Areas that require occasional review
    b. Frequency of review for updates
        1. Areas that require regular review
        2. Areas that require occasional review
XV. Appendixes
    A. Special Resources for Business Resumption
    B. Special Guidelines for Managers Dealing with Disaster-Related Stress
    C. Business Continuity for Microcomputers
    D. Inventory Control Form and Instructions
    E. Equipment Requirements
    F. Decision Matrices
    G. Critical Time Periods (daily or seasonal)
    H. Cross-Training Requirements and Responsibilities Matrix
    I. Typical Resources Allocation Plan (TRAP) Charts
    J. Test Schedules
    K. Test Worksheets
    L. Preparedness Overview
    M. Network Diagrams
    N. Off-Site Storage Inventories

Exhibit 11-2. Sample outline of business continuity plan. (continued)

O. Critical Functions
P. Staff Emergency Contact Information
Q. Vendor Emergency Contact Information
R. Vendor Contracts
S. Emergency Organizational Charts
T. Management Succession List
U. Agreements for Alternative Work Space
V. Temporary Agencies
W. Functional Systems Overview
X. Emergency Telephone Numbers
Y. Control of Building Contents (e.g., equipment and supplies)
Z. Special Salvage Vendors
AA. Purchasing Department's List of Vendors
BB. Procedures for Preserving Damaged Records
CC. List of Personnel Who Need Access to the Plan
DD. Notification Sequence
EE. Organizational Chart for Business Resumption Command Center
FF. Emergency Medical Information
GG. Emergency Housing Information
HH. Emergency Transportation Information
II. Business Resumption Control Center Notification
JJ. User Area Notification

Note:*For simplicity, this section of the outline shows a general building outage recovery plan that is used for all locations. Some organizations may find it necessary to have a separate recovery plan for each location.

The plan should be reviewed and updated on a regular basis; a plan is only as effective as its maintenance and updating program. Changes in departmental or company operations can quickly render a plan obsolete. A thorough maintenance and updating program prevents this.

Development of a business continuity plan may seem like a long and tedious process with no immediate benefit to the company. However, over the long term, a well-developed and well-maintained plan can help ensure that the company stays in business when a disaster strikes.

Chapter 12
Corporate Contingency Planning

Michael D. Cannon

CONTINGENCY PLANNING IS NOT A PROJECT THAT ENDS WHEN THE RECOVERY MANUAL IS WRITTEN. The contingency planning process is a corporatewide program that must continue to grow with the company it serves. This chapter addresses the process of developing and auditing the corporate contingency plan. An audit checklist for the corporate contingency plan is provided in the Appendix.

In the past, contingency planning was thought to be necessary for only information systems-related activities. Now it is considered to be a necessity for every business function of an organization. Auditors must be aware of contingency planning requirements and alert management of any deficiencies. The changes and growth that an organization experiences must also be taken into account when a contingency plan is being developed.

CONTINGENCY PLANNING METHODOLOGY

To adequately discuss the contingency planning process, the methodology must be addressed. This methodology has been described by various authors as a five-, six-, seven-, or eight-step process. This chapter combines these steps into a four-phase approach.

Exhibit 12-1 represents the contingency planning methodology. The methodology is a continuous process that must take into consideration both the information systems environment and the individual business units. The discussion that follows the chart explains each of the four phases.

Business Risk Assessment

The objective of the risk assessment phase is to determine the priority of the critical business units. As a result of this phase, the major areas of

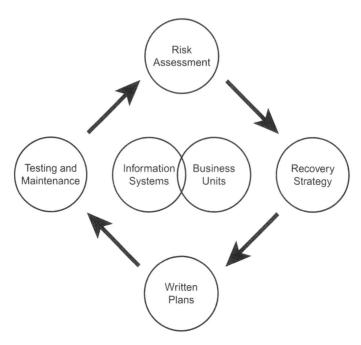

Exhibit 12-1. Contingency planning program — four phases.

exposure for the company are determined. This phase begins with interviews of each business unit's management. The interviews are performed using a structured approach that determines how critical the business unit is to the organization. Each business unit's management answers questions developed in advance. Questions and topics that are discussed include the following:

- What are management's title and functional responsibilities?
- How many persons are employed?
- What are the department's critical functions?
- What are the exposures if functions cannot be continued?
- From whom are inputs received?
- To whom are inputs provide?
- Do documented contingency plans exist? Have they been tested?
- What computer applications are considered essential?
- Is there a records-retention program? Is it documented?
- Do backup procedures exist?
- What are the minimum recovery requirements (e.g., people, supplies, and equipment)?
- How quickly must critical functions be restored?

When performing interviews, the interviewee is given two scenarios. The first scenario states that the business unit's information systems connectivity to the main computer is no longer available because of an information systems disaster. The second scenario states that the business unit's work space is no longer available because of a local disaster. During the discussion of these two scenarios, the impact on the business unit (e.g., loss of customers, loss of revenue, and legal and regulatory issues) is determined. Using this information, priorities can be determined for the recovery of each business unit. The risk assessment phase must be updated periodically (i.e., annually or bi-annually) to maintain an accurate priority list of business units.

Recovery Strategy Development

The objective of the recovery strategy phase is to determine the specific recovery requirements (e.g., number of people, special equipment, supplies, support services, and vital records) and to determine an appropriate recovery location for each critical business unit based on priority. The recovery location must be easy to move into so that normal business activity can begin immediately. Telephone and data lines should be in place, or installation should be preplanned to take place within 24 hours after notification of an emergency.

If a business unit is destroyed, its recovery strategy should designate space that can be obtained quickly. Space is one of the most important aspects of contingency planning and recovery. Without space critical business activities cannot be conducted. To determine the amount of space that is necessary, the number of people required to implement recovery (depends on the business unit) must be known. This number can be multiplied by the required amount of square feet for each workspace (approximately 50 to 100 square feet per workspace) in a recovery environment.

Space is the most elusive recovery strategy requirement, because empty space is a waste of corporate assets. Some companies use training rooms, conference rooms, or warehouses as designated recovery locations. Other companies that do not have extra space available lease backup space, or they subscribe to a business unit recovery facility from an outside vendor.

Writing the Recovery Plans

The objective of this phase is to document the contingency plans in a standard manner throughout the organization. The contingency planning and recovery manual must be useful for training, testing, and recovery purposes. Typically, the manual contains the following sections:

- policy statement
- plan overview
- emergency procedures
- notification and activation procedures
- explanation of the recovery organization structure

- recovery team descriptions
- recovery plan procedures
- recovery services (e.g., vendors, equipment, critical personnel, and telephone numbers)
- appendix

Normally, a contingency planning software package is used to enter data into the contingency planning manual and to maintain it on a periodic basis (e.g., annually or semi-annually). Some of these software packages enable users to follow a checklist during the development of a written contingency plan by using microcomputer-based tools (e.g., database, word processing, graphics, and software-specific utilities). Purchasing a contingency planning software package from a reputable vendor can ensure ongoing enhancements of the product.

Testing and Maintenance of Plans

The objective of this phase is to train the recovery team personnel in the use of the contingency planning and recovery manual. Testing should be designed to determine:

- the state of readiness of the individual departments to cope with a major disaster
- the ability of multiple departments and support units to effectively work together
- whether recovery inventories stored offsite are adequate to support the recovery of all business functions
- whether the plan has been properly updated and maintained by the recovery teams and the departmental contingency planning coordinator

Two basic types of testing can be performed to accomplish the preceding goals. Sometimes the word "exercise" is substituted for "test" to avoid the pass-or-fail viewpoint. The first type of test is commonly known as the walk-through exercise. When performing this exercise, the business unit brings together its critical personnel in a conference room or other meeting place to discuss the written contingency plan. The business unit manager walks through the sections of the manual, and he or she reviews procedures for accuracy and trains the participants on the activities to be performed in the event of a disaster.

The second type of exercise is known as a mock-disaster exercise. This type of exercise requires more planning than a walk-through exercise. The mock-disaster exercise simulates an actual disaster and requires that multiple business units interact with each other to recover from the disaster. The contingency planning coordinator and other members of the mock-disaster project team work together to develop a realistic scenario and test criteria. Unlike the walk-through exercise, the mock-disaster exercise can be performed unexpectedly. An unexpected exercise can determine if the critical personnel are available; if they are not available, it can determine if the alternates are capable of performing the same critical activities.

After testing is completed, the written procedures should be updated. Maintenance procedures consist of two general categories (i.e., scheduled and unscheduled). Scheduled maintenance is essentially time-driven, while unscheduled maintenance is event-driven. Scheduled maintenance occurs as a result of a scheduled review of the plan. Reviews are predictable and are scheduled at annual or semiannual intervals. Unscheduled maintenance is unpredictable and cannot be scheduled. The submission of actual change data should originate from the team leader or manager whose area of responsibility is affected. The following situations may require the unscheduled maintenance of the contingency plans:

- the transfer, promotion, or resignation of critical recovery personnel
- significant modification of basic functions or data flow requirements
- results of conducting a risk assessment
- changes in business or operating environment
- changes in the communication network
- changes in off-site storage facilities or methods
- improvements or physical change of the organizational structure
- recent acquisition or merger with another company
- new application platform development
- the discontinuance of an application system

REGULATORY ISSUES

Several regulatory issues should be addressed when developing a corporate contingency plan. The following sections address these issues and provide descriptions of requirements.

Financial Institution Requirements

The Federal Financial Institutions Examination Council (FFIEC) interagency policy on contingency planning for financial institutions addresses the need for corporatewide contingency planning by all financial institutions and their servicers. This policy states that strategies should be developed to minimize loss and to recover from significant disruptions in normal business activities. Furthermore, it recommends that these strategies must address:

- centralized and decentralized operations
- user department activities
- communications (voice and data) systems
- business functions linked to service bureaus
- recovery plans by the service bureaus

The FFIEC is concerned that many financial institutions and service bureaus have not sufficiently addressed the risks associated with the loss of or extended disruption of business operations. For example:

- Many contingency plans do not consider all the business units in the organization.
- Many serviced institutions have not coordinated contingency planning activities with their service bureaus.
- Many information systems service bureaus have not established contingency plans.
- Many contingency plans (e.g., information systems and business unit plans) have not been adequately tested.

The FFIEC requires that financial institution senior management and boards of directors establish policies, procedures, and responsibilities for comprehensive contingency planning. In addition, they must review and approve the institution's contingency plans annually, documenting them in the board minutes. If the institution uses a service bureau for information processing, management must evaluate the service bureau's contingency plan and ensure that the institution's contingency plan is compatible with its service bureau's plan.

Standards and Exchange Commission Requirements

The Foreign Corrupt Practices Act (FCPA) of 1977 requires that publicly held companies keep books, records, and accounts that accurately and fairly reflect the transactions and dispositions of the assets of the issuer, and that they devise and maintain a system of internal accounting controls sufficient to assure that:

- Transactions are executed in accordance with management's general or specific authorization.
- Transactions are recorded as necessary to permit preparation of financial statements in conformity with GAAP and to maintain accountability for assets.
- Access to assets is permitted only in accordance with management's general or specific authorization.
- The recorded accountability for assets is compared with the existing assets at reasonable intervals, and appropriate action is taken with respect to any differences.

According to the FCPA, a company must have an organizational structure, control procedures, and techniques that safeguard its assets, check the accuracy and reliability of its accounting data, promote operational efficiency, and encourage adherence to prescribed managerial policies. As a result, management must be concerned about the effectiveness of all organizational controls, including contingency planning for information systems and the individual business units.

Federal and State Requirements

The Internal Revenue Service (IRS) wants corporations to maintain complete and accurate records. When the IRS performs an audit, a company may be required to produce business records that cover three or more years. If the IRS suspects fraud, they can examine records spanning ten or more years. No statute of limitations exists for tax fraud. If a company loses its backup financial data because of a fire, flood, or other type of disaster, it may be penalized for lack of adequate documentation. States have their own regulations affecting business resumption planning. Some states (e.g., California) require businesses to be prepared for certain recurring natural disasters (e.g., hurricanes, earthquakes, or floods). Government agencies often contractually require that suppliers have business resumption capabilities. Many government bid requests require evidence and some contractual guarantee of a bidder's business continuity capability.

CONTINGENCY PLANNING TRENDS

A viable information systems business continuity plan and business unit resumption plan are essential to the development of a comprehensive corporate contingency planning program. These parts have evolved into major components of any organization.

Information Systems Business Continuity Plans

During the 1970s, business continuity planning was the terminology used to describe the process that required the offsite backup of computer software and data files on magnetic tape. As computer systems became more sophisticated and businesses became more dependent on these computer systems, consideration was given to computer hardware recovery. During the 1980s, several computer vendors began offering hot site subscription services. These services offered compatible computers and peripherals to the subscriber for testing business continuity plans and for recovery purposes in the event of a disaster.

During the 1970s and 1980s, disasters that involved computers were uncommon. However, during the 1990s, major disasters (e.g., earthquakes, hurricanes, fires, floods, and bombs) have caused problems in business computers and network operations. It is common for major corporations to spend five hundred thousand to one million dollars per year on hot site services and to test business continuity plans two, four, or six times per year.

Business Unit Resumption Planning

During the 1990s, the frequency of disasters has caused contingency planners and senior management to be more concerned about the continued processing of critical business units. As a result, hot site vendors are offering workstation recovery services. These workstations normally include a desk, a chair, a telephone, and a microcomputer. The cost of the subscription is based on the number of workstations required to recover the critical business units, plus special equipment (e.g., LAN servers, telephones).

Some companies are developing business unit resumption centers using training areas, conference rooms, warehouse space, or unoccupied company-owned office space. The key to business unit resumption planning is available space that is separate and distinct from the normal office building. It should also be easily wired for data and voice telephone lines.

Corporate Contingency Planning Program

For the corporate contingency planning program to work, a contingency planning coordinator must be appointed. This person (whether full-time or part-time) must be given adequate resources to put the plan in place and maintain it. The contingency planning coordinator must be able to work with all levels of personnel from clerical to senior management. This person should be familiar with the business unit's operations, as well as the information systems aspects of the company. The role of the contingency planner should include the following items:

- performing a risk assessment periodically
- determining business unit impact if a disaster occurs
- developing viable recovery strategies
- integrating contingency plans with emergency response procedures
- identifying command center procedures and defining management's role
- developing and fully implementing the plan
- developing corporate awareness and training programs
- preparing and participating in testing of the contingency plan
- documenting and evaluating the results of the tests
- updating the contingency plan after testing

CURRENT ISSUES AND TRENDS

The corporate contingency plan is growing in acceptance and importance. Because of this growth, certain issues are becoming more important to the success of plan implementation. These issues are covered in the following sections.

Types of Disasters

A variety of disasters can occur in the operations of an organization. The following categories of disasters are common to most organizations:

- breakdowns in data and voice communications
- local office or building floor damage

- significant building damage, but not areawide
- areawide damage (e.g., earthquake or tornado)

In the event of an emergency that disrupts operations, specific procedures may be followed to determine if the recovery plan is to be activated. Depending on the severity of the disaster, the backup plan may include providing for alternate recovery facilities that are prewired for critical equipment and communications.

Nonstop Processing

Many corporations must provide nonstop processing capabilities for their business units. For example, brokerage firms must be able to make trades of securities for their customers within a moment's notice. If the customer buys or sells securities expecting a certain price, late processing is not acceptable because of a disaster. As a result, brokerage firms, major banks, and other financial institutions have developed contingency plans that allow them to mirror all of their transactions on a duplicate or redundant computer system. In the event of an unexpected computer system breakdown, the redundant computer system takes over immediately without missing a transaction.

Another example of an industry that requires nonstop processing is the airline industry. If the reservation system of a major airline is unable to process the endless stream of customer travel requirements, the airplanes may be grounded until the computer system is restored. Airlines have redundant computer systems and networks to insure uninterrupted service.

New Technology

Today critical application systems are processed on LANs within the business unit. However, procedures for backup and recovery of these systems are lacking in most cases. Business units are developing processing centers at remote sites, and they must be connected by communication media to corporate headquarters. To protect critical business units from communications failures, diverse communications network contingency plans must be implemented. In the future, consideration should be given to new technologies and how they can be recovered before they are installed.

Compliance with Corporate Standards

Many of a company's assets and business methodologies are linked to each other and provide critical daily support to key operations. Without the timely recovery of these key processes, less-than-desirable levels of service are provided to customers. This environment, combined with the fact that disaster may take any form and strike at any time or place, requires that it be corporate policy to maintain a state of preparedness.

Senior management must mandate corporate policy to institute and maintain a contingency planning program that renews critical business units (in the event of a major interruption to normal business activity) in a timely fashion and with minimal disruption to the business.

When new departmental procedures or information systems are developed (or existing ones modified) contingency planning and recovery capabilities should be included in the basic design criteria. Each major change must be reviewed for the contingency planning and recovery requirements that might be affected by the change. It is the responsibility of departmental management to include recovery procedures for new or modified systems and procedures affecting their department. It is also the responsibility of departmental management to notify the contingency planning coordinator of any changes.

The company should provide funding, develop and maintain standards and procedures, periodically test, and institute guidelines that ensure adherence to the corporate contingency planning policy. It is the responsibility of management at all levels to ensure compliance with the corporate contingency planning policy.

Audit Participation in Testing

The internal audit department should be involved in all tests of critical contingency plans. The auditor's role includes the following activities:

- determining if the test objectives are met
- identifying the test assumptions
- documenting the time line of the test
- verifying that all outside communications are working
- documenting the problems encountered during the test
- documenting what external resources are involved
- verifying that all test transactions are accurately processed
- identifying issues that lead to plan improvements

Reporting Findings to Senior Management

The reporting phase of the contingency planning audit begins with the rough draft of the audit report. The auditor then conducts a closing conference, in which audit findings are reviewed with the contingency planning coordinator. In the closing conference, the auditor and the contingency planning coordinator should review and consider the following questions:

- What are the audit findings?
- What is the significance of the findings?
- What recommendations are suggested by the findings?

In the closing conference, the contingency planning coordinator has the opportunity to challenge the findings. Based on the closing conference, the auditor may revise the audit report. The report is then ready to be issued to business unit and senior management.

RECOMMENDED COURSE OF ACTION

It is unfortunate that some organizations do not consider a corporate contingency planning program until they are affected by a disaster. Government agencies and major corporations are requiring that business partners have a comprehensive contingency plan. Senior management must support the contingency planning program in order for it to succeed. Appointment of a contingency planning coordinator is a key factor in showing commitment to the program. Information systems technology and communication networks are becoming more complex. As a result, sophisticated contingency plans must be developed and implemented. These contingency plans must be tested on a regular basis and kept up to date to ensure a swift recovery. Using the information contained in this chapter, each business unit of the organization can evaluate its risks, develop recovery strategies, write detailed action plans, and test the plans on a regular basis.

Chapter 13
Business Continuity Planning: Trials and Tribulations

Steve Watts

THE NEED FOR SOME FORM OF BUSINESS CONTINUITY OR DISASTER RECOVERY PLANNING IS BECOMING INCREASINGLY APPRECIATED. Recent, well-publicized events have raised the level of awareness of the need to address the situation.

Whether operating within the government sector or private business, the basic issues to be addressed are fundamentally the same. Quite often, governmental departments and agencies might have established emergency procedures, to be activated in the event that certain circumstances arise — for example, emergency operational responses. If this is so, then the planning initiative should interface with these existing arrangements.

Quite often, the task can appear considerable, and a host of questions invariably arise:

- How can plans be made for an organization of this size?
- Where does one start?
- Who will do the work?
- How long will it take?
- Who will take responsibility for it?

A structured approach, initiating the task from a logical standpoint such as this, can do much to dispel these considerations. But even so, a number of pitfalls and obstacles can frequently arise in preparing the plan, resulting from some such basic issues as sources of funding, responsibilities not being fully assigned, the plan not reflecting true core requirements, and an attempt to completely duplicate processes and activities. Lessons learned from previous experience should enable these traps to be avoided from the outset.

RISK MANAGEMENT APPROACH

While there are a number of stages to be addressed, the planning process represents one component of the overall risk management approach; it should not be viewed in isolation from existing business protection activities.

Put simply, every organization, whether in the private or public sector, has resources it considers necessary to protect, and for this purpose will have installed certain safeguards. Depending on the expected impact caused by the loss of the resources, a contingency should be in place against the failure of these safeguards.

While the understanding of how a plan should be produced, how it should be constructed, and what it should contain, can differ widely, there are many factors that, if they are not observed, can considerably reduce the effectiveness of the final plan. Too often, the development of a plan is viewed as a one-off undertaking, subject to the constraints of any other project. Having stated previously that it should be viewed as an extension of risk management, it must also be considered to be a process — not an event.

Once the plan is completed, mechanisms must be put into place for its proper administration, maintenance, and testing, particularly as the business evolves and the requirements and expectations of the plan change.

BUSINESS CONTINUITY RESPONSIBILITY

For business continuity to be successfully addressed, the responsibilities for each stage of its development must be assigned. It is important that responsibilities are correctly apportioned throughout the organization. The basic responsibility lies with senior management; only such people will be in a position to apply resources and, more importantly, make the necessary judgments. This is illustrated later by way of example. Too often, a person in a relatively junior position is allocated the job in isolation, and is expected to make the kind of decisions that could determine whether the organization survives the disruption or goes under.

Many organizations offering warm site recovery services occasionally come across the misconception that recovery would be performed at a high level, into which departmental functions would simply dovetail with a minimum of involvement. A further basic responsibility, therefore, lies with departmental management. At the time of disruption, recovery management personnel will provide them with the resources previously identified as necessary for recovery. Suitably equipped, they will be responsible for the recommencement of their specific business processes, including the management of work backlogs.

In many cases, for reasons unknown, the existence of the plan is one of the organization's best-kept secrets. Therefore, an additional benefit of the proper assignment of responsibilities is that a high degree of awareness should be created. In turn, this will assist in the implementation of the plan.

Incorporated within the plan will be a nominated recovery management team. As the name implies, the prime function of this team will be the management of the recovery; it will also act as a facilitator to the departmental management, as recovery proceeds. The composition of the recovery management team is important. It is recommended that the most senior manager of the site not be automatically put forward as a candidate for team leader. Personnel who are ideally suited for inclusion on this team are usually those of a practical nature, and who also possess a degree of authority.

Senior management will have an important role to play: form a crisis management team, deal with the press, and provide strategic advice to the recovery management team. One of the golden rules of business continuity planning is that, over the disruption period, the normal decision-making processes should be replicated as far as possible. For example, under normal working conditions, senior management would not involve itself in the ordering of replacement furniture, so why should it under disruption conditions?

It is imperative that the plan correctly reflects business requirements, never losing sight of core business activities.

To the uninitiated, the temptation to form a committee to assemble and compile a plan based on intuition must be avoided. The end result of such an approach will raise more questions than it answers, will discourage the organizers, and is unlikely to achieve anything of substance.

BUSINESS CONTINUITY STRATEGY

Management is understandably anxious to see a plan in place. However, the actual production of the final plan can often be a comparative non-event, compared with the preparatory work that precedes it. Despite this, other influences too often enter into the planning sphere. Information services (IS) has been particularly strong so far as this is concerned, primarily because of its involvement in the development of the discipline.

From a historical viewpoint, the need for an organization to have access to some form of computing recovery facility was often questionable, and was often looked upon as an unnecessary overhead. Since those early days, methods of providing recovery have been developed to a high degree of sophistication. Recovery planning became more prominent as the reliance upon information processing grew. Initially, when batch systems predominated, loose reciprocal arrangements often existed between users of compatible computer systems for mutual emergency processing. This has increasingly become viewed as risky, inadequate, and unenforceable. Empty shell ("cold sites") facilities were then offered, on the basis that the computer facility itself and supporting environmental systems were difficult to reinstate within acceptable time scales; the actual computer equipment was easily available and could be installed within the nominated time.

To compensate for the shortcomings of these methods, companies emerged, offering access to a compatible machine in return for an annual subscription fee — warm sites. As the true requirements and commitment were realized by the companies providing the service, the level of sophistication of their offerings rose, both in proportion to that of the equipment, and to the level of reliance placed on it. As a result of this development, IS management developed a considerable degree of expertise, understanding, and skill, and often came to dominate this field within the organization.

The situation to be avoided is known as the "glasshouse syndrome." Using a multi-story building to illustrate the point, the result of the plan could be a fully recovered and functioning computer center, located on the top floor; whereas the lower floors — where the people who would use the services provided by the computer center were previously located — are in a state of devastation because there was no plan for their displacement.

During the course of a plan audit, recently carried out on behalf of a major United Kingdom organization, the recovery strategy of the IS function was examined. Recovery was centered on an old site, which it was estimated would take six weeks to equip and become fully operational. The need for business processes to plan for recovery was recognized; as a result, departments were essentially requested to "tread water" for six weeks, after which time, normal information services would resume.

The implications of this situation were demonstrated when the payroll department was investigated as part of the audit. Under disruption conditions, the recovery strategy of the department was to pay salaries and wages by duplication of the previous week's payroll. Notwithstanding the fact that this approach had not been agreed to with the workforce in advance, in the opinion of the payroll manager, payroll duplication would only be acceptable for a three-week period before severe industrial relations problems could be expected. Clearly, this counters the recovery strategy of IS.

A further example of the misdirection of the planning effort was that of a major utility that, at the time, was considering the effectiveness of its IS recovery strategy. IS management argued that the most cost-effective way that backup could be required was the construction of an additional in-house computer center — a "hot site." This would effectively split the equipment between the two locations and provide a higher degree of resilience. The justification for the expenditure on the second center was that the high volume of payments processed each day could be delayed, or even lost, with the disablement of the computer center.

However, when senior management of the utility was consulted, a different story emerged. While it recognized that the computer center was central to the processing of payments, the single most important activity in which the organization was engaged was the provision of clean, unpolluted water; any monetary losses could be recouped at a later date. As a result, recovery resources could have been seriously misdirected.

The purpose of this example is to illustrate the need to correctly deploy recovery resources in strict accordance with business requirements. This determination can only be made and confirmed by senior management. The intention is not to criticize the efforts made by IS departments, but to increase both the level of resilience and the ability to recover services. Their service should be considered one of a number of support services, of which there could be several. Examples of additional support services are communications (both data and voice), telemetry, and office facilities. A support service could also be provided by a third party, which would lessen the degree of direct control, but nevertheless would need to be included in the plan.

RESOURCING

A fundamental of recovery planning is that the intention of the exercise is not to immediately uplift and duplicate the entire organization at an alternative site. The aim is to identify those activities defined as being truly vital to the survival of the organization, and to ensure that facilities are in place to secure their recovery.

Appearing within the plan documentation should be an inventory of resources that have been identified as necessary to carry out these vital functions. This again would be a responsibility of departmental management, as only it would have intimate knowledge of the business processes and what would be needed to carry them out. Resources to be identified include personnel (numbers, skills, positions), equipment, computer systems, records, data, and documentation. An important aspect of this process is to identify the sources from where the resources would be obtained.

SUMMARY

In summary, recovery planning can have a different meaning to different people. This was illustrated during a recent planning exercise carried out at a foreign bank. The contents of a fire-resistant safe were identified as being items essential at the time of disruption. Detailed investigation indicated that it correctly contained backup documentation, authenticator keys, and, possibly of greater importance to the bank's staff, a copy of the golf club membership!

Chapter 14
The Business Impact Assessment Process

Carl B. Jackson

WHY BUSINESS IMPACT ASSESSMENT? The reason that the business impact assessment (BIA) element of the business continuity planning (BCP) methodology takes on such significance is that it sets the stage for shaping a business-oriented judgment concerning the appropriation of resources for recovery planning efforts.

Our experiences in this area have shown that, all too often, recovery alternative decisions such as hot sites, duplicate facilities, materials stockpiling, etc., are based on emotional motivations, and not on the results of a thorough business impact assessment. The bottomline in performing BIAs is the requirement to obtain a firm and formal agreement from the management group as to precise maximum tolerable downtimes (MTD). The formalized MTDs must be communicated to each business unit and support service organization (i.e., IT, Network Management, Facilities, etc.) that support the business units, so that realistic recovery alternatives can be acquired and recovery measures developed.

THE FIVE-PHASED APPROACH TO BCP

The BIA process is one phase of an overall approach to the evolution of BCPs. The following is a brief description of a five-phase BCP methodological approach. This approach is commonly used for development of the business unit (resumption) plans, technological platform, and communications network recovery plans.

- **Phase I: BCP Project Scoping and Planning** — This phase includes an examination of the organization's distinct business operations and information system support services in order to form a project plan to direct subsequent phases of the activity. Project planning activities involve defining the precise scope, organization, timing, staffing, and other issues so that the project status and requirements can be articulated throughout the organization, and chiefly to those departments

0-8493-0907-7/00/$0.00+$.50
© 2001 by CRC Press LLC

and personnel who will be playing the most meaningful roles in the BCPs development.

- **Phase II: Business Impact Assessment** — This phase involves developing a grasp of the proportion of impact individual business units would sustain subsequent to a significant interruption of computing and communication services. These impacts may be *financial,* in terms of dollar loss or impact, or *operational* in nature, such as the inability to deliver and monitor quality customer service, etc.
- **Phase III: Develop Recovery Strategy** — The information collected in Phase II is employed to approximate the recovery resources (i.e., business unit or departmental space and resource requirements, and technological platform services and communications networks requirements) necessary to support time-critical business functions. During this phase, an appraisal of recovery alternatives and alternative cost-estimates are prepared and presented to management.
- **Phase IV: Recovery Plan Development** — This phase includes the development of the actual business continuity or recovery plans themselves. Explicit documentation is required for execution of an effective recovery process and includes both administrative inventory information and detailed recovery team action plans, among other information.
- **Phase V: Implementation, Testing, and Maintenance** — The final phase involves establishing a rigorous testing and maintenance management program as well as addressing the initial and ongoing testing and maintenance activities.

BIA PROCESS DESCRIPTION

As mentioned above, the intent of the BIA process is to assist the organization's management in understanding the impacts associated with possible threats, and to employ that intelligence to calculate the maximum tolerable downtime for reliance upon time-critical support services and resources. For most organizations, time-critical support services and resources include:

- personnel
- facilities
- technological platforms (all computer systems)
- software
- data networks and equipment
- voice networks and equipment
- vital records
- data, etc.

IMPORTANCE OF DOCUMENTING A FORMAL MTD DECISION

The BIA process comes to a conclusion when the organization's senior management group has considered the impacts to the business processes due to outages of vital support services and then makes a formalized decision on the MTD they are willing to live with. This includes a decision to communicate that MTD decision(s) to each business unit and support service manager involved. Why is it so important that a formalized decision be made? Because the failure to document and communicate precise MTD information leaves each manager with imprecise direction on (1) selection of an appropriate recovery alternative method; and (2) the depth of detail which will be required when developing recovery procedures, including their scope and content.

We have seen many a well-executed BIA with excellent results be wasted because the senior management group failed to articulate their acceptance of the results and to communicate to each affected manager that the time requirements for recovery processes had been defined.

USE OF BIA QUESTIONNAIRES

There is no question that the people-to-people contact of the BIA process is the most important component in understanding the potential a disaster will have upon an organization. People run the organization, and can best describe business functionality and their business unit's degree of reliance on support services. The issue here, however, is deciding what is the best and most practical technique for gathering the information from these people.

There are different schools of thought about the use of questionnaires during the BIA process. Our opinion is that a well-crafted questionnaire will provide the structure needed by the BCP project team to consistently acquire the required information. This consistent questioning structure requires that the same questions be asked of each BIA interviewee — reliance can be placed on the results because answers to questions can be compared one to another, and the comparisons are based on the same criterion.

While we consider a questionnaire to be a valuable tool, the structure of the questions in the questionnaire itself is subject to a great deal of customization. This customization of the questions depends largely upon the reason why the BIA is being conducted in the first place.

The BIA process can be approached differently depending upon the needs of the organization. Each BIA situation should be evaluated in order to understand the underlying purpose to properly design the scope and approach of the BIA process. BIAs may be desired for several reasons, including:

- initiation of a BCP process where no BIA has been done before as part of the five-phase BCP methodology (Phase 2)
- reinitiating a BCP process where there was a BIA performed but now it needs to be brought up-to-date
- conducting a BIA in order to justify BCP activities which have already been undertaken (i.e., the acquisition of a hot site or other recovery alternative)
- simply updating the results of a previous BIA effort to identify changes in the environment and as a basis to plan additional activities
- initiating a BIA as a prelude to considering the beginning of a full BCP process for understanding or as a vehicle to sell management on the need to develop a BCP

BIA INFORMATION-GATHERING TECHNIQUES

There are various schools of thought regarding how to best gather BIA impact information. Conducting individual one-on-one BIA interviews is popular, but organizational size and location issues sometimes make conducting one-on-one interviews impossible. Other popular techniques include group exercises and often the use of an electronic medium (i.e., data or voice network) or a combination of all of these. The following points highlight the pros and cons of these interviewing techniques:

One-on-one BIA interviews — The one-on-one interview with organizational representatives is the preferred manner in which to gather the BIA impact information, in our opinion. The pros of this are that you have the ability to discuss the issues face-to-face and observe the person. This one-on-one discussion will give the interviewer a great deal of both verbal and visual information concerning the topic at hand. In addition, personal rapport can be built between the interviewee and the BIA team, with the potential for additional assistance and support to follow. This rapport can be very beneficial during later stages of the BCP development effort if the persons being interviewed understand that the BCP process was undertaken to help them get the job done in times of emergency or disaster. The minus to this approach is that it can become very time consuming and tends to stretch the length of the BIA process.

Group BIA interview sessions or exercises — This type of information-gathering activity can be very efficient in ensuring that a lot of data are gathered in a short period of time and can speed the BIA process tremendously. The problem with this type of an approach, if not conducted properly, is it can result in a meeting of many people without much useful information being accurately recorded for later consideration.

Electronic media — Especially these days, the use of voice, data, video conferencing, etc., media are popular. Many times, the physical size and diversity as well as the structural complexity of the organization lends itself to this clean information-gathering technique. The pros are that distances can be diminished and travel expenses reduced, and that the use of auto-mated questionnaires and other data-gathering methods can facilitate the capture of tabular data and make the ease of consolidation of this informa-tion possible. Less attractive, however, is that this type of communication lacks the human touch, and sometimes ignores the importance of the abil-ity of the interviewer to read the verbal and visual communications of the interviewee. Especially worrisome, however, is the universal broadcasting of BIA-related questionnaires. These inquiries go to an uninformed or little informed group of users on a network, whereby they are asked to supply answers to qualitative and quantitative BIA questions without regard to the point of the question or the intent of the use of the result. Such practices almost always lend themselves to misleading and downright wrong results. This type of unsupported data-gathering technique for purposes of formu-lating a thoughtful strategy for recovery should be avoided.

Most likely, however, your organization will need to use a mix of these suggested methods, or use others suited to the situation and culture of the enterprise.

CUSTOMIZING THE BIA QUESTIONNAIRE

There are a number of ways in which a BIA questionnaire can be con-structed and/or customized to adapt itself for the purpose of serving as an efficient tool for accurately gathering BIA information. There are also an unlimited number of examples of BIA questionnaires in use by organiza-tions. It should go without saying that any questionnaire, BIA or otherwise, can be constructed so as to elicit the response one would like to derive. It is important that the goal of the BIA be in the mind of the questionnaire developers so that the questions asked and the responses collected will meet the objective of the BIA process.

BIA QUESTIONNAIRE CONSTRUCTION

Exhibit 14-1 features an example of a BIA questionnaire. Basically, the BIA questionnaire is made up of the following types of questions:

- *Quantitative Questions* — These are the questions the interviewee is asked to consider to describe the economic or financial impacts of a potential disruption. Measured in monetary terms, an estimation of these impacts will aid the organization in understanding loss poten-tial, in terms of lost income as well as in an increase in extraordinary expense. The typical qualitative impact categories might include:

Exhibit 14-1. Sample BIA questionnaire.

Introduction
- Business Unit Name
  - Date of Interview
  - Contact Name(s)
  - Identification of business unit (BU) function
- Briefly describe the overall business functions of the BU (with focus on time-critical functions/processes, and link each time-critical function/process to the IT application/network, etc.) and understand the business process and the systems/applications interrelationships

Financial Impacts
- Revenue Loss Impact Estimations (revenue or sales loss, lost trade discounts, interest paid on borrowed money, interest lost on float, penalties for late payment to vendors or lost discounts, contractual fines or penalties, unavailability of funds, canceled orders due to late delivery, etc.)
- Extraordinary Expense Impact Estimations (acquisition of outside services, temporary employees, emergency purchases, rental/lease equipment, wages paid to idle staff, temporary relocation of employees, etc.)

Operational Impacts
- Business Interruption Impact Estimations (loss of customer service capabilities, inability to serve internal customers/management, etc.)
- Loss of Confidence Estimations (loss of confidence on behalf of customers, shareholders, regulatory agencies, employees, etc.)

Technological Dependence
- Systems/Business Functions/Applications Reliance Description (attempt to identify specific automated systems/processes/applications that support BU operations)
- Systems Interdependencies Descriptions
- State of existing BCP measures
- Other BIA-related discussion issues

---

revenue or sales loss, lost trade discounts, interest paid on borrowed money, interest lost on float, penalties for late payment to vendors or lost discounts, contractual fines or penalties, unavailability of funds, canceled orders due to late delivery, etc. Extraordinary expense categories might include: acquisition of outside services, temporary employees, emergency purchases, rental/lease equipment, wages paid to idle staff, and temporary relocation of employees.

- *Qualitative Questions* — While the economic impacts can be stated in terms of dollar loss, the qualitative questions ask the participants to estimate potential loss impact in terms of their emotional understanding or feelings. It is surprising how often the qualitative measurements are used to put forth a convincing argument for a shorter recovery window. The typical qualitative impact categories might include loss of customer services capability, loss of confidence, etc.

- *Specialized Questions* — Make sure that the questionnaire is customized to the organization. It is especially important to make sure that both the economic and operational impact categories (lost sales, interest paid on borrowed funds, business interruption, customer inconvenience, etc.) are stated in such a way that each interviewee will understand the intent of the measurement. Simple is better here.

Using an automated tool? If an automated tool is being used to collect and correlate the BIA interview information, then make sure that the questions in the database and questions on the questionnaire are synchronized to avoid duplication of effort or going back to interviewees with questions that might have been handled initially. A word of warning here, however. we have seen people pick up a BIA questionnaire off the Internet or from a book or periodical (like this one) and use it without regard to the culture and practices of their own organization. Never, ever, use a noncustomized BIA questionnaire. The qualitative and quantitative questions must be structured to the environment and style of the organization. There is opportunity for failure should this point be dismissed.

BIA INTERVIEW LOGISTICS AND COORDINATION

This portion of the report will address the logistics and coordination while performing the BIA interviews themselves. Having scoped the BIA process, the next step is to determine who and how many people you are going to interview. In order to do this, there are some techniques you might use:

- *Use Organizational Charts to Compile Lists of Interviewees* — You certainly are not going to interview everyone in the organization. You must select a sample of those management and staff personnel who will provide you with the best information in the shortest period. In order to do that, you must have a precise feel for the scope of the project (i.e., technological platform recovery, business unit recovery, communications recovery, etc.) and with that understanding you can use:
    1. *Organizational Chart Reviews* — The use of formal, or sometimes even informal organization charts is the first place to start. This method includes examining the organizational chart of the enterprise to understand those functional positions that should be included. Review the organizational chart to determine which organizational structures will be directly involved in the overall effort and those that will be the recipients of the benefits of the finished recovery plan.
    2. *Overlaying Systems Technology* — Overlay systems technology (applications, networks, etc.) configuration information over the organization chart to understand the components of the organization that

may be affected by an outage of the systems. Mapping applications, systems, and networks to the organization's business functions will aid tremendously when attempting to identify the appropriate names and numbers of people to interview.

3. *Interview Technique* — This method includes conducting introductory interviews of selected senior management representatives in order to identify critical personnel to be included in the BIA interview process.

- *Coordinate with the IT Group* If the scope of the BIA process is recovery of technological platforms and communications systems, then conducting interviews with a number of IT personnel could help shorten the data-gathering effort. While IT users can often provide much valuable information, they should not be relied upon solely as the primary source of business impact outage information (i.e., revenue loss, extra expense, etc.).

- *Send Questionnaire out in Advance* — It is a useful technique to distribute the questionnaire to the interviewees in advance. Whether it is in hard copy or electronic media format, the person being interviewed should have a chance to review the questions, be able to invite others into the interview or redirect the interview to others, and begin to develop the responses. You should emphasize to the people who receive the questionnaire in advance to not fill it out, but to simply review it and be prepared to address the questions.

- *Schedule One-Hour Interviews* — Ideally, the BIA interview should last between 45 and 75 minutes. We have found that it sometimes can be advantageous to go longer than this, but if you see many of the interviews lasting longer than the 75-minute window, then there may be a BIA scoping issue which should be addressed, necessitating the need to schedule and conduct a larger number of additional interviews.

- *Limit Number of Interviewees* — It is important to limit the number of interviewees in the session to one, two, or three, but no more. Given the amount and quality of information you are hoping to elicit from this group, more than three people can deliver a tremendous amount of good information that can be missed when too many people are delivering the message at the same time.

- *Try to Schedule Two Interviewers* — When setting up the BIA interview schedule, try to ensure that at least two interviewers can attend and take notes. This will help eliminate the possibility that good information may be missed. Every additional trip back to an interviewee for confirmation of details will add overhead to the process.

CONDUCTING THE BIA

When actually explaining the intent of the BIA to those being interviewed, the following concepts should be observed and perhaps discussed with the participants:

- *Intelligent Questions Asked of Knowledgeable People* — Based loosely on the concept that if you ask enough reasonably intelligent people a consistent set of measurable questions, you will eventually reach a conclusion which is more or less the correct one. The BIA questions serve to elicit qualitative results from a number of knowledgeable people. The precise number of people interviewed obviously depends on the scope of the BCP activity and the size of the organization. However, when consistently directing a well-developed number of questions to an informed audience, the results will reflect a high degree of reliability. This is the point when conducting qualitatively oriented BIA — ask the right people good questions, and you will come up with the right results!
- *Ask to Be Directed to the Correct People* — As the interview unfolds, it may become evident that the interviewee is the wrong person to be answering the questions. You should ask who else within this area would be better suited to address these issues. They might be invited into the room at that point, or you may want to schedule a meeting with them at another time.
- *Assure Them That Their Contribution Is Valuable* — A very important way for you to build the esteem of the interviewee is to mention that their input to this process is considered valuable, as it will be used to formulate strategies necessary to recover the organization following a disruption or disaster. Explaining to them that you are there to help by getting their business unit's relevant information for input to planning a recovery strategy can sometimes change the tone of the interview positively.
- *Explain That the Plan Is Not Strictly an IT Plan* — Even if the purpose of the BIA is for IT recovery, when interviewing business unit management for the process of preparing a technological platform recovery plan, it is sometimes useful to couch the discussion in terms of … "a good IT recovery plan, while helping IT recover, is really a business unit plan." Why? Because the IT plan will recover the business functionality of the interviewees business unit as well, and that is why you are there.
- *Focus on Who Will Really Be Exercising the Plan* — Another technique is to mention that the recovery plan that will eventually be developed can be used by the interviewees, but is not necessarily developed for them. Why? Because the people that you are talking to probably already understand what to do following a disaster, without referring to extensive written recovery procedures. But the fact of the matter is that following the disruption, these people may not be available. It may well be the responsibility of the next generation of management to recover, and it will be the issues identified by this interviewee that will serve as the recovery road map.

- *Focus on Time-Critical Business Functions or Processes* — As the BIA interview progresses, it is sometimes important to fall back from time to time and reinforce the concept that we are interested in the identification of time-critical functions and processes.
- *Assume Worst-Case Disaster* — When faced with the question as to "When will the disruption occur?" The answer should be, "It will occur at the worst possible time for your business unit. If you close your books on 12/31, and you need the computer system the most on 12/30 and 12/31, the disaster will occur on 12/29." Only when measuring the impacts of a disruption at the worst time can the interviewer get an idea as to the full impact of the disaster, and ensure that the impact information can be meaningfully compared from one business unit to the next.
- *Assume No Recovery Capability Exists* — In order to reach results which are comparable, it is essential that you insist that the interviewees assume that no recovery capability will exist as they answer the impact questions. The reason for this is that when they attempt to quantify and/or qualify the impact potential, they may confuse a pre-existing recovery plan or capability with no impact, and that is incorrect. No matter the existing recovery capability, the impact of a loss of services must be measured in raw terms so that as you compare the results of the interviews from business unit to business unit, the results are comparable (apples to apples, if you will).
- *Order of Magnitude Numbers and Estimates* — The financial impact information is needed in orders of magnitude estimates only. Do not get bogged down in minutiae as it is easy to get lost in the detail. The BIA process is not a quantitative risk assessment! It is not meant to be. It is qualitative in nature and, as such, orders of magnitude impacts are completely appropriate and even desirable. Why? Because preciseness in estimation of loss impact almost always will result in arguments about the numbers. When this occurs, the true goal of the BIA is lost, because it turns the discussion into a numbers game, not a balanced discussion concerning financial and operational impact potentials. Because of the unlimited and unknown varieties of disasters that could possibly befall an organization, the true numbers can never ever be precisely known, at least until after the disaster. The financial impact numbers are merely estimates intended to illustrate degrees of impacts. So skip the numbers exercise and get to the point.
- *Stay Focused on the BCP Scope* — Whether the BIA process is for development of technological platforms, end user, facilities recovery, voice network, etc., it is very important that you do not allow scope creep in the minds of the interviewees. The discussion can become very unwieldy if you do not hold the focus of the loss impact discussions on the precise scope of the BCP project.
- *There Are No Wrong Answers* — Because all the results will be compared with one-another before the BIA report is forwarded, then you

can emphasize that the interviewee should not worry about wrong answers. As the BIA process evolves, each business units financial and operational impacts will be compared with the others, and those impact estimates which are out of line with the rest will be challenged and adjusted accordingly.

- *Do Not Insist upon Getting the Financial Information on the Spot* — Sometimes the compilation of financial loss impact information requires a little time to accomplish. We often will tell the interviewee that we will return within a few days to collect the information, so that additional care can be taken in preparation — making sure that we do actually return and pick up the information later.

- *The Value of Push Back* — Do not underestimate the value of push back when conducting BIA interviews. Business unit personnel will, most times, tend to view their activities as extremely time-critical, with little or no downtime acceptable. In reality, their operations will be arranged in some priority order with the other business processes of the organization for recovery priority. Realistic MTDs must be reached, and sometimes the interviewer must push back and challenge what may be considered unrealistic recovery requirements. Be realistic in challenging, and request that the interviewees be realistic in estimating their business units MTDs. Common ground will eventually be found that will be more meaningful to those who will read the *BIA Findings and Recommendations Report* — the senior management group.

Interpreting and Documenting the Results

As the BIA interview information is gathered, there is considerable tabular and written information that begins to quickly accumulate. This information must be correlated and analyzed. Many issues will arise here and there will be issues and some follow-up interviews or information-gathering requirements. The focus at this point in the BIA process should be as follows:

- *Begin Documentation of the Results Immediately* — Even as the initial BIA interviews are being scheduled and completed, it is a good idea to begin preparation of the *BIA Findings and Recommendations Report* and actually start entering preliminary information. The reason is two-fold. The first is that if you wait to the end of the process to start formally documenting the results, it is going to be more difficult to recall details that should be included. Second, as the report begins to evolve, there will be issues that arise where you will want to perform additional investigation while you still have time to ensure the investigation can be thoroughly performed.

- *Develop Individual Business Unit BIA Summary Sheets* — Another practical technique is to document each and every BIA interview with its own *BIA Summary Sheet*. This information can eventually be used directly by importing it into the *BIA Findings and Recommendations Report* which can also be distributed back to each particular interviewee to authenticate the results of the interview. The *BIA Summary Sheet* contains a summation of all the verbal information that was documented during the interview. This information will be of great value later as the BIA process evolves.

- *Send Early Results Back to Interviewees for Confirmation* — By returning the *BIA Summary Sheet* for each of the interviews back to the interviewee, you can continue to build consensus for the BCP project and start to ensure that any future misunderstandings regarding the results can be avoided. Sometimes you may want to get a formal sign-off, and other times the process is simply informal.
- *We Are Not Trying to Surprise Anyone!* — The purpose for diligently pursuing the formalization of the BIA interviews and returning to confirm the understandings from the interview process is to make very sure that there are no surprises later. This is especially important in large BCP projects where the BIA process takes a substantial amount of time and there is always a possibility that someone might forget what was said.
- *Definition of Time-Critical Business Functions/Processes* — As has been emphasized in this chapter, all issues should focus back to the true time-critical business processes of the organization. Allowing attention to be shifted to specific recovery scenarios too early in the BIA phase will result in confusion and lack of attention toward what is really important.
- *Tabulation of Financial Impact Information* — There can be a tremendous amount of tabular information generated through the BIA process. It should be boiled down to its essence and presented in such a way as to support the eventual conclusions of the BIA project team. It is easy to overdo it with numbers. Just ensure that the numbers do not overwhelm the reader and fairly represent the impacts.
- *Understanding the Implications of the Operational Impact Information* — Oftentimes, the weight of evidence and the basis for the recovery alternative decision is based on the operational rather than the financial information. Why? Usually the financial impacts are more difficult to accurately quantify because the precise disaster situation and the recovery circumstances are hard to visualize. We know that there will be a customer service impact because of a fire, for instance. But we would have a hard time telling you with any degree of confidence what the revenue loss impact would be for a fire that affects one particular location of the organization. Since the BIA process should provide a qualitative estimate (orders of magnitude), the basis for making the hard decisions regarding acquisition of recovery resources are, in many cases, based on the operational impact estimates rather than hard financial impact information.

Preparing the Management Presentation

Presentation of the results of the BIA to concerned management should result in no surprises for them. If you are careful to ensure that the BIA findings are communicated and adjusted as the process has unfolded, then the management review process should really become more of a formality in most cases. The final presentation meeting with the senior management group is not the time to surface new issues and make startling results public for the first time.

In order to achieve the best results in the management presentation, the following suggestions are offered:

- *Draft Report for Review Internally First* — Begin drafting the report following the initial interviews. By doing this, you will be capturing fresh information. This information will be used to build the tables, graphs, and other visual demonstrations of the results, and it will be used to record the interpretations of the results in the verbiage of the final *BIA Findings and Recommendation Report*. One method for accomplishing a well-constructed *BIA Findings and Recommendation Report* from the very beginning is to record, at the completion of each interview, the tabular information into the BIA database or manual filing system in use to record this information. Second, the verbal information should be transcribed into a *BIA Summary Sheet* for each interview. This *BIA Summary Sheet* should be completed for each interviewee and contain the highlights of the interview in summarized form. As the BIA process continues, the BIA tabular information and the transcribed verbal information can be combined into the draft *BIA Findings and Recommendations Report*. The table of contents for a BIA Report may look like the following:

Exhibit 14-2. BIA report table of contents.

1. Executive Summary
2. Background
3. Current State Assessment
4. Threats and Vulnerabilities
5. Time-Critical Business Functions
6. Business Impacts (Operational)
7. Business Impacts (Financial)
8. Recovery Approach
9. Next Steps/Recommendations
10. Conclusion
11. Appendices (as needed)

- *Schedule Individual Senior Management Meetings as Necessary* — As you near the time for the final BIA presentation, it is sometimes a good idea to conduct a series of one-on-one meetings with selected senior management representatives in order to brief them on the results and gather feedback for inclusion in the final deliverables. In addition, this is a good time to begin building grassroots support for the final recommendations that will come out of the BIA process and concurrently give you an opportunity to practice making your points and discussing the pros and cons of the recommendations.

- *Prepare Senior Management Presentation (Bullet Point)* — Our experience says that senior management level presentations, most often, are better prepared in a brief and focused manner. It will undoubtedly become necessary to present much of the background information used to make the decisions and recommendations, but the formal presentation should be in bullet point format, crisp, and to the point. Of course, every organization has its own culture, so be sure to understand and comply with the traditional means of making presentations within your own environment. Copies of the report, which have been thoroughly reviewed, corrected, bound, and bundled for delivery can be distributed at the beginning or the end of the presentation depending upon circumstances. In addition, copies of the bullet point handouts can also be supplied so attendees can make notes for reference at a later time. Remember, the BIA process should end with a formalized agreement as to managements intentions with regard to MTDs, so that business unit and support services managers can be guided accordingly. It is here that that formalized agreement should be discussed and the mechanism for acquiring and communicating it determined.
- *Distribute Report* — Once the management team has had an opportunity to review the contents of the BIA Report and have made appropriate decisions and often given other input, the final report should be distributed within the organization to the appropriate interested individuals.

NEXT STEPS

The BIA is completed when formalized senior management decisions have been made regarding (1) MTDs, (2) priorities for business unit and support services recovery, and (3) recovery resource funding sources. The next step is the determination of the most effective recovery alternative to be selected. The work gets a little easier here. We know what our recovery windows are, and we understand what our recovery priorities are. We now have to investigate and select recovery alternative solutions that fit the recovery window and recovery priorities expectations of the organization. Once the alternatives have been agreed upon, the actual recovery plans can be developed and tested, with organization personnel organized and trained to execute the recovery plans, when needed.

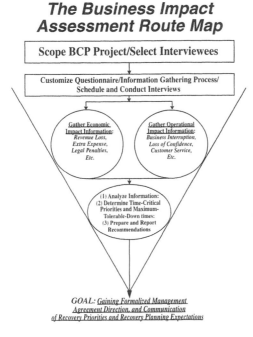

The Business Impact Assessment Route Map

Scope BCP Project/Select Interviewees

Customize Questionnaire/Information Gathering Process/
Schedule and Conduct Interviews

Gather Economic
Impact Information:
*Revenue Loss,
Extra Expense,
Legal Penalties,
Etc.*

Gather Operational
Impact Information:
*Business Interruption,
Loss of Confidence,
Customer Service,
Etc.*

(1) Analyze Information:
(2) Determine Time-Critical
Priorities and Maximum-
Tolerable-Down times:
(3) Prepare and Report
Recommendations

GOAL: *Gaining Formalized Management
Agreement Direction, and Communication
of Recovery Priorities and Recovery Planning Expectations*

Exhibit 14-3. The Business Impact Assessment Route Map.

SUMMARY

The process of business continuity planning has matured substantially since the 1980s. No longer is BCP viewed as just a technological question. A practical and cost-effective approach toward planning for disruptions or disasters begins with the business impact assessment. Exhibit 14-3 depicts the BIA Route Map — a visual presentation of the process.

The goal of the BIA is to assist the management group in identification of time-critical processes, and in recognizing their degree of reliance upon support services (i.e., IT, voice and data networks, facilities, HR, etc.). Time-critical business processes are prioritized in terms of their maximum tolerable downtime, so that senior management can make reasonable decisions as to the recovery costs and time frames that they are willing to fund and support.

This chapter has focused on how organizations can facilitate the BIA process. Understanding and applying the various methods and techniques for gathering the BIA impact information will be the key to success.

Only when senior management formalizes their decisions regarding recovery time frames and priorities can each business unit and support service manager formulate acceptable and efficient plans for recovery of operations in the event of disruption or disaster. It is for this reason that the BIA process is so important when developing efficient and cost-effective business continuity plans.

Exhibit 14-4. BIA do's checklist.

To-do's when doing business impact assessments:
- Customize the BIA questionnaire
- Focus on time-critical business functions/processes
- Assume worst-case disaster
- Assume no recovery capability exists
- Obtain raw numbers in orders of magnitude
- Return for financial information (don't wait for it during the interview)
- Go back and affirm that these same people agree with the output
- Get a formalized decision from senior management so that precise plans can be made by lower-level managers (MTD timeframes, scope and depth of recovery procedures, etc.)

Conducting the Interview:
- When interviewing BU personnel, explain that you are here to get the information you need to help IT build their recovery plan. But the IT recovery plan is really for the business units. We are obtaining BU input as an aid in ensuring that IT constructs the proper recovery planning strategy.
- Interviews last 45 minutes and no longer than 1 hour and 15 minutes.
- The number of interviewees at one session should be at best one, and at worst three. More than that and the ability of the interviewer to take notes is questionable.
- If possible, at least two personnel should be in attendance at the interview. Each should have a blank copy of the questionnaire on which to take notes.
- One person should probably not perform more than four interviews per day. This is due to the need to successfully document the results of each interview as soon as possible and because of fatigue factors.
- Never become confrontational with the interviewees. There is no reason that an interviewee should be made defensive in their answers to you unless they do not properly understand the purpose of the BIA interview.
- Relate to the interviewees that their comments will be taken into consideration and documented with the others, and that they will be requested to review, at a later date, the output from the process for accuracy and to provide their concurrence.

Chapter 15
Selecting the Right Business Continuity Planning Strategies

Ken Doughty

THE FIRST STEP IN DEVELOPING A CUSTOMIZED BUSINESS CONTINUITY PLAN (BCP) IS TO CONDUCT A BUSINESS IMPACT ANALYSIS. This comprehensive risk evaluation and business impact analysis (BIA) will identify the organization's core business processes and their critical dependencies. Because the organization's recovery strategy must be based on the recovery of the core business processes and their critical dependencies, the strategy ultimately selected may be two-tiered:

- **Technical:** desktop, client/server, midrange, mainframes, data and voice networks, third-party providers
- **Business:** logistics, accounting, human resources, etc.

Once the organization's executive management has signed off on the BIA report and endorsed the recovery of the recommended core business processes and the priority of recovery, BCP recovery strategies must be developed for each business process.

Ideally, all business units should participate in the development of these BCP recovery strategies. As experienced staff in the business unit's understands their business processes, they should be approached to suggest recovery strategies.

A recovery strategy workshop is an ideal forum to develop the BCP recovery strategy with input from the business units. This will ensure that there is ownership of the BCP strategy and the "plan" by the business units.

RECOVERY STRATEGY WORKSHOP

The purpose of the recovery strategy workshop is to identify appropriate recovery strategies for each core business process and the risks associated with each strategy. Of particular interest are recovery strategies that are *low* risk and *cost-effective.* Too often, there is a greater emphasis on cost and benefits without consideration given to the risks associated with the recovery strategy.

The BCP coordinator (i.e., the person responsible for developing, implementing, and maintaining the organization's BCP) must select the right recovery strategy and must also minimize the risks associated with that strategy. The BCP coordinator should be the workshop facilitator because he or she has a deep knowledge of business continuity planning, risk management training, as well as a good understanding of the organization's strategic objectives and processes. Business unit attendees should have a good working knowledge of their business processes.

Recovery Strategies

During the workshop, the BCP coordinator will assist the business unit staff to in identifying BCP recovery strategies for each core business process. It is not unusual to find that the initial recovery strategy suggested by the workshop attendees to be high risk and not cost-effective.

As a case study, take a look at the banking sector and one of its core business processes, that of processing customer checks and exchanging checks with other banking institutions.

At the workshop, attendees would identify a number of BCP recovery strategies for processing checks. For example:

- service level agreement with another bank to process all work
- branch network processes all credits and service level agreements with another bank to complete check processing
- branch network to processes all credits and forwards all checks to an intrastate/interstate center for final processing
- forward all work to an intrastate/interstate center for processing
- do nothing

Strategy Risks

To continue this case study for the core business process of processing checks, the workshop attendees (with the assistance of the BCP coordinator) would identify a range of recovery risks, that may be applicable (see Exhibit 15-1).

Assessing Risks

The BCP coordinator, with assistance from the workshop attendees and utilizing the BCP recovery strategy risks (as per Exhibit 15-1) and a risk

Exhibit 15-1. Recovery risks.

No.	Risk description
1.	Damage to the banks brand (i.e., reputation)
2.	Customer impact — financial and service
3.	External service level agreement (SLA) partner not compliant with agreement
4.	Hold over (delayed processing)
5.	Time frame lag
6.	Funding of recovery
7.	Resource shortage — staff
8.	Resource shortage — skills
9.	Resource shortage — equipment
10.	Resource shortage — stationery/stores
11.	Internal coordination
12.	External coordination
13.	Logistics — transportation of staff, work, etc.
14.	Employee's union
15.	Legislative requirements
16.	Third party suppliers — non provision of services
17.	Denial of access to alternate processing site(s)
18.	Internal/external communications
19.	Incompatible information technology
20.	Internal SLA partner not compliant with agreement
21.	Physical security over source documents

assessment methodology (e.g., AS4360 Risk Management — refer to Exhibit 15-2), assesses each recovery strategy and the associated risks. A risk assessment matrix is then applied for likelihood and consequences to derive a risk score.

Each recovery strategy score is then risk ranked to provide an indication of the level of risk associated with each recovery strategy (refer to Exhibit 15-3).

The BCP recovery strategy that offers the lowest levels of risk in execution and the greatest opportunity of success in the event is to be costed.

RECOVERY STRATEGY COSTS

There are two levels of costs: pre-event and event costs. Pre-event costs are incurred in either implementing risk mitigation strategies or allocation of resources (including human and financial) and capital expenditure on developing the necessary infrastructure for the BCP recovery strategy. These costs may include, for example:

Exhibit 15-2. Risk management methodology.

Table 1: Likelihood of event table.

Descriptor	Meaning
Almost Certain	The event is expected to occur in most circumstances.
Likely	The event will probably occur in most circumstances.
Moderate	The event should occur at some time.
Unlikely	The event could occur at some time.
Rare	The event may occur only in exceptional circumstances.

Table 2: Consequences of event table.

Descriptor	Meaning
Catastrophic	Complete disaster with potential to collapse activity.
Major	Event that, with substantial management, will be endured.
Moderate	Event that, with appropriate process, can be managed.
Minor	Consequences can be readily absorbed; however, management effort is required to minimize impact.

Table 3: Risk assessment matrix.

	Likelihood					
Consequences	Almost certain	Likely	Moderate	Unlikely	Rare	Irrelevant
Catastrophic	High	High	High	High	Significant	N/A
Major	High	High	High	Significant	Significant	N/A
Moderate	High	Significant	Significant	Moderate	Moderate	N/A
Minor	Significant	Significant	Moderate	Low	Low	N/A

Where the risk value meanings are:

High	High risk — detailed research and management planning required at high levels.
Significant	Significant risk — senior management attention needed.
Moderate	Moderate risk — specific risk management process(es) must be developed.
Low	Low risk — can be managed by routine procedures.

From AS4360 – Risk Management – Standards Australia.

- **Information technology**
  - hot site: fully operational computer center, including data and voice communications
  - alternate LAN server: a LAN server fully configured ready to be shipped and installed at the same site or alternate site
  - physical separation of telecommunications network devices (previously centralized) to reduce the likelihood of a single point of failure
  - establishment of service level agreements with BCP recovery company (i.e., hot, warm, or cold sites and mobile).

- — duplication of telecommunications network (another telecommunication carrier, switching capability, etc.)
- — creation of a full-time BCP Team that is responsible for maintaining and testing the organization's technical BCP.
- **Equipment.** The purchase and maintenance of redundant equipment at alternate site (e.g., microfilm readers, proof machines, image processors, etc.), particularly if there is a long lead-time to source and procure equipment.
- **Third-party service providers.** Third-party service providers are requested to develop a BCP requirement to meet organizational (customer) requirements. Some proportion of this cost may be borne by the organization requesting this functionality/facility be provided.

  Dependency on third-party service providers for business continuity purposes is a major concern to BCP coordinators. Once third-party service providers have been identified as critical to the day-to-day operations of the business, BCP coordinators are to seek assurance that these service providers have a demonstrable BCP in the event of disaster striking their organization.
- **Service level agreements (SLA).** The costs associated with the external suppliers to readily provide services and often also products (non-IT) in the event of a disaster.
- **Vital records.** A vital record program that identifies all critical records required for post-recovery core business processes. Costs may be incurred in the protection of these records (e.g., imaging, off-site storage, etc.) to ensure that they will be available in the event of a disaster.

Event costs are incurred in implementing the BCP strategies in the event of a disaster. The costs are an estimation of the likely costs that would be incurred if the BCP were activated for a defined period (e.g. one day, seven days, 14 days, 21 days, 30 days). These costs would include, but are not limited to:

- **activation of SLA:** often a once up cost plus ongoing costs until services/products are no longer required (cessation of disaster)
- **staffing** (overtime, temporary, contractors, etc.)
- **logistics** (transportation of staff and resources, couriers, etc.)
- **accommodation costs** (hire/lease of temporary offices, accommodation for staff and other personnel)
- **hire/lease or procurement of non-IT resources** (e.g., desks, chairs, tables, safes, cabinets, photocopiers, stationery, etc.)
- **hire/lease or procurement of IT resources** (e.g., faxes, hand-sets, printers, desktop PCs, notebook computers, terminals, scanners, etc.)
- **miscellaneous costs** (e.g., insurance deductible, security and salvage of assets at disaster site, clean-up of disaster site, emergency services costs, etc.)

Exhibit 15-3. Case study.

Banking sector: Processing checks Bank core process: check processing (deposits and checks) and exchange

BCP Strategy 1	Risks	Assigned risk rating
SLA with another bank to process all work	1. Brand damage	Moderate
	2. Customer impact	Low
	3. Other banking party non-compliant with SLA	High
	4. Hold-over	High
	5. Timeframe impact	High
	6. Funding	Low
	7. Staff shortage	High
	8. Equipment shortage	Significant
	9. Logistics	High
	10. External coordination and cooperation	Moderate
	11. Stationery/stores	Low
	12. APCA requirements	Moderate
	13. Other legislative requirements	Significant
	14. Internal/external communications	Moderate

BCP Strategy 2	Risks	Assigned risk rating
Branch network process all credits and SLA with another bank to complete check processing	1. SLA banking party not compliant	Low
	2. Hold-over	Significant
	3. Timeframe impact	High
	4. Funding	Low
	5. Staff shortage	High
	6. Equipment shortage	Moderate
	7. Internal coordination and cooperation	Moderate
	8. Logistics	Moderate
	9. Union	Significant
	10. External coordination and cooperation	Moderate
	11. Skills shortage	Moderate
	12. APCA requirements	Significant
	13. Other legislative requirements	Moderate
	14. Internal/external communications	Moderate

BCP Strategy 3	Risks	Assigned risk rating
Branch network processes all credits; forward all checks to an interstate Day 1 OPC for processing	1. Hold-over	High
	2. Timeframe impact	High
	3. Funding	Low
	4. Staff shortage	Significant
	5. Equipment shortage	Moderate
	6. Internal coordination and cooperation	Moderate
	7. Logistics	Significant
	8. Union	Moderate
	9. Stationery/stores	Low
	10. APCA requirements	Significant
	11. Denial access to alternate premises	Moderate
	12. Internal/external communications	Moderate

Exhibit 15-3. Case study. (*continued*)

BCP Strategy 4	Risks	Assigned risk rating
Forwards all	1. Brand damage	High
work to an	2. Customer impact	High
interstate	3. Hold-over	High
Day 1 OPC for	4. Timeframe impact	High
processing	5. Funding	Low
	6. Staff shortage	High
	7. Equipment shortage	Significant
	8. Internal coordination and cooperation	Moderate
	9. Logistics	High
	10. Union	Significant
	11. Stationery/stores	Moderate
	12. APCA requirements	Significant
	13. Denial access to alternate premises	Moderate
	14. Internal/external communications	Moderate

BCP Strategy 5	Risks	Assigned risk rating
Do nothing	Not considered, as it is unrealistic strategy	Not Applicable

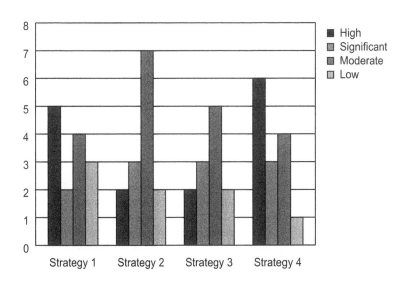

The BCP coordinator is to determine that all pre-event and event costs have been included and are reasonably accurate. Ideally, the BCP coordinator should request an independent party, for example the organizations' audit department, to review the cost components and value to ensure they all complete and accurate.

RECOVERY STRATEGY RISKS VERSUS COSTS

Once the costs (pre-event and event) have been determined, an analysis of the recovery strategy risks versus costs is to be performed. The objective of this analysis is to select the appropriate recovery strategy, which is balanced against risk and cost.

For example, using the case study above, the recovery strategies that offer the lowest risks for implementation are:

- *Strategy 2*: Branch network processes all credits and SLAs with another bank to complete check processing and exchange checks
- *Strategy 3*: Branch network to process all credits and forward all checks to an interstate center for final processing and check exchange

An analysis of Exhibit 15-4 indicates that:

- Strategy 2
  - highest risk of the two strategies being considered for implementation
  - pre-event cost of $150K per annum for the service level agreement
  - lowest event cost of the two strategies of $730K

Exhibit 15-4. Costs of two strategies.

BCP strategy	Pre-event costs	Accumulative event costs					Total costs
		1 day	1 Week	2 Weeks	3 Weeks	4 Weeks	
Strategy 2	$150K per annum	$75K	$255K	$375K	$515K	$730K	$880K
Strategy 3	Nil	$150K	$415K	$875K	$1.2M	$3.2M	$3.2M

- Strategy 3
  - lowest risk of the two strategies being considered for implementation
  - no pre-event costs
  - highest event cost of the two strategies by $3.2M
  - longer the outage there is an accelerating increase in the event costs

The decision to be made is whether the organization is prepared to accept higher risks with lower event costs, or a lower risk strategy with higher event costs. In other words it is a trade-off between risks the organization is prepared to accept and the costs the organization is prepared to spend.

However, where two strategies are of equal risk and similar cost value, then a third element is brought into the evaluation process — benefits. The benefits, including tangible and intangible, for each strategy are to be evaluated against the risks associated with the recovery strategy.

Further, the benefits are to be considered in the short and long term, that is, the "added" value to the organization that is operating in a dynamic and competitive market.

SUMMARY

Organizations that undertake Business Continuity Planning often do not spend the time to analyze the risks associated with the selected BCP recovery strategy, to determine if it is low risk and the cost of implementation is acceptable.

The BCP coordinator's role is enhanced by ensuring that the "right" BCP recovery strategies are selected for the organization.

The reality is that in the event of a disaster, selecting the "wrong" strategy may actually exacerbate the disaster. This potentially may lead to the organization going out-of-business. However, by performing a risk versus cost analysis of the BCP strategies, the BCP coordinator will reduce the potential exposures the organization will face in the execution of the Business Continuity Plan (i.e., implementation of the recovery strategy) and strengthening the recovery process.

Chapter 16
Business Continuity in the Distributed Environment

Steven P. Craig

TODAY'S ORGANIZATIONS, IN THEIR EFFORTS TO REDUCE COSTS, ARE STREAMLINING LAYERS OF MANAGEMENT WHILE IMPLEMENTING MORE COMPLEX MATRICES OF CONTROL AND REPORTING. Distributed systems have facilitated the reshaping of these organizations by moving the control of information closer to its source — the end user. In this transition, however, secure management of that information is placed at risk. Information Technology (IT) departments must protect the traditional system environment within the computer room, plus develop policies, standards, and guidelines for the security and the protection of the company's information base. Further, the IT staff must communicate these standards to all users to enforce a strong baseline of controls.

In these distributed environments, IT personnel are often asked to develop system recovery plans outside the context of an overall business recovery scheme. Recoverability of systems, however, should be viewed as only one part of business recovery. Information Systems (IS), in and of itself, is not the lifeblood of a company; inventory, assets, processes, and people are all essential factors that must be considered in the business continuation design. The success of business continuity planning rests on a company's ability to integrate systems recovery in the greater overall planning effort.

BUSINESS RECOVERY PLANNING: THE PROCESS

Distinctive areas must be addressed when formulating a company's business continuity plan that follow the stages of the scientific process; namely, statement of the problem, development of a hypothesis, and testing of the hypothesis. Most importantly, as with any scientifically developed process, the Disaster Recovery Planning Process development is iterative. The testing phase of this process identifies whether or not the plan will work in practice … not just in theory. It is imperative that the plan and its assumptions be tested, tested, and retested. The important distinction about business continuity planning, and the importance of its viability, is what is at stake — namely, the survivability of the business.

The phases of a viable business continuity plan process are:

- awareness and discovery
- risk assessment
- mitigation
- preparation
- testing
- response and recovery

Some of these phases can be combined, depending on the size of the company and the extent of exposure to risk. However, these phases are distinct and discussed more in length in the following sections.

Awareness and Discovery

Awareness begins when a recovery planning team can identify both possible threats and plausible threats to business operations. The more pressing issue for an organization in terms of business recovery planning is that of plausible threats. These threats must be evaluated by recovery planners and their planning efforts, in turn, will depend on these criteria:

- the business of the company
- the area of the country in which the company is located
- the company's existing security measures
- the level of adherence to existing policies and procedures
- management's commitment to existing policies and procedures

Awareness is also education. Part of the awareness process consists of instructing all employees on what exposures exist for the company and themselves; what measures have been taken to minimize those exposures; and what their individual roles are in complying with those measures.

Pertaining to systems and information: what exposures are there; what information is vital to the organization; and, what information is proprietary and confidential to the business? Also with respect to systems, another question that needs to be addressed is, when is an interruption considered to be catastrophic as opposed to operational? Again, this needs to be answered on a company-by-company basis. In an educational environment, the systems being down for two to three days may not be considered catastrophic; however, in a process control environment (e.g., chemicals or electronics), a few minutes of downtime might be catastrophic.

Discovery is determining the extent of the exposure and the extent of recovery planning and of the security measures that should be taken. Based on the response to the awareness question as to what is plausible, there are more questions to be asked. What specific operations would be impacted by the exposures? What measures are in place or could be put in place to minimize those exposures? What measures could be taken to remove the exposure?

Risk Assessment

Risk assessment is a decision process that weighs the cost of implementing preventative measures against the risk of loss from not taking any action. There are qualitative and quantitative approaches to risk analysis, of which there are full text references written on the subject. Typically for the systems environment, in terms of outright loss, two major cost factors arise. The first is the loss from not conducting business due to system downtime. The second is the replacement cost of the equipment. The unavailability of systems for an extended period of time is the easiest intuitive sell, as it is readily understandable by just about everyone in today's organizations as to how much they rely on systems.

The cost to replace systems and information, however, is often not well understood, at least not from a catastrophic loss point of view. In many instances, major organizations, when queried on insurance coverage for systems, come up with some surprising results. There will typically be coverage for mainframes and mid-range systems, as well as coverage for the software for these environments, but when it comes to the workstations or the network servers, they are deemed as not worth enough to insure. Another gaping hole is the lack of coverage for the information itself. The major replacement cost for a company is the recreation of its information base.

Further, the personal computer (PC), no matter how it is configured or what it is hooked up to or how extensive the network, is still perceived to be a stand-alone unit from a risk assessment point of view. Although many companies have retired their mainframes and fully embraced an extensive client/server architecture to fully manage their businesses, and fully comprehend the impact of the loss of its use, they erroneously look at the replacement cost of the unit rather than the distributed system as the basis of risk.

Risk assessment is the control point of the recovery planning process. The amount of exposure a company believes it has, or is willing to accept, determines how much additional effort the company will put forth on this process. Quite simply, companies with no plan are taking on the full risk of exposure, assuming that nothing, at least nothing severe, will ever happen to them. Companies that have developed plans have decided on the extent of risk assumption in two ways: (1) they have identified their worst-case scenario, and (2) they have made decisions based on how much they will expend in offsetting that scenario through mitigation, contingency plans, and training. Risk assessment is the phase required to gel a company's management perspective, which in turn supports the goal to develop and maintain a companywide contingency plan.

Mitigation

Mitigation has two primary objectives: lessen the exposures and minimize possible loss. History teaches several lessons in this area. One can be sure that companies in Chicago now think twice about installing data centers in the basement of buildings after the underground floods of 1992. Bracing of key computer equipment and of office furniture has become popular in California due to the potential injuries to personnel and the threat of loss of assets from earthquakes. And, forward-thinking companies in the South and southern Atlantic states are installing systems far from the exterior of the buildings and windows because of the potential damage due to hurricanes.

Once again, from a more operational perspective, one can read story after story in the trade journals about backup schemes gone awry, if there was a backup performed at all! Although it is a simple concept, to make a backup copy of key data and systems, it is a difficult one to enforce in a distributed systems environment. To wit, as systems have been distributed and the end user has been empowered, the regimen of daily or periodic backups has diminished. The end user has been empowered with the tools but not given the responsibility that goes along with the use of those tools. This author recently went into a company, one of the leaders in the optical disk drive market, and found that it did perform daily backups to the optical disk (using its own product) of its accounting and manufacturing systems, but never rotated the media and never thought to take it off site! Any event impacting the hardware (e.g., fire, theft, earthquake) would have also destroyed the "only backup" and the means of business recovery for this premier company.

Preparation

This phase of the disaster planning process delineates what must be done in addition to the mitigation taken, should an event occur. Based on the perception of what could happen, who will take what actions? Are alternates identified for key staff members that may have been injured as a result of the event? Can the building be occupied? If not, where will temporary operations be set up? What supplies, company records, etc., will be required to operate from a temporary facility? What computer support will be required at the temporary location? Will a hot site be used for systems and telecommunications? What vendors and service providers need to be contacted; and further, is there access to their off-hours phone numbers, emergency numbers, or home phone numbers? These are all questions that need to be addressed, contingencies established, and the plans documented as an integral part of the disaster preparedness process.

Testing

As mentioned above, the testing phase proves the viability of the planning efforts. If there are omissions in the plan, or invalid assumptions, or inadequately postulated solutions … this is when one wants to find these things out. Not at the time of an actual event! Additionally, organizations do not remain static; the elements of change within an organization and its environment dictate a reasonable frequency of testing. This is the phase of the plan that one must afford to reiterate until one is comfortable with the results and that the plans will work in time of crisis. A subsequent section in this chapter covers testing more in-depth and proposes a testing strategy made available by the use of distributed systems.

Response and Recovery

Most everyone carries auto insurance, home insurance, professional liability insurance, and life insurance, yet one hopes never have to use it or rely on it. Well, this is the phase of the contingency plan one hopes to never use! This part of the plan details which individuals will take on specific roles as part of predetermined teams, trained to address the tasks of emergency response, assessment of damage, cleanup, restoration, alternate site start-up, emergency operations center duties, and whatever else managing through a crisis might demand.

Every phase of the planning process, prior to this phase, is based on normalcy. The planning effort is based on what is perceived to be plausible. Responses are envisioned to cover those perceptions, and are done so under rational conditions. Remember that people are an integral part of the response and recovery effort. Dealing with a catastrophic crisis is not a normal part of everyday life or of someone's work load.

Expect very different reactions from individuals you may think you knew well under severe stress. A simple example, one may have experienced is being trapped in an elevator for several minutes. Within a couple of minutes, an individual's personalities, anxieties, and fears start to surface. Some will begin to panic; others will start taking control of the situation. Here again, testing the plan can afford some insight as to how team members will react. Ideally, one will be able to stage some tests that will involve role playing so as to give team members a sense of what they may be exposed to and the conditions they will have to work under.

DEPARTMENTAL PLANNING

Time and time again this author has been asked to help a company develop its business resumption plan, only to be asked to focus just on the systems and ignore everything else; for the most obvious reason — cost. As it turns out, if a company receives an action item as a result of an audit, it is typically a part of an IT audit and thus only targeted at the systems of a company. In turn, the company focuses only on the audit compliance, thus viewing business continuity as an expense, rather than as an investment in business continuity.

Having a plan that addresses data integrity and systems survivability is a good start, but there is a lot more to consider. Depending on the nature of the business, telecommunications availability, as an example, may be much more important than systems availability. In a manufacturing environment, if the building and equipment were damaged, getting the systems up and running would not necessarily be the most important priority.

A company's business continuation plan is, in fact, a compilation of its departmental plans. It is essential that each department identify its own processes and subsequent priorities of those processes. Overall company-wide operating and recovery priorities are then established by the company's management, based on the input supplied by the departments. Information Technology (IT), as a service department to all other departments, is subsequently in a much better position to plan recovery capacity and required system availability based on their inputs, priorities, and departmental recovery schedules.

Information Technology's Role

IT should not be responsible for creating the individual departmental plans for the rest of the company, but it can and indeed needs to take a leadership role in the departmental plan development. IT has generally been the department that has the best appreciation and understanding of information flow throughout the organization. IT is therefore in the best position to identify and assess the following areas.

Interdepartmental Dependencies. Many times in reviewing a company's overall plan and its departmental plans and their subsequent priorities, conflicts in the priorities will arise. This occurs because the departments tend to develop their plans on their own without the other departments in mind. One department may downplay the generation of certain information, knowing it has little importance to its own operations, but it might be vitally important input to the operation of another department. IT can typically identify these priority discrepancies simply by being able to review each of the other department's plans.

External Dependencies. During the discovery process, recovery planners should determine with what outside services end-user departments are linked. End-user departments often tend to think of external services as being outside the scope of their recovery planning efforts, despite the fact that dedicated or unique hardware and software are required to use the outside services. At a minimum, make sure the departmental plans include the emergency contact numbers for the services and any company account codes that would permit linkage to the service from a recovery location. Also inquire as what provisions the outside service provider may have to assist the company in its recovery efforts.

Outsourced Operations. A 1990s' trend in corporate strategic directions was the outsourcing of entire department operations. The idea was to focus the company's resources on what it does best, and outsource the functions that it believes other companies could better handle as part of their expertise and focus. The idea sounds good in theory, but in practice this was a mixed bag of tricks. The bottom line of this strategic direction was that it would add to the bottom line. Based on what is being published on the subject, the savings may only have been a short-term result, and in fact, very costly in the long run. From a contingency planning perspective, what happens if the idea does not work? How does a company rebuild an information systems department from scratch?

With respect to recovery planning, this is a key area that requires involvement at the earliest stages possible, including the review of contract wording and stipulations. This is an area in which the contractor has to be an integral partner, with as much ownership and jointly owned risk as the acquiring company. In many disasters, the Information Systems staffs are the first responders for business recovery. Will the contractor be as willing to take on this role? The recovery planner needs to validate that the on-site outsourced contractors are as well trained on response and recovery as the other internal departments. The area of systems is so integral to the recovery capability of the other departments that is it imperative that the outsourced information systems personnel be well versed in the recovery needs and response priorities of all of the departments they are there to support.

Collectively, the outsourcer may have considerably more resources available to it than the customer; however, it must be agreed to contractually that the contractor will bring its resources to bear in the event of the customer's catastrophe. Normally, these outsourced arrangements start off with the greatest of intentions, but once things get under way and the conditions of systems, documentation, and operations are established, anything outside the scope of the contract is doable, but with incremental cost. Costs were what was intended to be cut when the outsourcing direction was decided on; raising these costs will be a tough sell. So, the recovery planner must be involved early in the development of any such outsourcing contract and be sure to protect the company's contingency planning interests.

Internal and External Exposures

Stand-alone systems acquired by departments for a special purpose are often not linked to a company's networks. Consequently, they are often overlooked in terms of data security practices.

For example, a mortgage company funded all of its loans via wire transfer from one of three stand-alone systems. This service was one of the key operations of the company. Each system was equipped with a modem and a uniquely serialized encryption card for access to the wire service. As one might guess, these systems were not maintained by Information Technology; there were no data or system backups maintained by the end-user department; and, each system was tied to a distinct phone line. Any mishap involving those three systems could have potentially put this department several days, if not weeks, in arrears in funding its loans. A replacement encryption card and linkage establishment would have taken as long as a month under catastrophic conditions to reestablish.

As a result of this discovery, a secondary site was identified and a standby encryption card, an associated alternate phone line, and a disaster recovery action plan were filed with the wire service. This one finding and its resolution more than justified the expense of the entire planning effort.

Another external exposure was identified for the same company during the discovery process, dealing with power and the requirements of its UPS capabilities. The line of questioning was on the sufficiency of battery back-up capacity and whether an external generator should be considered as well for longer term power interruption. An assumption had been made that, even in the event of an area-wide disaster, power would probably be restored within 24 hours. The company had eight hours of battery capacity, which would suffice for the main operational shift of the company. At first, this author was in agreement with them, knowing that the county's power utility company had a program of restoring power on a priority basis for the larger employers of the county. When this observation was mentioned to them, the author was corrected. They were in a special district and actually acquired their power from the city and, as a business, would have power restored only after all the emergency services and city agencies were restored. The restoration period was unknown. The assumption of power restoration within 24 hours was revised and an external generator was added to the uninterruptable power supply system.

Systems themselves should not be the only type of exposure one looks for. In a recent client discovery walkthrough, a protracted construction project was under way. The existing computer room (on the eighth floor of a 20-story highrise) was being remodeled to house the company's latest generation of computers and telecommunications equipment. The room had originally been designed with stand-alone air conditioners, a UPS system, secured entry, and a raised floor. Sprinklers had been eliminated from the room to avoid potential water damage and a Halon fire suppression system had been installed.

As a result of the construction, the computer equipment was temporarily moved to the adjoining computer technician's room. As one might guess, the technician's room had none of the protections that had been developed for the computer room. However, while there were short-term exposures (for length of the construction period), this was a known calculated risk. The actual exposure discovered was the computer room itself. During construction, the Halon fire suppression system and alarms had been turned off, as well as the stand-alone air conditioning systems within. In addition, a considerable amount of packing material had accumulated within the room, so much so that it was stacked from floor to ceiling. The room was hot, from the lack of air conditioning. This was a fire waiting to happen. A fire needs fuel, oxygen, and heat — all three readily existed in the room. If a fire were to start, there were no active fire suppression capabilities within the room and, with the alarms being turned off, it would have been well under way before the other building detection systems would have been alerted. A fire located here would have easily knocked out the central computing capability and telecommunications for the entire corporation, as well as potentially destroying several floors of this corporate tower. Transition periods can be the times of greatest vulnerability for any company, as existing detection and protection systems are temporarily shut down. The recovery planner needs to know that the planning process is reiterative; if the assumptions of the plan change, a review of all of the process steps is in order.

Apprise Management of the Risk

It is entirely management's decision on how much risk it is willing to take or deem what risks are unacceptable. However, as IT identifies the various risks, it is their responsibility to make management aware of those risks. This holds true across the board on all security issues, be they system survivability issues (disaster recovery) or confidentiality or system integrity issues.

A company having its key system client files breached from the outside, or a sales representative's laptop stolen with those key client files contained within, can be potentially more devastating to a company's operations than a prolonged power outage.

Apprise Management of Mitigation Cost

There seems to be a tremendous amount of frustration in IT departments these days, as departments have been right-sized and yet have to manage more complex systems than ever before. Many of the things that one will uncover will have such an obvious risk that obtaining approval for any mitigation campaigns should be relatively easy to obtain. Other system-related topics are more intangible or in some cases deemed as being a "nuisance," and are admittedly a tougher sell.

To cope with today's organizational demands and yet still feel good about the job it is performing, IT personnel responsible for this planning effort must adapt to the changing times, anticipate the risks, and present to management the mitigation options and their associated costs — knowing that management will make a decision with the company's best interest in mind.

POLICIES

The best approach to begin an implementation of a system or data safeguard strategy is to first define and get approval from management on the policy or standard operating procedure that requires the safeguard be established. In assisting a community college in putting together a disaster recovery plan for its central computing operations, it was discovered that numerous departments had isolated themselves from the networks supported by the IT group. The reason for this departure was the belief that the servers were always crashing, which was a cause for concern some three years ago, but is no longer true. Yet, to date, these departments (including Accounting) were processing everything locally on their hard drives with no backups whatsoever. This practice, now three years old, needed to be dispelled, as a disaster such as a fire in the Accounting department would severely disrupt, if not cause a cessation of, the college's operations altogether. One of the other satellite campuses of the district went entirely its own route, setting up its own network with no ties to the central computing facility — with absolutely no backups at all.

The plan basically went back to the fundamentals: distribute the responsibility for data integrity along with the distributed system capability. A college policy statement on data integrity was made to the effect that:

- The recoverability and correctness of digitized data, which resides on college-owned computer systems and media, is the responsibility of the individual user. The ultimate responsibility of ensuring the data integrity for each departmental workstation rests with the department/division administrator.

- Information Technology will provide the guidelines for data backups. Adherence to these guidelines by the users of the college-owned workstations is mandatory.

Establish Recovery Capability

Based on the inputs from the departments of the company and the company's overall priorities, IT is challenged with designing an intermediate system configuration that is adequately sized to permit the company's recovery, immediately following the event. This configuration — whether it be local, at an alternate company site, or a hot site — needs to initially sustain the highest priority applications, yet be adaptable to expand to address other priorities, depending on how long it make take to reoccupy the company's facilities and fully restore all operations back to normal. One needs to consider, for example, that the key client/server applications may be critical to company operations, whereas office automation tools may not.

Restore Full Operational Access

Information Technology's plan also needs to address the move back from an alternate site and what resources will be required to restore and resume full operations. Depending on the size of the enterprise and the disaster being planned for, this could include hundreds to thousands of end-user workstations. At a minimum, this step will be as complex as moving the company to a new location.

Planning for the Distributed Environment

First and foremost, what are the marching orders? What is the extent the plan is to cover? Is it just the servers? Is it just the computers directly maintained by the IT department? Or is it the entire enterprise's systems and data your responsibility? Determining the extent of recovery is the first step; that is, defining the scope of the project. The project scope, the overall company priorities, and the project funding will bracket the options one has in moving forward. But what follows in the next sections are some of the basics no matter what the budget. As one reads through them, one will find that many of these ideas are founded in sound operational management — as they should be.

Protecting the LAN. There are two primary reasons why computer rooms are built: (1) to provide special environmental conditions, and (2) for control. Environmental conditions include air conditioning, fire-rated walls, dry sprinkler systems, special fire abatement systems (Halon, FM-200), raised flooring, cable chaseways, equipment racking, equipment bracing, power conditioning, and continuous power (UPS systems), etc. Control includes a variety of factors, namely access, external security, and internal security. All these aspects of protection (mitigation steps taken to offset the risk of fire, theft, malicious tampering, etc.) are built-in benefits of the computer room. Yet if one walks around company facilities today, one is likely to find servers and all sorts of network equipment on desktops in open areas, on carts with wheels, in communication closets that are unlocked or with no conditioned power — yes, they are truly distributed and open. What is on those servers or accessible through those servers ... just about anything and everything important to the company.

Internal Environmental Factors. A computer room is a viable security option, although there are some subtleties to designing one specifically for a client/server environment. If the equipment is to be all rack mounted, racking can be suspended from the ceiling, which still yields clearance from the floor, thus avoiding possible water damage. Notably, the cooling aspects of a raised floor design, plus its ability to hide a morass of cabling, are no longer needed in a distributed environment.

Conditioned power requirements have inadvertently modified computer room designs as well. If an existing computer room has a shunt trip by the exit but stand-alone battery backup units are placed on servers, planners must review computer room emergency shutdown procedures. The idea of the shunt trip was to "kill all power" in the room, so that if operational personnel had to leave in a hurry, they would be able to come back later and reset systems in a controlled sequence. However, when there are individual battery backup units that sustain equipment in the room, the equipment connected to them will continue to run, even after the shunt is thrown, until the batteries run out.

Rewiring the room for all wall circuits to run off the master UPS, in proper sequence with the shunt trip, is one way to resolve this conflict. However, if the computer room houses mainframe, mid-range, and client/server equipment, a different strategy might be required. Many of the client/server systems are designed to begin an orderly shutdown once the cut-over to battery power has been detected. This is not the case with all mid-range and mainframe systems.

There are instances when it would be better to allow an orderly shutdown to occur, a short-term power outage for example. While other times, an instant shut-off of all power would be required, as in the case of a fire or an earthquake.

The dilemma rests with the different requirements of the system platforms; the solution lies in the wiring of the room. One option is to physically separate the equipment into different rooms and wire each room according to the requirements of the equipment it contains. Another solution is a two-stage shunt approach: a red shunt would immediately shut off all power, as was always intended; a yellow shunt would cut all power except from the UPS, allowing the servers to initiate an orderly shutdown on their own.

Room placement within the facility is also a consideration, as pointed out earlier. If designing a room from scratch, identify an area with structural integrity, avoid windows, and eliminate overhead plumbing.

Alternate fire suppression systems are still a good protection strategy for all the expensive electronics and the operational, on-site tape backups within a room. If these types of systems are beyond the budget, consider multiple computer rooms (companies with a multiple-building campus environment or multiple locations can readily adapt this as a recovery strategy). Equip the rooms with sprinklers, and keep some tarpaulins handy to throw over the equipment to protect it from incidental water damage (a broken sprinkler pipe, for example). A data safe may also be a worthwhile investment for the backup media maintained on site. However, if one goes through the expense of using a safe, train personnel to keep it closed. In eight out of ten site visits where a data safe is used, this author finds the door ajar (purely as a convenience). The safe only provides the protection to the media when it is sealed. If the standard practice is to keep it closed, then personnel will not have to second-guess, under the influence of adrenaline, whether or not they shut it as they evacuated the computer room.

If a company occupies several floors within a building and maintains communication equipment (servers, hubs, modems, etc.) within the closets, then treat them as a miniature computer room as well. Keep the doors to the closets locked and equip the closet with power conditioning and adequate ventilation.

Physical Security. The other aspect of a secured computer room is control: control (both internal and external to the company) of access to the equipment, cabling, and backup media. Servers out in the open are prime targets for a range of mishaps — from innocent tampering to outright theft. A thief, in stealing a server, not only gets away with an expensive piece of equipment, but a potentially large amount of information, which, if the thief realizes it, may be several times more valuable and marketable than the equipment.

With regard to the previously mentioned college satellite campus that had no backups of the information contained within its network, this author explained to the campus administration, which by the way kept their servers out in the open of their administration office area that was in a temporary trailer, that a simple theft (equipment with a street value of $2000) would challenge their viability of continuing to operate as a college. All their student records, transcripts, course catalogs, instructor directories, financial aid records, and more were maintained on their servers. With no backups to rely on and their primary source of information evaporated, they would be faced with literally thousands of hours to reconstruct their information bases.

Property Management. Knowing what and where the organization's computer assets (hardware, software, and information) are, at any moment in time, is critical to recovery efforts. This may sound blatantly obvious; but remember, one is no longer talking about the assets just within the computer room. Information Technology needs to be aware of every workstation used throughout the organization; whether it is connected to a network or not (this includes portables); what its specific configuration is; what software resides on it; and what job function it supports. This is readily doable if all hardware/software acquisitions and installations are run through the IT department, the company's policies and procedures support that control (meaning that all departments and all personnel willingly adhere to the policies and procedures), and property management inventory is properly maintained. Size is a factor here. If one manages an organization with a single server and 50 workstations, this may not be too large a task; however, if one supports several servers and several hundred workstations, then one can appreciate the amount of effort this can entail.

Data Integrity. Information is the one aspect of a company's systems that cannot be replaced, if lost or destroyed, simply by ordering another copy or another component. One may have insurance, hot-site agreements, or quick replacement arrangements for hardware and global license agreements for software, but the data integrity process is entirely up to the Information Technology Specialist and the Disaster Recovery Planner; they are the individuals that need to ensure that the company's information will be recoverable when needed. It all goes back to the risk of loss as to how extensive a data integrity program one needs to devise — from policies, to frequency of backups, to storage locations, to retention schedules, to the periodic verification that the backups are being done correctly. If just starting the planning process, mitigation efforts should focus on this area first. None of the other strategies to be implemented will count if there is no possible recovery of the data.

Network Recovery Strategies. As Information Technology, one's prime objective with respect to systems contingency planning is system survivability. This means that one has provisions in place, albeit limited capacity, to continue to support the company's system needs for priority processing through the first few hours immediately following the disaster.

Fault Tolerance vs. Redundancy. To a degree, what one strives for is fault tolerance of the company's critical systems. Fault tolerance means that no single point of failure will stop the system. This is many times built in as part of the operational component design of the system. Examples include mirroring of disks, use of RAID systems, shadowed servers, and UPSs to multiple T1s for wide-area communications. Redundancy, duplication of key components, is the basis of fault tolerance. Where fault tolerance cannot be built in, a quick replacement or repair program needs to be devised. Moving to an alternate site, either one of the company's, or a facility that is under contract for emergency support (i.e., a hot site), is a quick replacement strategy.

Alternate Sites and System Sizing. Once the priorities of a company are fully understood, sizing the amount of system capacity required to support those priorities, in the first few hours, through the first few days and weeks after a disaster can be accomplished. If planning one's own recovery site using another company location, or establishing a contract with a hot-site service provider, one will want to adequately size the immediate recovery capacity. This is extremely important, as most hot-site service providers will not allow requirement modification your requirements once a disaster is declared.

The good news with respect to distributed systems is that the hot-site service providers offer options for recovery — from using their recovery center; to bringing self-contained vans to your facility, equipped with your required server configuration; to shipping replacement equipment for what was lost, assuming facility is still operable.

Adequate Backups with Secure Off-site Storage. This process must be based on established company policies that identify vital information and detail how its integrity will be managed. The workflow of the company and the volatility of its information base will dictate the frequency of backups. At a minimum, backup should occur daily for servers, and weekly or monthly for key files of individual workstations.

Workstation-based information continues to be one of the greatest vulnerabilities for most companies. There is so much vital information stored locally on these workstations with little or no backup. If individuals have taken the precaution of creating backups, they are typically stored right next to the workstations, leaving the company exposed to any type of catastrophic disaster. The recovery planner must insist that the company proactively address this issue through policy and through providing the means for effective workstation backups.

Planners must decide when and how often to take backups off-site. Depending on a company's budget, off-site could be the building next door, a bank safety deposit box, the network administrator's house, the branch office across town, or a secure media vault at a storage facility maintained by a company that is in the business of off-site media storage. Once the company meets the objective of separating the backup copy of vital data from its source, it must address the accessibility of the off-site copy.

The security of the company's information is also of vital concern. Security has several facets: if at a branch office, where do they safeguard the copy; if at the network administrator's house, where is it kept; and what about the exposure to the media during transit? There are off-site storage companies that intentionally used unmarked, nondescript vehicles to transport a company's backup tapes to and from storage. This makes a lot of sense because information is valuable and in an attempt to secure it, one does not want to be advertising who one is using and where one is storing the complete system backups.

Several products assist the LAN administrator with these backup issues. Some of the products offer highly compressed, encrypted backups of workstations and other servers. The compression techniques require very little in the way of bandwidth, and thus even work very effectively in remote backups of laptops using the Internet. The concept of vaulting, running mirrored data centers in separate locations, has been implemented by larger corporations that traditionally had the means to invest in the communications capabilities and the system redundancy. This type of capability is now made possible through these new tools. It is possible today to either work with off-site storage vendors to remotely back up at their facility or, if the company has multiple locations, to readily implement vaulting at the client/server level. Either way, recovery options are facilitated via dial-up access to key recovery systems and data.

Adequate LAN Administration. Keeping track of everything the company owns — with respect to its hardware, software, and information bases — is fundamental to a company's recovery effort. The best aid in this area is a solid audit application that is periodically run on all workstations. This assists in maintaining an accurate inventory across the enterprise, as well as providing a tool for monitoring software acquisitions and hardware configuration modifications. The inventory can be extremely beneficial for insurance loss purposes. It also provides accurate records for license compliance and application revision maintenance.

Personnel. The all-too-often-overlooked area of systems recovery planning is the system's personnel. Will there be adequate system personnel resources to handle the complexities of response and recovery. What if a key individual is impacted by the same catastrophic event that destroys the systems? This event could cause a single point of failure.

An option available to the planner is to an emergency staffing contract. A qualified systems engineer hired to assist on a key project that one never seems to get completed (e.g., the network system documentation) may be a cost-effective security measure. Once that project is completed to satisfaction, the company can consider structuring a contractual arrangement that, for example, retains the engineer for one to three days a month to continue to work on documentation and other special projects. The contract could also stipulate coverage for staff vacations and sick days, and should guarantee that the engineer will be available on an as-needed basis should the company experience an emergency. The advantage of this concept is the maintenance of a well-trained and well-versed resource of the company's systems, should one need to rely on them during an emergency; one has coverage for the company during employee personal leaves, andone has systems documented.

TESTING

The timeless adage with regard to business success being "location, location, location" is adapted here. The *pro forma* success of a business recovery plan will be most influenced by the extent of the "testing, testing, testing" of its plan. Testing and training are the reiterative and necessary components of the planning process that keep the plan up-to-date and maintain the viability of recovery.

Tests can be conducted in a variety of ways: from desk checking, reading through the plan and thinking through the outcome, to full parallel system testing, setting up operations at a hot site or alternate location, and having the users run operations remotely. The full parallel system test does generally prove that the hot-site equipment and remote linkages work, but does not necessarily test the feasibility of the user department's plans, as it is a system test. Full parallel testing is also generally staged with a limited amount of time, which adds the pressure of "getting it done" and "passing" because of the time restriction.

Advantages of the Distributed Environment for Testing

Distributed client/server systems — because of their size and modularity — permit a readily available, modifiable, and affordable system setup for testing. They allow for a testing concept that can be coined "cycle testing."

For those readers with a manufacturing background, this draws a direct parallel to cycle counting: a process whereby inventory is categorized by value and counted several times a year rather than a one-time physical inventory. With cycle counting, inventory is counted all year long, with portions of the inventory being selected to be counted either on a random basis or on a preselected basis. Inventory is further classified into categories, such that the more-expensive or critical inventory items are counted more frequently, and the less-expensive items less frequently. The end result is the same as taking a one-time physical inventory: by the end of a calendar year, all the inventory has been counted. However, the cycle counting method has several advantages: (1) operations do not have to be completely shut down, while the inventory is being taken; (2) counts are not done under the pressure of "getting it done," which can result in more accurate counts; and (3) errors in inventories are discovered and corrected as a part of the continuous process.

The parallels to cycle testing are straightforward. Response and recovery plan tests can be staged with small manageable groups so as not to be disruptive to company operations. Tests can be staged by a small team of facilitators and observers on a continual basis. Tests can be staged and debriefings held without the pressure of "getting it done" — allowing the participants the time to fully understand their role and critically evaluate their ability to respond to the test scenarios and make necessary corrections to the plan. Any inconsistencies or omissions in a department's plan can be discovered and resolved directly amongst the working participants.

Just as the more critical inventory items can be accounted for on a more frequent basis, so can the crucial components required for business recovery (i.e., systems and telecommunications). With the widespread use of LANs and client/server systems throughout companies today, the Information Systems department is afforded more opportunity to work with the other departments in testing their plans and ... getting it right.

SUMMARY

Developing a business recovery plan is not a one-time static task; it is a process that requires the commitment and cooperation of the entire company. In order to perpetuate the process, Business Recovery Planning must be a company-stipulated policy as well as a company-sponsored goal. The organizations that adopt this company culture-oriented posture are the ones whose plans are actively maintained and tested, and whose employees are well-trained and poised to proactively respond to a crisis. The primary objective of developing a Business Resumption Plan is the survivability of the business.

An organization's Business Resumption Plan is, in fact, an orchestrated collection of its Departmental Response and Recovery Plans. Information Technology's plan is also a departmental plan; however, in addressing the overall coordination of the departmental plans, IT is typically in the best position to facilitate the other departments' development of their plans. With respect to the continuing trend of distributed processing permeating throughout organizations, IT can be of particular help in identifying the organization's interdepartmental information dependencies and external dependencies for information access and exchange.

There are some basic protective security measures that should be fundamental to the IT plan, no matter what the scope of disasters being planned for. From operational mishaps, to industrial espionage, to area-wide disasters, the Information Technology plan must addresses the following:

158

- adequate backup methodology with off-site storage
- sufficient physical security mechanisms for the servers and key network components
- sufficient logical secxurity measures for the organization's information assets
- adequate LAN/WAN administration, including up-to-date inventories of equipment and software

Last, in support of an organization's goal to have its Business Resumption Planning process in place to facilitate its quick response to a crisis, the plan must be sufficiently and reiteratively tested and the key team members sufficiently trained. When testing is routinely built into the planning process, it becomes the feedback step that keeps the plan current, the response and recovery strategies properly aligned, and the responsible team members postured to respond. Once a plan is established, testing is the key process step that keeps the plan viable. Plan viability equates to business survivability.

Chapter 17
Details Overlooked in Contingency Plans

Jonathan R. King

IDENTIFYING ISSUES BEFORE THEY ARISE IN AN ACTUAL DISASTER IS THE CHALLENGE FOR THE ENTIRE CONTINGENCY PLANNING TEAM. There are many details that should be included in a contingency plan but, in fact, rarely are. This chapter stresses the importance of some basic, commonly overlooked details that IT auditors and contingency planners must plan for.

Most large companies have some form of contingency plan. Usually, the plans address only high-level issues in their strategy to recover from a crisis. This is not to say that all contingency plans are inadequate, because many businesses have highly detailed plans and conduct extensive tests. Yet for the most part, the issues that are raised in this chapter do not fall into the standard contingency risk scenarios. As a result, they are not planned for. Furthermore, these commonly overlooked details are usually uncovered at the most inopportune time — during a disaster. Although most of these issues are not significant by themselves, when merged with the problems arising from the process of recovering from a disaster, they can cause needless confusion and irritation to staff and management. These overlooked contingency components can be categorized into two general groups: people issues and communication issues. The chapter concludes with some general topics that should be considered when discussing contingency planning.

PEOPLE ISSUES

During a disaster, whether the entire organization or just the IS staff relocates to the alternative work site, people issues arise that must be addressed in the contingency plan. In the big picture, people issues center around the ability of employees to actually get work done. It could be the recovery team staff or the user departments that must be able to access the computer to perform daily business transactions. Several details have to be examined that all highlight the general question: Has management addressed and supplied the necessary items so that the people that are sent to the alternative site can effectively do their jobs?

Does the Relocation Site Have Enough Workstations to Accommodate the Staff of IS or User Departments?

Many commercial disaster site vendors provide only limited access to terminals or workstations, and even fewer provide office space for management and users at the relocation site. For companies that do not have other facilities (i.e., branch offices or warehouses) users can relocate to, the contingency plan should describe the contacts made with real estate companies to identify buildings suitable for relocation of the business operation. This job usually falls into the hands of the properties and physical plan manager.

The plan must identify the real estate company contact along with a summary of the discussions held and the services anticipated to be available. In some cases, this step may be difficult to manage because many real estate companies will not keep this type of relationship active if they see no direct business advantage. Most large cities currently have underused office space that could be leased fairly quickly to serve this purpose. The real estate firms need to focus on identifying buildings with adequate communications facilities, and the contingency plan should address the availability of dial-up or dedicated communications lines from the recovery site to prospective user relocation sites. In addition to the IS data communications details, the ability to establish the office phone systems (e.g., PBX and phone mail) should be considered in the search for potential business operation alternative facilities.

Are Records and Supplies Critical to Business Recovery at the Relocation Site Secured Appropriately?

If company records (e.g., operating manuals, customer lists, account numbers, and other data used in conducting business) are kept at the recovery site, they must be secured by company representatives. Furthermore, these records and documents must be kept current or they could become worthless to the recovery team during a disaster. A person or a list of users (if users are to maintain their own information) should be identified in the contingency plan as being responsible for making updates to the stored materials. In addition, internal audit should test to see that appropriate physical controls are in place and that a log is kept that shows updates to the recovery site's stored inventory. The auditor should determine whether the frequency of updates is adequate to provide up-to-date information at the relocation center.

Do Staff Members Have Access to Common Business Supplies at the Relocation Site?

If the contingency tests reveal that this topic has been covered, consider the company fortunate, because this level of detail is seldom addressed by contingency planners. Even during tests, people do not perceive the need for employees to have access to the most basic of office supplies because the contingency test team either does not fully parallel an actual disaster or they bring with them only the few supplies needed to execute the test plan. Business continuity vendors usually do not supply basic business items such as letterhead, paper, pencils, tape, or staplers. Relocation sites belonging to the company (i.e., branch or subsidiary company offices) require that the disaster staff canvas supply rooms and secretaries' desks to get these necessary supplies.

Have Arrangements Been Made with Hotels Near the Relocation Site for Housing the Recovery Team Staff?

Some companies have their alternative processing sites in remote locations, and hotel accommodations are usually limited in many cases. The contingency plan should identify primary and backup relationships with two or three hotels near the relocation center. Ancillary questions that must be explained include how the room charges are to be handled. Does the staff know if room charges will be billed directly to the company or individually expensed by each staff member?

Are Cafeteria Facilities Provided at the Relocation Site or Nearby Restaurants for Food Service?

Few commercial disaster site providers have cafeteria service, so this issue should be researched by management. Staff should not have to stop their recovery work for long periods to get something to eat. This issue is much more important for the remote disaster facilities that dictate significant travel time to the nearest restaurants. In the cases in which local restaurant facilities do not exist or are inadequate, the contingency plan should identify relationships with one or two food service companies. In most areas, food service companies can provide limited service to supply the needs of the recovery team while at the remote site.

Does the Contingency Plan Guide Staff in the Use of Rental Cars and Other Forms of Transportation During the Disaster?

The contingency plan should address the need for recovery staff to travel after reaching the alternative site. The recovery team may have to remain at the alternative site for a period of time that probably will require some rotation to take place (e.g., going home on weekends or for family emergencies). Most contingency plans cover the transportation to the alternative site but not local travel and travel back to the home-operations city after the recovery is complete; rental cars are the norm in most cases. The contingency plan should identify any preferred rental car companies with which the company may have existing agreements. Other questions to be addressed include how transportation is to be paid for and whether maps of the local vicinity around the relocation site are provided.

163

Has Management Determined in the Contingency Plan Document the Method of Supplying Cash Advances to Staff for Miscellaneous Expenses While at the Relocation Site?

Management at the recovery site should be entrusted to approve miscellaneous expenses and issue advance checks to recovery staff in order to cover justifiable expenses incurred during the disaster. Company checks should be held in reserve for contingency use and authorized for use by the senior contingency officer and his or her designated backup.

The main issue is for employees not to be handicapped by problems other than those caused by the actual disaster. Because employees usually work long hours to get the business back online, details such as not having a place to eat or sleep become important to maintaining staff morale and productivity.

COMMUNICATIONS ISSUES

Network communications issues are not the only issues to be addressed in contingency planning. Issues must be raised for all aspects of communications, including those outside of IS network or data communications recovery. People must be able to perform their job responsibilities for a recovery to be considered successful, and this usually requires an effective communications system. Arrangements or at least discussions should take place with phone and communications equipment providers to evaluate the availability of telephone circuits, phone equipment, and reassigning home company phone lines to the alternative site. It is assumed that communications hardware (e.g., controllers and multiplexers) are included in the IS hardware replacement agreements with vendors. Many disasters prevent employees from entering offices in which phone equipment continues to function properly, so phone systems must be able to be operated remotely. A phone mail system should be able to be changed remotely so its initial greeting message can instruct employees where to report or to check phone mailboxes for specific instructions.

When a Disaster Occurs, Can Management Notify Groups of Personnel of Where to Meet?

Getting the word out is the first major concern of the business continuity team. The team has to know where to meet and whom to call for specific instructions. This can be designed into the business continuity plan using manual or automated devices or some combination of the two. The manual process usually involves a list of team member home addresses and phone numbers. For this process to be successful, the phone number list must be kept current. Phone mail systems can assist in contacting team members. A group message can be distributed to disaster team members on phone mail. Team members are called and beeped on pagers and instructed to call into phone mail for details on the disaster and further instructions. This saves the person who is calling the team members from having to describe the disaster details to each person called — a significant time saver.

Currently, several devices are on the market that are designed to automatically call phone numbers on the business continuity team and give a short message. These devices are so sophisticated that their logic places calls to members on the basis of hierarchy and nature of the disaster. They can be thought of as databases connected to modems. A helpful feature of many of these devices is the audit trails that tell management who has been successfully notified of the disaster.

Has a Person or Department Been Designated to Communicate with the Public and the News Media?

The contingency plan should identify an employee and backup responsible for communicating with the media and the type of information to be furnished to the media. During disasters, news media seek information from many sources. A person should be identified in the contingency plan as the company representative for all official statements. Other employees should be instructed to direct all news media questions to the designated company representative. In addition, the contingency plan should have a section containing guidelines for dealing with the news media or include a prepared statement. Many companies have realized that it is better to provide the news media with a statement on the disaster than to see or read the competitor's interjected opinions of the situation, because if the news media does not get the story from the company, they will surely look elsewhere. Bad press can damage company goodwill and business reputations, which may take, in some cases, years to undo.

How is User Department Management Not Directly Affected by the Disaster Notified of the Execution of the Contingency Plan?

Internal company communications should be addressed in the contingency document to determine when and how the management and staff not directly affected by the disaster will be told of the event. Many times the lack of information causes people not involved in the recovery process undue tension. There should be policies on direct communication of the event to company employees.

Questions and rumors center around the ability of the company to recover from the accident and the possible impact on job security. Senior company management should address the event, in general terms, to all interested employees to ease concerns and describe the recovery process in progress — highlighting the merits of the well-designed contingency plan that is bringing the crisis under control. For companies that have phone mail systems, a general greeting message can be created to state that a disaster has occurred and then any specifics, such as calling supervisors or instructing the handling of communications with the recovery team.

Will a Phone List Be Generated and Distributed Shortly After Arrival Showing Extensions of Key Management and Support Staff at the Alternative Site?

Company management and user departments will need to call the recovery team for various reasons. Most commercial facilities will not function as a switchboard for the relocated company staff. A person should be assigned the job of drafting a list of staff and corresponding phone extensions and send them by fax to key company personnel — senior and user department management not situated at the alternative site. User management should be kept informed of recover status and when they can start to recover their application systems once the IS systems are properly functioning.

Has Courier or Messenger Service Been Investigated to Facilitate the Transfer of Data, Reports, and Documents Between the Relocation Site and User Departments and Customers?

Users will require reports and other physical materials from the recovery site, unless a truly paperless environment exists. Agreements with courier or messenger service providers should be investigated by management for inclusion in the contingency plan. For companies that do business with customers that usually send data or documents directly to the company's data center, management has to reroute these materials to the alternative site during a contingency. This means either contracting with a courier service to transport materials from the damaged site to the alternative site or contacting customers to inform them to send the materials to the alternative site's address until the crisis is resolved. If customers are not expected to modify their handling of data, the company should contract with its own courier service so that the move to the contingency site is transparent to dealings with the customer — taking into consideration the period of downtime until the system is recovered.

Have All Customers Been Briefed on the Contingency Plan and How the Execution of the Plan would Affect Their Dealings with the Company?

Continuity of the business relies on customer relationships, and one of the most important factors is trust that the business will be in existence to provide service. Customer trust is enhanced if the customer feels that the company has taken steps to ensure that it can recover in the event of a disaster. In the optimal situation, contingency tests should involve customers when user application systems incorporate online customer functions such as preedit or input transactions or customer database inquiries. Contingency tests should include establishing communications to customers from the alternative site. Certainly, customer involvement in contingency testing is a must for companies whose IS department serves as a service bureau for other businesses.

GENERAL CONTINGENCY PLANNING TOPICS

Some additional, general issues should be covered in reviewing any contingency plan and relate to many of the topics already discussed. The point is how closely the planning document comes to supplying the requirements of the business recovery team.

Are Changes Made by User Departments and IS Properly Integrated into the Contingency Plan on a Timely Basis?

For IS, this includes software changes that should be reflected in the contingency configuration (i.e., changes in operating system software and parameters, network software and node definitions, hardware configuration). For users, this relates to changed or new application systems, desk procedures, key management and staff responsibilities, and any other change that affects the existing contingency plan documentation. This is when changes to phone contact lists of key individuals should be addressed. Auditors must ensure that the procedures are in place to keep the contingency plan updated and that those procedures are functioning effectively.

To What Extent Do the User Departments Participate in the Contingency Tests?

A few years ago, few companies were devoting resources to the area of contingency planning; in recent years, the trend began to highlight contingency planning as business continuity planning. Today, in supporting the current challenges of contingency planners, companies are investing more resources and demanding better assurances of recovery in the event of a disaster.

The days of contingency teams composed only of IS staff are changing, as senior management realizes the tremendous impact that IS has on the continuity of the entire enterprise. Business recovery is now the direction of contingency planning, and therefore users must ensure that they can recover from any disaster involving IS. When the tests are conducted, users should participate as necessary, ensuring that the business recovery plan is functional and realistic. Business recovery in the user sense means:

- recovery of IS systems and communications
- starting the application systems (e.g., order entry, purchasing, payroll, general ledger)
- carrying forward logged transactions up to the point of the disaster or failure

- balancing to known values (e.g., hash total, batch totals, total transactions)
- closing the application
- reopening for a new business day

This step is the true test of any contingency plan. If a company has multiple tests of the disaster plan annually, at least one should include user participation. In addition, selected or major customers should be included in the test to determine whether the company can actually conduct business in a normal fashion after a catastrophe. Senior management, users, and customers get a better feeling about the continuity of the business when they are involved at this level of recovery testing.

RECOMMENDED COURSE OF ACTION

Auditors should keep the following question in mind when reviewing the contingency plan or witnessing testing: How would an actual business continuity team function in the particular situation and where might problems occur? Furthermore, an auditor should attend the contingency tests to ensure that the existing control structures designed for IS and user departments remain in place during the test. Separation-of-duties controls are easily disregarded during a disaster, when the premise is to do anything to get the system back online. However, it is during a disaster that a breakdown in controls can have a significant impact on financial systems and data (i.e., fraud or unintentional modification of data) that may go undetected. The auditor can offer beneficial recommendations for changes to the contingency planning document for a business standpoint.

Chapter 18
Restoration Component of Business Continuity Planning

John Dorf
Marty Johnson

EVERYONE UNDERSTANDS THE IMPORTANCE OF DEVELOPING A BUSINESS CONTINUITY PLAN (BCP) TO ENSURE THE TIMELY RECOVERY OF MISSION-CRITICAL BUSINESS PROCESSES FOLLOWING A DAMAGING EVENT. There are two objectives, however, and often, the second objective is overlooked. That is: Return to normal operations as soon as possible. The reason for the urgency to return to normal operations is that backup and work-around procedures are certainly not "business as usual." Backup capabilities, whether due to the loss of primary premises or primary data, probably only include those business activities that are critical to getting by. The longer a company must operate in this mode, the more difficult the catch-up will be. There are several steps that can be taken in advance to prepare for the timely, efficient return to normalization. The purpose of this chapter is to discuss the steps and resources to ensure total recovery. In addition, it is important to understand how to handle damaged equipment and media in order to minimize the loss associated with a disaster.

Restoration includes the following:

1. Handling damaged equipment and media in order to minimize the loss
2. Salvaging hard copy and electronic media
3. Performing damage assessment and the resulting disposition of damaged facilities and equipment
4. Determining and procuring appropriate property insurance

0-8493-0907-7/00/$0.00+$.50
© 2001 by CRC Press LLC

5. Identifying internal and external resources to perform restoration activities
6. Developing, maintaining, and testing your restoration plan

This chapter will help you understand the issues related to each of these items and be a resource for developing the necessary information for inclusion in your BCP program.

The more time that passes before the salvation of hard copy and electronic media, the greater the chance that the data or archival records will be permanently lost. However, if you rush to handle, move, dry, etc., media and do not do so in the correct manner, you may worsen the situation. Therefore, to ensure minimizing the damage you must act quickly and correctly to recover data and restore documents. This also applies to the facilities and infrastructure damage.

Having telephone numbers for restoration companies is not enough. The primary reason is in the event of a regional problem like flooding, ice storms, etc., you will have to wait for those companies that have advance commitments from other companies.

Another important issue associated with restoration is insurance. It is imperative you understand what is covered by your insurance policy and what approval procedures must be completed before any restoration work is performed. There are many stories about how insurance companies challenged claims because of disagreements concerning coverage or restoration procedures. Challenges from insurance carriers can hold up restoration for extended periods of time. Below are two examples showing the importance and magnitude of effort involved with restoration following a disaster.

1. The 1993 World Trade Center bombing illustrates the potential magnitude of a cleanup effort. Over a 16-day period, 2700 workers hired by a restoration contractor, working round the clock in three shifts, cleaned over 880,000 square feet of space in the twin towers and other interconnected facilities. Ninety percent of the floors in the 110-story towers had light amounts of soot, while 10 percent suffered heavier damage.

2. In 1995, Contra Costa County, California, suffered almost $15 million in arson-related fire damage to four county court houses over a three-week period. In all, 124,000 files had to be freeze-dried and restored at an estimated cost of $50 per document.

A good restoration program will not guarantee you will not have a problem with your insurance carrier. The following is an example of how a disagreement between an insured and insurer can delay restoration of your business:

In 1991, a 19-hour fire at One Meridian Plaza in Philadelphia destroyed eight of the 38 floors in the building. It took six years of legal maneuvering to settle the claim between the building owners and the insurers. Each party disagreed with the other over the extent of the restoration. For most of the six years, the parties' difference amounted to almost $100 million. The owners believed that the floors above the 19th floor had to be torn down because the steel beams supporting the structure had moved four inches and could not be certified as safe. The insurance company disagreed and argued that the building could be repaired without tearing down the floors. The owner and insurer also disagreed over the extent of environmental cleanup caused by the fire. Eventually, the matter was settled out of court for an undisclosed sum.

UNDERSTANDING THE ISSUES

For all damaged or destroyed property a company must understand when they need to try to restore the property, and when it can just be replaced. A critical issue concerning restoration is really the handling of documents and electronic media. Handling of the physical damage is more easily accomplished and more straightforward. The handling of vital records, however, is more difficult. The vital records may only be needed if an original contract is challenged, or is needed from a corporate entity standpoint. How a company deals with this exposure is not an easy determination. Some companies build facilities that are protected from most hazards to critical documents and data. The issue concerning having both a protected environment and duplication becomes a business issue; how much insurance is enough. Therefore, any time a company only has a single copy of vital documents and data, you must develop a strategy of what you would do if those records are damaged. This is a dilemma for many companies where duplicate copies cannot be maintained. Insurance companies have millions of pages of archived contracts and other legal documents that may not be feasibly copied. Other industries such as financial services handle equity certificates and other legal tender that perhaps cannot be copied as a normal course of business.

A company should develop a restoration plan in conjunction with performing a vital records review. This way the restoration of business-critical items can be assessed along with the alternatives of providing replication. Insurance coverage must be evaluated and coordinated with the restoration plan and other components of your Business Continuity Planning.

HOW TO SELECT RESTORATION SERVICE PROVIDERS

It is not difficult to find a service provider to clean up the rubble following a flood or fire. It is much more difficult to find a service provider that knows how to dry the soaked documents to best ensure their usability. It also takes a lot of expertise to handle fire-damaged documents and magnetic media to restore information.

The normal care for selecting any critical supply chain partner should be used. For a restoration company, however, you do not have the ability to ask for a pilot program. There are many sources of information to identify restoration companies, including local, state, and federal agencies. In addition, the Internet is an excellent source for both planning information, and resources.

Your own insurance carrier is also a good source of service provider information. Additionally, many insurance carriers have a partnership with recovery firms so that a firm is authorized to do certain work and deal directly with the insurance carrier to ensure there are no misunderstandings about the work to be performed.

WHERE DOES INSURANCE COVERAGE FIT INTO YOUR RESTORATION PROGRAM?

The subjects of restoration and insurance are closely intertwined as, in most cases, property insurers are expected to pay for the majority of the cost of any restoration. The settlement of a property insurance claim can be a complex, time-consuming, and vexing issue, even for a seasoned insurance professional. The insured often do not understand their coverage and routinely overestimate the amount of the loss or assume that a claim is covered when it is not. Insurers and their representatives may communicate poorly with the insured as to the nature of the coverage, the information required to adjust the claim, and the timetable to be expected. Both sides need to cooperate and communicate clearly so that reasonable expectations are established quickly and conflicts can be resolved in a timely manner.

The discussion on insurance will include a brief overview of standard commercial property insurance policies and common problems during the claim settlements process.

Property Insurance Overview

Property insurance can be purchased with many options, which serve to tailor the standard policy language to the specific needs of the policyholder. Therefore, it is important that business owners take the time to review their needs with their insurance agent, broker, or advisor, so that the resulting insurance purchase reflects those needs before a loss occurs. This will help avoid future misunderstandings with the insurance company in the event of a claim.

Property insurance can be purchased on either a named perils or All Risks form. The All Risk form covers all causes of loss that are not specifically excluded in the policy form and provides broader protection to the insured than a named perils form. Under a named perils form, the insured bears the responsibility of proving that damage to their property was caused by one of the enumerated causes of loss. Use of the All Risk form shifts the burden of proof onto the insurer to prove that a particular loss was not covered by the policy. Insurers avoid the use of the phrase "All Risk" and use the phrase "Special Form" to describe this same coverage.

The property policy valuation clause is a second area of frequent misunderstanding by policyholders. That is, if a loss occurs, on what basis will the policyholder be compensated for the loss or damage to their property. Insurers offer two basic valuation choices: actual cash value (ACV) or replacement cost coverage. ACV is defined as the cost to repair or replace the lost or damaged property with property of like kind and quality *less physical depreciation*. For example, suppose that a commercial refrigerator purchased five years ago and expected to have a useful working life of 10 years is burned up in a fire. Assuming that the refrigerator had been well maintained up to the time of the loss, the insurance company adjuster might offer to settle the claim for 50 percent of the cost today of a new refrigerator of similar design, quality, and capacity. It should be noted that the lost or damaged property will be valued as of the date of the loss and not on the basis of the original cost.

Replacement cost valuation means that the policyholder will be compensated on the basis of new for old. That is, the policyholder is entitled to compensation on the basis of the cost to repair or replace the lost or damaged property with property of like kind and quality with no deduction for physical depreciation. As noted above, the determination of the replacement cost of the damaged or lost property takes place as of the actual date of loss.

Regardless of whether ACV or replacement cost valuation is chosen, the policyholder needs to make sure that the amount of insurance purchased accurately reflects the current replacement cost value of the insured property. This is necessary to avoid a co-insurance penalty being applied that could reduce any loss adjustment.

If replacement cost coverage is chosen, then in the event of loss or damage to the covered property, the insured must actually repair or replace the lost or damaged property. Otherwise, the insurance company is usually only required to reimburse the insured on an ACV basis.

Finally, the insurance company will never pay more than the applicable amount of insurance that has been purchased by the policyholder. This last provision underscores the need for business owners to adequately assess the replacement cost value of their property at the time the policy is placed.

We have not included an in-depth discussion of the topics of Business Interruption or Extra Expense insurance in our discussion of property insurance because it is beyond the scope of this chapter. These coverages go hand-in-hand with adequate property insurance coverage. Business interruption coverage pays for lost earnings and continuing expenses during the period of time the business is shut down. Extra expense coverage pays for the additional costs to maintain business during the shutdown period. The absence or insufficiency of either of these coverages can jeopardize the survival of the business that is jeopardized because of a lack of financial resources during the restoration period. Detailed records of all expenditures to maintain the operations of the business (extra expense) should be kept and included in the claim. The business interruption portion of the claim will be based on the lost earnings of the business as compared with periods preceding the loss.

In addition to standard property insurance coverage, business owners should discuss with their insurance advisors the need for additional insurance coverage in the following areas:

- boiler and machinery
- valuable papers
- accounts receivable
- electronic data processing (EDP)

Property insurance policies exclude coverage for damage caused by:

- explosion of steam boilers, steam pipes, steam engines, or steam turbines
- artificially generated electric current, including electric arcing, that affects electrical devices, appliances, or wire
- mechanical breakdown, including rupture or bursting caused by centrifugal force.

Such damage may be covered under boiler and machinery insurance policies. Boiler and machinery policies have many characteristics similar to property policies. In the event of a loss, these insurers often provide assistance in the repair or replacement of the damaged equipment. They also provide statutorily required inspection services.

Valuable papers coverage under a standard commercial property insurance policy is limited to $2500. Valuable papers coverage may be important for businesses where the destruction of documents would cause the business to suffer a monetary loss or to expend large sums in reconstructing the documents. The limit of insurance under a standard property policy can be increased to meet a desired need. The ISO (Insurance Services Office) valuable papers form defines valuable papers and records as "inscribed, printed, or written documents, manuscripts, or records." Money and securities, data processing programs, media, and converted data are not covered. Coverage for loss or destruction to money and securities can be found in Crime insurance policies. Data processing programs, media, and data can be covered under EDP policies. Care needs to be exercised in estimating the cost of reconstructing documents so that adequate limits of insurance can be purchased.

If accounts receivable records are damaged by an insured cause of loss, this type of coverage will pay the business owner amounts due from customers that he is unable to collect as a result of the damage to his records, collection expenses in excess of normal collection costs, and other reasonable expenses incurred to reestablish records of accounts receivable. This coverage can be purchased as an endorsement to a commercial property insurance policy. Again, care must be exercised in setting an adequate amount of insurance.

Electronic data processing (EDP) coverage is a must for organizations that rely heavily on data processing or electronic means of information storage. EDP coverage can provide All Risk coverage for equipment and data, software and media, including the perils of electrical and magnetic injury, mechanical breakdown, and temperature and humidity changes, which are important to computer operations. In addition, the coverage can include the cost of reproducing lost data, which is not available under a standard commercial property insurance policy.

Property Insurance Claims Settlement Process

Exhibit 18.1 provides a broad overview of the claim settlement process. The last row underscores the importance of complete and well-organized

Exhibit 18-1. The claim settlement process.

- Report the event to the property insurance company immediately. Depending on the specific items damaged and the nature of the damage it may be appropriate to notify the boiler and machinery insurer as well.
- Prevent further damage to covered property.
- Obtain property repair/replacement estimates or appraisals and prepare and document the claim. If business interruption and also extra expense are going to be claimed, extensive additional documentation may be needed. (If a business interruption loss exceeds $1 million, the insured should consider hiring accountants experienced in documenting such claims.)
- Submit documentation to the insurance company adjuster and cooperate with the adjuster in his investigation and adjustment of the claim.
- Request authorization to proceed with repairs or the purchase of major items.
- If appropriate, request a partial payment of the claim from the insurance company.
- Negotiate the final claim settlement with the insurance company adjuster.
- Submit a sworn proof of loss to the insurance company.
- Receive claim settlement.

documentation and open communication during the claim settlement process. These two factors are major reasons why claims settlements are delayed or even end up in litigation. The items shown in this table are important steps to include in your restoration plan.

The claims settlement process is adversarial by its nature. The insured party is intent on maximizing its potential recovery under its insurance policy, while the insurance company is trying to minimize its exposure to the insured's claim. This does not mean that the claim settlement process must be nasty or unpleasant. The parties should work together in good faith in arriving at a reasonable settlement of a claim. The insurance carrier will be less likely to raise substantive issues if they believe that the insured is not trying to take advantage of the situation. Likewise, if the insurer establishes reasonable ground rules at the beginning of the process, they should expect the insured to be forthcoming with the information requested in a timely manner. While it is usually in the insured's best interests to provide complete and well-organized documentation, the insured should not overwhelm the insurance company and should only provide the documentation necessary to substantiate the amounts requested, keeping ancillary documentation available in the event that the insurance carrier requests additional information.

The insurance adjuster is an individual assigned by the insurance company to handle a claim on its behalf. The adjuster may be an employee of the insurance company or may work for an independent firm hired by the insurance company. Adjusters will be the key contact between the insurer and the insured. Their responsibilities include determining the cause of a loss, the nature and scope of damage to the property, whether the policy covers the damages claimed, to what extent property should be repaired or replaced and the corresponding cost, and finally the amount that the insurance carrier is willing to pay in settlement of the claim. The adjuster also acts as a quarterback in determining whether other specialists need to become involved.

Depending on the size and complexity of the claim, the insurance carrier may selectively involve accountants, lawyers, and other specialists in the claim settlement process. These specialists are working on behalf of the insurance carrier and not the insured. While the insured should not be unduly alarmed if the insurance company employs such specialists, the insured may be well advised to consider employing his own specialists to work on his behalf in calculating the claim in order to be on a more equal footing with the insurance company.

The agent or broker who placed the insurance can provide guidance and assistance to the insured in handling the claim. This should be expected, since the broker or agent has received compensation to arrange the insurance. Smaller brokers sometimes lack the capability to be of much assistance in a claim situation.

The responsibilities of the policyholder in the event of a loss are spelled out in most insurance policies. They include prompt notification of the insurer, protecting the covered property from further damage, providing detailed inventories of the damaged and undamaged property, allowing the insurance company to inspect the damaged property, take samples, and examine the pertinent records of the company, providing a sworn proof of loss, cooperating with the insurer in the investigation and settlement of the claim, and submitting to examination under oath concerning any matter relating to the insurance or the claim.

Willis Corroon, a large multi-national insurance broker, recommends that the following steps be taken immediately following a loss:

- Make sure that the loss area is safe to enter.
- Report the claim to the agent and to the insurer.
- Restore fire protection.
- Take immediate action to minimize the loss.
- Protect undamaged property from loss.
- Take photographs of the damage.
- Identify temporary measures needed to resume operations and maintain safety and security, and the costs of those measures.
- Consult with engineering, operations, and maintenance personnel as well as outside contractors for an initial estimate of the scope and cost of repairs.
- Make plans for repairing the damage.

WHAT'S INCLUDED IN A RESTORATION PLAN?

After a disaster such as a fire or hurricane, the natural inclination is to assume that documents, computer records, equipment and machinery, and high-tech computers and other data processing equipment that appear to be unusable or severely damaged should be scrapped and replaced. However, before anything is done, experts should be brought in to assess the damage and determine short- and long-term courses of action. The short-term course of action is intended to stabilize the situation at the disaster location so as to prevent further damage from occurring. The long-term strategy is to determine which items can be salvaged and repaired and what items should be replaced.

Although notification to the insurance company should be one of the first steps taken after a disaster has occurred; do not wait for the insurance adjuster to show up before implementing stabilization procedures. It is a common insurance policy requirement that the insured take steps to prevent additional damage from occurring after a disaster. Such post-loss disaster mitigation should be part of a comprehensive business continuity plan. If no plan exists, then common sense should prevail.

Your restoration plan should include the following:

- Ensure life safety at the disaster location.
- Reactivate fire protection and other alarm/life safety systems.
- Establish security at the site to keep out intruders, members of the public, the press, as well as employees who should not be allowed in the disaster area unless they are directly involved in damage assessment or mitigation efforts.
- Cover damaged roofs, doors, windows, and other parts of the structure.
- Arrange for emergency heat, dehumidification, or water extraction.
- Separate damaged components that may interfere with restoration, but do not dispose of these components because restoration experts and the insurance adjuster will want to inspect them.
- Take photographs or videotape of the disaster site as well as damaged and undamaged property.
- Bring in experts in document/records restoration and qualified technical personnel to work on computer and communications equipment and systems, machinery and furniture, wall and floor coverings, and structural elements.
- Maintain a log of all steps taken after a disaster, noting time, location, what has been done, who did it, as well as work orders and invoices of all expenditures relating to the disaster.

After the disaster site has been secured and stabilized and the extent of damage assessed, contracts should be negotiated with qualified restoration contractors. The insurance company adjuster may be able to recommend qualified contractors. The adjuster should be consulted before any contracts are awarded.

The extent of the restoration possible depends on the type of property damaged, the nature of the damage, and the extent and speed of post-disaster damage minimization. Another factor is the level of expertise brought in to assess and recommend restoration strategies as well as the quality of the restoration contractors brought in to do the work.

Here are some generalized comments on the restoration of paper documents, magnetic media (computer disks and tape), and electronic equipment and machinery.

Water damage is one of the most prevalent forms of damage to paper-based documents. Restoration efforts need to begin immediately if documents are to be saved. Water should be pumped out of the area as quickly as possible. The area also needs to be vented to allow air to circulate. Cool temperatures will help preserve water-soaked documents until actual restoration work can begin. Bringing in a freezer unit such as a refrigerated trailer (capable of being held at 0 degrees F) to store the documents will help slow down mold damage. Before freezing, documents should be cleaned and handled with extreme care. Documents should be kept in blocks (i.e., not pulled apart) as this will prevent additional deterioration. Documents that are not thoroughly soaked can be dried using dehumidification. Freeze-drying water-soaked documents will produce good results. Sterilization and application of a fungicidal buffer will help prevent further mold damage. Dehumidification and freeze-drying can take from one to two weeks to be completed.

Damaged computer tapes and diskettes need to be restored within 72 to 96 hours of a disaster to be effective. Water-damaged diskettes can be opened and dried using isopropyl alcohol and put into new jackets. Then the information is transferred onto new disks. Tapes can be freeze-dried or machine-dried using specialized machinery. The data on the tapes is then transferred to new media. Soot- and smoked-damaged diskettes need to be cleaned by hand, and then data transfer can take place.

Equipment and machines need to be evaluated on a case-by-case basis. There are specialist firms that can evaluate and recommend repair/restoration strategies for equipment. These firms may also do the repairs, or they may recommend shipping the damaged equipment to the manufacturer or utilize other shops to do the restoration. In general, insurance companies will not authorize replacement of damaged equipment with new or refurbished equipment unless the cost to repair the item exceeds 50 percent of its replacement cost. Smoke, soot, and other contaminants can be removed from equipment and replacement parts when damaged parts cannot be adequately cleaned. Occasionally, the original manufacturer may balk at substantially repairing damaged equipment, claiming that the repair will prove inadequate or will void the manufacturer's warranty. They are usually interested in selling new equipment. In such cases, insurance companies may be able to purchase replacement warranties (to replace the original manufacturer's warranty) from a warranty replacement company to satisfy the insured. The replacement warranty will be for the period of time remaining on the original manufacturer's warranty.

WHAT ARE THE COSTS FOR A RESTORATION PROGRAM?

The costs associated with restoration are more "at time of disaster" costs and would be covered by insurance. Having a thorough restoration strategy and plan will help to scope the insurance needed, and may even save money for those who are over-insured due to the lack of knowledge.

The primary cost of a program are the people resources necessary to develop and maintain the capability.

An approach to matching insurance needs with the potential cost to restore data and infrastructure is to start with your insurance carrier. Determine the types of restoration covered with different policies and then compare the coverage with restoration company estimates. Costs are usually based on square feet, type of media, etc.

Restoration of critical equipment is usually procured through the source of the equipment. This may include staged replacement parts or quick-ship components. Sometimes there is an incremental charge to maintenance fees to guarantee expedited service or replacement.

ENSURING PROVIDER CAN AND WILL PERFORM AT TIME OF DISASTER

Restoration is a service not dissimilar to maintenance for critical IT and facility operations. In the event of an emergency, any delay can cause a significant financial impact. You should view restoration in this same light. Therefore, expand the same diligence you would to selecting a service provider for ensuring business *continuation*, to selecting one for ensuring timely business *resumption*.

TESTING YOUR RESTORATION PLAN

Once a restoration plan has been implemented, it should be tested as part of a company's BCP program. The purpose of testing will be to validate that the plan:

1. meets the business needs in terms of timeframe
2. reduces the exposure to the loss of documents and data to an acceptable level
3. remains in compliance with insurance requirements
4. is current and the level of detail is sufficient to ensure a timely, efficient recovery

Testing is a primary means of keeping the restoration plan current. Regular tests with varying scope and objectives prevent the program from becoming too routine. As with any testing program, you start out simple and build on successes. Initially, it may involve contacting your service providers and verifying the following:

- You would be able to reach them at any hour, on any day.
- They should be able to respond within the expected timeframes.

Other tests may involve your restoration team members' awareness of the plan, ability to perform the tasks, and coordination with other "recovery and return to normal" activities.

In some cases, a company's need for restoration services actually diminishes. As IT solutions become more robust and the need for nonstop processing increases, more and more companies employ remote, replicated data. In this case, if the primary copy of data is lost, a second, equally current, copy is available. Therefore, if a company had services for the restorations of electronic media, it may not be necessary.

RESTORATION PLAN WITHOUT A BCP PLAN

Even if your company does not have a BCP program, it is still prudent to have ready resources to provide restoration services if needed. A company that does not understand the need for a BCP program will not allocate resources to develop a restoration strategy. A fallback would be to coordinate with your insurance carrier so they understand the critical nature of your vital records and single points of processing failure so they can procure the appropriate resources to get the job done.

CONCLUSION

A restoration strategy is one that can be implemented relatively easily and at minimal cost. Have your insurance carrier explain the types of hazards and restoration techniques, and if in a bind, work with their approved service partners.

Since time is of the essence when it comes to recovering damaged vital records and sensitive equipment, a BCP team should be assigned specific restoration responsibilities. Restoration should be a close second when it comes to recovering your business following a disaster.

Getting Support for Your Restoration Program

The most difficult task in developing a restoration capability and plan is to get internal manpower resources approved to help with the work. There may be some reluctance to go to management and suggest there is a need to prepare for the potential damage to critical property after management has spent money to supposedly eliminate the risk.

Everyone has seen news reports of damage due to floods, fires, and explosions. What most people do not know is that there is significant technology available to recover the critical data from damaged vital records. In addition, there are service providers who will guarantee replacement equipment within pre-established timeframes for a fixed subscription fee.

The important task is for the owner of critical business data and processing equipment to educate himself and his management that preplanning can significantly reduce the impact from potential loss of data.

Next Steps to Planning for Restoration

Below is an outline of steps to be performed to design and implement a restoration strategy to further protect a company's informational and physical assets.

I. Assess the needs
   A. What insurance coverage currently exists for the recovery and restoration of vital records following an event?
   B. What are the coverage options available for restoration of archival data and documents, as well as data needed to fully recover business processing?
   C. What are the business risks in terms of single copies of vital records?
   D. What are the business risks associated with the loss of equipment and facilities?

II. Develop a restoration strategy
   A. Identify alternatives to either eliminate single points of failure or reduce the impact of lost or damaged property.
   B. Perform a cost/benefit analysis of viable alternatives.
   C. Obtain approval and funding for appropriate alternatives.
   D. Implement the preventative and restoration strategies.

III. Develop a restoration plan and ongoing quality assurance
   A. Incorporate restoration into the existing BCP program.
   B. Assign restoration roles and responsibilities.
   C. Coordinate restoration with the risk management department and other BCP efforts.
   D. Develop ongoing plan maintenance tasks and schedules.
   E. Perform periodic tests of restoration capability.

Chapter 19
Systems and Communications Security During Recovery and Repair

C. Warren Axelrod

DURING DISASTERS, WHEN ALL INFORMATION SYSTEMS AND COMMUNICA-
TIONS STAFF ARE FOCUSED ON SYSTEM RECOVERY AND REPAIR, COMPUTER
AND COMMUNICATIONS FACILITIES AND INFORMATION AND NETWORK
RESOURCES ARE CRITICALLY VULNERABLE. Security procedures are often
ignored, and security controls are often not in place. This chapter presents
guidelines for the data security administrator, who must ensure that security and integrity of data and facilities are not further compromised during
the recovery and repair of systems and communications networks.

Many organizations assign resources to primary security controls and
contingency planning, but few plan beyond the initial recovery process. As
information technology (IT) systems become larger, more dispersed, and
increasingly linked together over local area and wide area networks (LANs
and WANs) and such public networks as the Internet, they become not only
more critical to organizations but also more vulnerable to abuse. The
occurrences of abuse and disaster are becoming more frequent and are
having greater impact as system size, distribution, and interconnections
increase. As a result, secondary backup measures and further protection
during the recovery process are becoming more critical as well as more
complex. Yet, data security during system backup and disaster recovery is
not usually addressed by most corporate contingency plans.

Computer systems and communications networks are most vulnerable
to breaches in security during backup and disaster recovery activities, in
particular. In addition, standard backup measures, such as creating multiple copies of data, programs, passwords, encryption keys, and procedures,

0-8493-0907-7/00/$0.00+$.50
© 2001 by CRC Press LLC

and storing these copies at a second location, expose systems to even greater risk of information leaks and security breaches.

Security systems traditionally focus on controlling access to secured facilities, computer software, data, and communications networks. Very little attention is paid to recovering, repairing, and preventing further damage to the security system itself. In some circumstances, fixing a damaged security system first, thereby preventing continuing damage, may be more important than recovering systems and data that remain vulnerable to further damage. After all, restoring a system and network makes little sense when the source of the initial breach is still active. However, circumstances do exist in which the systems and networks are so critical that they must be restored as quickly as possible despite the risk of subsequent breaches.

In this chapter, both the backup of security systems and security procedures during backup and recovery are discussed.

SECURITY AND RECOVERY BASICS

Computers and communications networks can be protected by applying the following six basic security functions: avoidance, deterrence, prevention, detection, recovery, and correction. The first three functions address the need to restrict access and limit the authority to have access; the last three are responses to unauthorized intrusions, abuse, or destruction of assets.

These security functions can be defined as follows:

- *Avoidance.* Removal or elimination of any threat to assets, the protection or removal of threatened assets from actual or potential danger, and not creating surplus vulnerable assets.
- *Deterrence.* Discouragement of action that threatens system security. Publicizing disciplinary actions previously taken or that will be taken if such actions are discovered.
- *Prevention.* Implementation of measures to protect assets from security breaches and from intentional or accidental misuse.
- *Detection.* Implementation of means to recognize potential threats to asset. Monitoring the computer and network environment to determine whether such a threat is imminent, is in process, or has already breached the preventative measures. Detection can include raising an alarm in event of a security breach.
- *Recovery.* Effort to return the system and networks to an operating condition.
- *Correction.* Introduction of new measures or improvement of existing measures to avoid, deter, or to prevent recurrences of security breaches and misuse of or damage to the computer systems and communications networks.

Data security systems should protect the following three major areas of vulnerability: access, misuse, and damage. Each area can be briefly described as follows:

- *Access.* The gaining of entry, physically or electronically, to computer resources, including software, data, the IT facility, or the communications network.
- *Misuse.* The manipulation of computer and network assets in a manner outside of or detrimental to the interests of the organization, whether or not any specific damage resulted.
- *Damage.* The modification or destruction of physical or logical computer and network assets.

In summary, the goal of computer and network security systems is to prevent unauthorized access to IT and communications systems and facilities. If such access does occur, misuse of or damage to the computer and communications assets must be prevented. If, despite such precautions, access is gained and damage occurs, it is necessary to recover the systems and networks from the intrusion and violation of assets and to take action to prevent recurrence.

Control of Access, Misuse, or Damage

Some security functions relate specifically to access control and are directed at preventing unauthorized intrusion. However, misuse and damage can result from a variety of causes, each of which may require different preventative measures and recovery procedures. Misuse or damage can be caused by either intentional misbehavior, negligence, or accident. Based on the six-stage breakdown of security functions previously outlined, Exhibit 19-1 shows which security functions are effective for controlling access and which work to limit misuse and damage.

As shown in Exhibit 19-1, the only security function that can be used to control authorized access is detection. That is, no preventative measures are taken if access is detected and observed to be legitimate. However, for unauthorized access, all available security control should be applied. If unauthorized access is detected, backup security should be implemented to prevent the potential recurrence of similar unauthorized access. As a simple example, if current security access codes, such as passwords, are used by someone not authorized to use the system, the codes should be changed immediately, and authorized users should be informed of the change. If users are responsible for changing their own passwords, they should be notified to make immediate changes.

It should be noted that in Exhibit 19-1 an additional step, repair, has been added to the sequence of security functions. When unauthorized access is detected, after invoking security measures to prevent further

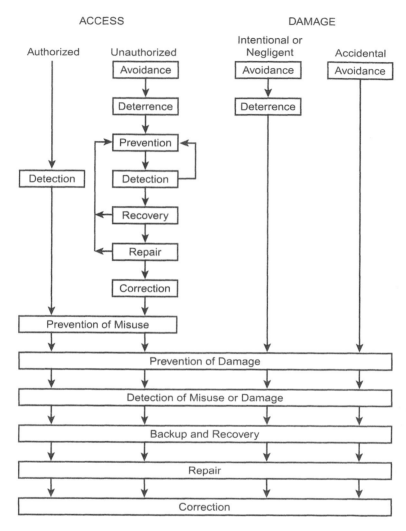

Exhibit 19-1. Measures for controlling access, misuse, and damage.

similar intrusions, an attempt should be made to recover from the intrusion and to repair or replace damaged or compromised security controls. As an extreme example, if attempted physical access results in an injured guard and a damaged door, it is necessary to replace the guard and repair the door to restore access security. Correction, as shown in Exhibit 19-1, is different from repair in that it involves changing preventative measures to make them more effective rather than fixing existing measures.

Avoidance and deterrence of damage refers to cases in which the damage is caused by an event other than access, such as a fire in the electrical wiring, a burst pipe causing a flood, or an earthquake. Securing a facility

186

against such damage involves such activities as equipment and facility inspections and worker training. To secure a system against intentional damage or accidental damage caused by negligence, all the avoidance measures should be taken. In addition, it is important to deter any actions that might result in physical damage.

Once access has been gained, whether authorized or not, misuse must be prevented. If misuse is not prevented, it must be at least limited so that it does not cause serious damage. Similarly, potential system abusers should be aware of disciplinary actions, and nonconformance to security guidelines should be noted and eliminated. Preventive measures against misuse and damage generally include access restrictions to systems, networks, and facilities, restrictions on potentially damaging activities (e.g., smoking or keeping open flames), the use of non-flammable and waterproof materials, the locating of computers and network equipment in secured areas, and the installation of protective devices (e.g., surge protection devices and automatic cut-off valves). It should be noted that, in cases of system and network recovery, the deadline requirements for returning the systems and networks to operation may dictate that recovery is only feasible if backup systems, networks, or facilities are available.

SECURITY DURING BACKUP

Once access, misuse, or damage is detected and the organization begins backup, recovery, and repair, security procedures should be followed to:

- Prevent further access, misuse, and damage due to continuance of the initial intrusion or cause of damage.
- Prevent access, misuse, and damage during the vulnerable backup and recovery processes.
- Prevent access, misuse, and damage during the repair process.
- Ensure that security controls do not unduly hinder the backup, recovery, and repair processes.

PREVENTION DURING RECOVERY

After the detection of unauthorized access, misuse, or damage, the highest priority of the data security administrator should be stemming further violations or abuses of the computer systems and networks, with the proviso that human safety should not be compromised. For example, if a fire is detected, the first consideration should be the evacuation of personnel to safety. Immediately after personnel safety is ensured, an attempt should be made to extinguish the fire, but only if the persons doing so are not at risk or are authorized fire fighters.

In the case of detecting unauthorized access to a system or network, the first step is to disconnect unauthorized users from the system, unless

187

apprehension of the perpetrators would be hindered or more harm would be caused to the organization than by allowing continued access. More harm would be caused, for example, if the entire system or network were shut down to stop further unauthorized access — depriving authorized users from performing their work.

The data security administrator should determine whether prevention of further intrusion and abuse is more harmful than continuation of the adverse practice. Because a decision made under such immediate pressure could easily be the wrong one, the rules of action should be carefully specified in advance and strictly enforced during an event. Because it is frequently during the initial moments of an emergency that decisions are most critical, rehearsals, simulations, and other training techniques are a crucial part of such contingency planning.

SECURITY DURING RECOVERY

When the source of abuse has been halted and the situation has been stabilized, recovering the system and facility begins. This may be achieved either on site or at off-site backup facilities.

Physical Access. Because backup and recovery frequently involves non-employees (e.g., fire fighters, messengers, or service engineers) the data security administrator should ensure surveillance of such persons while they are on the premises or handling confidential information. Alternatively, security may be achieved if only authorized persons are allowed access to sensitive areas of information. This may be done by designating emergency personnel in advance. Ironically, emergency surveillance is often conducted by temporarily employing unknown security guards who are unfamiliar with the environment.

Transfer of Data. Transferring confidential, valuable information (e.g., magnetic tapes, reports, or disk packs) to backup sites and returning these media, plus any new information created at the backup site, presents many opportunities for corruption or theft of information. Backup and recovery often necessitate the use of more vulnerable public communications networks, rather than more secure, private data communications networks so that exposures have to be anticipated and the preventative actions taken.

Examples of various approaches to achieving security during backup and recovery are listed in Exhibit 19-2 and are discussed in detail in the following sections.

Physical Access Control. Physical access at the primary and backup sites and access to information and materials in transit can be controlled by retaining reliable security guard service. Temporary security services should be selected in advance, and their references should be checked

Exhibit 19-2. Backup and recovery security procedures.

Security control	Backup and recovery procedure
Physical Access	
Guards, On Site	Contract for guard service in advance and preassign employees to guard duty.
Guards, in Transit	Contract in advance with secured transportation service for relocating media and equipment
Electronic Card Entry System	Provide emergency batter backup for security systems dependent upon electricity and provide for manual override system invoked by authorized personnel. Set up contingency access procedures in advance.
Voice and Data Communications Networks	Provide security on contingency lines and equipment equivalent, if possible, to primary networks.
Logical Access	
Passwords	Ensure that existing system passwords can be used on backup systems or issue special contingency passwords. Ensure that changes to the primary system are reflected in the contingency system.
Security Software	Provide comparable and compatible security software and contingency systems.
Dial-up Procedures	Provide contingency dial-up numbers for authorized personnel. Pre-specify contingency call-back numbers if the system is designed to hand up and call the user back. Set up equipment and software and specify telephone numbers in advance.
Network Security	Ensure that network security measures (e.g., encryption for data, scrambling for voice) are compatible with the backup systems and that changes to the primary system are reflected in the contingency system.

carefully to avoid hurried, reactive decisions. Unreliable guard service can negate many of the security controls of backup and recovery. At the same time, contingency access procedures should be developed at both primary and backup sites and for primary and backup communications network facilities, and authorized employees and the guard service should be familiar with these procedures. If electronic entry systems are employed, an alternative method for gaining access should be provided in case the electronic systems are disabled.

Communications Security. Backup communications networks should be armed with security controls. Securing of backup networks is often more difficult than for primary networks, because backup communications lines are often public. Communications backup procedures should accommodate the need to inform users of new changes in dial-up procedures, encryption keys, and communications log-on procedures, when appropriate, and other necessary contact information.

Securing data over public communications carriers can include encryption, error detection codes, positive Acknowledgment, or echoplexing. These methods verify message integrity but do not control access. The retention of encryption capability is an issue particularly during the recovery process because it means making the required encryption keys available at multiple locations and ensuring that the mechanisms are in place to transfer host or client locations without compromising the security effected by encryption.

Logical Access Controls. It is imperative either to update access passwords and procedures on the backup copies of the system or to have a means of informing users of their backup passwords in case the backup system is activated. Backup passwords should be distributed in the same secure manner as primary passwords. In addition, the security software for the backup system must be continually updated. It would compound a disaster if, after a successful move to a backup site, users were unable to gain access to the system because the security software was not compatible with the primary system or had not been updated to reflect changes in the primary systems and networks.

In summary, specific security measures to ensure continuing system integrity should be appended to every recovery procedure.

Special Security Provisions

The efficiency and effectiveness of the recovery process can be compromised if the same security measures designed to protect the systems and networks under normal operation are implemented during recovery. Security measures must be designed specifically for contingency situations. These security controls must allow for the unusual and urgent requirements of a recovery environment yet still offer protection during a very vulnerable situation.

The most fundamental and significant aspects of security during the recovery phase are that security controls appropriate in normal situations do not work best during disaster recovery and that special provision must be made in the security procedures to account for such differences. As a simple example, many data centers do not allow system programmers to gain physical access to the computers and prevent applications programmers from having access to production systems. However, during a disaster, a programmer may be critical to effecting a specific recovery. The security procedures must allow for certain individuals to have, in emergency situations, controlled privileged access that may not be available to them under normal operating conditions.

SECURITY DURING REPAIR AND CORRECTION

Frequently, when a disaster has passed and the risk to systems and networks has been reduced, there is a tendency to relax security and repair procedures. Repair and reconstruction often proceeds without the diligence and concentration afforded the recovery process; however, major dangers can result from such relaxation.

First, if another damaging event occurs before the completion of the repair and correction process, the organization may be left without backup or primary systems and networks. Whereas it is improbable that two independent, damaging events will occur in rapid succession, the repair process itself can pose added risk (e.g., welding or high-voltage electrical repair work can increase the risk of fire or further electrical outages). Also, some events have anticipated potential subsequent effects, such as aftershocks from an earthquake or structural damage from a fire or flood resulting in the shifting or collapse of a building.

Second, the repair process usually involves persons (e.g., contractors, electricians, vendors' technicians) who are not familiar with normal, daily operations. The probability of security breaches and abusive or damaging actions increases because of these individuals. A conflict frequently arises between the urgency in repairing damage and the need to plan and control the repair and reconstruction process carefully. Because many types of damage are difficult to predict, setting up contingency plans is impractical or infeasible for any but the most likely incidents. For example, most facilities have procedures for fire prevention and control and for personnel evacuation. Planning for repairs following a fire is often done only after an event when the extent of the damage is known. Much confusion can be eliminated, however, if some simple procedures are followed, such as keeping an up-to-date list of names and telephone numbers for all relevant vendors, contractors, suppliers, and employees. On the other hand, preparation for repair and reconstruction for very rare events, such as a chemical spill, might be handled after the event rather than planned in advance. Basic contingency arrangements, such as ensuring that a full set of floor plans and equipment and network layouts is stored at another location, should be made.

A reasonable procedure is to make preliminary plans for repairing damage caused by the most likely events, but planning for repairing improbable types of damage does not make sense. Even less justifiable is planning for reconstruction before the event, although names and telephone numbers of contractors and related services should be retained on site. However, special security procedures should be followed during the repair process.

RECOMMENDED COURSE OF ACTION

Risks to computer system and network integrity — through security breaches, misuse, and damage — are amplified considerably after such abuses occur, when the IT and communications environment is in a vulnerable state. Therefore, guarding against further abuses is especially important during the recovery and repair phases following the initial problem. The first line of defense is to ensure that there are fall-back procedures and resources in the event that the primary security system is damaged or otherwise compromised. This helps prevent subsequent breaches. If damage to the computer systems and communications networks occurs despite all precautions, and a recovery and repair process is initiated, security controls, based on those outlined in Exhibit 19-2, should be implemented during the recovery and repair process.

Section IV
Business Continuity Planning for Communications

Chapter 20
Network Business Continuity Planning

Nathan J. Muller

STRATEGIES FOR PROTECTING COMPUTER RESOURCES FROM POTENTIAL DISASTER ARE RECEIVING AN INCREASING SHARE OF ATTENTION; however, the links between hosts and terminals actually deserve the lion's share of attention. Digital facilities are sensitive to a variety of anomalies that can degrade performance, resulting in transmission errors, retransmission delays, and, at worst, prolonged network downtime.

Because there are many more links than host computers, there are more opportunities for failure on the network than in the hosts themselves. Consequently, a business continuity plan that takes into account such backup methods as the use of hot sites or cold sites without giving due consideration to link-restoral methods ignores a significant area of potential problems.

Fortunately, corporations can use several methods to protect their data networks against downtime and data loss. These methods differ mostly in cost and efficiency.

NETWORK RELIABILITY

A reliable network continues operations despite the failure of a critical element. The critical elements are different for each network topology.

Star Topology

With respect to link failures, the star topology is highly reliable. Although the loss of a link prevents communications between the hub and the affected node, all other nodes continue to operate as before unless the hub suffers a malfunction.

The hub is the weak link in the star topology; the reliability of the network depends on the reliability of the central hub. To ensure a high degree of reliability, the hub has redundant subsystems at critical points: the control logic, backplane, and power supply. The hub's management system can enhance the fault tolerance of these redundant subsystems by monitoring their operation and reporting anomalies. Monitoring the power supply, for example, may include hotspot detection and fan operation to identify trouble before it disrupts hub operation. Upon the failure of the main power supply, the redundant unit switches over automatically or manually under the network manager's control without disrupting the network.

The flexibility of the hub architecture lends itself to variable degrees of fault tolerance, depending on the criticality of the applications. For example, workstations running noncritical applications may share a link to the same LAN module at the hub. Although this configuration might seem economical, it is disadvantageous in that a failure in the LAN module puts all the workstations on that link out of commission.

A slightly higher degree of fault tolerance may be achieved by distributing the workstations among two LAN modules and links. That way, the failure of one module would affect only half the number of workstations. A one-to-one correspondence of workstations to modules offers an even greater level of fault tolerance, because the failure of one module affects only the workstation connected to it; however, this configuration is also a more expensive solution.

A critical application may demand the highest level of fault tolerance. This can be achieved by connecting the workstation to two LAN modules at the hub with separate links. The ultimate in fault tolerance can be achieved by connecting one of those links to a different hub. In this arrangement, a transceiver is used to split the links from the application's host computer, enabling each link to connect with a different module in the hub or to a different hub. All of these levels of fault tolerance are summarized in Exhibit 20-1.

Ring Topology

In its pure form, the ring topology offers poor reliability to both node and link failures. The ring uses link segments to connect adjacent nodes. Each node is actively involved in the transmissions of other nodes through token passing. The token is received by each node and passed on to the adjacent node. The loss of a link not only results in the loss of a node but brings down the entire network as well. Improvement of the reliability of the ring topology requires adding redundant links between nodes as well as bypass circuitry. Adding such components, however, makes the ring topology less cost-effective.

Bus Topology

The bus topology also provides poor reliability. If the link fails, that entire segment of the network is rendered useless. If a node fails, on the other

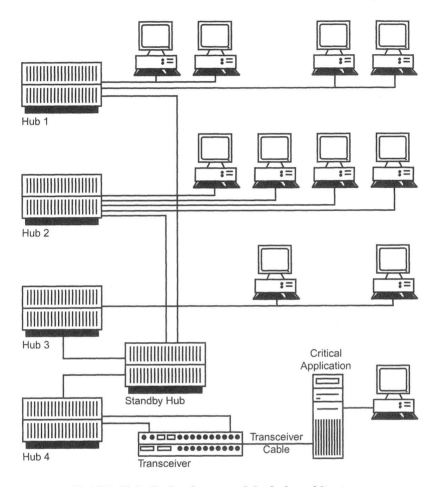

Exhibit 20-1. Fault tolerance of the hub architecture.

hand, the rest of the network continues to operate. A redundant link for each segment increases the reliability of the bus topology but at extra cost.

NETWORK AVAILABILITY

Availability is a measure of performance dealing with the LAN's ability to support all users who wish to access it. A network that is highly available provides services immediately to users, whereas a network that suffers from low availability typically forces users to wait for access.

Component Availability

Availability on the bus topology depends on the load, the access control protocol used, and length of the bus. With a light load, availability is virtually ensured for any user who wishes to access the network. As the load increases, however, so does the chance of collisions. When a collision

197

occurs, the transmitting nodes back off and try again after a short interval. The chance of collisions also increases with bus length.

With its multiple paths, a mesh topology, which is a variation of the bus topology, provides the highest degree of interconnectivity, which implies that the network is always available to users who require access.

A network based on a star topology can only support what the central hub can handle. In any case, the hub's LAN module can handle only one request at a time, which can shut out many users under heavy load conditions. Hubs equipped with multiple processors and LAN modules can alleviate this situation somewhat, but even with multiple processors, there is not usually a one-to-one correspondence between users and processors. Such a system would be cost-prohibitive.

The ring topology does not provide the same degree of availability as does a mesh topology but still represents an improvement over the star topology. The ring has a lower measure of availability than the mesh topology because each node on the ring must wait for the token before transmitting data. As the number of nodes on the ring increases, the time interval allotted for transmission decreases.

METHODS OF PROTECTION

In today's distributed computing environments, with so much information traversing public and private network, network managers must be acquainted with the available protection methods to ensure uninterrupted data flow and guard against data loss. On a WAN, the choices include carrier-provided redundancy and protection services, Customer-Controlled Reconfiguration, bandwidth on demand using ISDN, and dial backup. On the LAN, the choices include various recovery and reconfiguration procedures, the use of fault-tolerant servers and wiring hubs, and the implementation of Redundant Arrays of Inexpensive Disks (RAID). All these methods are discussed in detail in the following sections.

Tariffed Redundancy and Protection

Among the traditional methods for protecting WAN facilities are the tariffed redundancy and protection services offered by such interexchange carrier as AT&T, MCI Communications Corp., and US Sprint Communications Co.

A reliable method for minimizing downtime on the WAN is to have redundant lines ready and waiting. When a link goes down, the standby facility can be activated until the source of the failure is determined and appropriate action taken to restore service. Having duplicate facilities is a prohibitively expensive option for most businesses because monthly charges accrue whether or not the facilities are used.

To minimize the effects of failed facilities on the same route, AT&T, for example, offers two special routing methods in conjunction with its digital and analog service offerings: diversity and avoidance.

Diversity. With diversity routing, designated groups of interoffice channels (i.e., AT&T's portion of the circuit) are furnished over physically separate routes. Each route entails installation and routing charges. A custom option for diversity furnishes the interoffice channels partially or entirely over physically separated routes when separate facilities are available. In this case, AT&T applies a special routing charge to each channel.

Avoidance. The avoidance option allows the customer to have a channel avoid a specified geographical area. The customer minimizes potential impairments, such as delay, that might be exacerbated by long, circuitous routes. It also enables the customer to avoid potential points of congestion in high-use corridors, which can block traffic. This option also gives customers the means to avoid high-risk environments that can be prone to damage from floods, earthquakes, and hurricanes.

Further Protective Capabilities

Although special routing can minimize the damage resulting from failed facilities by allowing some channels to remain available to handle priority traffic, special routing makes no provision for restoring failed facilities. AT&T has attempted to address this issue with its automatic protection capability and network protection capability.

Automatic Protection Capability. Automatic protection capability is an office function that protects against failure for a local channel or other access for the ACCUNET T1.5 and ACCUNET T45 services. Protection of interoffice channels is provided on a one-to-one basis through the use of a switching arrangement that automatically switches to the spare channel when the working channel fails. To implement this capability, a separate local access channel must be ordered to serve as the spare, and compatible automatic switching equipment must be provided by the customer at its premises.

Network Protection Capability. Whereas AT&T's automatic protection capability guards against the failure of a local access channel, its network protection capability is designed to guard against the failure of an interoffice channel. Protection is furnished through the use of a switching arrangement that automatically switches the customer's channel to a separately routed fiber-optic channel on failure of the primary channel.

Dial Backup

Over the years, dial backup units have come into widespread use for rerouting modem and digital data set transmissions around failed facilities.

Dial backup units are certainly more economical than leasing redundant facilities or opting for reserved service or satellite-sharing arrangements.

This method entails installing a stand-alone device or an optional modem card that allows data communication to be temporarily transferred to the public switched network. When the primary line fails, operation over the dial backup network can be manually or automatically initiated. At the remote site, the calls are answered automatically by the dial backup unit. When the handshake and security sequence are completed and the dial backup connection is established, the flow of data resumes. On recovery of the failed line, dial backup is terminated in one of two ways: a central site attendant manually releases the backup switch on the dial backup unit, or, when in the automatic mode, the dial backup unit reestablishes the leased line connection and disconnects the dial network call upon detection of acceptable signal quality.

Customer-Controlled Reconfiguration

Management capabilities, such as customer-controlled reconfiguration available using AT&T's Digital Access and Crossconnect System (DACS), can be a means to route around failed facilities. Briefly, the DACS is a routing device; it is not a switch that can be used for setting up calls (i.e., a PBX switch) or for performing alternate routing (i.e., a multiplexer switch). The DACS was originally designed to automate the process of circuit provisioning. With customer-controlled reconfiguration, circuit provisioning is under user control from an on-premises management terminal.

With customer-controlled reconfiguration, however, a failed facility may take a half hour or more to recover, depending on the complexity of the reconfiguration. This relatively long period is necessary because the carrier needs time to establish the paths specified by the subscriber through use of a dial-up connection.

A recovery time of 30 minutes may seem tolerable for voice traffic, in which the public switched network itself is a backup vehicle, but data subscribers may need to implement alternate routing more quickly. Therefore, AT&T's DACS and customer-controlled reconfiguration service, and the similar offerings of other carriers, are typically used to remedy a long-term failure rather than to rapidly restore service on failed lines.

ISDN Facilities

T1 multiplexers offer many more functions than does DACS with Customer-Controlled Reconfiguration. In fact, the instantaneous restoral of high-capacity facilities on today's global networks calls for a T1 networking multiplexer with an advanced transport management system.

An ISDN-equipped T1 networking multiplexer offers yet another efficient and economical means to back up T1 and Fractional T1 facilities. With ISDN, the typical time required for call setup is from 3 to 10 seconds. An appropriately equipped T1 multiplexer permits traffic to be rerouted from a failing T1 line to an ISDN facility in a matter of seconds rather than hours or days, as is required by other recovery methods.

With ISDN, the user pays for the primary rate local access channels and pays for the interoffice channels only when used because these charges are time and distance dependent — just like ordinary phone calls.

With AT&T's high-capacity ISDN channels, users can avail themselves of the ISDN for backing up fractional or full T1 lines rather than pay for idle lines that may only be used occasionally during recovery. This is accomplished through a T1 multiplexer's capability to implement intelligent automatic rerouting, which ensures the connectivity of critical applications in an information-intensive business environment.

When confronted with congestion or impending circuit failure, the intelligent automatic rerouting system calculates rerouting on the basis of each likely failure. During a failure, the system automatically recalculates optimal routing, based on current network conditions. After restoration, the system again automatically calculates the most effective rerouting, should a second failure occur on the network. In this way, the system is always ready to handle the next emergency.

Because applications require different grades of service to continue operating efficiently during line failures, circuits must be routed to the best path for each application, not just switched to available bandwidth. This ensures that the network continues to support all applications with the best response times.

To avoid service denial during rerouting, voice transmissions can be automatically compressed to use less bandwidth. This can free up enough bandwidth to support all applications, both voice and data.

DDS Dial Backup

Despite carrier claims of 99.5 percent availability on digital data services (DDS), this seemingly impressive figure still leaves room for 44 hours of annual downtime. This amount of downtime can be very costly, especially to financial institutions, whose daily operations depend heavily on the proper operation of their networks. A large financial services firm, for example, can lose as much as $200 million if its network becomes inoperative for only an hour.

An organization that cannot afford the 44 hours of annual downtime might consider a digital data set with the ability to "heal" interruptions in transmission. Should the primary facility fail, communication can be quickly reestablished over the public switched network by the data set's built-in modem and integral single-call dialback unit.

Sensing loss of energy on the line, the dial-backup unit automatically dials the remote unit, which sets up a connection through the public switched network. Data is then rerouted from the leased facility to the dial-up circuit. If the normal DDS operating rate is 19.2K bps, dial restoral entails a fallback to 9.6K bps. For all other DDS rates — 2.4K, 4.8K, and 9.6K bps — the transmission speed remains the same in the dial-backup mode. Downspeeding is not necessary.

While in the dial backup mode, the unit continues to monitor the failed facility for the return of energy, which indicates an active line. Sensing that service has been restored, the unit reestablishes communication over it. The dial-up connection is then dropped.

RECOVERY OPTIONS FOR LANS

The LAN is a data-intensive environment requiring special precautions to safeguard one of the organization's most valuable assets — information.

The procedural aspect of minimizing data loss entails the implementation of manual or automated methods for backing up all data on the LAN to avoid the tedious and costly process of recreating vast amounts of information. The equipment aspect of minimizing data loss entails the use of redundant circuitry as well as components and subsystems that are activated automatically upon the failure of various LAN devices to prevent data loss and maintain network availability.

Recovery and Reconfiguration

In addition to the ability to respond to errors in transmissions by detection and correction, other important aspects of LAN operation are recovery and reconfiguration. Recovery deals with bringing the LAN back to a stable condition after an error, and reconfiguration is the mechanism by which the network is restored to its previous condition after a failure.

LAN reconfigurations involve mechanisms to restore service upon loss of a link or network interface unit. To recover or reconfigure the network after failures or faults requires that the network possess mechanisms to detect that an error or fault has occurred and to determine how to minimize the effect on the system's performance. Generally, these mechanisms provide:

- performance monitoring
- fault location
- network management

- system availability management
- configuration management

These mechanisms work in concert to detect and isolate errors, determine errors' effects on the system, and remedy these errors to bring the network to a stable state with minimal impact on network availability.

Reconfiguration. Reconfiguration is an error-management scheme used to bypass major failures of network components. This process entails detection that an error condition has occurred that cannot be corrected by the usual means. Once it is determined that an error has occurred, its impact on the network is assessed so an appropriate reconfiguration can be formulated and implemented. In this way, normal operations can continue under a new configuration.

Error Detection. Error detection is augmented by logging systems that keep track of failures over a period of time. This information is examined to determine whether trends may adversely affect network performance. This information, for example, might reveal that a particular component is continually causing errors to be inserted onto the network, or the monitoring system might detect that a component on the network has failed.

Configuration Assessment Component. This component uses information about the current system configuration, including connectivity, component placement, paths, and flows, and maps information onto the failed component. This information is analyzed to indicate how that particular failure is affecting the system and to isolate the cause of the failure. Once this assessment has been performed, a solution can be worked out and implemented.

The solution may consist of reconfiguring most of the operational processes to avoid the source of the error. The solution determination component examines the configuration and the affected hardware or software components, determines how to move resources around to bring the network back to an operational state or indicates what must be eliminated because of the failure, and identifies network components that must be serviced.

Function Criticality. The determination of the most effective course of action is based on the criticality of keeping certain functions of the network operating and maintaining the resources available to do this. In some environments, nothing can be done to restore service because of device limitations (e.g., lack of redundant subsystems) or the lack of spare bandwidth. In such cases, about all that can be done is to indicate to the servicing agent what must be corrected and keep users informed of the situation.

Once an alternate configuration has been determined, the reconfiguration system implements it. In most cases, this means rerouting transmissions, moving and restarting processes from failed devices, and reinitializing software that has failed because of some intermittent error condition. In some cases, however, nothing may need to be done except notify affected users that the failure is not severe enough to warrant system reconfiguration.

For a WAN, connections among LANs may be accomplished over leased lines with a variety of devices, typically bridges and routers. An advantage of using routers for this purpose is that they permit the building of large mesh networks. With mesh networks, the routers can steer traffic around points of congestion or failure and balance the traffic load across the remaining links.

Restoral Capabilities of LAN Servers

Sharing resources distributed over the LAN can better protect users against the loss of information and unnecessary downtime than a network with all of its resources centralized at a single location. The vehicle for resource sharing is the server, which constitutes the heart of the LAN. The server gives the LAN its features, including those for security and data protection, as well as those for network management and resource accounting.

Types of Servers. The server determines the friendliness of the user interface and governs the number of users that share the network at one time. It resides in one or more networking cards that are typically added to microcomputers or workstations and may vary in processing power and memory capacity. However, servers are programs that provide services more than they are specific pieces of hardware. In addition, various types of servers are designed to share limited LAN resources — for example, laser printer, hard disks, and the RAM mass memory. More impressive than the actual shared hardware are the functions provided by servers. Aside from file servers and communications servers, there are image and fax servers, electronic mail servers, printer servers, SQL servers, and a variety of other specialized servers, including those for videoconferencing over the LAN.

The addition of multiple special-purpose servers provides the capability, connectivity, and processing power not provided by the Network Operating System and file server alone. A single multiprocessor server combined with a network operating system designed to exploit its capabilities, such as UNIX, provides enough throughput to support five to ten times the number of users and applications as a microcomputer that is used as a server. New bus and cache designs make it possible for the server to make full use of several processors at once, without the usual performance bottlenecks that slow application speed.

Server Characteristics. Distributing resources in this way minimizes the disruption to productivity that would result if all the resources were centralized and a failure were to occur. Moreover, the use of such specialized devices as servers permits the integration of diagnostic and maintenance capabilities not found in general-purpose microcomputers. Among these capabilities are error detection and correction, soft controlled error detection and correction, and automatic shutdown in case of catastrophic error. Some servers include integral management functions (e.g., remote console management). The multiprocessing capabilities of specialized servers provide the power necessary to support the system overhead that all these sophisticated capabilities require.

Aside from physical faults on the network, there are various causes for lost or erroneous data. A software failure on the host, for example, can cause write errors to the user or server disk. Application software errors may generate inaccurate values, or faults, on the disk itself. Power surges can corrupt data and application programs, and power outages can shut down sessions, wiping out data that has not yet been written to disk. Viruses and worms that are brought into the LAN from external bulletin boards, shareware, and careless user uploads are another concern. User mistakes can also introduce errors into data or eliminate text. Entire adherence to security procedures are usually sufficient to minimize most of these problems, but they do not eliminate the need for backup and archival storage.

Backup Procedures. Many organizations follow traditional file backup procedures that can be implemented across the LAN. Some of these procedures include performing file backups at night — full backups if possible, incremental backups otherwise. Archival backups of all disk drives are typically done at least monthly; multiple daily saves of critical data bases may be warranted in some cases. The more data users already have stored on their hard disks, the longer it takes to save. For this reason, LAN managers encourage users to off-load unneeded files and consolidate file fragments with utility software to conserve disk space, as well as to improve overall system performance during backups. Some LAN managers have installed automatic archiving facilities that move files from users' hard disks to a backup data base if they have not been opened in the last 90 days.

Retrieving files from archival storage is typically not an easy matter; users forget file names, the date the file was backed up, or in which directory the file was originally stored. In the future, users can expect to see intelligent file backup servers that permit files to be identified by textual content. Graphics files, too, are retrieved without having the name, backup date, or location of the file. In this case, the intelligent file backup system compares the files with bit patterns from a sample graphic with the bit patterns of archived files to locate the right file for retrieval.

As the amount of stored information increases, there is the need for LAN backup systems that address such strategic concerns as tape administration, disaster recovery, and the automatic movement of files up and down a hierarchy of network storage devices. Such capabilities are currently available and are referred to as system storage management or Hierarchical Storage Management.

Levels of Fault Tolerance

Protecting data at the server has become a critical concern for most network managers; after all, a failure at the server can result in lost or destroyed data. Considering that some servers are capable of holding vast quantities of data in the gigabyte range, loss or damage can have disastrous consequences for an information-intensive organization.

Depending on the level of fault tolerance desired and the price the organization is willing to pay, the server may be configured in several ways: unmirrored, mirrored, or duplexed.

Unmirrored Servers. An unmirrored server configuration entails the use of one disk drive and one disk channel, which includes the controller, a power supply, and interface cabling, as shown in Exhibit 20-2. This is the

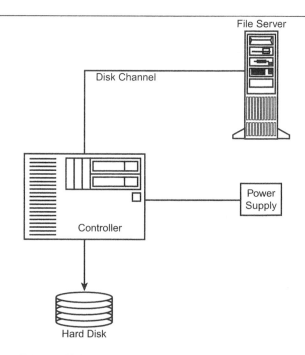

Exhibit 20-2. Unmirrored disk drive configuration.

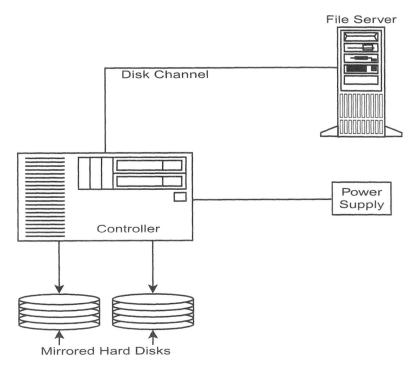

Exhibit 20-3. Configuration for disk mirroring.

basic configuration of most servers. The advantage is chiefly one of cost: the user pays only for one disk and disk channel. The disadvantage of this configuration is that a failure in either the drive or anywhere on the disk channel could cause temporary or permanent loss of the stored data.

Mirrored Servers. The mirrored server configuration entails the use of two hard disks of similar size. There is also a single disk channel over which the two disks can be mirrored together, as shown in Exhibit 20-3. In this configuration, all data written to one disk is then automatically copied onto the other disk. If one of the disks fails, the other takes over, thus protecting the data and ensuring all users have access to the data. The server's operation system issues an alarm notifying the network manager that one of the mirrored disks is in need of replacement.

The disadvantage of this configuration is that both disks use the same channel and controller. If a failure occurs on the channel or controller, both disks become inoperative. Because the same disk channel and controller are shared, the writes to the disks must be performed sequentially — that is, after the write is made to one disk, a write is made to the other disk. This can degrade overall server performance under heavy loads.

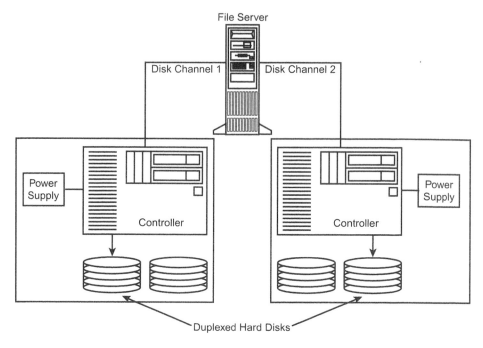

Exhibit 20-4. Disk duplexing configuration.

Disk Duplexing. In disk duplexing, multiple disk drives are installed with separate disk channels for each set of drives, as shown in Exhibit 20-4. If a malfunction occurs anywhere along a disk channel, normal operation continues on the remaining channel and drives. Because each disk uses a separate disk channel, write operations are performed simultaneously, offering a performance advantage over servers using disk mirroring.

Disk duplexing also offers a performance advantage in read operations. Read requests are given to both drives. The drive that is closest to the information responds and answers the request. The second request given to the other drive is canceled. In addition, the duplexed disks share multiple read requests for concurrent access.

The disadvantage of disk duplexing is the extra cost for multiple disk drives, also required for disk mirroring, as well as for the additional disk channels and controller hardware. However, the added cost for these components must be weighed against the replacement cost of lost information plus costs that accrue from the interruption of critical operations and lost business opportunities. Faced with these consequences, an organization might discover that the investment of a few hundred or even a few thousand dollars to safeguard valuable data is negligible.

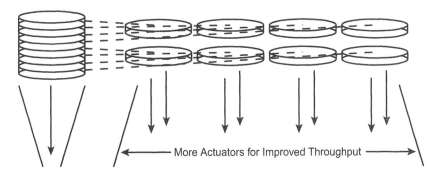

Exhibit 20-5. Redundant arrays of inexpensive disks.

REDUNDANT ARRAYS OF INEXPENSIVE DISKS (RAID)

One method of data protection is growing in popularity: Redundant Arrays of Inexpensive Disks. Instead of risking all of its data on one high-capacity disk, the organization distributes the data across multiple smaller disks, offering protection from a crash that could wipe out all data on a single, shared disk. Exhibit 20-5 illustrates RAID. Other benefits of RAID include:

- Increased storage capacity per logical disk volume.
- High data transfer or input/output rates that improve information throughput.
- Lower cost per megabyte of storage.
- Improved use of data center floor space.

RAID products can be grouped into the categories described in the following sections.

RAID Level 0

Technically, these products are not RAID products at all, because they do not offer parity or error-correction data to provide redundancy in the event of system failure. Although data striping is performed, it is accomplished without fault tolerance. Data is simply striped block-by-block across all the drives in the array. There is no way to reconstruct data if one of the drives fails.

RAID Level 1

These products duplicate data that is stored on separate disk drives. Also called mirroring, this approach ensures that critical files are available in case of individual disk drive failures. Each disk in the array has a corresponding mirror disk, and the pairs run in parallel. Blocks of data are sent to both disks simultaneously. Although highly reliable, Level 1 is costly because each drive requires its own mirror drive, which doubles the hardware cost of the system.

RAID Level 2

These products distribute the code used for error detection and correction across additional disk drives. The controller includes an error-correction algorithm, which enables the array to reconstruct lost data if a single disk fails. As a result, no expensive mirroring is required. The code, however, requires that multiple disks be set aside to do the error-correction function. Data is sent to the array one disk at a time.

RAID Level 3

These products store user data in parallel across multiple disks. The entire array functions as one large, logical drive. Its parallel operation is ideally suited to supporting imaging applications that require high data-transfer rates when reading and writing large files. RAID Level 3 is configured with one parity (i.e., error-correction) drive. The controller determines which disk has failed by using additional check information recorded at the end of each sector. However, because the drives do not operate independently, every time an image file must be retrieved, all the drives in the array are used to fulfill that request. Other users are put into a queue.

RAID Level 4

These products store and retrieve data using independent writes and reads to several drives. Error-correction data is stored on a dedicated parity drive. In RAID Level 4, data striping is accomplished in sectors rather than bytes or blocks. Sector-striping offers parallel operation in that reads can be performed simultaneously on independent drives, which allows multiple users to retrieve image files at the same time. Although multiple reads are possible, multiple writes are not because the parity drive must be read and written to for each write operation.

RAID Level 5

These products interleave user data and parity data, which are then distributed across several disks. Because data and parity codes are striped across all the drives, there is no need for a dedicated parity drive. This configuration is suited for applications that require a high number of input/output operations per second, such as transaction processing tasks that involve writing and reading large numbers of small data blocks at random disk locations. Multiple writes to each disk group are possible because write operations do not have to access a single common parity drive.

RAID Level 6

These products improve reliability by implementing drive mirroring at the block level so data is mirrored on two drives instead of one. Up to two drives in the five-drive disk array can fail without loss of data. If a drive in the array fails with RAID Level 5, for instance, data must be rebuilt from the parity information spanned across the drives. With RAID Level 6, however, the data is simply read from the mirrored copy of the blocks found on the various striped drives. No rebuilding is required. Although this results in a slight performance advantage, it requires at least 50 percent more disk capacity to implement.

Vendors continually tout the effectiveness of various RAID solutions. In truth, the choice among RAID solutions involves tradeoffs between cost, performance, and reliability. Rarely can all of these requirements be satisfied simultaneously, especially when trying to address high-availability, large-scale storage needs.

OTHER CONSIDERATIONS

As more businesses interconnect their computers at remote locations and run critical applications over a WAN, they are discovering that financial and operational losses can mount quickly in the event of internetwork downtime. Businesses of all types and sizes are recognizing that business continuity plans are essential, regardless of the particular computing environment. The business continuity plan should be a formal document that has been signed off by senior management, IS management, and all department heads. The following items should be addressed in any business continuity plan.

Uninterruptible Power Supplies (UPSs)

UPSs are designed to provide temporary power so attached computer systems and servers can be shut down properly to prevent data loss. UPSs are especially important in WANs. Because of the distance among links, sometimes reaching thousands of miles, WANs are more susceptible to power problems than LAN segments. Therefore, using battery backups to protect against fluctuations and outages should always be the first line of defense.

Although most central sites have UPSs, many remote sites typically do not, usually as a cost-savings measure. However, battery backup can be very inexpensive, costing only a few hundred dollars, which is cheap compared to the cost of indeterminate network downtime. Moreover, some UPSs have Simple Network Management Protocol capabilities, which lets network managers monitor battery backup from the central management console. For instance, every UPS can be instructed using simple network management protocol (SNMP) to test itself once a week and report back if the test fails. The network manager can even be notified if the temperature levels in wiring closets rise above established thresholds.

Generators

To keep computers operating during a prolonged loss of power, a generator is required. The difference between a UPS and a generator is the generator is capable of supplying much more power for longer periods of time. Using a fuel source, such as oil, a generator can supply power indefinitely to keep data centers cool and computers running. Because generators can cost tens of thousands of dollars, many companies unwisely decide to skip this important component of the business continuity plan.

Unless an organization has experienced a lengthy outage that has disrupted daily business operations, this level of protection is often hard to justify. However, many office buildings already have generators to power lighting and elevators during electrical outages. For a fee, tenants can patch into the generator to keep data centers and networks operating.

Off-Site Storage

Mission-critical data should be backed up daily or weekly and stored off site. There are numerous services that provide off-site storage, often in combination with Hierarchical Storage Management techniques. In the IBM environment, for example, this might entail storing frequently used data on a Direct Access Storage Device for immediate usage, whereas data used only occasionally might go to optical drives, and data that has not been used in several months would be archived to a tape library.

Carriers, computer vendors, and third-party firms offer vault storage for secure, off-site data storage of critical applications. Small companies need not employ such elaborate methods. They can back up their own data and have it delivered by overnight courier for storage at another company location or bring it to a bank safety deposit box. The typical bank vault can survive even a direct hit by a tornado.

In addition to backing up critical data, it is advisable to register all applications software with the manufacturer and keep the original program disks in a safe place at a different location. This minimizes the possibility of both copies being destroyed in the same catastrophe. Software licenses, manuals, and supplementary documentation should also be protected.

Surge Suppressors

In storm-prone areas like the Southeast, frequent electrical storms can put sudden bursts of electricity, called spikes or surges, on telephone lines. These bursts can destroy router links and cause adapters and modems to fail. To protect equipment attached to telephone lines, surge-suppression devices can be installed between the telephone line and the communications device. Surge suppressors condition the power lines to ensure a constant voltage level. Many modems and other network devices have surge suppressors built in. The business continuity plan should specify the use of surge suppressors whenever possible, and equipment should be checked periodically to ensure proper operation.

Spare Parts Pooling

Most companies can afford to stockpile spare cables and cards but not spare multiplexer and router components that are typically too expensive to inventory. Pooling these items with another area business that uses the same equipment can be an economical form of protection should disaster strike. Such businesses can be identified through user group and association meetings. The equipment vendor is another source for this information.

After each party becomes familiar with the disaster recovery needs of the other, an agreement can be drawn up to pledge mutual assistance. Each party stocks half the necessary spare parts. The pool is drawn from as needed and restocked after the faulty parts come back from the vendors' repair facilities.

Switched Digital Services

Carriers offer an economical form of disaster protection with their networks of digital switches. When one link goes down, voice and data calls are automatically rerouted or switched to other links on the carrier's network. Examples of switched digital services are switched 56K bps, Integrated Services Digital Network, and frame relay. Many routers now offer interfaces for switched digital services, allowing data to take any available path on the network. The same level of protection is available on private network, but it requires spare lines, which is often a very expensive solution.

Multiple WAN Ports

A well-planned internetworking system avoids single points of failure. This entails equipping nodes with redundant subsystems, such as power, control logic, network cards, and WAN ports. Routers, for instance, need multiple WAN ports so if a primary line goes down, the router can automatically use the backup line on another port.

Even branch sites with remote-access routers should have multiple WAN ports. If the first line goes down, the remote router is programmed to autodial into a second line on another port, which remains inactive until needed. The second port can dial up a switched 56K line that is paid for on a usage basis.

Links to Remote Sites

WANs of three or more sites often link the remote locations to the primary site but not to each other. Though this strategy saves linkage costs, it risks leaving remote workers stranded should the main office's services go down. To keep branches up and running, inexpensive links should be established among them. The links' bandwidth should be adequate to keep critical systems communicating.

As long as backup circuits are available, routers can run a routing protocol that understands link states and can reroute around points of network failure. The Routing Information Protocol, often used in smaller WANs, does not support link states, but the Open Shortest Path First protocol does. open shortest path first (OSPF) runs on TPC/IP networks and is the protocol of choice for larger internetworks.

Periodic Testing

It is advisable to test the business continuity plan periodically to check assumptions and to find out whether the plan really works. After giving users advance notice, the network manager can come in after business hours, unplug one of the communication links, and see what happens. If something unexpected occurs, it is necessary to fine-tune the business continuity plan and test again.

With certain types of network equipment, such as multiplexers and switches, several disaster-simulation scenarios can be programmed in advance and stored for emergency implementation. With the integral network modeling capability of some T1 multiplexers, network planners can simulate various disaster scenarios on an aggregate or node level anywhere in the network. This offline simulation allows planners to test and monitor changing conditions and determine their precise impact on network operations.

Any outage should be treated as an unannounced test of the business continuity plan. Network managers should determine if the response was adequate and if the response can be improved.

Worst-Case Scenarios

Planning how to provide communications connectivity based on the assumption that the entire network is inoperable is a sound business practice, especially for organizations in areas of the country that can suffer widespread damage from hurricanes, tornados, floods, and earthquakes. Whole nodes may have to be replaced to get the network back into proper operation, requiring advanced arrangements with suppliers so the necessary equipment can be obtained on very short notice instead of when it comes off a production run.

Many vendors of switches, hubs, routers, and multiplexers offer network recovery services at a reasonable cost and guarantee equipment delivery within 24 hours of the request. Even carriers offer business continuity services. AT&T Global Information Solutions, for example, offers crisis management services designed to allow customers to occupy a regional AT&T crisis center within two to four hours after a disaster. The customer gets fully restored voice and data communications and computer-ready floor space.

Some companies specialize in business continuity services. SunGard Recovery Services Inc., for instance, offers customers a hotsite backup center for mainframe computers. The company also addresses the needs of PC-based environments and offers PC software that helps identify which services are critical to operations. Its overnight assistance program rushes equipment — PCs, servers, and modems, as well as bridges, multiplexers, and routers — to any customer site. As part of its mobile recovery program, SunGard maintains a fleet of trailers that are ready for dispatch to customer sites for use as temporary work space.

Training

Often overlooked in the business continuity plan are provisions for training, essential because in an emergency reactions to impending disaster must be automatic. End users must save data and shut down applications at the first sign of trouble. Network managers must be able to assess quickly the criticality of numerous alarms and respond appropriately. Help desk operators must be able to determine the nature and magnitude of the problem to address end user concerns. LAN administrators must be able to determine the impact of the problem on local networks.

Insurance

The business continuity plan should provide for the periodic review of the organization's insurance policy. Of particular concern is to what extent information systems, network components, and applications software are covered in the event of a disaster. The policy should be very specific about what the insurance company does and does not cover. Ambiguities must be resolved before a disaster occurs, not after.

Reviews also provide an opportunity to add provisions for system or network upgrades and expansions that occurred in the time since the policy was initially written. Though this may add to the policy's cost, it is still much less compared to the wholesale replacement of equipment that falls outside of the insurance contract.

Risk Assessment

The business continuity plan should include a review of the physical layout of data centers, wiring closets, floor and overhead conduits, and individual offices that contain computers and data communications equipment. All equipment and cabling should be kept in a relatively safe place and not exposed to objects that are likely to fall and cause damage should disaster strike. Desks, tables, shelves, and cabinets should be solid enough to safely fasten equipment to them, to survive minor earthquakes. Whenever possible, equipment should not be positioned under water sprinklers. These and other precautions can even lower insurance costs.

CONCLUSION

The methods mentioned in this chapter are only a few of the many network restoral and data protection options available from carriers, equipment vendors, and third-party firms. As more businesses become aware of the strategic value of their networks, these capabilities are significantly important to organizations. A variety of link-restoral and data-protection methods can provide effective ways to meet the diverse requirements of today's information-intensive corporations that are both efficient and economical. Choosing wisely from among the available alternatives ensures that companies are not forced into making cost/benefit trade-offs that jeopardize their information networks and, ultimately, their competitive positions.

Chapter 21
Business Recovery Planning for Communications
Leo A. Wrobel

MOST BUSINESSES DEPEND ON THEIR TELEPHONE NETWORKS TO KEEP CUSTOMER COMMUNICATIONS OPEN. Lost service spells lost revenue. This chapter discusses the preliminary activities involved in getting a communications recovery planning project approved. Low-cost strategies to help prevent voice communications outages from occurring or to minimize their disruptive effect are emphasized. The information is intended to help IS and user managers who are assessing the risks in their organizations or are preparing to evaluate more advanced network protection measures.

Computer business continuity centers, which were merely a concept 10 years ago, currently represent a three-quarter-of-a-billion-dollar industry that serves to protect critical information systems. Surprisingly, however, of the 80 or more major computer outages that have led to the activation of a computer recovery facility since 1986, only a fraction resulted from an actual computer failure or from such incidents as flood, fire, or sabotage. In fact, the chief source of disaster has been telecommunications disruptions. In other words, organizations have had to mobilize expensive computer recovery facilities simply to use their telephones.

All told, there were no fewer than six major network failures in 1991 alone, affecting New York (three times), Washington, D.C., Atlanta, Los Angeles, and locations in New England. These failures do not include the scores of smaller, more regional disasters that happen frequently but do not make national news. One such incident involved a software failure in the central office of a Dallas telephone company that cut off phone service to a major hospital for more than three hours. In another incident, lightning struck a major long-distance carrier's facility, producing a day-long network outage. Hundreds of cable and fiber-optic cable disruptions also occur yearly that virtually isolate users, even though they may be unaware of the disruption.

These disruptions take on a whole new dimension as the trend toward business automation and, in particular, online systems continues. Incoming 800 numbers and online point-of-sale terminals are ubiquitous in a modern economy. Companies have become highly dependent on the network for key elements of operations and customer service. When the telephone stops ringing, so does the cash register.

This chapter discusses the preliminary work needed to get a communications recovery planning project approved. It then reviews the major threats to voice communications and recommends some low-cost strategies to eliminate avoidable risks and minimize the impact of risks that cannot be eliminated.

BUSINESS'S RELIANCE ON COMMUNICATIONS

Many professionals in the business continuity and IS management fields have had to take a hard look at the communications network. Contingency planning is always time-consuming and complicated, even when the manager's efforts are directed toward a more familiar IS environment. Compiling a contingency plan for the communications network is especially complicated; still, the responsibility falls, for better or worse, on the business enterprise.

A great deal of interest is centered on how to safeguard voice communications as part of an organization's overall business continuity plan. Failures of voice networks have plagued users over the past few years with ever-increasing frequency and severity. As a result, companies and business continuity service providers are designing more broad-based business recovery solutions in which voice communications plays an integral part.

For example, in a service-oriented company, the average workstation serves as the front-line interface to the customer. Incoming calls are answered and some type of information processing takes place in real time — an order is taken, a product is sold, or a service is rendered. These activities generate the cash flow that supports the business. Airline and transportation companies, bank card validation centers, or various inbound or outbound marketers rely heavily on workstation-based computing.

In each case, the lowest common denominator is the person who calls in, requests a service, or purchases a product. In a service company, when the telephone is not answered, revenue is not produced. No amount of additional support personnel, money, or other resources can alter this fact.

ASSESSING THE IMPACT OF LOSS OF SERVICE

A properly designed business recovery plan for such companies must require that not only individual workstations be restored but also incoming telephone service that turns customer calls into revenue for the company. Restoring computer function matters little if the customer cannot make use of it. On the surface, this example seems to reflect common sense; in practice, recovery of communications can be difficult to achieve without preplanning.

The company may, for example, use a wide array of communications services, including incoming 800 numbers, outgoing WATS lines, Direct Inward Dial circuits, custom circuits (e.g., private data and voice lines), and software-defined networks. It may also employ automated call-distributing (ACD) systems and other special call-handling equipment that resides on site.

The risk to the company, then, includes not only internal threats to resident equipment from fire, flood, and sabotage (as in computer contingency planning) but threats from outside sources. Both can have an equally devastating effect on operations when disaster strikes. The major area of external exposure is undoubtedly the communications network.

PRELIMINARY ACTIVITIES IN RECOVERY PLANNING

A persistent problem in addressing the need for network protection is the availability of funds and the required management support for these resources. Justifying money and people for disaster planning is difficult no matter how urgent the need. Developing a full-scale communications recovery plan is also a long-term project that has an average life of two or more years. One logical method of addressing the recovery planning project is to deal with it in three phases.

Defining the Exposure in an Executive Summary

Phase one examines what the business is really trying to protect and why. It involves a preliminary study of critical business systems. Senior managers in the major business units must be asked to estimate what the financial damage to the overall company would be in the event of a communications outage affecting a critical system (e.g., a telemarketing center or order desk) for the duration of n days. The resulting figures are then cross-checked with other departments and with corporate financial managers to provide a reliable (although not exact) assessment of financial loss. The final report or presentation is made to senior management. This report must always concentrate on the business, not the technical, issues. Assigning a dollar value to an hour or day of downtime is an excellent strategy for obtaining management support, in terms of both money and personnel, to continue the project.

Educating Personnel and Setting Audit Standards

The IS department and internal audit function usually have defined and documented acceptable standards for auditing a data center's ability to recover from a disaster. A similar set of standards should be developed for the communications department and for the network itself. Phase two involves formulating these standards through a cooperative effort among departments. The result of this effort is a document everyone can claim ownership of and that ensures continuity so that all the involved departments — IS, communications, operations, and internal audit — are prepared for the third phase (implementation) of the project.

Implementing the Network Business Continuity Plan

It is not unusual for the implementation of a network recovery plan to take anywhere from 18 to 30 months. Whereas phase one involves only a high-level assessment of exposure, this phase deals with the specifics of the plan and requires detailed interviews with users and department managers and with personnel from virtually every internal department, from human resources to building security.

The depth of study required accounts in part for the long time frame for implementing the plan. However, to be considered a true business recovery plan, it must include input from all departments. Contingency planners must tap the appropriate personnel to provide necessary information on market share, salaries (required to estimate losses in productivity in the event of a disaster), or legal issues. In addition, most of the organization's equipment and network vendors need to become involved and major network modifications may have to be made over time.

During this phase, the company will remain exposed to many types of communications disasters; however, it can take a few proactive steps almost immediately to decrease the exposure. Much of the capital-intensive part of the task has already been paid for by the acquisition of the hardware set in place by the telephone companies. A local or long-distance carrier network can perform many business continuity functions; the organization must simply learn how to take advantage of them. By knowing how to avail itself of such technology — and by taking a few rudimentary steps before disaster strikes — an organization can improve its resistance to telecommunications disruptions immeasurably and at low cost.

Identifying the Four Threats to Voice Communications

One way to gain an understanding of the nature of the various threats to voice communications integrity is to divide the threats into four categories:

1. The loss of the network's switching capability (e.g., a software glitch)

2. The loss of a network serving facility (e.g., a central office fire)
3. Isolation from a network provider's serving facility (e.g., a cut cable)
4. An internal disruption (i.e., a disruption inside the company's building)

Each of these threats is discussed in the following sections along with an example and some suggestions for steps that can either prevent such outages from occurring or minimize their disruptive effect. The focus is on low-cost alternatives that can be undertaken with relative ease. This information is intended to help IS managers who are assessing similar exposure in their organizations or are preparing to evaluate more advanced network protection measures.

LOSS OF NETWORK SWITCHING CAPABILITY

The most notable example of this type of outage was the January 1990 failure of the AT&T network that resulted from a glitch in software that was, ironically, designed to increase reliability in the network. Approximately 50 percent of AT&T's regular traffic volume was blocked for most of a business day. Hardest hit were companies that depended on incoming 800 services or software-defined network services.

The fact that Fortune 1000 companies had alternative carriers mattered little because incoming 800 numbers are not portable, or transferable, between carriers. Consequently, a user whose incoming AT&T 800 numbers were inoperative because of the outage could not have its other carriers process those calls, even if the connection to these carriers was available. Software-defined networks were similarly affected because they rely solely on the switching services of a single carrier, in this case AT&T

Long-Distance Access Codes

During this type of outage, outbound services at least can be easily restored through the use of the long-established 10XXX dialing pattern. The surprise resulting from the AT&T incident was just how uninformed users were about the availability of 10XXX dialing or five-digit dialing codes. Because all major carriers can be dialed through an equal access end office, a disrupted long-distance user can in essence dial around a problem by selecting the access code for a long-distance carrier not affected by the outage (see Exhibit 21-1).

For example, an AT&T user who would usually dial 1 (214) 733-6870 could have instead dialed 10222, 1 or 0, then the regular number to complete the call on the MCI network. Similarly, the five-digit code 10333 would access US Sprint. It is ironic to think that the most widely available and useful — and least expensive — alternative for restoring long-distance calling

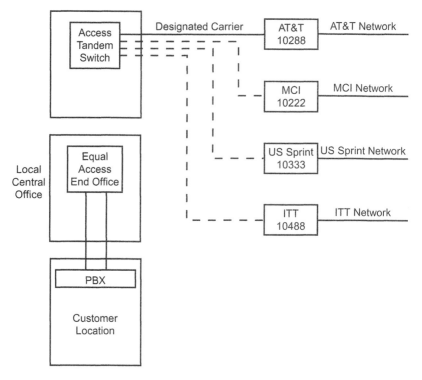

Exhibit 21-1. Using 10XXX dialing.

capability was unknown to so many users. Companies would be prudent to keep a listing of such codes on hand at all times, because the long-distance company may not be able to provide them when an outage occurs. These codes are a cost-effective insurance measure against long-distance outages.

LOSS OF A NETWORK SERVING FACILITY

In any business, a total loss of a major facility is always a possibility, and communications providers are no exception. There have been dozens of cases of telephone central offices being rendered inoperable over the past 10 years. Causes have included fires, floods, lightning, tornadoes, hurricanes, switch failure, and human error. The most far-reaching central office disaster occurred in May 1988 in Hinsdale, Illinois, when a fire in a suburban Chicago central office affected not only the 49,000 local telephone subscribers but more than half a million other users nationwide.

Central office disasters are always messy; they affect a large area and the damage is not limited to basic dial-tone service. Other services that may be affected are data and voice private line circuits; cellular, paging, and long-distance access lines; and 911emergency trunks. Given the magnitude of such disasters, however, a few measures can be taken at low cost by alert contingency planners who think ahead.

Command and Control Emergency Response

Cellular telephones operate from mobile telephone serving offices (MTSOs) that are often diverse from an affected central office. Although only a limited number of cellular phones can be used in a given area because of limitations of the cellular network, they are indispensable for command and control.

Other technologies not to be overlooked are radio telephones and two-way radios. Radio telephones can often be used for phone patches back to the public network by way of repeaters, whereas two-way radios are useful for communications in the immediate area.

After police, fire, and other emergency services, the next class of service restored following a major central office disaster is usually pay telephones. Because Asynchronous Transfer Mode and other banking operations may be down for a significantly longer time, managers should keep some cash on hand, some of it in quarters, for incidentals.

ISOLATION FROM A SERVING FACILITY

A cable cut is probably the most common cause of a communications disruption. A cut cable can affect any of the thousands of high-capacity fiber-optic lines that crisscross the United States.

One well-publicized AT&T outage in New York was caused by a technician who unknowingly cut the wrong underground fiber-optic cable. Unfortunately, this particular fiber contained a 1.7G-bps carrier, or about 240,000 circuits (about 60 percent of New York's capacity, by some estimates).

Often there is precious little that can be done about human error. People are fallible and accidents will happen, even to the best-prepared companies. Reasonable precautions include enforcing strict adherence to written policies as well as to procedures for maintenance and safety. Effective change control management of major software upgrades and revisions can also be an effective way to prevent disruption.

Assessing Communications Rights-of-Way

Telephone, electric, fiber-optic, gas, water, television, and other services are usually installed in the same public rights-of-way, mainly along streets and thoroughfares. In many cities, especially older ones like New York, Boston, and Philadelphia, these rights-of-way date back decades. The result is that when contractors dig to repair or install facilities, they are never quite sure what they will hit on the way down.

Although being invisible makes a telephone cable facility more secure, it makes it vulnerable in other ways. Record keeping can be a problem, for example, when rights-of-way have been in continuous use for decades or more. Some companies have begun to use innovative schemes for installing communications facilities by laying fiber-optic cable in abandoned steam tunnels and subway tunnels. Although this eliminates one problem by making the facility more accessible, it can create another by making the facility visible and therefore vulnerable to disruptions caused by vandalism or tampering by unauthorized personnel.

There are many methods to protect and diversify cables in a network. One inexpensive precautionary measure that addresses part of the problem is to meet with the account representative of the local operating company to assess the company's exposure in this area. Many times, alternate or diverse routing is available in the company's service area for little or no cost.

Alternate and Diverse Routing. IS managers should understand the terminology and the difference between alternate and diverse routing. Many users, and the telephone companies for that matter, use the terms interchangeably.

Generally, alternate routing refers to any cable facility that is different from the facility to which the company is currently assigned. Diverse routing refers to the use of not only a different facility but a completely different physical path. Most telephone companies can provide alternate routing with relative ease. Diverse routing is trickier, especially if the business is located far from its serving central office. An examination of the entrance facilities to the building is also recommended; it undermines the purpose of diverse routing if new facilities are simply brought in through the same building conduit. All construction activity in the vicinity of a business must also be taken into consideration.

Pair Gain Units. Central offices and cables are not the only items to consider when the organization is assessing vulnerability in rights-of-way. Other components of the network that should be considered are telephone pedestals and pair gain units. The most common pair gain unit is called an SLC-96 pair gain unit (SLC stands for subscriber loop carrier). In areas where cable facilities are in short supply, distances are long, and laying new cable is expensive, these units are used to carry 544 simultaneous circuits on 16 pairs of copper cables. A fiber version also exists.

Pair gain units work exceptionally well and have been broadly accepted by the local operating companies; however, pair gain units, pedestals, and fiber-optic repeaters are uniquely vulnerable to traffic hazards and can be suddenly disabled by an accident. For example, if a driver runs a car into a central office, a totaled car might be the only physical consequence. A similar collision with a pair gain unit would destroy the equipment, thereby isolating users. This is the same consequence as a total central office disaster, although probably for a shorter time because the equipment takes less time to replace.

INTERNAL DISRUPTIONS

Some of the least expensive insurance available to ensure network integrity involves the dedication of someone's time. It is a prudent idea to personally involve people from the IS department, because many contingency planning rules for the data center hold true for the communications network.

IS Manager's Checklist

A walkthrough of the site will enable IS managers to assess potential problems and to check that adequate precautions are being taken to protect the organization's communications equipment. A checklist of problems to look for would include the following items:

- Are all telephone closets and PBX rooms locked and accessible only to authorized personnel?
- Do cable risers in multistory buildings pass through telephone closets belonging to other companies? Do they similarly restrict access, or do others have access to the organization's cables from other telephone closets? Are flammable materials stored in lower cable closets? Are the risers into the closets fire-stopped?
- Are backup copies of PBX software and assignments made regularly? Are they stored off site and included in the IS department's regular pick-up schedule?
- Are similar power conditioning schemes employed in the switch room as in the computer room? If not, can the switch room use computer room resources already in place, such as power conditioners and UPS equipment? (The IS department's expertise in the area of power conditioning is valuable and should be shared.)
- Are sprinklers, air-conditioning pipes, and regular building plumbing located above the equipment? Do low sprinkler heads exist over pathways where equipment is rolled in? Are pipes in an area where they might freeze?

Infrared Scanning

The same technology that allows space satellites to look through clouds can be employed to identify electrical faults and shorts in walls before they cause fires. Infrared scanning is highly recommended for businesses residing in older buildings with dubious wiring or in new ones to reveal slipshod construction. AT&T and other companies provide infrared scanning (also called thermographics) service.

RECOMMENDED COURSE OF ACTION

The interruption of critical business systems and communications networks is a risk that is often ignored until a disaster happens. Corporate management must shoulder the cost of a business continuity planning project. One way to influence corporate management is to initiate a study to quantify the extent of the company's dependence on the network and to quantify the impact loss of service would have on the company in terms of:

- lost sales (i.e., direct revenues)
- lost market share
- lost customer confidence
- lost productivity (e.g., idle employees)
- legal liability issues

These are terms that are understandable to executive management, and they will assist contingency planners in securing the necessary support and funding for the business continuity planning project. These figures must be quantified with the corporate controller, the vice president of marketing, the sales vice president, or corporate counsel, as appropriate. Consultants and outside resources can also be brought in when necessary.

Establishing standards is another part of the business continuity planning project. Just as the organization has standards for the data center, standards for the network should be devised in connection with such physical security issues as fire protection and access control. Other issues directed toward the network itself — for example, when backup circuits are appropriate — must be included as well. All departments in the organization must have input to this process to ensure uniformity and compliance.

After a formal network recovery plan has been implemented, all new services should be ordered with business continuity in mind. It is easier, for example, to require a switch, modem, or multiplexer vendor to provide guaranteed replacement times for equipment before the contract is signed. Otherwise, the organization could end up having to pay extra for the same service later.

The task of business continuity planning for the communications network need not be put off because of budgetary constraints. There are many concrete actions the IS manager can and should be taking, both independently and with the aid of vendors, to protect the organization's critical network resources. Fault-tolerance in the network does not happen overnight. It evolves over time, through the collective impact of even the most minimal efforts, such as those described in this chapter. Any steps that can be taken, however small, result in a higher level of service to the company's customers and greater peace of mind to the organization.

Chapter 22

Documenting a Communications Recovery Plan

Leo A. Wrobel

THE GROWING COMPLEXITY OF COMMUNICATIONS SYSTEMS means that almost every organization today has a local area network (LAN) administrator whose possible absence during a disaster mandates the development of a well-documented communications recovery plan that can be executed by people unfamiliar with an organization's systems. This chapter reviews the basic components of such a plan, particularly the need for accurate and up-to-date hardware and software inventory forms.

Technical services personnel often respond tersely when asked by management to produce a business continuity plan for a communications system. They view such a request as a no-confidence vote and the plan as a test of their ability to perform a recovery in the event of a disaster.

Competency, however, is almost never the issue. In most large organizations, the technical services and communications staffs are capable of recovering from a disaster under virtually any circumstances. Often, the very people controlling the recovery process are those who actually designed and built the communications system in the first place. They know where every wire in the organization runs and have memorized the telephone number of every major equipment vendor and service supplier. In the event of a disaster, these employees would undoubtedly pull together in an almost superhuman effort.

Problems with business continuity occur when an organization's key personnel, such as the local area network (LAN) administrator, are unavailable for any reason during a disaster. Because of the growing complexity of LAN technology, one of the most effective tests of a business continuity plan is to assemble the disaster response team and remove the LAN administrator from the exercise. Loss of a LAN administrator who knows everything about a system can be devastating.

The need for a communications recovery plan should therefore be presented to technical services staff from the perspective that someone unfamiliar with the system may have to execute the plan. The goal of every organization should be to document its communications recovery plan in a systematic format that can be followed by any reasonably trained technical services personnel, whether they be from a vendor, a rental company, a major supplier, or a carrier company.

DEVELOPING AN INVENTORY OF COMMUNICATIONS HARDWARE

Business continuity personnel need to know several details about the organization's hardware, including:

- type and model number
- software packages residing on the hardware
- software revision numbers
- date of purchase and cost
- criticality to operations
- power requirements

Other helpful items include:

- the name, address, and telephone number of the manufacturer
- the local distributor or depot for the equipment
- the location of secondary-market hardware suppliers, who can be instrumental in providing equipment during a disaster

Exhibit 22-1 provides an example of a hardware inventory form that can aid recovery personnel in making quick command decisions. For example, if a four-year-old piece of equipment is depreciated over a five-year period, recovery personnel may decide to replace rather than to repair it. Such information is extremely useful when many decisions must be made rapidly and under tense circumstances.

A separate inventory should also be kept of all hardware maintained by an organization at a business continuity center. The inventory should contain some fairly minute detail, such as whether the hardware is on a movable rack or requires dollies, and the type of power plug the equipment requires.

MAINTAINING ACCURATE INVENTORIES

The best method for keeping track of hardware necessary for restoring communications is through a process called data importing.

Automated Data Importing

Importing is essentially a means of finding data bases and repositories of information within the organization that are reasonably up to date.

**Exhibit 22-1. Hardware inventory form for emergency replacement
and restoration.**

Component:

_____

Purpose:

_____

Manufacturer:

_____

Serial Number:

_____

Associated Software:

_____

Criticality Rating (1,2,3,4):

_____

Date of Purchase:

_____

Vendor Name and Telephone Number:

_____

Remarks:

_____

For example, when a piece of hardware is purchased, a document or file for the equipment is archived somewhere within the organization. Sometimes, the contract and the documentation for the equipment goes to the accounting department for amortization purposes. In other cases, the files become part of the personal file of the communications manager or analyst. The optimal situation is for them to be stored and accessible on a LAN. In any case, recovery planners should locate and identify these repositories of inventory data so they can be automatically imported into the recovery plan.

There are good reasons for taking this approach. The price of some of today's hardware and the necessity for any mission-critical equipment to be protected by a business continuity plan means that the savvy technical services manager often includes business continuity in the selection criteria for major hardware purchases. Such equipment includes automated call distribution units; Private Branch eXchange; major bridges, routers, and gateways; LAN networks; and mainframe computers. It is much more cost-effective to negotiate roll-in replacement guarantees when a vendor is vying for business than to try to add these services later. Yet, given today's levels of staff turnover, failure to import information on such guarantees and on maintenance contracts into the recovery plan could result in a future LAN manager needlessly paying for a business continuity plan for equipment already protected.

Organizations that make heavy use of internetworked LANs have an advantage because they can automatically transfer files between interconnected departments in several ways without human intervention. For example, when object linking Microsoft Word files, a technical services manager can key in on a specific file name in the accounting department to ensure that updates to a hardware repository file are transferred to the appropriate file in the recovery plan.

Manual Updating

Importing can also be accomplished through a sneaker net — assigning a key person or division to regularly go to the department containing files on equipment, make a floppy disk copy of the appropriate file, and update the recovery plan. But under the pressures of work, busy technologists can easily overlook this task, causing the recovery plan to be dangerously outdated. Updating this way therefore requires that staff realize the importance of the recovery planning process and that the process be enforced, to the point of withholding raises when the task is not performed.

ADDITIONAL COMPONENTS OF AN UP-TO-DATE PLAN

Importing Information on Personnel and Vendors

Up-to-date telephone numbers for personnel and critical equipment vendors are essential to the successful implementation of a business continuity plan. Once again, this means importing data from reliable sources regularly and, preferably, without human intervention.

Consider employees' home telephone numbers, which are found in several places, such as human resources and the company telephone directory. Care must be taken to ensure that the data contained in these sources is up to date. Here again, importing is best done by object linking files together, but it can also be accomplished through use of a sneaker net and floppy disk.

Telephone numbers for key hardware vendors and suppliers can often be found in the network control center, help desk, or other operational environment whose personnel have day-to-day contact with vendors and are often the first to know about changed telephone numbers. Because operations staff are usually regularly involved in escalation procedures, their departments generally document information on second- and third-level management within the vendor community.

Developing an Inventory of Software

Communications recovery planners must also develop an inventory of all software required for operation of mission-critical communications equipment. This inventory should include:

- acquisition date
- original cost
- license number
- version number

Exhibit 22-2 provides an example of a software inventory form.

Equipment Room Diagrams

Equipment room diagrams should show all installed communications hardware and delineate any special environmental specifications such as

Exhibit 22-2. Software inventory form for emergency replacement or restoration.

Software Package:

Purpose:

Supplier Name and Telephone Number:

License Number:

Version Number:

Criticality Rating (1,2,3,4):

Location Where Software Can Be Purchased or Replaced:

Remarks:

Exhibit 22-3. Useful appendices to a business continuity plan.

- Emergency Phone Lists of Management and Recovery Teams
- Vendor Callout and Escalation Lists
- Inventory and Report forms
- Carrier Callout and Escalation Lists
- Maintenance Forms
- Hardware Lists and Serial Numbers
- Software Lists and License Numbers

Team Member Responsibilities
- Network Schematic Diagrams
- Equipment Room Diagrams
- Contract and Maintenance Agreements
- Special Operating Instructions for Sensitive Equipment
- Cellular Telephone Inventory and Agreements

air flow, temperature, and power needs. The diagrams should also outline equipment footprints, clearances, and any other information useful to a network installer. They form part of the appendices that should accompany a thorough recovery plan. See Exhibit 22-3 for a list of the information that should be contained in these appendices.

Importing Components of the Corporatewide Plan

Technical recovery planners should consider importing components of the corporatewide recovery plan dealing with global policy issues. It makes little sense for a technical recovery planner to write procedures for such companywide concerns as loss of a building, physical security, fire and bomb-threat procedures, purchasing, and media affairs. In these cases, the technical recovery planner should direct the reader of the communications recovery plan to the relevant section of the corporate plan. In most cases, the LAN or network recovery plan itself will probably end up being imported into a corporatewide recovery plan for execution by an emergency management team. The process is reciprocal.

Assigning Technical Teams

It is advisable to split a technical recovery plan into numerous subsections managed by technical teams. Such sections include LAN management, voice communications, data communications, and the emergency network control center. Each of these functions has assigned day-to-day responsibilities, and the team assigned to each will have specific responsibilities during a disaster. A network control center or help desk, for example, could take on a very different function in a disaster by helping to maintain command and control.

THE REAL REASONS FOR DISASTER PLANNING

All companies use automated systems to conduct business and all suffer when these systems fail. Whether they are LANs or other communications systems, automated systems should not increase the risk to a company merely because they are convenient. A communications recovery plan should therefore accurately focus on restoring a business'core operations, or the items most crucial to its profitability, in the event of a disaster. Exhibit 22-4 presents the seven R's of a successful business continuityplan.

RECOMMENDED COURSE OF ACTION

A business continuity plan is a complex road map of how to rebuild an organization after a disaster. It should be written for execution by a reasonably well-educated technical person in the event key personnel are unavailable.

A thorough recovery plan includes input from all major vendors, suppliers, and departments and must import data from accurate sources. It should delineate recovery tasks systematically and clearly and strike a balance between cumbersome detail that discourages reading and a cursory explanation understandable only to people familiar with a system.

It can take two years or more to complete a successful recovery plan, but the effort is well worth the protection the plan affords an organization.

Exhibit 4. The seven R's of a successful business continuity plan.

1. Recognition of Need for Planning
   — Protect Human Life.
   — Recover Critical Operations.
   — Protect Competitive Position.
   — Preserve Customer Confidence and Good Will.
   — Protect against Litigation.

2. Response
   — Reacting to Initial Report of a Disaster.
   — Notifying the Police, Fire, and Medical Personnel.
   — Notifying Management.
   — Establishing the Executive Management Team (EMT).
   — Filing Initial Damage Assessment Reports to the EMT.

3. Recovery
   — Assisting the EMT in Preparation of Statements.
   — Opening a Critical Events Log for Auditing Purposes.
   — Using Modified Signing Authority for Equipment Purchases.
   — Obtaining Necessary Cash.
   — Maintaining Physical Security.
   — Arranging Security at the Damaged Site, the Recovery Center, and Emergency Funds Disbursement Centers.

4. Restoration
   — Coordinating Restoration of the Original Site.
   — Restoring Hardware Systems.
   — Restoring Software Systems.
   — Restoring Power, the UPS, and Common Building Systems.
   — Replacing Fire Supression Systems.
   — Securing the Building.
   — Rewiring the Building.
   — Restoring the LAN.
   — Restoring the WAN.

5. Return to Normal Operations
   — Testing New Hardware.
   — Training Operations Personnel.
   — Training Employees.
   — Scheduling Migration Back to the Original Site.
   — Coordinating Return to the Original Site.

6. Rest and Relaxation
   — Scheduling Compensatory Timeoff.

7. Reevaluate and Reassess
   — Reviewing the Critical Events Log.
   — Evaluating Vendor Performance.
   — Recognizing Extraordinary Achievements.
   — Preparing Final Review and Activity Report.
   — Aiding in Liability Assessments.

Chapter 23

Adding Communications Network Support to Existing Business Continuity Plans

Leo A. Wrobel

A BROAD-BASED BUSINESS RECOVERY PLAN MUST ADDRESS THREE CRITI-
CAL COMPONENTS: physical space for employees, connection to information systems essential to the conduct of core business operations, and telecommunications facilities that turn these systems into revenue generators
for the company. There are several ways to dovetail communications systems into an organization's existing business continuity plan for its mainframe computer room.

PHASE 1: BUSINESS RISK ANALYSIS

What the Organization Needs to Protect and Why

This first phase involves preliminary identification of mission-critical
communications systems. It may be necessary to run a series of executives
interviews within the company to identify core business systems as well as
the communications systems that support those activities. Examples
include inbound call centers, customer service lines, engineering or HR
departments, sales departments, and divisions involved in financial filings
for the company.

Management may need to be convinced that recovery planning for the
communications network is an important and essential component of the
overall business recovery plan. A helpful technique is to draft a white

0-8493-0907-7/00/$0.00+$.50
© 2001 by CRC Press LLC

paper assessing the risks to the company and presenting them in nontechnical language that management can understand. To be most effective, a white paper to management should outline the big four areas in which communications systems disruptions cause a loss to the company. These include:

1. lost sales
2. lost market share
3. lost customer confidence
4. loss of productivity

These are all things management can understand and subscribe to. Focusing on these issues will further the cause within the organization.

PHASE 2: UPDATING PROCEDURES

The second phase of a successful communications systems recovery planning effort involves becoming up-to-date in business continuity planning methodologies for the network. IS may want to consider establishing some type of liaison with service providers geared around the business continuity effort. It is also time to talk to related departments within the organization, such as security personnel and facility management, which may already have business continuity plans that network support plans can be rolled into.

Operating and Security Standards

One of the most significant tasks in phase 2 is documenting a set of operating and security standards for communications systems. These standards are essentially the basic operating practices for the network, and they are designed for two reasons.

The first reason is to ensure that disasters are prevented before they happen. Policies and procedures help maintain network integrity and prevent disasters. Standards that prevent disasters include policies on the management of combustibles — for example, no smoking policies, training in the use of fire extinguishers, and standards for change management when making software changes to mission-critical systems such as PBX or multiplexers.

The second reason is to ensure that the emergency procedures dovetail gracefully with the operational environment. By working together, related departments such as IS, computer operations, LAN management, facility management, and others can avoid the perception that they are trying to impose a solution on another department. This approach also ensures continuity between the departments.

The following basic security standards should exist:

236

- Equipment rooms lock and sign-in logs exist for people entering and leaving the area.
- PBX class-of-service indicators are backed up daily and stored off site, similar to procedures in the computer room.
- Passwords are changed frequently for dial-in maintenance access to critical multiplexers, PBXs, and voice mail systems.
- Trash is not permitted to accumulate in equipment room. There is a no smoking policy. Basic housekeeping procedures exist within the equipment room.
- If possible, the equipment room is located in an area other than the basement. Any water problems that develop anywhere within the building will ultimately end up in the basement.
- There are regular surveys of the cable routes between the organization and the local service provider.
- Infrared scanning equipment is used to pick up heat sources within computer or telecommunications rooms and thus help avert fire. Such equipment is available from fire protection contractors and other sources.
- Power is separated from electrical cables. In addition to being a cause of noise and interference, electrical cables in telephone cable racks are also a safety hazard, sometimes leading to catastrophic fires.
- Fire-retardant cable is used in equipment rooms. In addition to the traditional Teflon cable that resists burning, there are also newer materials available, such as Halar, Kevlar, and Stolsis. Permanent virtual circuit, or PVC cable, can burn and produce nauseous fumes. When water is poured on burning Permanent virtual circuit cable, it creates acid compounds that can rapidly destroy equipment.
- Emergency instructions are prominently posted in the PBXs room and adequate command and control exists to send messages rapidly should something go wrong.

An additional checklist of standards is presented in Exhibit 23-1. Other standards are geared specifically toward the recovery process itself. For example, if emergency procedures call for a list of home telephone numbers for employees who need to be called back to work, something must be documented in the operational environment to ensure that list exists in the first place. Responsible people should also be assigned to keep the list up-to-date. Similar policies must be in place for equipment inventories, vendor callout lists, and other components of the emergency plan that rely on the standards to execute properly.

The last part of Phase 2 involves making long-term recommendations for the network. Because it is usually impossible to scrap equipment that is already installed, much of this equipment may have to be phased out over time to allow for business continuity plans. At minimum, specific recom-

Exhibit 23-1. Checklist of communications systems standards.

- Password protection of remote maintenance port dial-in access, DISA, and DATA dial-in.
- Fraud protection on DISA through use of caller ID, DISA, and other methods.
- Smoking ban in effect in equipment room.
- Separate power breakers for sensitive telecommunications equipment.
- Instructions posted for human safety and for graceful equipment shutdown in equipment rooms.
- Back-up power tested frequently.
- Lightning protection where applicable.
- Emergency lighting.
- Equipment room: locked door, sign-in logs, posted emergency procedures.
- Water pipes labeled, under-floor moisture detectors installed, plastic sheeting or drape equipment stored nearby.
- Sign-off procedures for major equipment or software changes.
- Policy of performing back-up before major telecommunications equipment changes.

mendations on long-term network changes to be executed at an appropriate future date should be made.

PHASE 3: DOCUMENTING THE PLAN

A solid, systematic set of business continuity procedures can be summed up using the seven R's of a successful recovery planning process.

Recognition. If a night security guard sees water coming under the door of the equipment room, who does this guard notify, and how, precisely, would the emergency call be routed through an organization?

Instructions should be displayed prominently within the room with call-out numbers for key technologists who may have to respond immediately to a disaster. Procedures might exist, for example, whereby the director of facilities would call the director of technical services in such an event and request an on-site representative. The facilities department must know what steps to take for human safety, such as shutting off power if the equipment appears wet. These and dozens of other issues have to be addressed to ensure that everyone is called quickly and can respond as quickly as possible to any type of facility disaster affecting communications systems.

Response. Once key personnel have been called, what exactly are they needed to do when they arrive on site? One suggested approach is to immediately open a critical-events log.

A critical-events log need not be more complicated than a small notebook or a handheld voice recorder. It is important, however, because many command decisions are going to be made in rapid succession and need to be tracked. This permanent record of command decisions will be useful later, either for assessing liability or for reassessing what went right and what went wrong in the recovery plan.

The name of the game in the response phase is to arrive on-site, execute a successful callout of key personnel and vendors, and make a report to management within 90 minutes or some prespecified time of the disaster, explaining how serious the disaster is, whether it will involve other departments to recover, and providing some estimate of how long it will take to recover, as well as whether a companywide recovery plan should be activated because of the communications system disaster.

Recovery. Getting back to business as soon as possible is the objective. This recovery process should be documented to a level where it involves technical personnel, such as LAN or mainframe personnel, to execute the plan in the event communications personnel are unavailable to effect the recovery process or are injured in the disruption itself.

It is important to note that recovery does not mean restoration of the original equipment; rather, it means restoration of the business process that the equipment provides, even if it is in some type of degraded mode. For example, a large department may have 50 telephones. In a disaster, the plan may be to provide only 25 telephones, but to add a second shift. Not everyone within the organization needs to work 8 to 5. This is why an understanding of the core business is so important to create a flexible and workable recovery plan. Telecommunications personnel will also have to be dispatched at this time to commercial computer recovery or business recovery centers to which the company subscribes.

Restoral. Close interdepartmental coordination is important during the restoral phase of a recovery process. For example, the communications systems manager has certain responsibilities for wiring, but a LAN manager has others, and the facility manager, responsible for electrical power, for example, has still others. These responsibilities should be carefully documented and delineated to ensure the correct type of wiring is installed.

Return to Normal Operations. When the emergency is over, it is then time to tear down any emergency configuration and go back to business as usual. If the recovery center is stable and operating, and the revenue stream of the company is firmly established, all new configurations still must be adequately tested before migrating back to the original site. This includes documenting in the recovery plan what constitutes a successful test before going back to the original network configuration.

Rest and Relax. Needless to say, after responding to a disaster, employees will be tired and stressed out and probably at their wit's end. Therefore, it is important to schedule compensatory timeoff so the staff can get some rest after what could have been several days or weeks of 12-hour shifts.

Regroup and Reassess. After any execution of the communications systems recovery plan, whether it is a test or a full-blown recovery implementation, it is important to go back and reassess how effectively the procedures worked and make adjustments within the plan. This is part of the reason for the critical-events log during the recognition phase of the recovery effort. Adjustments that are made after tests or activation of the plan strengthen the plan in the long run, so that it can be expected to execute more flawlessly the next time.

Other considerations in a successful communications systems recovery plan include:

- *Defining a meeting place to coordinate recovery activity.* This could be any suitable real estate located off-site. It should also be equipped with a small contention of telephones, fax machines, and supplies, and serve as the focal point for command and control for recovery activity. It may also house the emergency management team (EMT) that coordinates the overall disaster response.
- *Defining an emergency management team of executives for communications systems disasters, and appropriate recovery teams for both the on-site and off-site recovery processes.* Teams and their designed back-ups should be defined for:
  — dispatch to a recovery facility
  — coordination of on-site recovery activities
  — retrieval of off-site magnetic media
  — administrative functions
- *Keeping employee callout lists and home telephone numbers current.* The best way to do this is to import them, perhaps over a LAN, from known reliable sources, such as human resources.
- *Establishing procedures for maintaining human life and safety when reentering damaged facilities.* These would be procedures such as immediately shutting off power and other precautions before entering a damaged facility.

- *Keeping an inventory of all equipment that will be required for the recovery process and all equipment installed on-site.* One way of doing this is to establish a liaison with the accounting department. Whenever new equipment is purchased and accounting receives a copy of the contract for the equipment purchased, accounting could be asked to update a database with such information as the equipment's serial number, software revision number, date of purchase, and number of months the equipment is amortized. In a disaster, this list can be created quickly and used as the basis for fast command decisions on whether to scrap or attempt to save damaged equipment, depending on when it was purchased and what the original price was.

Lastly, be sure the plan adequately defines the roles between communications systems personnel and those from other departments, such as LAN management, operations, and facilities, to ensure coordination during a recovery implementation. Procedures on where to get cash, how to arrange travel, and how to purchase new equipment, for example, may be documented already within the organization by one of these other groups; these procedures can be adopted in the communications systems plan.

CONCLUSION

This chapter has reviewed the processes that must be documented in a successful communications systems recovery plan. The most important component of the plan is its ability to bring various departments within the organization together to ensure a seamless recovery process and a flawless execution of a companywide recovery plan. Whether the disaster is confined to the communications systems (in which case IS must recover on its own) or is a companywide disaster (in which case the department becomes a supporting player), the level of detail in the recovery plan directly influences how well it executes and how well protected the assets of the company are. In short, a detailed communications systems recovery plan equates to a higher level of network services and greater peace of mind to the company.

Section V
Maintenance and Testing of Business Continuity Plans

Chapter 24
Strategies for Developing and Testing Business Continuity Plans

Kenneth A. Smith

BECAUSE OF THE INCREASING DEPENDENCE OF BUSINESSES ON THEIR INFORMATION, PLANNING FOR THE RECOVERY OF AN INTERRUPTION TO IT FUNCTIONS HAS BECOME A TOP PRIORITY. In the past, companies focused solely on recovery of their large mainframe centers. Now, with information spread throughout the organization, a more comprehensive form of recovery planning and testing is essential. Comprehensive business recovery solutions must include not only large systems recovery but the recovery and testing of midrange systems, networks, and work groups. This chapter presents steps for developing and testing a comprehensive business resumption plan. It reviews specific plan development stages, testing objectives, and actual testing approaches. Finally, it offers basic guidelines and recommendations for a test plan that helps to ensure business continuity.

Comprehensive business resumption planning is growing beyond the walls of the data center. Business's growing dependence on multiple computing platforms and increasingly sophisticated communications networks is making companies more vulnerable to disaster. Actual disasters are highlighting the importance and vulnerability of distributed computing systems, even while mainframe recovery is becoming more reliable. Business continuity must address these evolving integrated and networked business environments.

Public awareness of the need for comprehensive business recovery is on the rise as well, probably largely because of the increase in major regional catastrophes during the past few years. The public sector is also getting involved, with increasing federal, state, and local government participation in comprehensive disaster planning.

Companies are reacting to this need by developing enterprisewide business continuity plans but are discovering a host of problems associated with comprehensive business recovery planning. These plans require far more participation on the part of management and support organizations than mainframe recovery planning. The scope is no longer limited to recovery; plans must integrate with existing disaster prevention and mitigation programs. These companywide resumption plans are costly to develop and maintain and are frequently prolonged, problematic, and unsuccessful.

Fortunately, there have been successes from which security specialists can learn. This chapter presents some of the lessons learned, including some of the tools, techniques, and strategies that have proved effective.

COMPREHENSIVE BUSINESS RECOVERY STRATEGIES

Successful recovery from disaster often depends on workable and timely alternative operating recovery strategies. A well-known set of recovery strategies, including some simple and relatively inexpensive commercial products and services, has made recovery planning feasible for large-scale mainframes and midrange computers. New solutions are becoming increasingly available for small computer configurations and business resumption (e.g., work group) recovery. These evolving solutions are based on experiences gained from a multitude of single-site and regional disasters.

Formal recovery planning and testing is an essential part of the total recovery solution. Companies that develop, maintain, and regularly test their business resumption plans recover far better and faster than those that are not prepared.

Exhibit 24-1 illustrates the scope needed for a companywide business continuity program. Business resumption should be thought of as an ongoing program, much like existing avoidance programs (e.g. security) and loss-mitigation programs (e.g. insurance).

Resumption planning is moving into departmental work groups. Executive management and the support organizations are also taking part in business resumption through integrated crisis incident management planning.

Numerous planning tools and strategies are available to help companies develop plans. The tools include commercially available software, consulting services, and several public-domain information sources. These tools and services are invaluable in reducing the effort, elapsed time, and cost involved in developing business resumption plans.

Exhibit 24-1. Scope of the companywide business continuity program.

Before discussing how to develop a plan, it would be useful to review the available strategies for both computer and work group recovery. The following sections examine these strategies.

Mainframe Systems

The choice of which mainframe recovery strategy to follow is based primarily on business recovery timing requirements, cost, and reliability. Hot sites are fast becoming the recovery strategy of choice for companies requiring rapid recovery. The commercial hot site is second only to an internally owned redundant site in terms of reliability and timing, and usually at less than 10 percent to 30 percent of the annual cost. In some areas (e.g., disaster support and telecommunications infrastructure), hot sites can actually provide a more reliable strategy than an internally owned redundant facility.

The potential strategies for mainframe and midrange computer recovery (discussed in the next section) are listed in Exhibit 24-2. Most organizations use multiple strategies, depending on the severity of the disaster and expected outage duration. During planning, different strategies may be identified for different applications, depending on the potential business consequences.

The recovery time frames in Exhibit 24-2 do not imply either minimum or maximum times; these figures represent actual company experiences following disaster. For example, in two recorded examples of a total data center loss, the rebuilding time was 6 months for one company and 12 months for the other. Most recoveries using commercial hot sites have been accomplished within 8 to 24 hours.

247

Exhibit 24-2. Mainframe and midrange recovery strategies.

Strategy	Recovery Time Frame	Advantages	Disadvantages
Repair or Rebuild at Time of Disaster	6-12 months	• Least cost	• Time to recover, reliability, and testability
Cold Site (private or commercial)	1-6 weeks	• Cost-effective • Time to recover	• Testability • Detail plans are difficult to maintain • Long-term maintenance costs
Reciprocal agreement	1-3 days	• Useful for specialized equipment in low- volume applications	• Not legally acceptable in some • environments Testability
Service Bureau	1-3 days	• For contingency planning (e.g. backup microfilm)	• Not available in large CPU environments
Shippable or Transportable Equipment	1-3 days	• Useful for midrange computing	• Logistical difficulties in regional business continuity
Commercial Hot Site	Less than 1 day	• Testability	• Regional disaster • Long-term commitment and integrity

When costs for mainframe recovery strategies are analyzed, it is important to realistically estimate personnel and equipment costs. In addition, the strategies should be planned out over a minimum three-to-five year period to ensure that the cost of maintaining and upgrading equipment is considered. Equipment resources for mainframe strategies should be defined at a fairly detailed level, because the cost of the incidental infrastructure and network can significantly affect actual costs.

Evaluating potential hot-site or cold-site recovery vendors is less clear-cut. Quality of service is most important but difficult to evaluate. Decisions are often made on the basis of technical and pricing criteria.

Midrange Systems

Effective business resumption planning requires that midrange systems be evaluated with the same thoroughness used with mainframes. The criticality of the midrange applications is frequently underestimated. For example, an analysis of one financial institution found that all securities investment records had been moved to a midrange system previously limited to word processing. Because it was viewed as office support, this system's data was not protected off site. Its loss would have meant serious if not irreparable damage to this company and its investors.

Midrange systems share the same list of potential recovery strategies as mainframes. In addition, shippable and transportable recovery alternatives may be feasible.

Cold-site and repair or replacement recovery timeframes can be much shorter for midrange systems (e.g., days instead of weeks), because many systems do not require extensive facility conditioning. However, care should be taken to ensure that this is true for specific systems. Some systems are documented as not needing significant conditioning but do not perform well in nonconditioned environments.

Special considerations should be given to turnkey system. Turnkey software vendors often do not package business continuity backup and off-site rotation with their systems. On the other hand, other turnkey vendors provide business continuity strategies as an auxiliary or additional cost service.

Companies using midrange systems frequently have mixed hardware and network platforms requiring a variety of recovery strategies and vendors. When recovery strategies are being evaluated, some cost savings can be realized if all of the midrange systems are considered at the same time. Another planning consideration unique to the midrange environment is the limited availability of in-house technical expertise. Recovery at the time of the disaster often requires people with extensive skills in networking, environmental conditioning, and systems support. A single hardware vendor may not be able to supply these skills in the mixed platform environments.

In an evaluation of the recovery timing strategy, special attention should be given to recovery timing issues on midrange systems. Some platforms are notoriously slow in restoring data.

Work Group Systems

The computer recovery strategies can be borrowed and adapted to work group recovery planning. However, the optimum choices frequently differ because of the different technical and logistical issues involved. As a result, numerous commercially available products and services are becoming available for work group recovery.

Exhibit 24-3. Work group recovery strategies.

Strategy	Recovery Time Frame	Advantages
Repair or Rebuild at Time of Disaster	1-3 days	• Ongoing cost for office space and equipment
Shippable or Transportable Equipment	1-3 days	• Ease of use • Reliability
Hot Site or Cold Site	Immediate	• Testability
Reciprocal Agreement	1-3 days	• Useful for specialized equipment in low-volume applications
Service Bureau	1-3 days	• Useful for daily contingency planning
Redundant Facility	Immediate	• Greatest reliability

Strategy	Disadvantages	Comments
Repair or Rebuild at Time of Disaster	• Availability risk	Rent space and buy replacement equipment Limited availability of special equipment and space
Shippable or Transportable Equipment	• Ongoing cost	Use commercial products and services
Hot Site or Cold Site	• Availability in regional disaster	Use commercial backup office space
Reciprocal Agreement	• Limited application capacity	Arrange office space (internal) and specialized facilities (external)
Service Bureau	• Not available for large CPU environments	Use commercial services (e.g., print shops and microfilm companies)
Redundant Facility	• High cost • Long-term commitment and integrity	Internal use only

The goal of work group recovery planning is to re-establish essential day-to-day business functions before the consequential effects occur. To accomplish this, most organizations find it necessary to relocate their employees to an alternative location or to relocate the work itself. Exhibit 24-3 lists the most common work group strategies.

In addition to these alternative operating strategies, work group planning has some unique and difficult computer recovery challenges. Businesses' dependence on desktop computing is growing far faster and with less control then did their dependence on mainframe and midrange systems. Disaster experiences are showing that many businesses are absolutely dependent on these systems and that the degree of disaster awareness and preparation is seriously and dangerously lacking.

Desktop Computers and Local Area Networks

Currently, the most common method of information protection is to back up data at a file server level and accept the business risk of the loss of microcomputer workstation data. In actual disasters, many companies have been found to be inadequately protecting their microcomputer-based information. The ultimate solution for desktop and local area network (LAN) information recovery rests in two major areas: standards and standards enforcement.

Planning for LAN recovery is made more difficult by the absence of standardized backup devices. Backup device technology changes frequently and is not always downward compatible. Some companies have found it difficult to acquire older compatible technology at the time of a disaster. Redundant equipment and meticulous testing may be the only feasible solution.

Technological obsolescence must be considered in any long-term LAN recovery strategy. Equipment purchased and stored off site (e.g., redundant strategy) rapidly becomes obsolete. Reciprocal agreements require that hardware remain compatible over time, which is often difficult.

An even more difficult planning consideration is network wiring. Companies are wiring their buildings with special network facilities (e.g., IBM Token Ring and Ethernet), making relocation to dissimilar facilities difficult. Companies with multiple facilities (e.g., campus environments) can sometimes use reciprocal arrangements if capacities are sufficient. In the absence of these facilities or in a regional disaster, shippable microcomputers that include preinstalled network capabilities are the safest alternative.

Lack of industry-standard communications hardware is a problem in local and wide area network recovery, making rapid replacement at the time of the disaster risky. Several shippable products (e.g., shippable bridges and gateways) are commercially available to assist local and wide area network recovery. When these tools are unavailable, stockpiling of redundant equipment is usually the only recourse.

Wide Area Networks

Business continuity planning for WANs is still in its infancy. Even though few companies are addressing recovery of wide area network, these networks are often installed to support vital business missions. For example, they are being installed to support such mission-critical functions as LAN-resident business applications, Electronic Data Interchange, and gateways to mainframes.

Recovery of a wide area network is primarily a network planning issue. WANs are typically connected using communications lines with massive bandwidth capabilities. Typically, the same type of network solutions for large mainframe-based networks are available for wide area network connections. Unfortunately, that massive bandwidth can also equate to large network expense.

Networking

That the communications infrastructure (both voice and data) is essential to daily business operations is well understood and accepted. Business impact studies have shown that networks must be restored in most locations at near-full production capacities, usually in a very short time. Some companies have found that the need for voice and data communications is actually higher than normal during a disaster.

Network recovery strategy decisions are driven by business timing requirements, choice of alternative processing decisions for computer recovery, work group recovery, and cost. The technical strategies and the menu of products and services are far too complicated to discuss here; however, the network strategy planning criteria are quite simple to describe.

Simply stated, network recovery strategies should address all technology and facilities required to reestablish connectivity. This includes person-to-person, person-to-computer, and computer-to-computer connections. All network components should be addressed and appropriate strategies decided on. For most components, the same recovery strategies previously described for computer and work group recovery can be applied.

The following sections discuss some of the special requirements of work group facilities and communications equipment.

Work Group Facility. Loss of a work group facility requires replacing all equivalent network components. These include telephones, terminals, control units, modems, LAN network wiring, and the PBX. These may be obtained at time of disaster using replacement or shippable strategies. They may already be in place in an existing redundant, reciprocal, or commercial hot-site or cold-site facility. The same set of planning issues and network business continuity strategies can be employed.

Access to Communications. A disaster may affect the communications infrastructure outside the work group facility (e.g., loss of phone lines or a central office). In this case, an entirely different set of strategies comes into play.

Two possible recovery strategies can be used: relocating to an alternative facility in which the infrastructure is in place or reconnecting to the surviving infrastructure through alternative facilities. Because of timing, these alternative communications facilities are usually redundant and can be quite expensive.

Electronic Vaulting. Electronic vaulting has gained wide attention as a business continuity strategy. Electronic vaulting allows critical information to be stored off site through means of a network transfer rather than traditional backup and off-site rotation. Electronic vaulting brings two major benefits: decreased loss of data and shortened recovery windows.

Commercial business continuity vendors provide both remote transaction journaling and database shadowing services. Several companies with multiple computer sites are using electronic vaulting internally on a variety of computer platforms. Electronic archiving is becoming fairly common in the microcomputer arena. Although use has been limited because of significant hardware and communications costs, these costs are expected to decline, making electronic vaulting more attractive in the future.

A DEVELOPMENT APPROACH

Presented in Exhibit 24-4 is a graphical representation of a simple but effective three-phase approach for developing a business resumption plan. The foundation phase of the development methodology is identification of business continuity business requirements. Once these requirements are fully understood, appropriate recovery strategy planning can be conducted. Finally, detailed resumption plans, or action plans, may be developed and documented. All three of these recovery phases involve the surrounding elements of personnel, recovery, resources, and planned recovery action.

Project Planning and Management

Before the first planning phase can be initiated, some thought should be given to project planning and management. Two of the first crucial activities

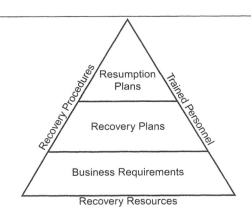

Exhibit 24-4. Recovery planning phases and elements.

within project planning are clearly defining the scope of the project and enlisting management support.

In larger companies (e.g., those with more than 500 to 1,000 employees), the sheer magnitude of the task may justify staging work group recovery planning. Usually computer business continuity planning should be done before or at the same time as work group recovery planning. The business requirements phase helps identify the areas that need to be planned first as determined by the consequences of losing those organizations.

Important business decisions must be made during the planning process regarding preparedness and eventual recovery issues. Active management support throughout the planning process is essential if the planning project is to be successful.

The success of the project is affected by selection of the development project team and distribution of planning responsibilities. Care should be taken to select a qualified project leader. The skills needed for an effective project manager or business resumption planner include:

- extensive large project management skills
- a thorough understanding of records and data protection concepts
- a basic understanding of network concepts and recovery capabilities
- outstanding communication skills, both written and verbal
- knowledge of business resumption concepts

Delegating responsibility for planning to individual work groups usually is not practical. Because of the learning curve and documentation skills, it is more cost-effective to lend a specific work group these skills in the form of a qualified project manager. In addition, many recovery planning decisions involve centralized strategy planning (e.g., determining how the voice network will be recovered or how the replacement of office equipment and departmental computers will be replaced), which would be better managed by a centralized project team.

On the other hand, some planning activities are more effective conducted at the individual work group level. For example, inventorying of equipment resources, identifying minimum acceptable configurations, and identifying specific implementation requirements are all handled best by departmental management. Responsibility for maintaining the recovery capability must remain the individual work group's responsibility because it must use the plan when a disaster occurs.

The following sections discuss the three phases of developing the business resumption plan.

Defining the Business Requirements

Once the project plan has been developed, actual business resumption planning can begin. The first and most essential step in this process is to gain an understanding of the business recovery requirements — that is, determining which functions must be recovered and when.

The business impact is often intuitively obvious without a formal analysis. For example, loss of a reservation system is a catastrophic event to an airline company. Other businesses and functions may need to conduct a formal Business Impact Analysis to quantify the potential impact and timing requirements. In either case, it is necessary to understand the consequences and timing of the negative business impact of a disaster to each work group. Most of the negative effects on the business develop in spurts over time. For example, an outage of a few hours may be acceptable, but cessation of business operations for a few days may be intolerable.

The business impact may be quantified in tangible values, such as revenue (e.g., income), loss of assets (e.g., warehouse shrinkage), or lost sales(e.g., underwriting support). The impact may also be intangible, affecting such areas as company reputation, client satisfaction, and employee morale.

Gathering and analyzing business impact information and the current level of preparedness is best done by the project management team working with work group management. Care should be exercised to identify the appropriate level of management; the size of the organization often dictates the level of analysis. Questionnaires should be used sparingly; besides the obvious difficulty in getting responses, questionnaire responses almost always miss unique characteristics and effects on some work groups.

Selecting Appropriate Recovery Strategies

Once the business recovery timing requirements are understood, the choice of an appropriate recovery strategy becomes a business risk issue rather than an emotional issue. Recovery strategies vary by cost and the speed at which business operations can be resumed. Recovery strategies providing very fast recovery (e.g., redundant facilities) are usually expensive. At the other end of the scale, strategies for replacement at the time of the disaster may lower ongoing costs but can take considerably longer. The choice of recovery strategies must weigh the potential impact from loss of the business functions, relative timing of the impact, and the cost of protection compared to the business risk.

Once the business recovery timing requirements are understood, a company can immediately eliminate those strategies that do not meet the business needs. The remaining strategies can then be analyzed on the basis of their relative merits and costs, resulting in an informed business decision.

It is important to note that companies always make a decision about recovery strategies. Companies without a formal recovery plan have implicitly chosen to use either a repair and rebuild strategy or a do not recover strategy, depending on how successful they are at identifying and storing essential data off site.

It is important to determine all strategies, not just the alternative computer processing strategy. For example, recovery of the voice network, the level of detailed planning, and the degree of training are all strategy issues that must be considered. As these recovery strategy decisions are weighed and decisions made (either explicitly or implicitly), these decisions should be documented along with the reasons for reaching the decision. Finally, any resulting exposures should be documented.

Developing Detailed Resumption Plans

The final phase of business resumption planning is the detailed resumption planning. Planning must address all three recovery elements: personnel, recovery resources, and recovery actions. A common mistake is to focus on personnel and recovery resource planning and to overlook planning and documenting the actual business resumption activities needed to resume operations.

Planning is best done in a series of working sessions conducted jointly by the project team and work group management. Testing is an integral part of the development process. Each of the following steps represents a work group planning session:

Step 1: Formulating the strategy
Step 2: Analyzing the implementation
Step 3: Validating the implementation
Step 4: Approving the recovery plans

The project team may assist the work groups in carrying out these steps. In addition, the project team is responsible for much of the preparatory work for these steps, because these team members have more knowledge of business continuity and more experience in writing plans. The work groups bring special knowledge of their particular areas to the planning process. The following sections discuss these steps in more detail.

Formulating the Strategy. The work group must review the business requirements and high-level recovery strategies and then formulate implementation plans and strategies. As a result of this planning session, recovery management and logistical issues will be defined and documented.

Analyzing the Implementation. A workflow analysis is a useful tool with which to conduct this planning. By reviewing how work is processed on a daily basis, the work group can identify which recovery actions would be required to recreate this environment in an alternative operating location.

Detailed planning should identify those individuals responsible for managing the recovery process. In addition, any key technical resources (internal or external) necessary for effecting recovery should be identified and documented within the recovery plan.

Logistical arrangements and administrative activities must be clearly documented in a plan. A frequent complaint of companies recovering from a disaster is that the logistical and administrative activities, particularly in regard to personnel, are inadequately planned.

Testing should be considered in planning the recovery activities. Resources should be documented in such a way that their presence may be validated during exercises. Information resources (e.g., vendor contacts and emergency phone numbers) should be usable during exercises.

Validating the Implementation. Once plans have been defined and documented, they should be validated through testing. This can be done in a manual exercise of the plan, comparing the plan's recovery actions against a hypothetical disaster scenario. Following this validation, iterative implementation planning sessions may be required.

Approving the Recovery Plans. In each step, recovery strategies, actions, and resources are documented. As a final step, the plans should be formally reviewed, accepted, and turned over from the project team to the respective work groups.

TESTING THE PLAN

There is no surer way to turn a business continuity manual into waste paper than to fail to frequently and periodically test the plan. Testing is critical in the development and ongoing maintenance of business resumption plans.

There are five important reasons why business resumption plans should be tested periodically. These reasons apply equally to traditional mainframe and midrange planning and work group recovery planning. The reasons are:

- Testing proves whether the recovery plan works and whether it can meet the business's recovery requirements.
- Testing the plan identifies the weak links in the plan, allowing them to be corrected before the plan is actually needed.
- Testing the plan is the primary employee training tool. Frequent testing of the plan enhances employees' familiarity with the strategies and implementation process and also raises general awareness levels.
- Periodic testing is necessary to comply with legal and regulatory requirements for many organizations. Although this is especially

relevant in the banking industry and some insurance companies, it is fast becoming a de facto regulatory requirement for all industries.

- Testing is a prudent business practice. The testing program protects the initial development investment, reduces ongoing maintenance costs, and protects the company by ensuring that the plan will work when a disaster occurs.

Testing is a universal term used in the business continuity industry. Unfortunately, testing has a negative pass/fail connotation carried over from school days. The term *testing* would be better replaced by such terms as *exercising* or *rehearsing*. Finding problems during a test should not be viewed as failure when it is really the basic reason for conducting the exercise. Attention should be focused on the positive, not the punitive. For the testing program to be successful, this attitude should be carefully communicated to employees.

Testing Approaches

An effective testing program requires different types of tests to cost-effectively examine all components of the plan. For the purposes of this discussion, testing can be categorized into four types:

1. *Desk checking or auditing.* The availability of required recovery resources can be validated through an audit or desk check approach. This type of test should be used periodically to verify stored, off-site resources and the availability of planned time-of-disaster acquisitions. Unfortunately, desk checking or auditing is limited to validating the existence of resources and may not adequately identify whether other resources are required.
2. *Simulations by walkthroughs.* Personnel training and resource validation can be performed by bringing recovery participants together and conducting a simulated exercise or plan. A hypothetical scenario is presented, and the participants jointly review the recovery procedures but do not actually invoke recovery plans. This type of exercise is easy to conduct, inexpensive, and effective in verifying that the correct resources are identified. More important, this testing approach helps train recovery personnel and validate the recovery actions through peer appraisal.
3. *Real-time testing.* Real-time testing is frequently done on the mainframe or hot-site backup plan and is gaining popularity in work group recovery planning. Real-time testing provides the greatest degree of assurance but is the most time-consuming and expensive approach. If only limited real-time testing is planned, priority should be given to high-risk areas.
4. *Mock surprise testing.* Surprise tests are a variation of the other three approaches but with the added dimension of being unanticipated.

This type of test is frequently discussed but rarely used. The inconvenience for personnel and the negative feelings it generates tend to outweigh its advantages. The benefits derived from a mock surprise disaster can be achieved by careful attention and implementation of controls to avoid the possibility of cheating during planned exercises.

These testing approaches can be combined into an unlimited variety of tests. For example, walkthroughs can be extended by actually performing some recovery activities (e.g., notifying vendors). Training facility equipment can be used to test replace-at-time-of-disaster strategies, alleviating the need to actually purchase replacement computers, desks, tables, and chairs.

A Matrix Approach to Testing

An orderly and organized approach to testing is necessary to ensure that all recovery strategies and components are being adequately validated. A matrix approach may be used to ensure that all plan components were adequately considered, as determined by their level of importance (e.g., business impact) and risk (e.g., reliability and complexity of recovery strategy). The matrix presented in Exhibit 24-5 illustrates this concept.

In this approach, one or more tests are identified for each component of the plan. The organization can develop a long-range (e.g., two-year) test program during which each element and component of the plan is verified or validated. The test program can then be reviewed and revised periodically (e.g., annually) on the basis of testing results, identified exposures, and training requirements.

Work groups testing approaches and frequency depend on the complexity of the organization. For ease of testing and awareness purposes, some plans may be separated and tested by phase (e.g., test alert notification and alternative-site restoration). In general, technical resources (e.g., computer systems or network recovery) require frequent real-time testing. Work group computing needs occasional real-time testing to ensure that the recovery strategies work when they are needed.

Some departments (e.g., outside sales and long-term strategic planning) have fairly low risk in recovery, allowing less rigorous testing to be done. Process-oriented departments (e.g., order processing, credit and collections, and plant scheduling) have greater risk and recovery complexities, justifying more frequent personnel training and recovery testing.

Conducting the Test: Guidelines and Techniques

There are several important ground rules that must be followed in developing a testing program. These are discussed in the following sections.

Exhibit 24-5. Test planning matrix.

TEST PLAN

PLAN RECOVERY COMPONENTS	Type of Test	Frequency of Testing	Comments
Crisis Management			
Data Center			
–Phase 1			
–Phase 2			
–Phase 3			
Work Group 1			
Work Group 2			
Work Group 3			
:			
Work Group n			

Limit Test Preparation. Test preparation should be limited to developing a test disaster scenario, scheduling test dates and times, and defining any exceptions to the plan. Exceptions should be limited to defining the test scope (e.g., testing only the notification component) or resource acquisition (e.g., substituting a training center for rented office space). Actual testing should follow the documented recovery procedures.

Avoid Cheating. An independent observer should be identified for each recovery test. Controls should be put in place to ensure that only resources identified in the recovery plans are used for the recovery effort. Exceptions to the recovery plan should be noted for subsequent follow-up. The object of limiting cheating is not to be punitive but to ensure that all activities and essential resources have been identified and will be available at time of disaster.

Document and Communicate Test Results. The results of the recovery test should always be documented, including follow-up activities, when possible. Corrective actions should be identified, responsibilities defined, and dates set.

Test results should be communicated to the participants and management in a positive manner. Successes should be clearly documented and recognition given to those contributing to the success. Likewise, identified problems should be stated in a positive manner with emphasis on the corrective actions.

Test Information Reconstruction. Difficulties in data restoration and recreation are usually discovered only through real-time testing. The off-site storage facility should be periodically audited to ensure that backups are present and safely stored. The ability to restore should be tested using the actual off-site backup media. When information recreation depends on other facilities (e.g., paper in branch offices or microfilm at the off-site vault), the ability to access this information should be verified. Sufficient volume should be tested to ensure that recovery actions are effective at production volumes.

RECOMMENDED COURSE OF ACTION

To develop an effective and comprehensive business resumption plan, companies should take advantage of the lessons learned from other companies and should approach disaster planning from a business perspective as well as a technical perspective. The course of action depends on the status of the organization's current business continuity plans and business priorities.

The following steps summarize how a company should expand its current plans into a comprehensive business resumption plan:

- Conducting realistic and critical evaluation of the current recovery program. This evaluation should clearly define the status of the entire business resumption plan scope, including incident crisis management, computer business continuity, and work group business resumption.
- Developing a project plan to expand the current program, using the development guidelines presented in this chapter. This involves:
  — Analyzing the business's recovery requirements.
  — Adopting appropriate recovery strategies to meet the recovery requirements.
  — Developing detailed recovery action plans necessary to implement the proposed recovery strategies.
- Developing an ongoing testing, training, and maintenance program for the business resumption plan.

Chapter 25
Maintenance and Update of Business Continuity Plans

Ken Doughty

EXECUTIVE MANAGEMENT'S COMMITMENT AND SUPPORT FOR A BUSINESS CONTINUITY PLAN (BCP) DOES NOT JUST MEAN ISSUING A POLICY ON BCP AND FUNDING ITS INITIAL DEVELOPMENT. Management commitment and support extends not only to developing the infrastructure for the implementation of the policy and ongoing maintenance of the plan, but also includes the on-going provision of critical resources (financial and human).

The infrastructure for updating the plan includes providing the necessary lines of communication to ensure that all changes in the organization that may have an impact on the BCP are communicated to the employee (e.g., BCP coordinator) charged with the responsibility of maintaining and updating the plan.

Too often, maintenance of the BCP is seen as an impost onto an often overloaded employee's existing duties. This is one of the main causes why the BCP is not updated — it is competing with the day-to-day duties of the employee.

BCP MAINTENANCE REGIME

Step 1: BCP Plan Ownership

A fundamental premise of successful business continuity planning is that plans should be owned by those who must actually carry them out in the event of an actual disaster. Unless ownership is assigned, any plans that are developed will not remain up-to-date, thereby increasing the risk to the organization of not recovering in a cost-effective and timely manner in the event of "disaster."

There are a various ways of assigning ownership of the BCP; for example:

- corporate
- business unit
- business process (or function)
- business application

Further, consideration is also to be given to the complexity of the BCP; that is, whether there are a number of BCPs within the organization (i.e., decentralized).

The decision to assign BCP ownership should be made at the executive level. This decision should be embodied in the organization's BCP policy. Additionally, to ensure compliance with the policy, a key performance indicator (KPI) should be designated for the maintenance and update of the BCP. This KPI will then be one of the measures to monitor the performance of each manager within the organization.

Once the BCP ownership has been defined, the assignment of the responsibility for development, maintenance, and testing of the plan(s) must be given due consideration by executive management. The organizational employee(s) charged with the responsibility of maintaining the plan(s) should be at a level of management that reflects the organizational commitment to BCP. This will also facilitate pro-active action being taken by subordinate managers in the execution of BCP maintenance.

Step 2: Sensitivity Analysis of BCP

A sensitivity analysis of the BCP needs to be undertaken on a regular basis to identify the elements that may be the subject of potential change. Exhibit 25-1 displays the elements that would be most sensitive to change.

Exhibit 25-1. Elements more sensitive to a change.

Element	Potential Source of Change
BCP strategy	Corporate/business unit plans
BCP decision-makers	Reorganization (structural changes)
BCP resourcing	Financial budget
BCP recovery team members	Staff turnover
BCP procedures	Various
Service level agreements	Change in service providers

The BCP coordinator needs to determine the change indicators and develop procedures to ensure that when the indicators are "set off," that the nature and timing of the changes are communicated in a timely manner.

Step 3: Amendment/Update of BCP

Upon receipt of communication that changes are to occur, or have occurred, that have an impact on the current BCP, the BCP coordinator needs to develop an action plan (i.e., identify tasks, prioritize tasks and timetable for the development/implementation of tasks) to update the BCP.

Depending on the size of the organization, the complexity of the BCP infrastructure (i.e., corporate/business unit BCPs) and the nature of the changes to the plan may require the BCP coordinator to establish a project (i.e., create a project mandate, funding, resourcing etc.).

It is important that sufficient time be allowed to develop the BCP amendments to facilitate the review of the amendments by the stakeholders before the BCP is updated, including testing, revision, publication, and distribution of the BCP. This is to ensure that the amendments are practical, fully understood by the BCP recovery team members, and easy to implement in the event of disaster.

Step 4: BCP Maintenance Schedule

An up-to-date BCP will provide a reasonable amount of assurance in the event of disaster that the organization will minimize the affects of a disaster to allow the organization to carry out, in some semblance of "normal" operations, while in recovery mode. Therefore, it is important that maintenance schedules and review procedures be developed and implemented.

The BCP coordinator should develop a maintenance schedule and associated procedures that include:

- corporate plan and business unit plan review
- risk management program review
- update of the business impact analysis
- sensitivity analysis of the BCP
- BCP gap analysis
- BCP procedures review
- third-party service providers agreement reviews
- BCP module testing
- BCP module testing results review
- update of the BCP from the BCP module testing

The results of the tasks undertaken in implementing the maintenance schedule should be communicated to executive management to ensure accountability of the BCP ownership function within the organization. Executive management should ensure that it receives regular reports (corporate governance) from the BCP owners.

Further, the organization's auditors (internal or external) should also undertake a review of the BCP(s) to ensure that the assertions (reports) of its BCP owners are up-to-date and accurate. Acquittance by the auditors that the BCP is up-to-date will support the premise that executive management has undertaken its fiduciary duties.

FORMULATION OF CHANGE CONTROL PROCEDURES

The BCP coordinator is required to periodically (at least annually) update the Business Impact Analysis (BIA) to determine that the BCP strategy is appropriate. Part of this process is to review the corporate and business planning process to assist in identifying potential risks resulting from planned changes to the organization's business environment.

Step 1: Review the Corporate and Business Plans
(Including the Strategic Information Technology Plan)

Today, organizations undertake the development of a corporate plan that provides the roadmap for the organization in the achievement of its mission, goals, and objectives, and details the strategies in the achievement of these objectives (see Exhibit 25-2). The corporate plan broadly details the organization's mission statement, strategic objectives, strategies for a defined period (generally two to five years), KPIs, and S.W.O.T. (Strengths, Weaknesses, Opportunities and Threats) analysis. As part of this planning process, the organization's business units develop business plans to support the organization in the achievement of its goals and objectives.

It is essential that the BCP coordinator be involved in the development of the corporate and business plans. This involvement should extend to identifying the impact on the organization's BCP(s) of the planned implementation of the macro and micro strategies by the organization and its business units. The rationale for BCP coordinators to be involved in the planning phase is that they can identify the risk and quantify the exposure that planned strategies will have on the organization's current and future BCP(s).

If the BCP coordinator is not involved in the planning phase, it is possible that the projected benefit to the organization of implementing a specific strategy may not only be outweighed by the cost of changing the BCP strategy, but also threaten the likelihood of recovery if disaster should strike the organization or its strategic trading partner(s).

There are a number of strategies that will impact the current BCP and its maintenance in the future. For example, the organization may be planning to:

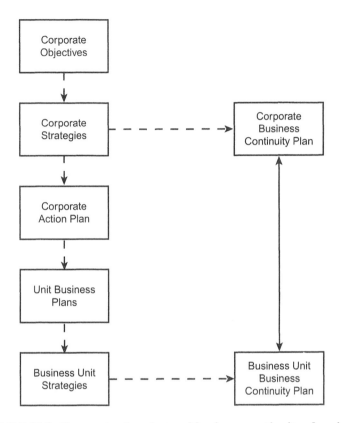

Exhibit 25-2. Corporate planning and business continuity planning.

- change its information technology environment (i.e., hardware/software platforms, outsourcing a part or all of its IT operations, changing the data/invoice communications network topology)
- relocation of the organization or business units to another city or state
- decentralize its IT operations
- change its business environment (e.g., property development to media — television)

All of these scenarios will have a dramatic impact on the current BCP strategy as well as maintenance of the plan.

From the planning process, the BCP coordinator should:

- document the planned changes (include organizational structure, staffing, and strategies) that are being considered/approved by executive management
- identify the specific areas where the BCP will be impacted
- evaluate the impact on the current BCP(s)

- develop new BCP strategies and procedures (where applicable)
- determine the cost of developing and implementing the new BCP strategies and procedures
- obtain executive management approval (include commitment) and funding (where applicable) for the implementation of the new BCP strategies and procedures
- develop an implementation plan (include training and testing) for the new strategies and procedures
- implement the new strategies and procedures

Step 2: Develop Procedures to Monitor Organizational/Operational Changes

The objective of maintaining the plan in a "state of readiness" is to reduce the likelihood of inappropriate decisions being made and decreasing the level of stress placed on BCP recovery team members in the event of disaster.

The BCP coordinator should also be concerned with the timeliness of the changes; that is, changes that may impact the plan should be conveyed as soon as possible to the BCP coordinator. Further, the BCP coordinator should have sufficient authority to ensure being informed of any changes no matter "how small." Testing of the plan should not be the only impetus to update the plan; organizational changes must be the primary driver to update the plan.

The BCP coordinator must review the corporate plan and business unit plans on a regular basis and develop change control procedures to monitor any planned or unplanned changes (e.g., business opportunities) to the plans. The procedures should also include the organization's relationship with its external service providers and key suppliers.

One of the major threats to BCP maintenance is where the organization is decentralized; that is, each business unit operates autonomously and reports to the corporate business entity on operational performance. The risk exists wherein the business unit might implement changes to its operations that may directly or indirectly affect the business unit or corporate BCP, or both. These changes may not have been documented in the business plan. The changes may have arisen, for example, as a result of an opportunity in the marketplace.

To ensure that these changes are communicated, organizational BCP policies and guidelines need to be developed, implemented, and enforced. A number of organizations today make it mandatory for *all* projects to include BCP as a project task sign-off item, regardless of the type of project (e.g., construction, engineering, logistics, IT, etc.). This ensures that each project addresses BCP during the planning process — rather than as an afterthought.

The BCP coordinator must develop strong communication links with each business unit to ensure that all changes in operations that may have an impact on BCP are communicated. This will ensure that the BCP is continually maintained up-to-date; otherwise, critical or subtle changes that may have an impact on the BCP strategies and plan(s) may go undetected.

Step 3: BCP Version Control

Version control, plan re-issue, and distribution can lead to a single point of failure in the successful execution of the plan in the event of disaster. Maintaining version control over the BCP(s) is a critical task because, in the event of a disaster, the various BCP recovery team personnel may undertake tasks that are no longer relevant, incorrectly executed, out of order, or, even worse, fail to undertake the critical tasks.

The BCP coordinator should to develop a version control standard and procedures for the re-issue, distribution, and circulation of BCP updates; and also ensure that there is a central record (e.g., a register) of the location and the authorized personnel who have copies of the plan. This is required to ensure that when the plan is updated, all copies of the plan are updated and old versions are removed. For example, the register should contain the following information:

- copy number
- name of recipient
- location
- date issued
- last updated
- update number

To ensure receipt of the revised BCP procedures, the BCP coordinator should request *positive* confirmation that the recipient has received the current version.

The organization has expended a large amount of money in the development and implementation of the plan. Therefore, it is essential that adequate security is maintained over the plan to prevent: (1) accidental or intentional destruction, and (2) unauthorized disclosure. Hence, the BCP coordinator should periodically undertake audits of the BCP recovery team members' BCP manuals to ensure that they have not only been maintained up-to-date, but also that they are secure from any unauthorized access (this includes off-site copies). *In toto,* the BCP coordinator should

- be ensured of the correct version
- that copies are issued only to authorized personnel
- that each copy has a accountable number
- that copies are secure from unauthorized access

Step 4: Testing BCP Changes

The success or failure of the BCP is measured against its objective of ensuring an orderly, timely, and cost-effective recovery from disaster. To measure how successful the BCP meets this objective is difficult without simulating a "real" disaster scenario. Therefore, organizations today undertake the following testing strategies: paper walk-through, "rolling" BCP testing, or full BCP testing.

Paper Walk-through. This approach is relatively inexpensive and can be conducted through a workshop environment using a structured walk-through methodology.

"Rolling" BCP Testing. By breaking the BCP into its various modules/components, each module/component can be tested throughout the year using a continuous "rolling" approach. Via this approach, each module/component is tested and the scope of each test can be expanded to include more than one module/component at a time. This approach ensures that every facet of the plan is tested. The advantage of this is that the impacts of testing on the organization's operations and cost are minimized.

Full BCP Testing. This approach can either be a "surprise" test or an organized test where all the BCP recovery team members are informed prior to the test being carried out.

The overall object of conducting the tests is to optimize BCP personnel experience, coordination, and provide assurance that in the event of a disaster there is every likelihood that the organization can recover in a cost-effective and timely manner.

However, testing of the BCP is perceived to be a costly exercise and hence there is general reluctance by executive management to undertake this. Therefore, the BCP coordinator must ensure that testing of the BCP outside of planned and budgeted testing should only be undertaken where there have been *significant* changes to the plan to warrant the cost of additional testing.

This is where the judgment of the BCP coordinator is critical, particularly where the potential risk and exposure may be intangible to executive management. The BCP coordinator will be required to justify the "additional" cost of testing the BCP due to changes enforced from organizational decisions.

SUPPORT TOOLS FOR THE MAINTENANCE OF THE BCP

Selecting the support tools to maintain and update the BCP is often a difficult choice for the BCP coordinator. The difficulty arises because of the number of software tools available to select from:

Exhibit 25-3. Considerations for selecting the appropriate software tools.

Software Organizational Parameters
- The complexity of the BCP
- The skill set of the personnel assigned the responsibility for updating the BCP (this where the BCP has been decentralized)
- Physical location of the personnel
- The availability of organizational resources (e.g., hardware, in-house software support, training, etc.)

Software Selection Criteria
- The software tool compliance with the organization's software architecture (detailed in the IT Strategic Plan)
- Support and ongoing maintenance from the software vendor
- Price/performance of the software
- Ease of use
- Functionality (including export of text and graphics)
- Report generation
- Query capabilities
- Security

- word processing packages (e.g., MS Word, WordPerfect, Lotus AmiPro, etc.)
- database products (e.g., Lotus Notes, MS Access, etc.)
- BCP software (LDRPS, BCPKickstart, PreCovery, Comprehensive Business Recovery, Business Continuity Planning Complete, Cassandra, etc.)

Further, the BCP coordinator might have to comply with the organization's system development methodology in the selection of software.

To select the appropriate software tools, the BCP coordinator should consider the items listed in Exhibit 25-3.

Each type of software tool (i.e., word processing, database products, and BCP software) will have its strengths and weaknesses. To ensure that the most appropriate software tool is selected may require the BCP coordinator to undertake a detailed evaluation of each of the products in accordance with the organization's system development methodology. This requirement can be waived if it has been decided that a word processing package will meet the basic requirements.

The system development methodology generally requires that:

1. The BCP coordinator prepare a User Requirement document which details:

- the mandatory and desirable functions of the software in order of priority,
- installation, testing, and implementation requirements,
- hardware and software architecture (compliance with the organization's information technology architecture).

2. To reduce the number of software packages for detailed evaluation including testing, the user requirements are matched to those of the selected software packages. The BCP coordinator must match the mandatory and desirable requirements with those offered by the software package(s) and eliminate those software packages which do not meet the requirements.

3. Each shortlisted software package must be trialed. However, there is reluctance by software vendors to provide a full version of the software on an evaluation basis. The majority of vendors have a demonstration version available.

4. The reasons for acceptance or rejection of each software package should be documented to a degree, which would stand scrutiny, by any interested party (e.g., auditors).

The BCP coordinator needs to review the software tool(s) on a regular basis. Specifically where due to organizational changes (e.g., change in hardware/software architecture, IT strategic plan, organizational growth/expansion, etc.), the BCP continues to grow/expand in size and complexity. Therefore, software tool(s) may not longer have the capacity and functionality to meet the BCP maintenance requirements.

SUMMARY

Executive management in many organizations today does not realize the organization's dependency on its BCP. Therefore, the maintenance and updating of the BCP is an essential element of the survival of the organization.

The BCP does not guarantee that the organization will recover in a cost-effective and timely manner in the event of disaster. However, an up-to-date BCP will provide reasonable assurance to executive management that the organization will minimize the effects of a disaster on its operations.

Management will only realize the value of its investment in the maintenance of the BCP when a real disaster strikes the organization. To ensure that management continually provides the resources in the maintenance of the plan, the BCP coordinator must continually "sell" the virtues of Business Continuity Planning to all the stakeholders.

Chapter 26
Testing Business Continuity Plans

Leo A. Wrobel

THE TRUE TEST OF A BUSINESS CONTINUITY PLAN IS WHETHER IT CAN UNCOVER FAILURE POINTS. Companies should consistently tighten testing criteria and review test results to ensure that a business continuity plan executes under a variety of conditions. A checklist of issues and errors tailored to specific business continuity teams aids in refining the test process.

Determining the effectiveness of a business continuity plan, or whether a plan works at all, is as crucial to the plan's development as the documentation of operating and security standards and recovery procedures. This chapter presents checklists of issues and errors that often occur during business continuity tests. It is based on an exercise conducted by a large fictitious company whose executive management team works in coordination with other logistical teams to oversee a highly visible disaster. Reviewing the functioning of these varied teams can help other IS managers develop or refine a test and ensure a more cohesive recovery exercise for their organizations.

THE EXECUTIVE MANAGEMENT TEAM (EMT)

At a minimum, an EMT should comprise a chief executive, a director of technical services, a building facilities manager, and a small administrative staff. It is called together only under specific circumstances, such as a destructive disaster that necessitates moving the company's primary place of business to a business continuity facility; an environmental disaster, such as a hazardous chemical spill, that poses a complicated public affairs problem; or a disaster that is considered a threat to investors, shareholders, or customers who depend on the organization and require a high level of public contact and reassurance. The primary requirement of an EMT is a predefined location — such as a training facility, hotel suite, or one of the executive's homes — to which the executives know to report after a disaster.

Activating the EMT

Successful activation of an EMT depends foremost on the ability to contact team members during the difficult and unusual circumstances a disaster poses. Several basic issues can arise during the notification process: Do key executives have unlisted telephone numbers that are not documented in the plan? Even if they do not, what if telephone service is out to the area? Do they have a backup, such as a pager or a cellular phone?

Contacting employees at their homes regarding disasters at the facility involves other more subtle issues. For example, what if an employee was at the facility when the disaster occurred? People making the calls to employee homes should be prepared to deal with hysterical relatives who may be hearing for the first time that a disaster has occurred at the facility where a loved one works. Providing a preapproved checklist that contains not only names and telephone numbers but also a brief procedure to follow when contacting employees' families can help circumvent these problems.

Once notified, the correct EMT members should assemble at the predetermined location or command center. Under already difficult conditions, EMT members may have trouble following directions to the command center. Planners should choose a location that is central enough for easy reach by team members. These issues can be mitigated in large part by establishing the command center at a landmark that has ready access to telephone service.

Operating the Command Center

The EMT needs to be able to begin work on arriving at the center. Several items must be immediately available to the EMT, such as telephones, fax machines, a small copier perhaps, and, although less apparent, a place to sit. Documenting the command center's setup allows technical personnel to ensure that the center can begin operations promptly.

To prevent EMT members from wasting precious time trying to figure out how to use emergency telephones, a basic touchtone analog telephone set should be used. Workers should be able to plug in a fax, laptop machine, or modem to the telephone as well.

The EMT must receive critical status and damage reports in the time frame prescribed in the recovery plan. A successfully activated EMT works with several logistical teams involved in the technical aspects of the recovery process. Once notified of the disaster, the teams fan out citywide or perhaps nationwide to implement the company's recovery plan. One team is dispatched to the business continuity center, if one is in use; another is dispatched to the affected facility to aid in restoration; and still more teams travel to perform such functions as retrieving stored magnetic media and picking up and delivering equipment.

Refining the Test Process

The importance of testing business continuity plans must be communicated, as well as the ability of even the most advanced organizations to learn something each time they test their recovery plan. To strengthen their company's plan, team members should make notes during and after the test. For effective updating, the plan and test procedures should be reviewed immediately following any test and activation, when memory is fresh. EMT members can learn lessons from the exercise, including what procedures they would change next time they test the plan. For example, EMT members may feel that recovery could have been facilitated by the representation of other areas in the company on the team, such as the real estate department and human resources.

TECHNICAL SERVICE TEAMS

Many organizations use commercial off-site business continuity facilities from a variety of sources. While these sources specialize in recovery, they cannot do the job alone. Several teams of technical service personnel must be mobilized to staff and configure a recovery center. Some of the most basic are suggested here.

Despite the trend toward distributed processing, mainframes are still used by many companies. The team responsible for what is generally the oldest but still core component in many recovery plans must be activated.

Mainframes, however, are only one component of a business and its recovery plan. Today a mainframe supports many functions that it did not support in the past. One of these things, of course, is LANs. Restoring LANs means more than restoring a server and wiring. To effectively restore a LAN business function, the three components of a business recovery solution are needed:

1. An attendant position
2. The data that resided on the LAN
3. The communications link that turns the employees using the LAN into revenue generators for the company. These links will play a prominent role in recovering LANs, both for voice and data communications.

Other teams involved in the recovery include field services teams comprising personnel who may normally support personal computers or terminals from a maintenance standpoint and can serve as emergency installation technicians for the new configurations.

Various engineering teams, or teams of senior analysts, may also be involved to provide high-level trouble-shooting and support when complex equipment configurations must be literally built overnight.

Mobilizing Technical Service Teams

Mobilizing technical service personnel involves many of the same issues as mobilizing the EMT. For instance, team members obviously will need easy-to-follow directions to the recovery center. Planners, however, must address additional factors. In cases of widespread disasters, as many as 50 percent of employees will go home to check on their homes and families before reporting to work. It is therefore imperative to test how the recovery plan would work in the absence of key technical personnel. Removing a few personnel in a simulation effectively tests how others will compensate.

Setting Up the Recovery Center

Commercial business continuity centers are shared by many organizations. A company must be aware that its site probably was used by others between tests and that configurations most likely were changed.

Personnel unfamiliar with a company's day-to-day environment will rely on diagrams and a documented recovery plan to set up equipment. The company's key technical people will know where equipment goes and how to set it up, but there is no guarantee they will be available during a disaster. Even when company personnel are present, they will be installing overnight what originally took years to create. Equipment service or installation manuals should be readily at hand in the event they are needed. Similarly, commercial recovery sources must provide on-site guides to demonstrate the subleties of equipment used at the center, such as complex matrix switches.

Restoring Communications

Technical service teams must deliver a report to the EMT within a prescribed time frame. Restoring communications is therefore one of the teams' priorities. If the recovery center does not provide regular touchtone analog telephones, personnel should be trained in advanced on the telephones at the center.

Efficient restoration of communications involves several tasks. When a large amount of technical equipment must be installed in a short time, keeping the same help desk or network control number enables vendors supporting the recovery process to contact a company easily, avoiding unnecessary delays. Dial-in data, switched digital service, and Integrated Services Digital Network links must also be successfully established.

The complement of telecommunications services that support data transmission for users must be checked in advance. One common problem with T1 links, for example, concerns the fact that most T1 local loops to recovery centers are shared among a broad user community. Because each customer using these links may be using a different line code for the T1, the links may have been reoptioned since a company's last disaster test and may not work without modification.

Procedures for reoptioning Channel Service Unit (CSUs) and other components that may have changed should be detailed in the recovery plan. The best test in all of these cases is a live test. Even if live production data is not transmitted, running a test pattern across these facilities can ensure that the telecommunications facilities are in tact, work properly, and would support data if necessary.

Data Delivery and Restoration

Data stored off-site must be delivered to the recovery center for such components as the mainframe and LAN ; telecommunications, switches, and multiplexers; the voice mail system; and automated call distribution (ACD) units. Procedures for retrieving mainframe and LAN data, which are typically stored off-site, are already in place. With coordination, telecommunications data may also be picked up during this procedure.

Problems in removing software from one system and reinstalling it on another stem from subtleties in operating systems or even minute differences in components such as tape drives. Although this problem is common, shortcuts that facilitate a more graceful reload on the new systems can be learned.

Evaluating Performance

Like members of the EMT, technical personnel should document what they learned from the exercise and what should be changed for the next test. Some of the issues requiring documentation are basic, such as whether the test equipment installed at the center for general use was surveyed in advance, appropriate for the company's test processes, and functioning properly. Even seemingly insignificant items, such as hand tools, should have been available and adequate. It is also highly recommended to request of principal equipment vendors that a representative be present at the recovery center, and to rate each vendor's response to the request.

No team can accomplish its goals without an overall environment reasonably conducive to the company's work environment. This issue is especially important in cases of distributed processing. While ergonomics may be a problem and people may be working on folding tables, the recovery assembly should help everyone get the job done. If not, team members should specify what is needed to bring the recovery center up to par.

Successful performance of tasks also depends on effective use of personnel at a time when personnel are at a premium. Team members should evaluate whether representatives of other areas of the organization would have facilitated work at the recovery center. Or, stated another way, they should ask whether an area was unnecessarily represented at the center. Someone who may be a fifth wheel at the recovery center could be reassigned to assist in restoring the damaged facility, for example.

Thorough documentation also includes communicating to management that the true test of a plan is whether it can uncover failure points. Consistent flawless results on recovery tests indicate that an organization should tighten its standards.

THE FACILITY RECONSTRUCTION TEAM

The facility reconstruction team comprises a complement of personnel who are dispatched to the damaged site to survey conditions, report to the EMT, and coordinate with local and emergency authorities. The team could include members of the company's building services group and representatives of the production, LAN, mainframe, telecommunications, or other divisions that have a high content of equipment in the building. Other teams, such as administrative or logistical supply teams, should also be considered, as well as a media affairs representative.

Again, testing criteria for the facility reconstruction team are similar to those discussed previously, with notable exceptions. A checklist for the reconstruction team follows.

Restoring the Damaged Facility

The Right People for the Job. Only employees required for the recovery process should assemble at the site after a disaster. Others who report to satisfy their curiosity may interfere with the recovery process, especially by tying up valuable cellular telephone frequencies with personal or unnecessary calls.

The specific complement of personnel who report to the damaged site depends on the type of disaster that has occurred. In the case of a fire, the building facilities manager should be present to interface with local emergency personnel who control the facility until it is deemed safe for entry. A knowledgeable building facilities manager could help these personnel decide issues more quickly. Similarly, in cases of a highly visible or widely broadcast disaster, a media affairs representative is needed to interact with the inevitable high volume of media presence. In almost all disasters, it is a good idea to have at least one security person on the team to assess the situation and determine whether additional security reinforcements are required to secure the building from theft.

A smoothly functioning reconstruction team also depends on clearly delineated responsibilities. Without them, conflicts or turf issues may develop over such issues as which department is responsible for rewiring the building. There are probably five different people in the organization (from facilities, LAN management, telecommunications, and other departments) who will believe themselves responsible for rewiring, so predefined responsibilities will avoid overlap, wasted efforts, and squabbles during the recovery.

Adequate communication among members is also a must. Team members should feel like a cohesive unit during the test. If they frequently feel out of touch with others, communications must be improved to foster cohesiveness.

Appropriate Equipment. Each member of the team that enters what may be a severely damaged facility needs certain standard equipment, such as a flashlight with a spare set of batteries; a hard hat; an identifying badge or, preferably, an identifying vest to quickly differentiate between employees and looters; a copy of the recovery plan; a small notebook to annotate critical events and document important command decisions made during the recovery process; and at least one roll of quarters in the event that a major telecommunication disaster renders other services unavailable or overwhelmed. The team should also have at least two cellular telephones, two two-way radios, two pagers to keep track of people on-site and expedite the recovery process, and at least one cellular fax and a laptop computer with a fax modem card to aid in reporting to the EMT in the prescribed time frame.

A Staging Area for Recovery Operations. When a building is totally inaccessible or lacks the required telecommunications, water, or sanitary facilities, facility reconstruction personnel should promptly report to a prearranged staging area for recovery operations, such as in a nearby hotel. Telephone numbers must be promptly diverted to the staging area. The network control number may be diverted to the recovery center, for example, for technical questions regarding mainframes or LANs. The help desk number, however, may be diverted to the staging area.

Notifying Professional Clean-Up Personnel. Professional clean-up companies have the answers to such questions as what to do with magnetic tapes that have been wet in a disaster (they should be put in the freezer). The companies use a freeze-dry process to save valuable data stored on magnetic media and similar processes for wet paper and smoke-damaged equipment. Immediate notification is crucial, since the processes must be performed within the first 48 hours following a disaster.

Evaluating and Documenting Test Results

Facility reconstruction personnel must evaluate similar issues as their colleagues on the EMT and technical service teams. Most important is whether an initial status report was dispatched to the EMT within the 90 minutes specified in most business continuity plans. Other issues include whether equipment was adequate, whether on-site vendor representatives were immediately summoned and current telephone numbers listed for them, whether the complement of team members was effective, and what should be changed for the next exercise.

CONCLUSION

The teams involved in a business continuity test have different tasks, goals, and needs, yet the testing procedure holds the same overriding message for all of them: Testing a plan is a learning experience. Organizations should not expect their first test to run perfectly, nor aim for perfect results each time they test. Testing until failure makes for a true test.

Once testing procedures become routine, criteria should be tightened, or key personnel removed from the process to ensure that the plan executes in a variety of circumstances. Successful testing of a plan provides greater peace of mind and assures management that the time and money spent in developing and honing the test was a wise investment.

Chapter 27
Changes that Could Affect the IS Business Continuity Plan

JoAnn Bozarth
Belden Menkus

AT ONE TIME, A REVIEW OF THE IS BUSINESS CONTINUITY PLAN EVERY TWO YEARS WAS RECOMMENDED. And, for some aspects of the plan, that recommendation still may be sufficient. But change is occurring so fast these days that a more frequent, perhaps even a continuing, review is needed to ensure that, as written, the plan reflects the organization's current information processing environment.

Changes in the IS environment can occur as a result of changes in technology, in the nature and mix of an organization's human resources, in the enterprise's direction, and in the potential threats to its continued operations. These changes can work together to create an IS environment where the recovery challenge is more complex, yet meeting it is more critical to business survival. In response to these changed recovery needs, organizations adopt what has been called "advanced" recovery technology and techniques to replace, or add to, their traditional recovery methods.

This chapter discusses some of the various types of changes, particularly the adoption of new ways of addressing recovery needs, that could affect the plan's currency and effectiveness. This chapter does not address the mechanics of auditing the plan for currency or of keeping the plan in sync with changes as they occur.

CHANGES THAT CAN AFFECT RECOVERY NEEDS

The types of changes discussed in this chapter section can affect the relevance of a business impact analysis (BIA) that may have been performed in the past as a part of the organization's contingency planning. A revised BIA that reflects the changes that have taken place and identifies and

0-8493-0907-7/00/$0.00+$.50
© 2001 by CRC Press LLC

quantifies their expected impacts on business operations usually reveals a need for enhanced IS recovery planning.

Changes in IS and End-User Departments

User departments and IS experience change in several areas as they adopt new computing and telecommunication technological offerings. Any of these changes that affect the recovery process should be incorporated into the business resumption plan. Examples of these new offerings include enterprise resource planning, E-commerce, and data warehousing. Organizations take up these new offerings as a way to solve real business problems. The trend is to integrate all of the affected applications and data into single databases and to enter all of the data online, making the only record of these transactions the electronic data itself. Moreover, the trend at one time toward distributing systems from IS out into the user departments is now reversing in some organizations toward bringing these systems back into IS for safety and control purposes. Where these changes occur, increasing reliance is placed on IS and the IS infrastructure.

In IS, some changes might be software changes and equipment configuration changes, such as alterations in operating system software functions and parameters, network software and node definitions, the hardware configuration, the telecommunication capabilities, and vendor offerings.

In the case of end users, these changes might be the adoption of new, or the modification of old, information processing applications or disk operating procedures. Also, key management and staff member responsibilities may change. These and any other revisions that impact the existing business resumption plan documentation should be incorporated into the plan. Not to be overlooked in plan currency maintenance are the changes to the contact lists of conventional voice telephone, cell phone, fax, and pager numbers, as well as the relevant e-mail addresses.

Changes in the Organization

Organizations may undergo major changes such as mergers or takeovers; reengineering of the organization's main business, even a refocusing of various aspects of its business, leading to the establishment of new business partnerships; or the actual control of the enterprise passing to a larger organization. (The last change may involve, for example, the control of a hospital passing to a health management organization, or the control of the organization passing to an acquiring conglomerate. In these situations, both IS production and its recovery may have to be synchronized with those of these other enterprises.) But even incremental changes may affect the plan's currency and utility. In the case of a major change, the business continuity plan may need more than updating. Its complete revision may be necessary.

Also, changes in approaches to filling personnel requirements, for example, the switch to the widespread use of temporary workers or telecommuters may impact recovery efforts and should be allowed for in the plan. For example, the existing plan provisions for onsite cleanup after a flood or fire may have to be altered to reflect the realities that have been imposed by these new approaches.

Other Changes

Individuals assigned to specific tasks and responsibilities under the existing IS business continuity plan no longer may be employed by the organization or may have taken positions in the organization that are inappropriate for their assignment under the plan. Or, they may not be familiar with changes made to the plan since their last exposure to it. (This may be true, as well, of the contact people assigned to the organization by the vendors who will play a role in the recovery effort.) Contractual arrangements with telecommunication and hardware vendors may have expired and not been renewed. Instead, other vendors may have been contracted with and their representatives may lack the desired familiarity with the provisions of the business continuity plan. Possibly, the key vendors who were expected to be involved in the operations restoration process cannot be counted on now. They may have gone out of business, or simply ceased to be a key vendor. The hot-site or similar alternate operations facility no longer may be large enough or have sufficient capability to fit current IS operational needs.

Any rise in the level of the existing corporate commitment to distributed computing should be reflected in the plan. As applications become increasingly interdependent, even low-priority applications can take on some of the attributes of criticality assigned to those applications that are most important to the organization's business survival. (This interdependence may involve a complicated set of differing relations with a changing mix of suppliers, principal customers, and divergent government bodies. And, it may include the handling of both complex graphics as well as conventional textual materials.)

CHANGES IN RECOVERY TECHNIQUES

Traditional recovery techniques may have informed the initial development and the subsequent revisions and reviews of the IS business continuity plan. The abandonment by the organization of any or all of those techniques in favor of implementing one or more of the so-called technologically advanced recovery techniques, since the last plan revision or review, may call for an extensive overhaul of the plan.

Why Organizations Change to Advanced Techniques

Technologically advanced recovery techniques are considered and adopted by organizations as senior executives come to realize the serious impact that unplanned interruption to critical applications can have on their business activities in a changed environment. A senior executive may have become concerned because of the disaster-related problems experienced by a competitor, another organization, or by the impact of natural disasters or other events on their industry or the geographic area in which the executive's organization does business. But, usually, the instrument that converts concern to a decision to turn to advanced recovery techniques is a revised BIA — one that identifies and quantifies the impacts in a changed environment if relying on conventional recovery methods currently in place.

An organization may select a combination of techniques to create a customized solution. Also, with limited resources and competing priorities, a phased approach for introducing such a solution may be required.

Which of the numerous advanced recovery options that an organization selects depends on the organization's key objectives for recovery as identified in the revised BIA. In the BIA, management establishes the recovery time objective (RTO) and recovery point objective (RPO). (Recovery time refers to the amount of time that elapses from the point when a business operation was disrupted until that operation is resumed and current business transactions can be applied. By contrast, recovery point reflects the age of the last-available data that was captured before the interruption. The closer these points are together, the greater the need for quick recovery.)

Other Factors that Affect the Selection Process

In addition to the possible impact on RTO/RPO of a given advanced recovery solution, other factors may play a role in an organization's selection of a particular solution. For example, because some of these solutions are more costly to implement than others, the balance of budget constraints against the impacts quantified in the BIA often define the selection process. Also, a consideration could be that the use of certain advanced recovery techniques, in contrast to certain others, may offer a projected reduction in the time required for completing recovery testing and a potential for carrying out more in-depth testing in the same timeframe.

Another consideration that could influence selection is that an organization's preferred telecommunication and business continuity vendors may not offer all of these solutions, limiting the acceptable available options. In that case (or if it is known that a vendor's operations could be affected at the same time that the organization's operations are impacted, such as when a flood or a tornado or hurricane occurs), the organization may recognize a need to develop in-house an advanced recovery capability.

Factors related to IS production could bear on the selection of advanced recovery technology. These deserve a bit more explanation because of their likely effect on the computing environment.

Factors Related to IS Production. Certain advanced recovery technologies offer the potential for improvement in several important aspects of IS production. These include the disk I/O response and throughput, and the response of the particular application that is affected, the tape write times, and database update performance. The possibility of improved IS production performance and a consequent improved return on investment may sway the selection process outcome to one solution or another.

Another IS production concern is whether a recovery methodology that is being considered for selection will provide for business continuity testing that does not disrupt the recovery capability of IS production. This provision is likely to require that the organization maintain separate copies of its data for testing purposes and for carrying out the actual recovery process.

IS production that involves the use of an advanced recovery site will be influenced in various ways if the telecommunication connection with that site is lost and then regained. In making a recovery solution selection, the reconnection effects of that solution may be considered. A main consideration could be whether the product is able to detect communication loss. How a product resynchronizes the principal and recovery sites after the restoration of communications is an important consideration. The state of the data can affect the ability of the organization to recover during this resynchronization, depending on the solution that has been chosen.

Advanced Recovery Techniques

A variety of technologically advanced recovery techniques are available. The variety of these offerings can be expected to grow as the business continuity-related uses of computing technology continue to develop. Advanced recovery offerings, in general, can be categorized as electronic vaulting mechanisms or structural mechanisms, as follows.

Electronic Vaulting Mechanisms. Electronic vaulting provides an alternative to the lengthy process of transporting and staging, as well as locating and having returned by some form of courier arrangement, particular backup records that are maintained on magnetic tape in a designated secure recovery location. Electronic vaulting is the process of routine bulk transmission of data to an appropriate recovery location. It can take several forms. These include remote transaction journaling, database shadowing, and remote mirroring.

Remote Transaction Journaling. This is based on the concurrent interception of the writes to a local database transaction log or journal and the transmitting of this intercepted data offsite in a real-time mode. This mechanism will provide a recovery point that will occur in an ideal setting. It will happen within seconds of the failure.

Database Shadowing. This is the aggressive combination of the maintenance of a point-in-time copy of a database on disk (essentially, it can be thought of as a standby database) as well as remote journaling with the regular, scheduled application of the log/journal updates to the database. Database shadowing is a flexible option for meeting a time-critical application-specific RTO. Database shadowing allows for application updates to be shadowed as often as may be required to meet the RTO. Applications requiring shorter RTOs will need more frequent updates to the database. Regardless of the recovery time required, here too the recovery point will occur within seconds of the failure.

Remote Mirroring. With remote mirroring, a duplicate copy of an organization's data can be maintained at a remote location. This permits a drastic improvement in recovery point and recovery time for the protected data. The two methods of remote mirroring are host-based software and controller-based software. Controller-based mirroring offers the ability to support enterprise storage recovery with a single product. Because IS personnel are managing a single product in this scenario, it is likely to require fewer resources, resulting in savings that offset some of the costs. Host-based mirroring offers the management of the recovery point to an absolutely consistent timestamp across all of the data protected in a defined group needing to be consistent.

All of these forms of electronic vaulting can be carried out either on a routine, or a specifically scheduled, basis. Electronic vaulting is suitable, in particular, to be maintained through a form of virtual private network (VPN) arrangement. Data can be moved through such an arrangement to the electronic vault at different logical levels — such as by tape volume, by disk volume, or by individual file, as defined by the requirements of the information processing application that must be recovered — but all provide for continuous maintenance of a remote copy of discrete data at a specific point in time.

Structural Mechanisms. Electronic vaulting may be complemented by using some combination of a standby operating system, a hot network node, system replication, and system fail-over.

Standby Operating System. This refers to maintaining a remote copy of the operating system on disk that is connected directly to the recovery processor. Doing this ensures that systems being protected can be hardware attached and restarted immediately at the recovery site at time of test or the occurrence of a disaster.

Hot Network Node. A hot network production node is one that is always ready to operate. A hot network node can be located in the same location as the recovery capability. Because the hot network node is always in use

286

and is monitored continually, the potential for its failure is minimized. Such an arrangement promises to alleviate the complexity and time-consuming difficulty of establishing network communications at the time of disaster by prestaging the restoration configuration, which eliminates or reduces error and excess recovery time impact. By this means, access to systems and data by those who need them is maintained, which is the basic requirement of an effective rapid recovery of those systems and data.

System Replication and System Fail-over. System replication provides a continuous operating environment by endlessly duplicating systems, data, and networks at a remote location. System fail-over functionality is the ability for the backup system to take over immediately from the production system at the moment of disruption. The addition of system fail-over functionality addresses both the RTO and the RPO constraints.

An IS Auditing Concept

The effectiveness of these advanced technology business continuity methods rests on the determined application of a concept that will be familiar to the IS auditor: consistent control of the techniques and the data that are used in them. Special attention should be given to means for keeping the selected and implemented technology in sync with the basic systems and for keeping the data current. Obsolete data should be purged from these recovery solutions promptly to avoid possible confusion or error in the recovery process.

CONCLUSION

The traditional two-year cycle of reviewing and revising the IS business continuity plan may not be adequate to ensure that the plan's contents reflect changes that affect recovery needs and recovery methods. This chapter discussed first a sampling of some of the changes that can affect recovery needs. It then discussed changes in recovery methods, beginning with some of the issues associated with selecting advanced technology recovery solutions and going on with a brief description of some of the advanced business continuity techniques that are available to address the changes in recovery needs.

Section VI
Business Continuity Manager's Tool Kit

Chapter 28
Business Continuity Planning Tools and Management Options

Jon William Toigo

MANY ORGANIZATIONS ARE FINDING THAT THE DECISION TO UNDERTAKE BUSINESS CONTINUITY PLANNING IS NO LONGER A MATTER OF CHOICE; it is a legal necessity. An effective business continuity plan can be developed either by a business continuity consultant or by in-house personnel. Consultants can bring considerable expertise and experience to the table and, in some cases, help overcome internal obstacles to the plan's development. The cost of consultant-developed plans, however, has put this service out of reach for most small and medium-sized organizations. This has led to an increased interest in in-house business continuity planning. Fortunately, there is now an increasing body of literature to help novices understand and implement business continuity planning; in addition, several software packages have been developed to aid in plan development and maintenance. This chapter reviews the merits of consultant-assisted business continuity planning, examines the available planning tools, and provides criteria for selecting a business continuity consultant or the right planning tool.

In the late 1980s, a legal doctrine emerged that placed personal liability on an organization's corporate officers for the protection of its automated systems and other information assets. Because of this legal liability for data loss, there has been an increased interest in business continuity planning, especially within financial institutions. For banks that participate in the U.S. Federal Reserve System, the office of the comptroller requires that boards of directors and bank management personally review and approve contingency plans that have been developed to safeguard their organization's systems and data. In other industries, the courts have repeatedly held for customers in suits against disaster-stricken companies that neglected to safeguard critical corporate assets — including information — before a disaster occurred.[1]

0-8493-0907-7/00/$0.00+$.50
© 2001 by CRC Press LLC

If the legal liability issue has led to an increased interest in business continuity planning, the record of recent disasters has further underscored and reinforced this interest. The National Fire Protection Association asserts that there were, on average, 83 fires per year in data centers and telephone equipment rooms from 1969 to 1983;[2] the actual number of smoke and rubble disasters covered by business continuity facilities during that period was six. However, in 1987,there were 18 highly publicized disasters in which organizations implemented business continuity plans and relocated operations to backup facilities. In every case, organization spokespersons attributed the survival of their businesses to the existence of a tested business continuity plan. These acknowledgments have led to a heightened perception of the threat of disaster, as reported in a 1988 Ernst & Whinney survey.[3]

The increased awareness of the need for business continuity planning has been accompanied by a marked rise in the memberships of contingency planning associations throughout the country. Popular IT journals that would rarely publish articles on contingency planning now feature special issues entirely devoted to the topic. In addition, new journals are being published that are dedicated to the subject of contingency planning.

In the business continuity services industry, the late 1980s and early 1990s have witnessed a boom of activity. In 1989, IBM Corp. announced a new Business Recovery Services offering, consisting of consulting services, mainframe- or minicomputer-based hot site facilities, and commercial cold sites. In addition, consulting firms report that they are busier now than ever before, and the major accounting and auditing firms (e.g., PricewaterhouseCoopers, Ernst & Young, KPMG, etc.) now offer contingency planning services to their clients.

Even with all of the evidence pointing to the benefits of business continuity planning, securing management commitment is difficult. In some cases, management may be reluctant to spend money to acquire the services and products it needs to implement the plan. This indicates a lack of understanding of the financial risks and exposures presented by disasters. Legal requirements that compel management to undertake planning must be communicated early. When legal exposure is not the primary factor, other risk factors must be cited to sell senior management (e.g., loss of clients or orders, high insurance premiums, unproductive use of time by employees who depend on computer resources, and inordinate expenditures for equipment and software that was not considered before the disaster). Once senior management gives the go-ahead, the first task facing the data manager is to decide who will develop the plan. One approach is to hire a consultant, and another is to develop the plan in-house. The following sections examine the arguments in support of each option.

THE CONSULTANT OPTION

Business continuity planning is no less complicated than a major systems development project. Recognizing the scope and complexity of business continuity planning, the data manager may be inclined to look to a consultant to manage the project.

Several factors support a decision to hire a consultant. Experienced consultants bring a set of proven tools to the project, which may mean the quick development of an effective plan. A practiced consultant understands the effective construction of a business continuity plan, asks the right questions, and typically knows who's who in the business continuity products and services industry. Consultants who work in a specific industry often tailor a methodology for business continuity planning to that industry, which reduces the amount of time needed to learn new skills and helps speed development. Further, consultants bring a fresh perspective to the process, spotting important recovery requirements that may be overlooked by employees.

Consultants are expensive, however. Ironically, this may be an advantage in some cases. Business continuity planning requires the interaction of users and information systems personnel. In many large IS operations, fractious functions (e.g., programming and systems operations) must cooperate. Frequently, the only way to have all parties work together efficiently is to impress upon them the considerable cost of the consultant. Similarly, because senior management has made an investment in the consultant's plan, it may be less inclined to withdraw the support needed to implement the plan.

Data managers who are charged with choosing a consultant should be aware of the many myths surrounding consultant-driven plans. Many managers believe that because consultant plans are written by experts, they are more effective. With the business continuity information and tools available to all contingency planners, however, even novice planners can develop an efficacious plan.

Another fiction is that only consultant plans are executed successfully. Although this used to be the rule, in the past few years there have been numerous instances of successful recoveries in organizations that developed their plan in-house. Along those same lines, many managers believe that auditors will accept only consultant plans; in fact, as long as the plan has been fully tested and demonstrated to be effective, auditors will accept it.

There is a common but false belief that employees of an organization using consultants do not need to be involved in developing the recovery plan. At a minimum, any organization will need to have at least one employee work with the consultant to develop the plan. If the consultant works entirely alone, the plan will not work because staff members will not understand their part in it.

Selecting the Right Consultant

To guard against making a contract with the wrong consultant, the data manager should take five initial steps. These are discussed in the following paragraphs.

1. Obtaining Qualifications. It is important to request in advance the name and background of the consultant who will provide business continuity services. Which organizations has the consultant served? Were these clients satisfied with the job? An inexperienced consultant, even one that is in contact with more experienced professionals, should be avoided. The ideal consultant possesses a solid grasp of information systems, understands the specific requirements of the client's business, and has developed satisfactory business continuity plans for at least two other organizations.

2. Requesting a Plan Proposal. The consultant should submit a proposal that details the phases, tasks, and milestones of the planning project. Most consultants work from generic methodologies that they can adapt to specific client requirements. With the increasing availability of commercial products for planning and managing contingency planning and business continuity projects, consultants can no longer portray their work as mysterious or otherwise beyond the reach of nonpractitioners.

3. Validating Proposed Time and Cost Estimates. A consultant cannot develop meaningful time and cost estimates unless consulting services are packaged as a fixed-price contract. The data manager should be particularly wary if the consultant quotes exact costs or completion times without having assessed the organization's requirements.

Estimates provided by the consultant can be of value to the data manager in several ways. For example, valid time and cost estimates are useful benchmarks when the proposals of various consultants are being compared, especially if each estimate is made on the basis of similar projects for comparable businesses. To ensure that the data presented in each proposal is as accurate as possible, the data manager should verify that all predictable costs, including the consultant's travel and lodging, are reflected in the estimated cost.

4. Negotiating Cost. Initially, consultants often market their premium service, offering the less expensive shared-responsibility approaches only if they sense they may be pricing themselves out of a contract. Faced with the prospect of losing business, a consultant can be notably creative in finding cost-saving measures. One manager reported that the cost of the plan development was cut by putting corporate word processing at the consultant's disposal to take care of all documentation and by designating one of the staff members to work full time with the consultant, replacing the assistant called for. Other managers have purchased a consultant's microcomputer-based business continuity planning tool, contracting with the consultant only for the initial analysis and data collection. The result: substantial cost reductions.

5. Assessing the Consultant's Relationships with Vendors. Many consulting firms have formal and informal relationships with vendors of business continuity products and services. In fact, some consultants argue that it is partly their extensive knowledge of and contacts within the industry that qualify them for the rates they command. These relationships can, in some cases, benefit the client organization. The client may thereby qualify for a discount on a fire protection system, off-site storage, or the use of a hot site.

The potential for misuse of these relationships is also present. An unethical consultant may be willing to forego the objective analysis of client requirements and recommend a product or service for which the consultant receives compensation. Therefore, it is important to know with whom the consultant has marketing agreements and how these agreements may translate into cost advantages. Most vendors will openly disclose special arrangements, particularly when they profit a potential client and, in the process, improve the marketability of their service.

THE IN-HOUSE OPTION

For many organizations, the use of consulting services is a luxury, a cost over and above the already expensive business continuity planning project that they must undertake to satisfy legal and audit requirements. Others take the view that any reasonably intelligent employee, equipped with management support and the technical details of an organization's system and network operations, can develop a competent business continuity capability.

The problems faced by organizations that elect to develop a contingency plan using in-house personnel are fourfold. First, many novice planners lack fundamental knowledge about the scope of business continuity planning. This problem is reflected by the inordinate amount of time spent by the novice planner who creates disaster scenarios and strategies for coping with them, or by the lengthy, theoretical dissertations on business continuity found in many internally developed plans.

The second problem confronting many do-it-yourself planners is one of procedure. Procedural difficulties arise from efforts to collect information from departmental managers and from outside agencies (e.g., fire department representatives, local civil emergency planners, and utility and telephone companies). Managers or planners who do not know the appropriate questions to ask or how to effectively manage interviews will confront major obstacles to plan development.

Vendor management is the third problem. If the planners are able to surmount the problems of scope and procedure and are able to develop an understanding of the needs and exposures that business continuity planning must address, they will still be thwarted by their lack of knowledge of commercially available products and services that help reduce exposure. Even if planners have a general knowledge of products and services, they may know little or nothing about product pricing or about the contracts that govern delivery of promised commodities.

Finally, there is a problem of plan articulation. The way a planner assembles information about systems, exposures, and recovery strategies into a business continuity plan document determines how useful the plan will be in an actual emergency and how difficult the plan will be to maintain. A well-written plan is structured so that only pertinent sections are given to recovery teams in an emergency and so that plan procedures can be implemented readily. The plan should be structured to be updated easily as the names of vendor contacts, recovery team members, detail of systems and network hardware, and software configurations change over time.

A partial solution to these difficulties is to use one of the numerous, commercially available business continuity planning tools: software packages typically designed for use on a microcomputer. Sometimes irreverently referred to as canned plans, these applications can provide scope, procedure, and format to business continuity planning projects.

WORD PROCESSOR-DRIVEN TOOLS VERSUS DATABASE-DRIVEN TOOLS

Business continuity planning tools come in a variety of forms. Some are simply boilerplate text documents, sold on diskette in American Standard Code for Information Interchange format. The user imports this plan into a word processor, and the plan can be modified or customized using word processor editing functions. Another type of packaged plan is database-driven. Both types of plans offer distinct benefits and are discussed in the following sections.

Word Processor-Driven Tools

There are several advantages to these plans, one of them being that the in-house planner is allowed to use familiar software (i.e., the word processor), which reduces the learning curve that frequently delays plan development. In addition, a text plan may be readily expanded to incorporate business continuity planning for user departments, for branch offices, or to account for other requirements that may not be part of the generic plan. Finally, word processor-driven plans are easy to maintain using the global search-and-replace function that is part of most business word processors.

Once customized, the word processed plan is printed like any text document. The format and the content of the plan can be redesigned to resemble other business plans or to accommodate company standards relating to document preparation.

Database-Driven Tools

Another type of plan is database-driven. The generic portion of the plan is incorporated into the fields on the data entry screens, and the data requested from the user is specific and detailed. As the data is entered onto the screens, several relational databases are compiled containing information about systems, networks, and personnel. Then, through the use of vendor-supplied queries and programs, the business continuity plan is printed out as a series of reports.

Advantages of this approach to planning tool design are the enhanced organization and management of data derived from a database structure. For example, all data pertaining to recovery teams (e.g., the names and emergency telephone numbers of each team member) is located in a single database, making it easier to update the information regarding such matters as employee turnover or changes of telephone numbers.

Other vendors have developed planning tools that integrate enhanced database software applications (e.g., project management software) with a generic business continuity plan, claiming the combination supports not only plan development and maintenance but implementation. One such package provides decision support software that can be used during a disaster to collect data on the progress of the recovery effort.

CRITERIA FOR SELECTING BUSINESS CONTINUITY PLANNING TOOLS

Regardless of the mode of presentation employed, the primary determinant of the microcomputer-based business continuity planning tool's effectiveness is the generic plan that it provides. Although this built-in plan is neither right nor wrong, it may be more or less appropriate to a specific organization and its business continuity planning requirements. Several planning tools should be evaluated by an in-house contingency planner before one is selected.

The in-house contingency planner should outline various criteria to aid in evaluating packages (as well as consultant-developed plans). Some criteria are suggested by the following questions, and these criteria are outlined briefly in the product evaluation checklist in Exhibit 28-1.

Product Identification

Product Name: _____

Vendor: _____

Address: _____

_____

Price: _____

	Yes	No	Comments
Scope			
Data Center Only			
Companywide			
Corporationwide			
Methodology			
Project Management			
(if No, state other)			
Plan Description (Check Yes if feature is provided)			
Generic Plan			
Action Plan			
Plan Activities			
Recovery Team Directory			
Vendor Information			
Equipment Inventories			
Records and Locations			
Network Descriptions			
System Descriptions			
Company Information			
User-Friendliness (Check Yes if feature is provided)			
User Interface (menus, windows, or mouse)			
Help Screens (contextual)			
Input Methods (nonredundant data entry, batch mode)			
Output Methods (diversity of reports, query language)			

Exhibit 28-1. Business continuity planning tools evaluation checklist.

Does the Tool Provide the Means for Developing a Business Continuity Plan for the Entire Organization? If business continuity planning is to be comprehensive, the selected planning tool must be able to handle plans for the recovery of more than hardware, software, and electronically stored data (e.g., telecommunications recovery) and for the restoration of company operations to an acceptable level. Most planning tools do not provide this capability in their generic, noncustomized form, despite vendor claims to the contrary. The contingency planner should determine, in advance, the degree to which the plan can be modified to meet the organization's needs.

Does the Planning Tool Require Adoption of an Approach to Recovery Planning That Differs from Methodologies Used in Other Planning Activities? Effective business continuity planning differs little from other types of business planning. Objectives are developed, tasks are derived from objectives, and criteria are set forth to gauge task and objective fulfillment. An experienced planner can use basic project management skills to develop and maintain an effective contingency plan; novice planners, however, may need more than a generic project management software package to develop their first plans. The package that a novice planner uses should not deviate drastically from a basic project management approach. If a manual is required just to understand the plan's methodology, it is probably not the most appropriate plan.

Is the Planning Tool Comprehensive? At a minimum, the essential sections in the plan are:

- *The action plan.* The order in which recovery activities must be undertaken to result in speedy business continuity.
- *Plan activities.* The tasks that must be undertaken in a recovery situation. These should be ranked in order of importance and related to an action plan.
- *Recovery teams and the notification directory.* The planning tool should have a location for recording the names of company personnel who will play a role in a recovery situation, as well as a list of telephone numbers for all personnel who must be notified in the event of a disaster.
- *Vendor information and contact directory.* The planning tool should provide a location for recording information about all vendors who will provide products or services during a disaster and the names and telephone numbers of vendor contacts.
- *Records requirements and locations.* The plan should include sections detailing the locations and types of vital records stored off site and the procedures for accessing them during recovery.
- *Equipment inventories.* An inventory of systems hardware and other equipment should be maintained in the plan, both for insurance purposes and for use as a checklist in plan testing.
- *Communications networks, line, and equipment requirements.* The plan should provide a description of network operations and communications line and equipment and of services recovery requirements.
- *Application systems software and hardware requirements.* This section should provide descriptions and should list the hardware necessary for operations and for meeting user hardware requirements.
- *Company information.* Information regarding an organization's lawyers, insurance policies, and lines of credit should be maintained in the plan document.

Is the Package User-Friendly? An excellent business continuity planning application should be as user-friendly as any other software package. In fact, given the specialized work of the package, the planning tool should be even more user-friendly. Some of the factors that contribute to user friendliness are:[4]

- *The user interface.* Complex packages should require less expertise from the user. This rule of thumb applies to nearly all applications. A well-designed package should provide menus, displays, and straightforward escape routes. Mouse controls might also be desirable, though system portability would be reduced if a fallback to cursor control is unavailable.
- *Help screens.* Contextual help screens are a definite advantage. Printed manuals are not as useful as help screens that can be invoked from anywhere in the program to explain how to avoid or repair errors and list available options.
- *Tutorials or samples.* A business continuity planning tool should give the user an idea of what an actual business continuity plan looks like. The microcomputer-based tool should come equipped with a sample that can be modified by the user to accommodate an organization's requirements.
- *Input.* Data input should be as simplified a procedure as possible. This is a key issue in determining which type of planning package — word processor-driven or database-driven — is best for a specific environment. The plan should be organized to reduce or eliminate redundant data entry. In addition, it may be useful if the planning tool allows the importation of outside files through batch conversion or some other method, because some of the information needed for the plan may have been assembled in another form or for another purpose and importing files will reduce duplicate entry.
- *Output.* The planning tool should be able to output an actual plan. The plan should be divided into sections by subject or task, and its form should be flexible enough to accommodate documentation standards.

What Is the Pedigree of the Planning Tool? Many business continuity planning tools were developed by consulting firms for the consultant's use at client sites. In some cases, the package was subsequently licensed for use by the client who then maintained the plan. Consulting firms began to customize their planning tools for business continuity backup facility vendors and their clients. Finally, direct sales to the client became a lucrative source of business for consulting firms. Hence, many tested, reliable planning tools were originally used to develop actual plans for specific organizations. Untested planning tools may produce inadequate plans, a fact discovered only after testing or — in the worst case — in an actual disaster. Therefore, the pedigree of the plan is extremely important.

These considerations aid in the selection of the best business continuity planning tool for a particular organization. In addition to these, the price of the planning tool, the availability of telephone support, and other factors that contribute to the selection of any software package are also important.

WHAT PLANNING TOOLS DO NOT PROVIDE

Business continuity planning tools can aid the in-house planner in many ways. They can provide an example of the structure of a plan, which may be unavailable from other sources. From this base, the planner can build and customize. Most tools also provide emergency action plans for reacting to disasters of varying destructive potential. This helps to set limits on the endless creation of scenarios that often strangles novice planners' efforts. Planning tools underscore the information that the planner must acquire. Knowing what questions to ask and having a format for entering responses can speed project completion.

However, business continuity planning tools are also limited in what they can provide. For example, no planning tool can provide the in-house planner with the skills needed to obtain the cooperation of departmental managers in assessing those systems that are critical. Planning tools do not provide planners with the skills required to evaluate vendor offerings, to negotiate contracts for hot-site services, or to develop effective off-site storage plans. Nor can a planning tool convince senior management of the need for business continuity planning.

On the other hand, planning tools can be used to articulate a plan for business recovery, a plan that can be tested, refined, and maintained. An effective tool will pay for itself in the time saved in maintaining the plan. This is arguably the greatest benefit business continuity planning tools can offer.

SOURCES OF INFORMATION ON PLANNING TOOLS

Generally, the best sources of information about business continuity planning and tools are professional contingency planning associations. The number of these organizations has increased dramatically over the past several years, and membership is booming.

Most contingency planning group members are business continuity or security planners from organizations within a specific geographic region. Members exchange ideas and information openly about their situations and offer advice and solutions from their own experiences. These groups can be valuable sources of new techniques and methods of plan development — from presenting the plan to management to deciding on the best records-salvaging strategy. Many associations are self-appointed watchdogs over the essentially unpoliced business continuity industry. The groups invite vendors to demonstrate products and provide insight into their particular expertise. In addition, most business continuity groups do not allow their vendors to interfere with candid appraisals of products and services, including business continuity planning tools.

CONCLUSION

Because of the costs associated with contracting a business continuity consultant, many organizations choose to develop a contingency plan in-house, either by using planning tools or by using a consultant for the initial stages of the development. Either choice is valid, but business continuity planning tools do not provide a comprehensive solution to an organization's business continuity planning needs. Only by careful study of the literature of business continuity planning and by interacting with other business continuity planners can novice planners obtain the competence to develop effective recovery capabilities for their firms. On the other hand, planning tools can be a useful adjunct in plan development activities by providing an example of plan format and by exposing the user to the plan's unique approach and method.

Notes

1. R.C. Miller, "Your Legal Liability in a Data Processing Disaster," *Disaster Recovery Journal* 1, no. 1 (1988).
2. J.W. Toigo, *Disaster Recovery Planning: Managing Risk and Catastrophe in Information Systems* (New York: Prentice Hall, 1988).
3. G. Dean and D. Bellm,"72% Cite Increase in Risks," *Disaster Recovery Journal* 1, no. 1 (1988).
4. H.A. Levine, *Project Management Using Microcomputers* (Berkeley, CA: Osborne McGraw-Hill, 1988).

Chapter 29
Choosing a Hot-Site Vendor

Philip Jan Rothstein

ANY ORGANIZATION THAT HAS DECIDED TO BACK UP CRITICAL IT OPERATIONS MUST DECIDE HOW IT WILL DO SO. Two common methods of operations backup are hot sites and cold sites. Hot sites are fully equipped, ready-to-run computer centers designed to be activated when a subscriber declares that a disaster has occurred. Cold sites are ready-to-use facilities without computers or communications equipment in place. Other options include using company-owned facilities. Although using a hot site can be an expensive option, an organization whose survival depends on its computer processing capability may find that it is ultimately the most cost-effective choice. This chapter provides some guidelines on choosing a hot-site vendor.

TYPES OF VENDORS

There are basically four categories of hot-site vendors. The first consists of organizations that are dedicated to disaster recovery. This includes the three companies that constitute the majority of the hot-site market, Comdisco Disaster Recovery Services, Inc., Sungard Recovery Services, Inc., and IBM Business Recovery Services. Each of these companies offers multiple locations and classes of service.

The second category of hot-site offerings comprises hardware vendors (other than IBM), including Hewlett-Packard, which provide recovery services primarily for their customers. Hewlett-Packard has alliances with other organizations to support multiplatform recovery capabilities.

The third category consists of regional, local, or specialty hot-site vendors. Companies that depend on multivendor computing environments or complex communications networks may find the hot-site services of many of these vendors to be too limited.

The fourth category is composed of mobile recovery sites. Mobile recovery sites provide the convenience of having a self-contained backup computer facility trucked or airlifted to or near the subscriber's premises. The time delay for transportation may or may not be acceptable. CSC Provident Mobile Recovery Systems, Sungard Recovery Services, XL/Datacomp, Inc., and Comdisco Disaster Recovery Services are among the firms that offer relocatable recovery sites. Some of the minicomputer equipment vendors also have truck- or van-mounted emergency systems.

INDUSTRY OVERVIEW

Since this chapter was last updated, the business continuity hot-site industry has continued an accelerating trend toward consolidation. Three major vendors constitute the vast majority of the industry segment: Comdisco Disaster Recovery Services, IBM Business Recovery Services, and Sungard Recovery Services. The remaining independent hot-site vendors consist of either computer hardware vendor captives (e.g., Hewlett-Packard) or "boutique" vendors focusing on either specific niches (trading floor recovery, mailing recovery, specialized computer environments) or specific geographic regions. Many of these captives or boutiques have formed alliances with one or more of the three major providers.

The second, accelerating trend since this chapter was last updated is the broadening of hot-site services to increasingly address mid-frame, client/server, and distributed computing environments, complex networks, and work-area recovery. As a result, the ability to handle complex, technologically sophisticated hot-site recovery capabilities at all may constrain vendor choices.

FACTORS FOR CHOOSING A HOT-SITE VENDOR

Before beginning the hot-site vendor selection process, the disaster recovery planner should ensure that all hot-site vendors to be evaluated provide equipment that is compatible with that of the organization. This will eliminate the time-wasting process of reviewing inappropriate candidates.

Capacity and Growth

Once the list of compatible vendors has been compiled, the ability of the hot-site vendor to handle the projected processing workload, data storage, and data communications volumes as well as physical space requirements should be considered. The business continuity planner not only should consider the organization's current needs but should project those needs at least through the duration of the prophot-siteosed hot-site contract. Flexibility on the part of the hot-site vendor in meeting a certain degree of unanticipated capacity requirements or in adapting to functional changes over time is essential.

Ideally, the hot-site vendor should guarantee the available capacity and space through the duration of the contract and provide reasonable assurance (preferably in the written contract) of future capacity that would support contract renewal.

In addition to computer space and processor storage capacity, noncomputer space needs should also be evaluated. Sufficient space should be available for storing magnetic tapes and other media, printer paper, and custom forms and operational documentation. Consideration should be given to work areas for the staff who will be operating the computer system and to office space for support staff who will work in proximity to the computer area. In the event of a lengthy stay at the hot site, additional office, storage, or other space may be needed.

Recovery Experience

The key test for any hot-site vendor is its performance during an actual disaster. The ratio of actual disaster recoveries to the total client base may be low — or even zero. Given that actual recoveries are relatively rare, it should be reasonable to expect that a hot-site vendor has never mishandled an actual recovery. The odds are that any vendor who fails in a client recovery would quickly be out of business. Therefore, contrary to expectations that emphasize vendor experience in recovering clients during disasters, vendor stability, technology and other factors tend to be weighted more significantly.

The extent of vendor participation in the development of the business continuity plan for clients who have successfully recovered can indicate the hot-site vendor's commitment to its clients. Interviewing clients who have experienced disasters can help uncover weaknesses.

Comdisco Disaster Recovery Services, IBM Business Recovery Services, and Sungard Recovery Services each have substantial experience supporting client recoveries.

Testing Capabilities

Without regular testing of the business continuity plan, the ability to recover at a hot site is shaky at best. Most hot-site vendors provide a testing allowance; some even insist contractually on a minimum level of subscriber testing. Most also participate proactively in client testing. The availability and convenience of testing and vendor support of the testing process can significantly affect the cost as well as effectiveness of business continuity; if it is inconvenient or costly to test, testing may not be performed adequately; as a result, in an actual disaster the recovery effort could be useless.

The frequency and duration of testing varies from vendor to vendor. Twenty-four to 72 hours of test time annually is typical. Additional test time can usually be arranged at extra cost. Any additional testing needs should be specified in the initial contract. The time to negotiate testing allowances is *before* signing a contract. Once an agreement is executed, additional test time may only be available at extra cost.

Availability of the hot site for testing should also be evaluated. Depending on the number of hot-site clients and their testing needs, the lead time to schedule a test could be significant. Some hot-site testing schedules are busiest on weekends, others on weekdays. It is a good idea to check into test schedules as early as possible.

Of course, a declared disaster preempts any testing at a hot site. Even test time scheduled well in advance may be unexpectedly cancelled or interrupted; provision for such an event may be appropriate in the vendor agreement as well as in test plans.

The hot-site vendor should be included in the process of initiating and orchestrating a test. On completion of the test, the vendor should be able to offer specific feedback and recommendations.

In some cases, remote testing may be necessary — or even more appropriate than on-site testing. Some vendors offer remote testing (and sometimes remote recovery) as an option, which could be particularly valuable if the hot site is far away.

Geography

The business continuity planner must consider location of the hot site in light of both recovery and testing. Costs for communications, transportation, and lodging are likely to be higher if the recovery site is farther away. On the other hand, a more distant site is less likely to be affected by a regional disaster (e.g., flood, hurricane, toxic contamination, or communications or power failure). In general, a hot site should be at least 25 miles away.

The business continuity planner should consider the impact of the hot site's location on personnel. In addition to affecting costs, a remote hot site requires that employees make an abrupt transition to a distant location for recovery; the disruption in their lives could hinder the recovery effort.

In the event the contracted hot site becomes unavailable because of a declared disaster by another client or for any other reason, an alternate hot site may be offered either at the same location or at a different location. It is important to make provisions in the recovery plan for the possibility of a different hot-site location. Issues related to logistics and possibly system configuration must be addressed, particularly if travel is involved.

Most of the same consideration used in situating a data center apply to the location of a hot site. A hot site should not be a in a high-risk location that is subject to external disruption. Access to transportation, including airports, interstate highways, and rail lines, is important to expediting business continuity and even more important in the case of a regional disaster. Such predictable occurrences as rush-hour traffic or the effects of inclement weather should not seriously impair access to the hot site.

Cost

Hot site costs fall into several categories. Some hot-site vendors offer testing and initial setup at no cost. Most charge a monthly or annual subscription fee to the organization for the ability to use their facilities and services when needed.

Subscription Fees. Subscription fees may range from a few hundred dollars to tens of thousands of dollars a month (for very large, complex mainframe environments).

Declaration Fees. Most hot-site vendors charge a one-time declaration, or activation, fee. This is designed in part to ensure that clients take the decision to declare a disaster seriously and in part to cover the vendor's immediate costs in supporting the client's recovery. These fees can range from a few thousand dollars to tens of thousands and are paid only when a disaster is declared.

Recovery Use. Once the hot-site vendor has received a declaration of a disaster, the clock usually starts ticking. In addition to hourly or daily use fees, there may be other time- or resource-related fees during the period of the actual recovery as well as during the subsequent operation at the hot-site facility.

Some hot-site vendors limit the amount of time a hot site may be occupied after a disaster is declared, so that the hot site can be returned to "ready" status for other clients. This may mean that it becomes necessary to relocate from the hot site in a matter of weeks after the disaster, possibly to a cold site within the same facility, or elsewhere. The length of time the hot site may be used should be defined in the contract, along with clear responsibilities for the additional work and expense should a relocation become necessary.

The return to normal operations following a disaster may involve additional costs and effort. This should be considered in recovery planning, testing, and budgeting.

External Costs. Expenses incurred on the client's behalf by the hot-site vendor are usually billable and should be identified explicitly, both for testing and in the event of a disaster declaration. These will likely include both one-time and duration-dependent costs, such as telecommunications connections or extra equipment rental.

Storage and Maintenance Costs. The vendor may charge a fee for locker or storage space used to store documentation, materials, supplies, and so forth if beyond the basic allotment. If dedicated equipment or network connections are necessary, it is likely the hot-site vendor will charge a fee covering space occupied, equipment maintenance and monitoring, electricity, etc.

Testing Costs. Testing at the hot site should be done at least once a year and, in many cases, as many as four to eight times a year. The hot-site vendor provides a testing allowance addressing time and resources. Additional costs may be incurred for testing beyond the basic agreement. Before an organization enters into a contract with a hot-site vendor, testing costs should be projected and reflected in the agreement.

Cost Increases. Some hot-site contracts have annual or other periodic cost increases. In addition, the costs for future increases to function or capacity should be negotiated and committed up front to the furthest degree practical. Hot-site contracts typically cover multiyear periods, because the upfront investment in establishing a working hot-site vendor-subscriber relationship may be substantial relative to ongoing costs.

Software Costs. Even if business continuity planning software is bundled with the hot-site subscription, there may be additional costs for options, enhancements, and annual software maintenance.

Other Costs. Specialized resources, vendor personnel time, and such direct expenses as office furniture, supplies, food, and external vendor fees, may be chargeable to the subscriber during testing as well as during a recovery. These costs should be identified in advance whenever practical. Costs associated with evaluating hot-site vendors and negotiating an agreement may include travel to vendor sites and legal costs.

Insurance. Insurance may cover some of the costs associated with recovery to a hot site. The hot-site vendor may be expected to provide the insurer with detailed documentation in order to obtain compensation from insurance coverage.

Technical Environment

As stated previously, the vendor's technical environment must be compatible with the client's configuration and environment. The vendor's technical staff should be well versed in the specifics of the client's environment.

In some cases, the vendor may provide operating system software, communications drivers, or other offerings that may or may not be under the subscriber's control or may be shared with other subscribers. Technical and technological compatibility must be an integral aspect of the contract.

Increasingly, client technical environments are becoming more complex and volatile. Information technology trends such as client/server, Internet connectivity, remote computing, and mobile computing have made the process of hot-site recovery planning and execution more difficult. The effective hot-site vendor will demonstrate flexibility as well as the ability to adapt and improvise as needed to cope with evolving client needs.

In addition, clients operating multiple computing platforms may find that hot-site vendors may house the recovery platforms in more than one location, or may operate a particular platform in only one location. The vendor's ability to deliver computing services through dedicated or public communications networks to the client's site will be essential to a successful recovery.

Recovery Center Facilities

The hot site should be operated as a going business, with appropriate attention to maintenance, testing, security, cleaning, and staffing. It should offer a professional environment appropriate to a facility that will house the subscriber's vital operations in a crisis.

Physical security and access control are especially important at a hot-site facility. Multiple clients may be testing or recovering concurrently within a facility housing multiple hot sites. Some hot-site facilities may share hardware (such as logically partitioned processors) and communications facilities. The client should understand the level of physical as well as logical security provided by the hot-site vendor and the mechanisms used to prevent security breaches and to detect violations.

The client may also wish to employ multiple levels of security clearance among its own personnel. For example, certain people may be permitted to enter the computer area or tape library, and others restricted to office work areas. Many hot-site vendors offer card-key access control systems that may be programmed to allow this.

The infrastructure of the hot-site facility is also important. Some (but not all) hot-site vendors provide alternate electric power sources, with uninterruptible power supply systems and backup generators. Redundant environmental systems are also common.

Some clients find it useful to store key documentation, including their business continuity plan and operating procedures, at the hot site. They may also store backups of key systems data to expedite the startup process. Many hot-site vendors provide limited storage or locker space for this purpose as well as limited space for such on-hand supplies as special printer forms. Arrangements can be made to ensure that the client can access this documentation or data.

Alternate Facilities

A hot site may be only part of a recovery solution for a client. Several hot-site vendors offer alternate facilities for computer recovery. These may include mobile, fully equipped, self-sufficiency, trailer-mounted computer rooms; "quickship" capabilities, with computer and support equipment rapidly delivered to the client location (or alternate recovery location); even self-contained electrical power generation and stand-alone communications facilities such as satellite or microwave links.

These alternate facilities may be integrated with the basic hot-site agreement or may be contracted separately. The client's recovery timeframe, economic constraints, technical environment and location should be weighted carefully when considering an alternate facility or hot site.

Communications Capabilities

In the past few years, communications capabilities have become one of the most critical aspects of disaster recovery. A backup computer configuration in a remote conditioned space is of little value if the computer cannot communicate effectively with the subscriber's business.

More than line access is involved. The vendor should play an active role in designing, implementing, and managing the backup network. Expertise and facilities should be in place to operate, troubleshoot, and reconfigure the network. Custom generation of network control software to meet subscriber needs should be possible. Spare capacity, redundancy, and diagnostic capabilities should be in place. Modems, multiplexers, patch panels, cables, dial backup units, and other components should be inventoried, tested, and ready to use when needed. The network capabilities should also be compatible with the subscribers' requirements.

It may prove necessary to install client communications equipment or circuits to the hot site in advance. The hot-site vendor may charge fees for the space occupied by client equipment, as well as for management, testing, and coordination.

Voice and other communications needs should be considered as well as data. Beyond basic PBX or Centrex service, the client may need to redirect incoming telephone calls and faxes to the hot site. Availability of automated call distribution systems, voicemail, and other specialized equipment should be considered if it is in use at the client's existing site.

Complementary Services

Some hot-site vendors offer a variety of complementary services that may be of value to the subscriber, including cold sites, electronic vaulting, planning software, off-site storage, or consulting support. In addition, some organizations may rely on such specialized equipment or services as laser printers, microform production or handling, check sorters or signers, and custom equipment. (There are even recovery facilities for trading operations.) Furthermore, such basic office needs as a telephone PBX, facsimile, copiers, or other components may be vital to a recovery effort. The vendor's responsibilities regarding this equipment should be specifically identified.

Vendors may also provide business continuity planning software. The software cost may be bundled with the hot-site subscription. This may or may not prove to be an advantage to the client: (1) the software may not be ideal for the client's specific plan development needs or environment; (2) annual software maintenance costs could become considerable; and, (3) upgrades or options for the software may be necessary at additional cost.

Therefore, in weighing the value of bundled software or services with a hot-site contract, the true value to the client organization should be considered, along with ongoing costs, if any, for maintenance.

Stability and History

Business continuity hot sites are a relatively new industry. Only a few companies have been active for more than 10 years. The business continuity planner should look for a company with a steadily increasing client base (to a declared maximum) and history of enhancement as an indication of stability. In addition, actual recovery experience is a powerful advantage that should not be overlooked; some hot-site vendors have not yet actually supported any declared client disasters. The continuing vendor consolidation in the business continuity hot-site industry, noted earlier, is an important factor. A hot-site vendor's policies, practices, philosophy, facilities, staff, and more may change if the vendor is acquired or merged. If a hot-site vendor fails, the cost and impact of reimplementing and retesting the business continuity plan with a new vendor may exceed the cost of the hot-site agreement.

The financial data, ownership, and history of a hot-site vendor can be a decisive factor in the selection process. Some companies have entered the hot-site business as an adjunct to their service bureau or other business. When an organization is checking references, service bureau clients should be considered separately from hot-site clients.

Contract Terms

The typical hot-site agreement duration ranges from 2 to 5 years. Subscription costs tend to decline dramatically with increasing terms beyond three years. An important tradeoff to consider is that client needs may change dramatically during the contract term.

Therefore, subscription fees should not necessarily be weighted as heavily in the decision process as such factors as costs associated with initial plan development, implementation and testing; transition costs if the client were to move to another vendor; or, excess or insufficient hot-site coverage as the client's configuration, recovery needs, or technology evolve.

Responsiveness and Flexibility

Business continuity requirements are likely to change over time. The hot-site vendor should be able to support such changes, although there may be additional costs. Most organizations find that the ability to change configuration or other aspects over time without renegotiating the base contract is valuable. In addition, the vendor's history of innovation and responsiveness to industry trends can indicate its commitment to its clients. The vendor should explicitly define the nature and extent of their commitment to new client technology, equipment, capacity, or functional needs.

The process of activating the business continuity plan is another area to look at with regard to responsiveness. The vendor should have an explicit, documented plan for the declaration process that meshes with the subscriber's business continuity plan.

Activation

The process and time delay associated with initiating a disaster declaration should be considered from both a recovery and financial perspective. Most vendors prefer that a client who is considering declaring a disaster first issue an alert, so that the vendor can begin preparations to support the client in the event the client formally declares a disaster. Generally, there is no cost to a client for alerting the hot-site vendor.

Once alerted by the client, the hot-site vendor should be able to rapidly activate the hot site if a disaster is declared. The hot-site agreement should be unambiguous with respect to activation timeframes as well as specific vendor and client responsibilities. However, it should be noted that the hot-site agreement typically contains limitations regarding the vendor's liability, hot-site availability, and adequacy of the facilities.

Personnel Support

The recovery center should not be merely a shell housing a computer. Subscriber staff will likely spend a great deal of time at the center conducting testing as well as carrying out recovery procedures in the event of a disaster. It is important that lodging, food, access to medical care, transportation, logistics, communications, and any other special needs of the personnel who will be assigned to the recovery team at the hot site be addressed by the hot-site vendor.

Most hot-site vendors provide such basic amenities as break rooms, vending machines, and coffee service. Some even provide more elaborate facilities, including basic on-site medical care, cots, and VCRs or video games for off-duty personnel. While not critical to a recovery effort, such conveniences can have great value in relieving the stress and inconvenience of a recovery.

Availability

Most hot-site vendors limit competition for their resources to ensure that they are able to serve any client promptly. The contract should limit the maximum number of subscribers to the hot site. Many vendors will not sign on a subscriber to the same facility as another subscriber in the same area (e.g., building, block, neighborhood, telephone central office, or power grid).

In addition, to improve the odds of being able to serve clients in the event of a regional disaster, some hot-site vendors offer alternative facilities or locations in case the primary hot site is already in use. Once a subscriber declares a disaster, it is completely dependent on that hot site; a fallback facility could become critical. This is particularly important if the vendor is limited to a single recovery facility and that facility was unavailable for any reason — already in use by another customer, or disabled by a local or regional disruption.

RECOMMENDED COURSE OF ACTION

The first question that a business continuity planner should ask before considering hot-site vendors is whether a hot site is really necessary and appropriate. Some organizations enter into hot-site agreements without fully considering other alternatives (e.g., cold sites or other company-controlled facilities) or contract with hot-site vendors before they are able to implement recovery procedures or to test. Without those procedures or thorough testing, a hot-site contract is nothing more than a costly piece of paper.

Once the organization has decided that a hot site is required, the disaster recovery planner must have a clear understanding of the requirements before contacting vendors. Examples of organizational requirements include:

- The minimal configurations and capacity necessary
- The most important factors in vendor selection
- The factors that would rule out a vendor from further consideration

A list of weighted selection factors should be prepared before vendors are contacted so that the most important considerations are identified and resolved early in the evaluation process.

The next step is to determine which vendors have the potential to meet the basic recovery requirements. Exhibit 29-1 lists some sources for general information about vendor offerings.

It is helpful to provide hot-site vendors with specific written requirements. Some vendors may decline to bid because of the organization's particular functional, capacity, or logistic requirements; by ruling them out early in the process, the business continuity planner can save much time.

Contacting current clients of the hot-site vendor is a vital step. Each of the factors affecting selection should be addressed to the extent practical with the vendor's clients as well as the vendor itself.

The list of potential hot-site vendors should be narrowed rather quickly; however, the business continuity planner should remember that vendor pricing is only part of the total cost and therefore avoid ruling out a vendor early on pricing alone.

Exhibit 29-1. Information sources for hot-site vendors.

Disaster Recovery Journal
P.O. Box 510100
St. Louis, MO 63151
314.894.0276
E-mail drj@drj.com
http://www.drj.com

The Rothstein Catalog on Disaster Recovery
Rothstein Associates Inc.
4 Arapaho Rd.
Brookfield, CT 06804-3104
203.740.7444
E-mail info@rothstein.com
http://www.rothstein.com

Survive! The Business Continuity Group
P.O. Box 5030
Branchburg, NJ 08876
1-800-SURVIVE
E-mail surviveusa@aol.com
http://www.survive.com

In addition to Survive!, numerous regional business continuity groups throughout the world provide access to information about hot-site vendors. Each of the above sources can provide information on these contingency groups.

Once a vendor has been chosen, it is imperative to ensure that the contract provides for all the organization's current and projected needs. Relationships with hot-site vendors may deteriorate because of unrealistic expectations made on the basis of oral or assumed agreements. Once a contract is signed, it may be difficult or costly to address additional expectations; a costly transition to a different hot-site vendor may be necessary, possibly even before the end of the contract term.

Chapter 30
A Proactive Approach to Improving the IS Business Continuity Plan

Belden Menkus

DIFFERENT ORGANIZATIONS USE DIFFERENT NAMES TO IDENTIFY THEIR PLAN OF ACTION TO RECOVER FROM INTERRUPTIONS TO BUSINESS OPERATIONS DUE TO NATURAL OR MANMADE DISASTERS. For simplicity, this chapter uses the term *business continuity plan*. Whatever name is selected, the organization's executives expect the IS business continuity plan's provisions to enable employees to restore expeditiously and in order of priority the organization's computing capabilities that have been disrupted by the occurrence of some type of disaster event. Yet, when actual disasters have occurred, organizations have found that reaching this desired goal was hindered because some of the issues that should have been addressed in the design stage of the business continuity plan were not.

Often these issues come to light only after disaster strikes an organization. In the recovery process, those employees responsible for realizing the recovery may find that much damage could have been avoided or diminished if certain steps had been taken before the disaster occurred. Some of those steps are the focus of this discussion.

ISSUES AND RECOMMENDATIONS

This chapter emphasizes a *proactive* approach by examining some of the issues that often are overlooked in the design of business continuity plans. The recommendations in this chapter can be incorporated into an organization's already existing IS business continuity plan. Also, these recommendations can guide the revision of an existing audit work program for assessing the IS business continuity plan. These recommendations are discussed in no order of priority. They are all important.

Local Fire Fighter Capability

Ensure that the local fire fighting unit is prepared to extinguish a blaze that involves electronic hardware. In particular, fire fighters should be equipped and trained to deal with the combustion of the complex plastic residues and the various toxic substances that the device components and the insulation that is used to coat the telecommunication and computing connection cables may release. (The members of most fire fighting units deal primarily with fairly straightforward blazes that occur in residences. Rarely do they encounter complicated fire extinguishing situations. This is true especially in suburban and rural localities, where the fire fighters may be volunteers with essentially limited training.)

Try to arrange for an annual familiarization visit by the members of the fire fighting unit that is most likely to respond to the organization's site. These individuals should be made aware, at least, of the placement of the major computing and telecommunication hardware units and their wiring ducts. And, training in the proper techniques for handling a fire involving toxic substances should be provided by the faculty of the nearest fire academy or similar entity.

Printed Forms

Provide for prompt replenishment of essential stocks of printed forms. (Even where laser printers are being used to produce such forms, it may be impossible to restore that capability during the immediate post disaster recovery period.) Identify which vendor has the negatives for each form which must be available during the recovery period. *Consider:* including a duplicate set of these negatives with the records that are maintained in secure off-site storage for use in the business continuity process. (Where electronic forms are being employed by an organization ensure that a current copy of the software that is used in their generation is maintained at the secure off-site storage location.)

Time Delay

Allow for a delay of at least 12 to 48 hours in beginning to restore operations after a fire is extinguished. This time will be required for the fire marshal's legally required investigation of the site of a blaze to identify its probable cause and to determine the possibility of arson being involved in the incident. In some localities, as well, the local building inspector or health department may be required to certify that the site remains suitable for human occupancy. During this period, employee and vendor representative access to the site and the removal or salvage of equipment, supplies and records will be restricted, at best. In some instances, such access may prove to be impossible for several days.

Funds Collection and Disbursement

Verify that an alternate means for collecting and disbursing funds exists if a major disaster occurs. In many such situations, such as a flood or an earthquake, the bank regulatory agency officials can be expected to close all of these institutions in the surrounding area for several days following the disaster. This action will be undertaken to permit the bank employees to concentrate on returning their institutions to normal operations.

Such a closing could have a critical impact, however, on the business continuity plans of the customers of the affected banks. Under this arrangement, they would be denied ready access to their organization's funds. Such a restriction could impact both the enterprise's funds collections and accounts payable processes. This could pose a significant economic recovery risk for those entities that must transfer funds domestically on a time-critical basis or internationally in any fashion. This will prove to be extremely critical in situations where so-called *electronic commerce* arrangements are in place. *One possible solution*: Negotiate a *standby* line of credit from an out-of-area bank or investment house, to be used only during a recovery from the occurrence of a disaster.

Utilities At Alternate Site

Assure that the required water, electric power, and telecommunication services are in place and ready for use at whatever site is to be used for essential computing and telecommunication operations during the post disaster period. Typically, at least eight to 36 hours must be allowed in the business continuity plan for the utility providers who are involved to activate any already in-place services capabilities. Three to five additional days must be allowed when new or additional utility services must be installed. And, in many rural localities this allowance should be doubled.

Telecommunications Capabilities

Validate that the telecommunications service providers who will be involved are prepared to divert incoming voice and data traffic from the organization's regular location to whatever site is to be used during the recovery process. Some local telecommunication enterprise central sites and the alternate carriers may not be prepared to divert call traffic in volume on short notice. The extra call load may create a queuing situation within the interoffice and network node trunk arrangements that will cause them to *busy out* this diverted traffic.

Possible Loss of Telecommunications Central Site

Allow for the possibility that the telecommunication enterprise central site itself may be lost. (Most likely, such a disruption would occur as the result of a fire.) Typically, central site service restoration will require several weeks to complete. The business continuity plan should allow at least three to five days for the installation and testing of a replacement switch. And the plans should allow at least an additional day for each 1500 local service links that must be restored. Normally, fire, police, and medical services will be given priority treatment during this process. However, other telecommunication enterprises that are not associated with those services can not be expected to receive special treatment during this time. *Consider:* Providing a so-called *bypass* microwave link for use during this period. If this is to be done, the hardware and electronic gear must be located on site in advance of the disaster occurrence.

Recovery Period Employee Work Space

Assure that there is suitable work space available for those employees who must be displaced during the business continuity process. Those individuals who are concerned directly with emergency operations should be relocated to a nearby contingency operations site. *Consider:* Furloughing customer service representatives, information processing application developers, and others whose work it may not be possible to support during the disaster recovery period.

Water Sprinkler Rating

*Confirm that the **rating** is adequate for whatever water sprinkler fire extinguishing mechanism which must be used in the environments in which any type of computing or telecommunicating is carried out.* It may not be feasible, for a variety of reasons, to install any form of carbon dioxide or other type of gaseous extinguishing capabilities in these areas. What is of concern in a sprinkler fire extinguishing mechanism is the environmental or *ambient* air temperature at which most of the individual sprinkler heads will operate to discharge water and begin the fire suppression process. A 165∞F rated water sprinkler fire extinguishing mechanism is the one that is used most commonly in these environments. (In many localities the building code or the fire marshal will insist that such a mechanism be installed. even where another type of fire suppression arrangement is in place.)

The individual water sprinkler heads in this sort of installation are designed to operate when the temperature of the fire sensing element in the head reaches between 160∞F and 170∞F. (The range of this relatively crude measure reflects the fact that these devices were meant originally for use in relatively simple warehouse and storage shed structures.) However, because of the comparatively primitive nature of the fire sensing process itself in such environments, the actual air temperature can reach 1000∞F before the extinguishing mechanism is activated. The availability of the protection that is provided by a water sprinkler fire extinguishing mechanism is far better than having no protection at all.

Ceiling Tiles

Insist that the tiles in the ceiling of any area in which computing or telecommunicating is carried out be anchored independently where a gas discharge fire suppression arrangement has been installed. This action will prevent the accidental dislodging of these tiles when the gas is discharged. (Normally these tiles are mounted loosely on a supporting metal framework in order to facilitate their removal to provide for access to the plenum area for the routine maintenance of the installed lighting and ventilation mechanisms. However, the air turbulence that may be created by the fire suppression arrangement gas discharge can send the individual loosely mounted ceiling tiles flying across the work area, causing injury to people and damage to property.)

Water and Moisture Removal

Assure that sufficient drainage has been provided for the prompt removal of any post disaster water accumulation in the area in which any type of computing or telecommunicating is carried out. Significant amounts of water can collect as a consequence of such things as natural flooding and the discharge of fire suppression mechanisms or the use of conventional hose streams to *knock down* the fire. (Most of this water will be very contaminated and will affect adversely the operation of the computing and telecommunication equipment. In addition, the dirt and debris that this water can contain may be considered by the inspectors who were mentioned earlier in this chapter to constitute a *public health hazard.*) Normally, the so-called *poured concrete with steel reinforcement* construction that has been used commonly over the past generation in office buildings does not provide such drainage. Some of the water and debris may be drained naturally through the building's interior stairways and elevator shafts.

Drainage alone, however, cannot be assumed to be able to remove all of the residual moisture. *Consider:* Installing and operating several dehumidification units during the post disaster recovery period.

Rubbish Removal

Verify that adequate provisions have been made for rubbish collection and removal during the post disaster site cleanup process. A fire, flood, or other disaster can generate rubbish in volumes that are much larger than most structures are designed to accommodate or than most building maintenance employees are equipped to handle. Among other things, the type and extent of the flooding that was mentioned earlier in this chapter can dissolve the glue that holds floor coverings in place. *Consider:* Renting several larger so-called *dumpsters* or *open bed* trailers to supplement the available trash removal equipment during the post disaster recovery period.

REALISTIC EXPECTATIONS

Finally, the main emphasis in the design of the business continuity plan should be on its practicality. It is unrealistic to expect that the impact of the disaster will be controlled readily and that the recovery process can be carried out in a neat and orderly fashion. In particular, the plan designers should look at business continuity from a *proactive* perspective.

Chapter 31
Reengineering the Business Continuity Planning Process

Carl B. Jackson

THE FAILURE OF ORGANIZATIONS TO ACCURATELY MEASURE THE CONTRIBUTIONS OF THE BCP PROCESS TO ITS OVERALL SUCCESS HAS LED TO THE DOWNWARD SPIRALING CYCLE OF THE TOTAL BUSINESS CONTINUITY PROGRAM. The recurring downward spin or decomposition includes planning, testing, maintenance, decline → re-planning, testing, maintenance, decline → replanning, testing, maintenance, decline, etc. The 1998 *Contingency Planning and Management/Ernst and Young LLP Business Continuity Planning Survey*[1] clearly supports this observation. According to the latest survey results, 63 percent of the respondents ranked BCP as being either *extremely important* or *very important* to senior management. This study indicates that decision makers have a high level of awareness regarding the importance of BCP. These findings contrast with other survey results which illustrate that execution and follow-through of the BCP mission is often lacking. These statistics include:

1. 82 percent of the respondents do not measure the cost/benefit of their BCP programs
2. Only 27 percent of the respondents' organizations train their people on how to execute the BCP
3. 33 percent of the organizations responding do not test their BCPs
4. Only 3.6 percent of the organizations base pay increases for BCP personnel on the success of the BCP program

Business Continuity Planning Measurements

These results also suggest a disconnect between top management's perceptions of BCP objectives and the manner in which they measure its value. In the past, BCP effectiveness was usually measured in terms of a pass/fail grade on a mainframe recovery test or on the perceived benefits of backup sites and redundant telecommunications capabilities weighed against the expense for these capabilities. The trouble with these types of metrics is that they only measure BCP direct costs and/or indirect perceptions as to whether a test was effectively executed. These metrics do not indicate whether a test validates the appropriate infrastructure elements or even whether it is thorough enough to test a component until it fails, thereby extending the reach and usefulness of the test scenario.

So, one might inquire as to what the correct measures to use are. While financial measurements do constitute *one* measure of the BCP process, others measure the BCP's contribution to the organization in terms of quality and effectiveness, which are not strictly weighed in monetary terms. The contributions that a well-run BCP Process can make to an organization include:

1. sustaining growth and innovation
2. enhancing customer satisfaction
3. providing for people needs
4. improving overall mission-critical process quality
5. providing for practical financial metrics

Each of these measurements is discussed later in this chapter.

A RECIPE FOR RADICAL CHANGE: BCP PROCESS IMPROVEMENT

During the 1970s and 1980s experts in organizational management efficiency began introducing *performance process improvement disciplines*. These process improvement disciplines have been slowly adopted across many industries and companies for improvement of *general manufacturing* and *administrative business processes*. The basis of these and other improvement efforts was the concept that an organization's *processes* (Process — see Definitions in Exhibit 31-1) constituted the organization's fundamental lifeblood and, if made more effective and efficient, could dramatically decrease errors and increase organizational productivity.

An organization's processes are a series of successive activities, and when they are executed in the aggregate, they constitute the foundation of the organization's mission. These processes are intertwined throughout the organization's infrastructure (individual business units, divisions, plants, etc.) and are tied to the organization's supporting structures (data processing, communications networks, physical facilities, people, etc.).

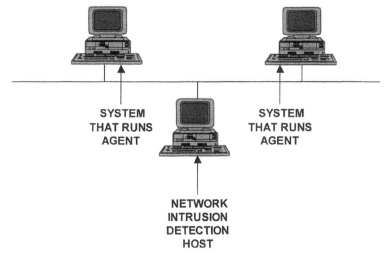

SYSTEM
THAT RUNS
AGENT

SYSTEM
THAT RUNS
AGENT

NETWORK
INTRUSION
DETECTION
HOST

Exhibit 31-1. Definitions.[5]

A key concept of the **Process Improvement and Reengineering** movement revolves around identification of process enablers and barriers (see Definitions in Exhibit 31-1). These enablers and barriers take many forms (people, technology, facilities, etc.) and must be understood and taken into consideration when introducing radical change into the organization.

The preceding narration provides the backdrop for the idea of focusing on business continuity planning not as a **project**, but as a **continuous process** that must be designed to support the other mission-critical processes of the organization. Therefore, the idea was born of adopting a continuous process approach to BCP, along with understanding and addressing the people, technology, facility, etc., enablers and barriers. This constitutes a *significant* or even *radical change* in thinking from the manner in which we have traditionally viewed and executed recovery planning. An example of a BCP process is presented in Exhibit 31-2.

Radical Changes Mandated

High management awareness and low BCP execution effectiveness, coupled with the lack of consistent and meaningful BCP measurements, call for radical changes in the manner in which we execute recovery planning responsibilities. The techniques used to develop mainframe-oriented disaster recovery (DR) plans of the '70s and '80s consisted of six distinct stages which required the recovery planner to:

1. establish a project team and a supporting infrastructure to develop the plans
2. conduct a threat or risk management review to identify likely threat scenarios to be addressed in the recovery plans
3. conduct a business impact analysis (BIA) to understand time-critical applications/networks and determine maximum-tolerable-downtimes
4. select an appropriate recovery alternative that effectively addresses the recovery priorities and time-frames mandated by the BIA
5. document the recovery plans
6. establish and adopt an ongoing testing and maintenance strategy

Shortcomings of the Traditional Disaster Recovery Planning Approach

This approach worked well when disaster recovery of *glass house* mainframe infrastructures were the norm. It even worked fairly well when it came to integrating the evolving distributed/client–server systems into the overall recovery planning infrastructure. However, when organizations became concerned with **business unit** recovery planning, the traditional DR methodology was ineffective in designing and implementing business unit/function recovery plans. Of primary concern when attempting to implement enterprise-wide recovery plans was the issue of **functional interdependencies**. Recovery planners became obsessed with identification of interdependencies between business units and functions, and the interdependencies between business units and the technological services supporting time-critical functions within these business units.

Losing Track of the Interdependencies

The ability to keep track of departmental interdependencies for BCP purposes was extremely difficult, and most methods for accomplishing this were ineffective. Numerous circumstances made tracking interdependencies difficult to achieve consistently. Circumstances affecting interdependencies revolve around rapid rates of change that most modern organizations are going through. These include reorganization/restructuring, personnel relocation, changes in the competitive environment, and outsourcing. Every time an organizational structure changes, the BCPs had to change, and the interdependencies had to be reassessed. The more rapid the change, the more daunting the BCP reshuffling. Because many functional interdependencies could not be tracked, BCP integrity was lost, and the overall functionality of the BCP was impaired. There seemed to be no easy answers to this dilemma.

Interdependencies Are Business Processes

Why are interdependencies of concern and what, typically, are the interdependencies? The answer is that, to a large degree, these interdependencies

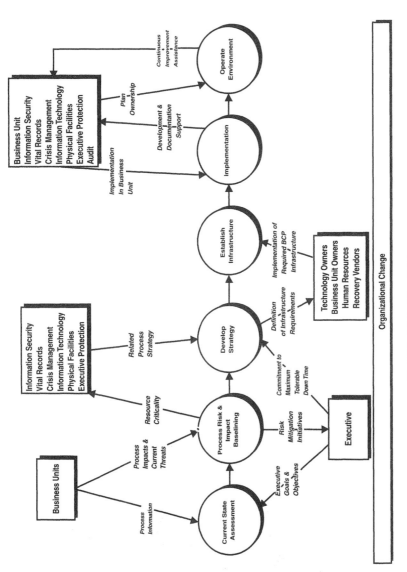

Exhibit 31-2. The BCP process.

are the **business processes** of the organization, and they are of concern because they must function in order to fulfill the organization's mission. Approaching recovery planning challenges with a business process viewpoint can, to a large extent, mitigate the problems associated with losing interdependencies, and also ensure that the focus of recovery planning efforts is on the most crucial components of the organization. Understanding how the organization's time-critical business processes are structured will assist the recovery planner in mapping the processes back to the business units/departments, supporting technological systems, networks, facilities, vital records, people, etc., and also will help the planner keep track of the processes during reorganizations and also during times of change.

THE PROCESS APPROACH TO BUSINESS CONTINUITY PLANNING

Traditional approaches to mainframe focused disaster recovery planning emphasized the need to recover the organization's technological and communications platforms. Today, many companies have shifted away from technology recovery and toward continuity of prioritized business processes and the development of specific business process recovery plans. Many large corporations use the process reengineering/improvement disciplines to increase overall organizational productivity. BCP itself should also be viewed as such a process. The following figure provides a graphical representation of how the enterprisewide BCP Process framework (see Exhibit 31-3) should look:

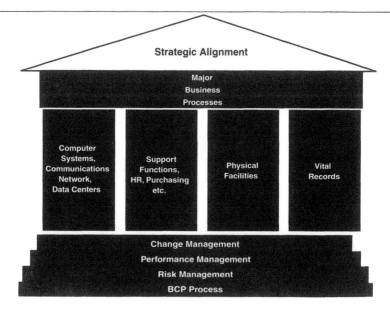

Exhibit 31-3. The BCP process framework.

At the base or foundation of the business continuity planning structure are the business continuity planning support subprocesses. These subprocesses are relevant and necessary to ensure that:

- business continuity plans are complete
- plans address all business issues
- business process owners take responsibility for their area's BCP
- staff are trained and capable of executing the recovery plans effectively

The four pillars are the core infrastructure and service elements required to effectively support the business processes of the organization.

- Basic infrastructure includes supporting resources/services (i.e., technological platforms, voice and data communications networks, etc.).
- Support functions include HR, Purchasing, etc., support mechanisms and external service providers (the virtual organization).
- Facilities refer to locations where the business may be carried out.
- Vital records are those records, manual and electronic, that are used to support time-critical business processes in the relevant business units, in addition to the traditional legal obligations pertaining to government and other statutory recordkeeping requirements.

Resting on the four supporting pillars are the key business processes which are required to keep the organization operating effectively after a disruption. The roof of the structure shows all these elements brought together and aligned with the strategies of the organization. It is within the overall context of the business strategies that BCP solutions are sought, evaluated, and prioritized.

While the base, columns, and roof of the continuity planning strategy are important and provide the strength of the structure, it is the business processes they support that determine the effectiveness of the business continuity plan.

MOVING TO A BCP PROCESS IMPROVEMENT ENVIRONMENT

Route Map Profile and High-Level BCP Process Approach

A practical, high-level approach to *BCP Process Improvement* is demonstrated by breaking down the BCP process into individual sub-process components, as shown in Exhibit 31-4.

While this route map appears complex, it goes far beyond the BCP approaches which have been used in traditional DR planning methodologies, including:

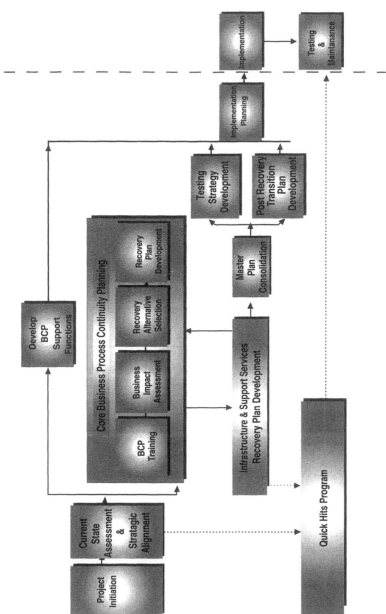

Exhibit 31-4. Sub-process components of BCP.

- Business Impact Assessment
- Strategy Selection
- Plan Development, Testing, and Maintenance

Within this route map, it is important to note that:

- Provision is made for the identification and initiation of immediate "quick hits," which are BCP-related recommendations that require urgent and immediate attention to provide protection in the short term) that can jump-start BCP initiatives. These initiatives can be effectively addressed without waiting until the end of the BCP process implementation project.
- Provision is made for introduction of Organizational Change Management components which will help facilitate deployment of the BCP process
- Emphasis is placed on co-development of recovery strategies.
- Development of business continuity plans must be business-process driven.
- Development of process-oriented recovery plans independently for each time-critical business process is critical to overall success.

The activities in each of the major stages of the BCP process improvement route-map are described below.

Stage 1 — BCP Process Initiation

During this stage, the foundation for the business continuity planning is established by developing the BCP process plan and obtaining approval. The BCP process plan is a detailed account of the work to be done, the resources that should be used, and the management practices that should be followed to control it.

Stage 2 — Current State Assessment and Strategic Alignment

In this stage the BCP process team should analyze the current state of the organization's business continuity and disaster recovery capabilities. A threat/risk management review should be conducted to identify threat categories, the estimated probability (high, medium, low) of each particular threat occurring, and the likely impact if the threat were to occur (High, Medium, Low).

Another activity of this stage is identifying strategic alignments. It is imperative that whatever business continuity plans and strategies are developed are aligned with the organization's overall business and technology plans.

Two portfolios of information result from this stage. The first stage consists of a portfolio of "quick hits," and the second stage consists of a portfolio of the core or key business processes for which comprehensive Business Continuity Plans must be developed.

Stage 3 — Develop Business Continuity Planning Support Processes

During this stage the key support elements of the Business Continuity Planning process are developed. To ensure that Business Continuity Planning is institutionalized, it must be integrated into the structure of the business. BCP program accountability must be defined and responsibilities allocated. Performance measurement criteria and processes must be developed. Policies and procedures must define how the organization plans to manage and execute the business continuity planning process.

A risk management framework should be developed that monitors business continuity risk factors and ensures that appropriate risk management and contingency action plans are maintained. Change management plans should also be developed that focus on how business and technical changes are incorporated into the Business Continuity Planning process.

Core Business Process Continuity Planning. The following four stages that make up this phase should be repeated for each *core business process* identified during the Current State Analysis.

Stage 4 — Business Continuity Planning Training

Business Process Owners and staff participating in this BCP Process should be trained in the fundamentals of Business Continuity Planning and receive basic instruction in:

- conducting Business Impact Assessments
- recovery Plan Development

The use of a knowledgeable and experienced person(s) from each of the organization's departments/business processes is vital to the success of this process. This should facilitate the preparation of viable continuity plans and procedures for each critical business process. It is also important to have these people involved during all stages of planning because they are most likely to be called upon to execute the user aspects of the continuity plan in the event of disruption.

Stage 5 — Business Impact Assessment

The purpose of the Business Impact Assessment stage is to understand the impact of a loss of business functionality due to an interruption of computing and/or infrastructure support services. Through an interview and information-gathering process these impacts should be measured quantitatively (financially) and qualitatively (operationally), such as confidence in the ability to deliver and track service to member institutions. The goal of the business assessment impact stage is twofold.

- *Resource Priorities for Recovery* — Each business process is identified and business impact information is gathered. Attention is then focused on those "time-critical business processes" requiring recovery within the maximum tolerable downtime (MTD), while placing non-time-critical business processes at a lower priority for recovery. Resource requirements for continuity of critical processes are determined.
- *Maximum-Tolerable Downtime* — The BIA helps to estimate the longest period of time a business process can remain interrupted before it risks its ability to ever adequately recover. Those business processes that require continuity within shorter time periods are defined as "time-critical," with the assumption they should receive priority attention following a disruption.

Once the analysis is complete, the BCP Process team should ensure that business units or support services management agree with the results. These results should then be formalized and presented to the responsible senior executive authority with recommendations and a request for authorization to proceed to the next BCP Process stage.

Stage 6 — Recovery Alternative Selection

Once the BIA is completed, the BCP Process team should identify available continuity strategy alternatives. Risk management options are considered during the strategy selection process, and issues such as risk avoidance, risk limitation, risk sharing, and risk transfer are analyzed. Criteria for evaluating available continuity strategies are determined. The primary objective of this stage is the development of a recovery alternatives matrix with an appropriate business case presented for the recommended continuity strategy.

Stage 7 — Recovery Plan Development

This stage involves documenting the continuity strategies that were determined in the steps above and organizing the information in a convenient format that can be used following a business interruption. The plans should address business process recovery team structures, emergency control center location(s), inventory information (i.e., people, equipment, documentation, supplies, hardware/software, vendors, critical applications, data processing reports needed, communications capabilities required, vital records, etc.), and high-level procedures to be followed. Business process managers and staff are responsible for providing additional detailed procedures, as required, to the continuity plan.

Vital records backup, storage strategies and plans are also reviewed during this stage.

Stage 8 — Infrastructure and Support Services Continuity Plan Development

During this stage, continuity plans are developed for the key support services and complex infrastructure services. The key drivers of the development of these plans are the infrastructure and service requirements identified and validated during the development of the business process recovery plans.

Stage 9 — Master Plan Consolidation

During this stage the individual Core Business Process Recovery Plans and the Infrastructure and Support Services Continuity Plans are consolidated and integrated into the organization's overall Crisis Management/ Continuity Plan. This acts as the central control and launch point in the event of a major service interruption or disaster. During the development of the overall Crisis Management/Continuity Plan, certain "global" issues are considered and planned for (e.g., damage assessment and disaster declaration procedures, location of emergency control centers, etc.).

Stage 10 — Testing Strategy Development

During this stage, an appropriate testing strategy is developed, ensuring the business continuity capability is periodically tested and evaluated. Testing strategies generally include definition of test scope and objectives, measurement criteria, test scripts, test schedules, post-mortem reviews, and test reporting.

Stage 11 — Post Recovery Transition Plan Development

After an interruption occurs and the business continuity plan is implemented, organizations find themselves operating in a non-normal mode and environment with no plans for resumption of normal operating procedures. During this BCP process stage, a high-level plan is developed to facilitate the transition back to a normal operating environment as quickly and efficiently as possible.

Stage 12 — Implementation Planning

During this stage, comprehensive implementation plans are developed for the Core Business Process Recovery Plans and Infrastructure and Support Services Recovery Plans that have been integrated into the overall Crisis Management/Contingency Plan. Implementation plans include the acquisition and installation of facilities and resources required to facilitate the continuity strategy.

Stage 13 — Quick Hits Program

The quick hits program identifies critical business continuity initiatives that require addressing in the short term in order to provide a level of comfort. This program enables organizations to provide partial services in the event of major service disruption or disaster. Solutions developed during this phase may be temporary or stop-gap solutions, until the enterprise-wide business continuity planning process is fully functional.

Stage 14 — Implementation and Testing and Maintenance Stages

These stages should become integral parts of the organization's business continuity program. The regular maintenance and testing of the business continuity plans and strategy help to ensure that:

- The continuity strategy stays viable;
- Plan documentation is current and accurate; and
- Team leaders are trained in the execution of continuity plan procedures.

HOW DO WE GET THERE? THE CONCEPT OF THE BCP VALUE JOURNEY

The **BCP Value Journey** is a helpful mechanism for co-development of BCP expectations by the organization's top management group and those responsible for recovery planning. In order to achieve a successful and measurable recovery planning process, the following checkpoints along the *BCP Value Journey* should be considered and agreed upon. The checkpoints include:

- *Defining Success* — Define what a successful BCP implementation will look like. What is the future state?
- *Aligning the BCP with Business Strategy* — Challenge objectives to ensure that the BCP effort has a business-centric focus.
- *Charting an Improvement Strategy* — Benchmark where the organization and the organization's peers are, the organization's goals based upon their present position as compared to their peers, and which critical initiatives will help the organization achieve its goals.
- *Becoming an Accelerator* — Accelerate the implementation of the organization's BCP strategies and processes. In today's environment, fast beats slow, and speed is a critical success factor for most companies.
- *Creating a Winning Team* — Build an internal/external team that can help lead the company through BCP assessment, development, and implementation.

- *Assessing Business Needs* — Assess time-critical business processes' dependence on the supporting infrastructure.
- *Documenting the Plans* — Develop continuity plans that focus on assuring that time-critical business processes will be available.
- *Enabling the People* — Implement mechanisms that can help to enable rapid reaction and recovery in times of emergency, such as training programs, a clear organizational structure, and a detailed leadership and management plan.
- *Completing the Organization's BCP Strategy* — Position the organization to complete the operational and personnel-related milestones necessary to ensure success.
- *Delivering Value* — Focus on achieving the organization's goals while also envisioning the future and handling all organizational changes which occur simultaneously.
- *Renewing/Recreating* — Challenge the new BCP process structure and organizational management to continue to adapt and meet the challenges of demonstrating availability and recoverability.

The Value Journey Facilitates Meaningful Dialogue

This *Value Journey* technique for raising the awareness level of management helps to both facilitate meaningful discussions about the BCP Process and to ensure that the resulting BCP strategies truly add *value*. As will be discussed later, this value-added concept will also provide additional metrics by which the success of the overall BCP process can be measured.

THE NEED FOR ORGANIZATIONAL CHANGE MANAGEMENT

In addition to the approaches of *BCP Process Improvement*, and the *BCP Value Journey* mentioned above, the need to introduce people-oriented *Organizational Change Management* (OCM) concepts becomes an important component in implementing a successful BCP process.

H. James Harrington et al., in their book *Business Process Improvement Workbook*,[2] point out that applying process improvement approaches can often cause trouble unless the organization manages the change process. They state that, "Approaches like reengineering only succeed if we challenge and change our paradigms and our organization's culture. It is a fallacy to think that you can change the processes without changing the behavior patterns or the people who are responsible for operating these processes."[3]

Organizational change management concepts, including the identification of people enablers and barriers and the design of appropriate implementation plans which change behavior patterns, play an important role in shifting the BCP project approach to one of *BCP Process Improvement*. The authors also point out that, "There are a number of tools and techniques that are effective in managing the change process, such as pain management, change mapping, and synergy. The important thing is that every *BPI* (Business Process Improvement) program must have a very comprehensive change management plan built into it, and this plan must be effectively implemented."[4]

Therefore, it is incumbent on the recovery planner to ensure that, as the concept of the BCP Process evolves within the organization, appropriate OCM techniques are considered and included as an integral component of the overall deployment effort.

HOW DO WE MEASURE SUCCESS? BALANCED SCORECARD CONCEPT

A complement to the *BCP Process Improvement* approach is the establishment of meaningful measures or metrics that the organization can use to weigh the success of the overall BCP process. Traditional measures include:

- How much money is spent on hotsites?
- How many people are devoted to BCP activities?
- Was the hotsite test a success?

Instead, the focus should be on measuring the **BCP Process** contribution to achieving the overall goals of the organization. This focus helps us to:

- Identify agreed-upon BCP development milestones
- Establish a baseline for execution
- Validate BCP Process delivery
- Establish a foundation for management satisfaction in order to successfully manage expectations

The *BCP Balanced Scorecard* includes a definition of the:

- Value Statement
- Value Proposition
- Metrics/Assumptions on reduction of BCP risk
- Implementation Protocols
- Validation Methods

Exhibit 31-5 illustrates the *Balanced Scorecard* concept and shows examples of the types of metrics that can be developed to measure the success of the implemented BCP Process. Included in this *Balance Scorecard* approach are the new metrics upon which the BCP Process will be measured.

Following this *Balanced Scorecard* approach, the organization should define what the *Future State* of the BCP Process should look like (see the preceding *BCP Value Journey* discussion). This *Future State* definition should be co-developed by the organization's top management and those

Balanced Scorecard

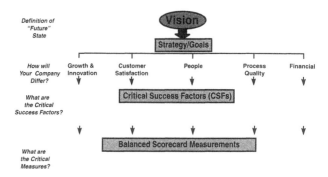

Exhibit 31-5. The balanced scorecard concept.

responsible for development of the BCP Process infrastructure. Once the *Future State* is defined, then the BCP Process development group can outline the BCP Process implementation critical success factors in the areas of:

- Growth and innovation
- Customer satisfaction
- People
- Process quality
- Financial state

These measures must be uniquely developed based upon the specific organization's culture and environment.

SUMMARY

The failure of organizations to measure the success of their BCP implementations has led to an endless cycle of plan development and decline. The primary reason for this is that a meaningful set of BCP measurements has not been adapted to fit the organization's future state goals. Because these measurements are lacking, expectations of both top management and those responsible for BCP often go unfulfilled. Statistics gathered in the *Contingency Planning and Management/Ernst and Young LLP Business Continuity Planning Survey* support this assertion. Based on this, a radical change in the manner in which organizations undertake BCP implementation is necessary. This change should include adapting and utilizing the *Business Process Improvement* (BPI) approach for BCP. This BPI approach has been implemented successfully at many *Fortune 1000* companies over the past 20 years. Defining BCP as a process, applying the concepts of the *BCP Value Journey*, expanding BCP measurements utilizing the *BCP Balanced Scorecard*, and exercising the *Organizational Change Management* (OCM) concepts will facilitate a radically different approach to BCP.

References

1. *Contingency Planning and Management*, April 1998. (The survey was conducted in the U.S. and consisted of 482 respondents drawn from *Contingency Planning and Management* magazine's domestic subscription list. Industries represented by respondents include "financial/banking" [20%]; "manufacturing/industrial" [14%]; and "government" [10%]).
2. H. James Harrington, Erick K. C. Esseling, Harm Van Nimwegen, *Business Process Improvement Workbook*, McGraw-Hill, 1997.
3. Harrington, p 18.
4. Harrington, p 19.
5. Harrington, pp. 1-20.

Chapter 32
Backup: The Forgotten Essential

Bruce Edwards

FROM THE EARLY DAYS OF COMPUTING, PRESERVING DATA THROUGH BACKUP PROCEDURES HAS ALWAYS BEEN A ROUTINE PART OF OPERATIONS, BECAUSE OF EQUIPMENT UNRELIABILITY, PROGRAMMER ERRORS, OR OPERATOR FOUL-UPS. Backup was simple with a full daily and perhaps a monthly tape sent offsite to keep the auditors happy. It was seen as basic operations insurance, and the idea of data as a vital corporate resource and essential for business continuity did not occur to IT departments.

In the 1980s, backup became a more demanding and sophisticated task. Corporations finally overcame the backlog of basic accounting systems and began to install business-critical systems, thus becoming almost totally reliant on IT. PCs often holding highly sensitive data were introduced and IT management, which had carefully built up controls and restrictions on access to mainframe corporate data, found systems being installed by users usually without any security or backup.

With the growth of LANs, computer management began to get back control of corporate data by restricting sensitive information to servers or the mainframe, and, by polling PCs and servers, ensured backup was done and unauthorized files removed. Rules began to be enforced as viruses forced corporate management to listen to IT security concerns.

The rise of client/server systems caused serious worries on database integrity if the network failed, and resulted in the implementation of "2 phase commit" to ensure transactions were completed. But the change to multiple databases on different machines using different operating systems has immensely complicated backup.

Now there is digitizing of voice, images, and video; Internet and intranet access; and integration of these into the corporate database through multimedia systems. How does one control and backup a networked system of these data types.

Electronic document management is in its infancy, but represents an entirely new problem. Huge quantities of data, much of it archival, will in future be held as electronic files, not on the old dusty filing shelves controlled by managers with a library or physical records management background. These vast repositories of data will require a discipline of culling for destruction if they are not to get out of control, and how to restore them if they should be destroyed in a disaster will be a new challenge.

In the same way, the growth of e-mail, with its attendant implications for privacy and the need to hold these documents for legal purposes, is creating a nightmare for IT departments as users demand access to more and more data.

These trends have already given new impetus to IT operations in safeguarding corporate data, but in many cases the challenge has proved to be too much. Auditors are concerned that many organizations cannot recover their operations from the backup media, nor are they keeping their data for the required statutory periods. The days when an organization could revert to manual processing are gone. More than ever before, backup strategy must be an essential part of any operation and IT recovery plan.

NEEDS ANALYSIS

Corporations now keep far more data online and will continue to do so as new storage devices enable even faster access to large volumes of previously hardcopy archived data with data warehouses and data mining techniques. But much of this material is not important or urgently required and should be graded to determine the security level for access and retrieval such as:

- *Secret:* information where the release would cause great harm (e.g., takeover details).
- *Proprietary:* information important to the competition or embarrassing to the company if it were released (e.g., pricing deals being negotiated).
- *Business use only:* data that would be costly to reproduce if it were lost (e.g., recreating the General Ledger).
- *Personal:* information that should be restricted internally (e.g., employee medical records, performance evaluations, etc.). Be especially careful with electronic mail messages.
- *Non-confidential* (the biggest group): data that requires no security clearance as it is already in the public domain and could be easily recreated, or where there is a legal requirement to disclose.

When information has been classified, security controls on its use and storage can be implemented. Highly confidential sensitive data should not be stored openly in a tape library. Data storage must be organized to restrict physical access and greater care taken of valuable information.

However, there is also the practical problem of how much data to hold online. Storage is still expensive and strategies are needed to decide what data must be immediately accessible, what can be held in cartridge dispensers, silos, or on optical discs, and what can be sent offsite.

This splitting of logical databases across several physical devices has led to the use of hierarchical storage software such as DFHSM and ASM2 as automated operational control became mandatory. Backup procedures must be able to not only recreate the databases under normal operating conditions, but may also have to rebuild them on different hardware in a disaster scenario.

MEDIA MANAGEMENT

Backup

The purpose of backup is to recover the system after a failure. Thus, backup is not just concerned with data but should also include the operating system, programs, and utilities. Data backup should occur daily and be designed for fast restoration of the stored data.

The biggest problem with backups is that users mostly — but not always — have to be denied access to the application. Techniques such as data compression can minimize the number of tapes and reduce time, but time can also be minimized using better procedures: daily, a partial backup is done of files that have had movement on them since the previous day; supplemented by a weekly backup taking a copy of the status of all files; and perhaps a monthly or end-of-period routine that looks at further copies of major files. Daily backups can also be incremental, although this may increase restoration time. The purpose of valuing data can now be seen, as daily, weekly, and monthly tapes may be kept for different time periods, depending on the sensitivity and value of data on them.

Distinguish between data files and operating information. Simplify backup and save time by grouping information into four main classes:

1. *Operating system:* operating system and utilities, communication protocols, network configurations, etc. Because this information rarely changes, try storing it on a different physical tape to make business continuity easier.
2. *Proprietary systems:* CDs of unmodified applications packages, file utilities, word-processing systems, etc.

3. *Applications systems:* in-house programs will have updates and changes but do not need to be backed up every day.
4. *Data files:* the main part of any backup are files that will be used on a daily, weekly, or monthly basis. They can be classified and stored either by system or, if a value procedure has been incorporated, they can be done by value within systems. Avoid backing up by physical device, especially if application databases are spread across devices; this could dramatically slow recovery because all devices have to be restored before database integrity checks can commence.

Backup is too frequently taken for granted. Have a formal procedure to check and review methods at least every six months, and make sure that this includes data integrity — because in business continuity, there is no second chance.

Archiving

Archiving is the storage of corporate records for a very long period of time (e.g., insurance policy history). Archiving should be planned well in advance, and access to stored data is rarely urgent — even when holding live databases. The most important difference between archiving and backup is that archiving needs to allow for hardware and software changes. With data being kept for a long time, it is essential that when files are required, they can be read; thus, be sure that the programs that process the data are also archived. Any organization that is contemplating changing from a proprietary system, to say servers running Windows NT, has a dilemma: how is archived data going to be read?

Archive tapes and cartridges, if properly stored under controlled environmental conditions, can last for years. But it is still a good idea to bring back tapes from offsite storage at regular intervals and test them.

WHY STORE OFFSITE?

What is wrong with a fireproof safe and a reciprocal arrangement with a company or another part of the organization down the road? Unfortunately, for business continuity, fireproof safes and reciprocal arrangements are simply not good enough. A fireproof safe is valuable for storing backup but should only be used to store tapes until they can be collected and taken offsite. If a fire were to occur, and the safe has fallen through six floors with three floors of rubble on top of it, how accessible are the tapes?

Storing tapes on a reciprocal basis nearly always fails. Procedures become lax and tapes do not go, records are not kept, and in an emergency, the media cannot be found. Can the backup be obtained quickly, at night and on weekends? The local bank vault is not much better. Where is the control?

Media storage is a case of the right premises and fixtures, controlled conditions, dust filters, and frequent checks and inspections, which is why using one of the specialist companies that have the correct facilities is essential. But even then care must be taken to ensure that data really is recoverable.

Check the premises where the data is being stored. Is it really fireproof, or is it a fire-rated shed inside a warehouse full of stored paper records? Are the delivery boxes flammable compressed fibro? Why are you bringing a fire risk into your site? Is the service provider reliable? If delivery errors are being made in normal operations, what sort of performance will there be under emergency conditions? Costs are important, but security is the real decider.

How often should data be removed to the off-site vault? Ask yourself: how long would it take to reconstruct lost data? And could reconstruction be done at all? Is the source data in a form where it could be rekeyed? It may cost a little more, but daily off-site storage is the only true security.

TESTING THE STRATEGY

Procedures

A written procedure for doing backup should consist of:

- normal routines for daily, weekly, and month-end backups
- trafficking the data to and from the off-site storage vault
- how to bring up the reserve or hot-site system using the backup media

Procedures should show how each application is backed up and on what frequency. In a complicated network where data is held on several file servers, show how these parts of the system are to be backed up, especially if they are not done as part of an overall software procedure. For free-standing PCs, detail who is responsible for collecting data from individual workstations.

Instructions for trafficking data to and from the off-site storage vault must include levels of authority and procedures for retrieving data. In a recent business continuity test, an unauthorized person was delegated in the plan to collect data from the off-site storage location, and recovery failed because the person was, correctly, not given the data.

In business continuity, the person doing the restore may not be the normal operator and therefore the instructions must be sufficient for another person to restore the system. An added complication is that the system on which the data is being restored may not be the same configuration as the original computer. Most procedure manuals concentrate on the recovery of lost application databases; but in a disaster, the total system would have to be restored. IT operations rarely bring a complete system up, and it is often these procedures that are lacking.

Stipulate how data integrity checks are to be carried out before the system is declared live. Remember that, for an online transaction system, this is not a simple exercise. Regularly recall media, and test that it contains the data specified and that it is really readable.

Testing

A complete test of backup media is a lengthy exercise but it can be done very effectively by breaking down testing into three categories. First check the operating system and utilities by bringing up a system using only the information stored on the tape. (Note that all necessary manuals must also be stored offsite.) This exercise will inevitably show a number of deficiencies in the backup procedures, and also will provide valuable information on the time to restore the system.

Once the operating system tests have been successfully carried out to a point where they are being done in the minimum time, next bring back the data. It is not necessary to bring back all the application systems. Select a relatively simple application and apply this application to the operating system that has been restored. Again, the tests will highlight the deficiencies in the backup media and will also give a good indication of the time to bring up the system.

Only when a series of applications has been successfully restored is it worth booking time on an external machine, or perhaps a development machine within the organization, and doing a full test of restoring the operating system, utilities, and all databases.

Testing is vital. It is only by doing tests that deficiencies in procedures, data held, and the time to recover can be proven. A recent study by auditors revealed that many organizations could not recover their systems from the data that they had stored in the off-site vault.

CONCLUSION

Without backup there is no recovery. The key to business continuity is preparation and attention to detail. When storing vital data offsite, remember to store the library system so that one can work out what is on each tape. And last, but not least, make sure that a copy of the restoration procedures is stored offsite.

Section VII
Auditor's Perspective of Business Continuity Planning

Chapter 33
Using Audit Resources in IT Business Continuity Planning

JoAnn Bozarth
Belden Menkus

EVALUATING IS BUSINESS CONTINUITY PLANS AND PARTICIPATING IN THE DEVELOPMENT OF THEM CONSUME VALUABLE AUDIT RESOURCES. While the implementation of audit management techniques and the use of relevant high-quality audit work programs are the principal means of stretching these resources, attention to the details described in this chapter can boost the effectiveness of those measures. This chapter discusses the importance of focusing on the goal of IS business continuity, several aspects of the plan that often are overemphasized or misunderstood, and the four main aspects of the IS business continuity plan on which to concentrate.

THE GOAL

The concept of anticipating possible disasters and planning ways of recovering from them is not new. And although the strategies and procedures for meeting new and changing challenges have evolved over time, the essential goal of disaster planning and recovery has remained the same. That goal is to protect and restore the organization's critical activities as soon as possible with little loss of revenue or operational control in order to enable the organization to meet its business objectives with minimum disruption. With that goal in mind, the decisive consideration in developing and evaluating an IS business continuity plan is that employees know their role in that process and recognize the realities of doing their part.

0-8493-0907-7/00/$0.00+$.50
© 2001 by CRC Press LLC

OVEREMPHASIZED AND MISUNDERSTOOD CONSIDERATIONS

Plan developers and evaluators will want to avoid spending resources on activities that do not aid in reaching the goal of disaster planning just described. Attention to several issues can help in staying focused on achieving the main purpose.

Misdirected Emphases

IS business continuity plans commonly include three issues that IS auditors dwell on unnecessarily in their evaluation of a plan. These issues relate to persuading management of the benefits of contingency planning, risk assessment, and the material characteristics of the written plan itself.

Persuasion. IS contingency planning advisers correctly recommend that top management and even IS management must be sold on the need for an IS business continuity plan and on the value that will accrue from having such a plan because unless they are so sold, the plan is likely to come to naught. However, planners and evaluators should be concerned less with the selling effort itself than with the resulting demonstrated commitment by management.

Risk Assessment. Assessing the potential risk to the organization from loss due to disaster is a necessary prelude to developing appropriate responses to the identified likely threats to the survival of IS operations and the probabilities that they will occur. A report of this activity and the results of this activity is an appropriate part of the written plan. As such, it must be reviewed in connection with the IS audit of the plan. However, IS auditors need not get bogged down in the details of this risk assessment report. Instead, they need to concentrate on the report's currency and the relevance of the risks it considers.

Risk assessment, regardless of the methodology used, is still largely a matter of (1) best-guess estimates by busy managers in the user departments and (2) IS-related damage or loss experience that may not be applicable to the organization or to its industry group. The application of a mathematical formula to these weights or rankings in the assessment process does not make them more valid, no matter how hard and firm the resulting numbers appear to be. Because both the basis for the estimates upon which the ratings have been made and the company's experience with actual losses may change over time, the risk assessment cannot be considered to be done once and never to be reconsidered or repeated. Provision should be made for the risk assessment to be redone periodically. In particular, the risks that are considered should distinguish between those that the company can control and those that it cannot. Such things as the disruption of electric power utility and telecommunication carrier services fall into this latter risk category.

Material Characteristics. In developing or evaluating the IS business continuity plan, the auditor will want to guard against being misled by the written plan's heft, formality, number of appendices and attachments, and attractive graphics and binding. These qualities are not necessarily proof of the plan's efficacy in preparing key individuals in the IS group to respond positively, realistically, and expeditiously whenever disaster hits. For example, a document's length may mean unnecessary wordiness that obfuscates. Or its heft may impede its handiness. Recognize that the artful use of graphics can help clarify procedures or directions, but that mere decoration or cuteness may obscure the document's lack of substance or may distract users at their moment of critical need for information.

Artificial Distinctions

Conventional wisdom regarding IS business continuity makes artificial distinctions between backup, recovery, and emergency operations. Such distinctions unnecessarily complicate both the planning and the recovery processes. To be successful, the business continuity process must be integrated completely.

Confusions

Planners and plan evaluators often tend to confuse the impact of real disasters with any interruption of processing activities. In the context of IS disaster planning, disaster is defined properly as "any condition or event that reduces materially or terminates the organizations's ability to process data on a timely and accurate basis." Using that definition, a power or communications outage lasting less than a single shift is **not** a disaster; a circumstance that without forewarning forces abandonment of a mainframe processing site or makes it impossible for employees to use some components of a client/server arrangement for an extended period of time **is** a disaster.

Underestimations

IS business continuity plans typically underestimate the number, extent, and possible severity of the threats that must be protected against. For example, plans for IS operational sites away from the West Coast may not consider an earthquake as a possible threat; yet there are active seismic faults in such areas as the Mississippi River Delta and metropolitan New York City. An earthquake measuring 5.0 on the Richter Scale was centered within 30 miles of Cleveland, Ohio. While earthquakes in that range are not considered by seismologists to be **major** earthquakes, they do have the potential for creating significant damage to water, gas, and electrical distribution facilities, as well as to telecommunications lines.

In all parts of the country, some IS disaster planners and plan evaluators underestimate the effect of the loss of telecommunications facilities. They assume that any post-disaster loss of telecommunications facilities will be relatively minor, the impact on message traffic will be comparatively limited, and repairs and service restoration will be completed expeditiously. That is no longer a reasonable assumption. For example, a fire in San Juan, Puerto Rico, destroyed a building that housed electronic switching equipment. In effect, the fire terminated all voice and data telephone traffic between the United States mainland and Puerto Rico. It also it interrupted this traffic between the U.S. mainland and Spain and those European countries where messages are routed normally through Spain. Among the IS activities impacted by this service loss were those in the securities, tourism, and banking industries. Multimillion dollar losses were apparently incurred. Reportedly, service was not fully restored after more than a week.

FOUR MAIN ASPECTS OF AN IS BUSINESS CONTINUITY PLAN

The continued ability of an organization's information systems to prevent or recover from a disaster is the sole reason for auditors to devote resources to assisting in the development of an IS business continuity plan or to evaluating one. An IS business continuity plan as a whole should deal with these four main aspects:

1. commitment to the IS business continuity preparedness effort on the part of both corporate management and MIS management
2. impact on corporate IS asset protection and post-disaster limitation of business disruption
3. functional and practical scope of the business continuity preparedness effort
4. operational effectiveness of the business continuity provisions

The following series of questions and discussions related to each of these aspects can be the vehicle for developing the plan or can be studied as background in preparing to conduct the plan evaluation. The ideal answer to each underlined question is "Yes" and the support for that answer should be specific and complete.

Management Commitment

Have sufficient funds to create and sustain this effort been included in the regular IS operating budget? Management should demonstrate its willingness to invest on a frequent and regular basis in such things as maintaining spare or backup facilities, staff training in business continuity preparedness responsibilities, and preparedness readiness tests. (The issuance of policy statements and comparable gestures are not an adequate measure of commitment on the part of corporate management or MIS management.)

Has responsibility for sustaining this effort been assigned to a key, or lead, person on the IS staff? Staff people will judge the degree of management commitment to this preparedness effort by the relative organizational status of the person selected to be responsible for making it succeed. This individual should not be a clerk, administrative assistant, or other junior staff member.

Was this a career advancement or promotion for the assignee? If not, management's commitment may be in doubt. When a "lateral arabesque" or a "testing of juniors" is evident in this assignment, staff people may discount the importance of the effort.

Is the assignee permitted to devote sufficient time to this task? The assignment should be real, and not just for the record. The task requires that the person actually monitor and manage the IS business continuity preparedness effort.

Is the assignee authorized to act as sole judge of when to invoke the IS business continuity plan? If the assignee is not senior enough to make that judgment or if such a decision requires committee action, that may indicate that management commitment to the effort is wanting.

Is the assignee authorized to manage the IS business continuity process through to the point at which normal operations can be reestablished?

Do responsible corporate, line, and IS management participate in and monitor the results of IS business continuity preparedness readiness tests? Among other things, provisions should be made for the representatives of the appropriate fire protection and emergency medical service groups to participate in these tests and to ensure that the software and data files used in client/server and other distributed computing arrangements are identified correctly and are included in the readiness tests. Additionally, consideration should be given to how possible access road closures and the disruption of mass transit arrangements will be handled.

Do corporate and IS management insist that identified plan and readiness test defects be remedied promptly? The expense of correcting these defects should be budgeted as a priority expenditure.

Impact of the Plan on Corporate IS Assets and on Business Disruption Limitation

Have those IS applications that are critical to sustaining operational continuity been identified? These particular applications may not always be obvious. For example, resumption of general ledger maintenance can often be delayed for days during the post-disaster period. Again, it may be feasible to have one of the organization's banks prepare the corporate payroll throughout the business continuity period on some sort of service bureau basis — using payroll lists that are deposited periodically with that service. Only those activities that are immediately related to such things as the restoration of customer service, cash flow, and compliance with essential governmental regulations should be identified as and designated as critical.

Does management support and enforce the designation of certain applications as noncritical during the business continuity process? Bear in mind that it is natural for managers to feel that whatever activity they are responsible for is critical — whether it is or not. Nevertheless, if an application does not contribute directly to the prompt resumption of vital business operations, it must be designated as noncritical.

Are the designations of critical and noncritical processing applications independently re-audited at least annually? The possible permanent discontinuation of the noncritical processing applications should be recommended to these managers.

Have users of these critical applications been made aware of whatever processing/response limitations may be imposed during the disaster recovery period? This notification should be supported by an appropriate ongoing educational effort — involving, say, periodic notices to the affected employees or the discussion of this situation in scheduled staff training sessions. (In evaluating the plan, verify this awareness — and that which should be reflected in the next two questions — by interviewing employees selected at random. Ask them to recount in their own words what they are to do when a disaster occurs and how they are to do it.)

Have the users of the noncritical applications been made aware that normal processing of these applications will be discontinued during the business continuity period?

Have these users been made aware of whatever alternate data handling methods will be followed during the recovery period? Here, too, this notification should be supported by an appropriate ongoing educational effort. Arrangements should be reviewed periodically for timely replacement of inoperable software and equipment.

Has management invested sufficient resources to ensure that suitable reserve and backup IS capabilities remain on what is essentially an immediate availability standby basis? The purpose of such a provision is to restore as promptly as possible processing of the critical systems mentioned earlier. If management has permitted this processing capacity to be utilized otherwise, commitment of it to the actual business continuity process will be delayed. If this processing capacity is being used, say, for testing by systems developers or for some sort of routine background processing, provision for expeditious processing recovery may be questionable.

Where online or so-called wide area network processing must be restored to support one or more critical applications, are arrangements in place for expeditious rerouting of carrier trunk service to the alternate operating site?

Have suitable arrangements been made for providing the staff to be involved in the recovery process with food, water, sanitary facilities, and sleeping space? Among the things to be checked are provisions for electrical, heating, ventilation, air conditioning, and communications facilities at this site. (Not initiating these arrangements before a disaster is an indication of lack of management commitment.)

Functional and Practical Scope of Plan

Is the IS business continuity plan based on some sort of modified worst-case scenario to avoid the understandable optimism that may afflict IS management when it is called upon to consider this sort of unpleasant possibility?

Are provisions for post-disaster IS functions and later restoration of the full scope of IS operations realistic? Have possible short-term and long-term delays in resuming operations been provided for?

Have provisions been made for the expeditious notification of key corporate customers of the nature and extent of IS service interruption, the time and date of its likely restoration on an emergency basis, and the impact upon their dealings with the organization in the interim? This notification is not the same as that mentioned earlier as being given to corporate IS service users. It is an especially critical consideration where direct order/payment interchange exists between a corporation and its key suppliers and customers.

Have arrangements been made for those members of the IS staff — and those of the larger organization served — whose use of IS facilities during the recovery period has been determined to be noncritical? Where will they be housed? What pre-use preparation — such as provision of electrical, heating, air conditioning, telecommunications facilities, and office equipment — will be required at that site? What commercial IS service and communications facilities will be made available to them? In the case of IS systems development and maintenance people, will they be furloughed during the recovery period? Will other employees, not a part of the IS staff but whose activities depend on corporate information systems, have to be furloughed during this period?

Have provisions been made for data center and communications switch site cleanup from the effects of a fire or flood? Normally, it will be necessary to contract specifically with people experienced in doing such cleanup.

Building maintenance people typically lack both skill and experience in handling such tasks.

Have provisions been made for the orderly restoration of normal IS operations at the close of the business continuity process? This involves resuming support of those activities and applications not sustained during the recovery period because they had been determined to be noncritical.

Have provisions been made to ensure that data integrity is not compromised during the entire recovery process? During this process, will unauthorized attempts to modify database content be detected promptly? Will attempts to subvert transaction routines be detected promptly?

Operational Effectiveness of Recovery Provisions

Are IS business continuity provisions for initiating restoration of operations realistic? For example, do they provide for a possible delay of up to 72 hours before efforts to restore operation on-site can begin? That is how much time may elapse after a fire officially is deemed to be out before the fire marshal or arson investigator involved will release the site for cleanup by the occupant. Again, can remotely stored tapes and DASDs be moved to an alternate operations site with sufficient haste to permit planned operations resumption as expeditiously as called for by the plan?

Are periodic IS business continuity plan tests scheduled during normal work hours when IS operations are at normal performance levels? While tests scheduled on third shifts or during weekends may be less disruptive of normal work practices, typically they are so unrealistic as to be essentially meaningless.

Are time-critical aspects of the IS business continuity plan included in these tests? As an illustration of this, is it verified that backup tapes and DASDs can be recovered and routers and similar devices regenerated as promptly as called for by the plan? Again, have hardware and software vendors demonstrated that they are able to replace destroyed devices and lost object code as promptly as called for by the plan? Written promises from a vendor representative do not meet this test requirement; actual demonstration of performance, insofar as is feasible, is what is necessary.

Have reliable provisions been made for the prompt notification of cessation of normal processing activities for those users geographically distant from the main IS operations site? These people should not be left until their screens go blank to learn that there is a problem. And, the notification process should include those customers and suppliers with whom virtual private network and similar open operations arrangements exist.

Is the IS business continuity plan reviewed independently — ideally by one or more executives who are not answerable to IS management — at least once every two years against the operational environment within which it must function to ensure that the plan and the environment remain in sync? For example, are individuals assigned to specific tasks and responsibilities under the IS business continuity plan still employed? Have they received suitable familiarization training covering that assignment in the recent past? As another example, does the program still reflect current contractual arrangements with communications and hardware vendors? Again, do key vendors who will be involved in the operations restoration process still exist? Also, is the hot-site or similar alternate operations facility of sufficient size and capability to fit current IS operational needs? And, does the IS business continuity plan itself reflect the level of the existing corporate commitment to distributed DP? Does the written plan reflect any technologically advanced recovery techniques (such as remote mirroring, electronic vaulting, standby operating system, and remote transaction journaling) that have been implemented by the organization since the last review?

CONCLUSION

The material presented here does not supplant the need for a managed approach to developing or evaluating business continuity plans. It can, however, provide awareness of the need to focus IS audit resources on the main aspects of business continuity planning and not to be distracted by those elements that may seem important but that do not contribute to the organization's ability to recover from a disaster.

Chapter 34
How IS Auditors Can Enhance Business Continuity Planning

Douglas B. Hoyt

ALTHOUGH ALMOST ALL SYSTEMS MANAGEMENT PROFESSIONALS AGREE THAT PROPER DISASTER OR CONTINGENCY PLANNING IS IMPORTANT, MANY THINK THEIR OWN ORGANIZATIONS' PLANS FALL SHORT OF WHAT THEY SHOULD BE. These planning deficiencies are generally due to a lack of senior management support, improper priorities, or simple procrastination. This chapter describes the steps for creating and maintaining a sound disaster plan. It also covers recent technological developments that can help in disaster planning and identifies support that can be obtained from five outside areas: software, consulting, backup facilities services, associations, and seminars. Case examples of effective methods are cited, and guidelines are included to help IS auditors evaluate existing plans.

Disruptions from earthquakes, tornadoes, volcanoes, and power and telephone outages have made managers aware of disasters that cannot be predicted but must be prepared for. Because computer operations are such an integral part of most organizations, the IS auditor's vision and leadership are essential to successful disaster planning. The potential dangers to information systems are increased by the widespread use of microcomputers, which are typically operated without centralized safeguards , by the vulnerability inherent in data transmission over local and wide area networks, and by other communications devices and techniques.

In addition, several legal considerations make sound business continuity plans necessary. The Foreign Corrupt Practices Act of 1977 makes corporate officers subject to fines for not properly protecting their companies' assets. Bank regulators expect and require suitable business continuity plans. Contractors with the federal government also must meet business continuity plan regulations.

DEFINING BUSINESS CONTINUITY PLANNING

In this chapter, business continuity planning includes preparations for handling events that could impair computer operations and telecommunications — as well as other vital activities of an organization — to minimize disruption and losses from the effects of disasters that are not preventable. The chapter also covers measures that can be taken to prevent disasters from occurring. (The terms *contingency planning* and *disaster recovery planning* are used synonymously. Because of the importance of considering the business as a whole, this chapter uses the term *business continuity planning*.)

A 1987 University of Texas survey showed that only 63% of 160 respondents had disaster plans, and 39% of those who had disaster plans had never tested them, though 85% said they heavily depended on computer systems.[1] There are many reasons for inadequate planning. Disaster planning is easy to delay because disasters rarely seem imminent. Preparation for possible future difficulties therefore receives lower priority than current real problems.

These reasons for insufficient disaster planning may seem valid, but the benefits of preparing and maintaining a workable business recovery plan far outweigh the excuses. According to the booklet *Business Recovery and Planning System*, an effective recovery plan:

- Minimizes potential economic loss.
- Reduces potential legal liability.
- Minimizes disruptions to operations.
- Ensures organizational stability.
- Provides the mechanism for an orderly recovery.
- Decreases potential exposures.
- Reduces the probability of occurrence or recurrence.
- Minimizes insurance premiums.
- Protects employees.
- Protects assets.
- Reduces reliance on key personnel.
- Minimizes decision making during a disaster.
- Reduces delays during the recovery process.[2]

ROLE OF THE IS AUDITOR AND OTHERS

The IS Auditor. The IS auditor should take the initiative in promoting, developing, and maintaining a sound and effective business continuity plan. Securing the necessary time and budget usually requires convincing senior management of the importance and value of business continuity planning.

Because information systems are the main element in business continuity planning, IS auditors are often asked to participate in business continuity planning for other vital functions. Information systems business continuity planning must at the very least be coordinated with planning for such other activities as earmarking alternative office facilities should the headquarters building be destroyed or ensuring that extra copies of legal documents be kept at a remote site in case the originals are burned or lost.

Systems Staff Members. Developing and implementing a business continuity plan requires the participation of many specialists within the systems organization. The systems staff members' individual business continuity planning responsibilities should be spelled out in their job descriptions as well as in the business continuity manual written as a part of the business continuity plan development.

Senior Management. Ideally, senior management should take the initiative in pushing for and supporting business continuity planning. In many cases, however, such initiative does not exist, and IS auditors must educate their superiors about why the plan is necessary and how it should be accomplished. Either way, management must authorize the time and expense required to develop and maintain a sound and effective business continuity plan and participate in determining policy issues that arise during planning.

Security Administration. The role of security administration varies widely among organizations. In some organizations, a strong security administration function plays a significant role in the development and maintenance of the business continuity plan.

Users. Users served by information systems are responsible for the system input and receive and use the system output. Their viewpoint is a valuable element in evaluating both potential risks to the system and alternative protective measures. It is essential that they be a part of the team effort to design and maintain the business continuity plans.

CREATING THE DISASTER PLAN

The following sections describe the steps involved in creating a business continuity plan. Because these steps typically overlap to some degree, they are not strictly sequential.

Assessing Vulnerabilities

The first logical action in developing a business continuity plan is to systematically determine events that could cause operations to cease or be severely disrupted and to assess the potential consequence of these events. The most effective means of doing this is to have the planning team brainstorm to come up with as many problems as possible (e.g., earth-quakes, fires, terrorism, loss of power, pipes breaking, downed phone lines, misbehavior by a disgruntled employee, or disruption to a key supplier). This should include even problems that may seem unlikely but are possible.

This step should also involve discussions with key executives in all areas of the organization to ensure that all important possibilities have been considered and to help pave the way for protective actions that will be recommended. The evaluation should be organized analytically by giv-ing some measures of the likelihood of each event and of the value of the damage that could result. In organizations with multiple locations, the functions and geography of the various locations must be taken into account during this evaluation process.

Using Outside Support

Many programs can help guide this vulnerability assessment. Some are combined with programs for planning the protective actions and maintain-ing the business continuity plans.

A variety of vendors are eager to furnish services to assist in business continuity planning. These services include software, which helps guide the planning process and manual preparation; consulting services, which provide evaluation and planning assistance; and facilities backup, which provides the buildings or hardware needed for business continuity. Micro-computer packages that provide business continuity planning support range from $350 to $14,500 or more for a single copy, with special rates for corporate licenses.

IS auditors can find many sources for information in addition to vendors, books, and magazines. To stay up to date in the field, it would be most help-ful for auditors to become active in one or more of the associations serving the field or to have their specialists who are responsible for developing and coordinating business continuity plans join and participate in these groups.

If a member of a systems staff needs greater knowledge or training in some specific business continuity planning area, the IS auditor should encourage attendance at a seminar or course at which the staff member may gain the required guidance and develop useful contacts with others who have common interests.

Gaining Senior Management Understanding and Support

The information and estimates gathered during the assessment of vul-nerabilities can help convince senior management of the need for a sound, effective, and continuing business continuity plan. If senior management is not already convinced at this stage, the IS auditor can use documentation of the possible dangers the organization faces as one means to help gain the necessary support for taking a proactive approach to business continuity.

Planning Software and Information Backup

Most computer operations have routines for backing up transaction data, databases, and related software programs so that if a problem occurs in processing, the backup can be used to immediately restart operations. However, a severe disaster (e.g., a fire that destroys a main computer center and its library) requires further measures if operations are to be reestablished within a reasonable time. Ideally, it is desirable to have two extra backups (each at a different location) so that survival during a crisis does not depend on only one backup. In addition, it is preferable that these safeguarded backups be transmitted off site immediately as records are created and modified, eliminating the risk and time otherwise required to reconstruct current records.

The IS auditor should identify all the software programs, databases, and transaction files that are important. After evaluating each item in relation to the cost of various backup approaches, the IS auditor should determine an appropriate backup location and method for each item. The location may be another site of the organization or may be provided by electronic, paper, and microfilm warehousing services. Most of these services provide pickup and delivery, have the appropriately controlled storage environments, and carefully document the movements to and from their storage facilities. IS auditors who are responsible for noncomputer business continuity planning should also ensure that other vital records are identified and safeguarded by extra copies at remote sites.

Planning Facilities Backup

Many considerations are involved in the selection of and arrangements for an alternative site for the information processing function if the original equipment cannot be used because of some disaster. The systems manager must weigh such recovery issues as the speed needed, the site's location and cost, and the reliability of the service provider if it is a vendor.

Hot Sites. These are the facilities provided by a vendor equipped with the necessary hardware and related equipment and ready to be used on demand by a customer. Customers pay a monthly fee to be on the list and usually pay another fee to reserve the facilities whenever they declare a disaster and still another fee when the facilities are actually used. Periodic tests are scheduled, for an additional fee, to make sure the conversion will work and to correct any errors.

Cold Sites. Cold sites are similar to hot sites, but without the basic computer hardware. The customer must arrange for hardware to be made available from a hardware vendor or hardware lessor.

Warm Sites. Warm sites are located near the customer's place of business and can be earmarked for use on a contingency basis. They have telecommunications and office facilities available but are not equipped for mainframe or minicomputer operations.

Portable Facilities. These are simply cold sites that can be moved in modules and assembled at the customer's location.

Alternative Locations. Organizations that have two or more facilities with identical computer equipment can sometimes plan to use their own alternative locations if one becomes inoperable because of a disaster. This arrangement is workable only if there is excess capacity available or if low-priority work can be deferred during the emergency. Some organizations may deem their computer operations so essential that they set up a completely redundant operation as a contingency safeguard. Although this is expensive, it is usually the most secure option because most vendors' services are available only on a first-come, first-served basis.

Mutual Agreement. Some organizations make reciprocal arrangements with other organizations that have similar hardware configurations. Mutual agreements generally do not work well, often because the important testing can be annoying and inconvenient to both parties and because during an actual disaster the servicing organization's processing needs take priority.

Hardware Lessors. At least one mainframe equipment lessor guarantees delivery of equipment specified by a customer within five days of the report of a disaster. This option can be combined with contracts for cold sites or portable facilities.

Coordinating with Non-Information Systems Function Recovery

Each organization's business continuity plan must encompass the possible dangers to the whole organization, not just to information systems. The systems manager must either take the initiative in resolving the contingency needs of noncomputer activities, or coordinate with the person assigned to computer business continuity planning for those other functions. Protective plans must be included for such vital functions as research and development, patents and legal activities, personnel, and manufacturing processes.

Preventing Disasters and Minimizing Their Effects

The IS auditor must coordinate decisions on the measures to take to prevent disasters and to minimize the consequences of disasters that cannot be prevented. This requires discussing decisions with the appropriate users and systems specialists, documenting the decisions, and implementing the actions chosen. These actions vary widely. They can include such preventive measures as drawing up a contract with a hot site vendor, buying plastic sheets to cover hardware in case pipes break, installing fire detectors, securing an uninterrupted power source, and making copies of vital legal records and storing them off site.

Planning the Steps to Take When a Disaster Strikes

The step-planning process involves deciding on and documenting the sequence of actions (and who is responsible for each action) to recover from all the possible disruptions that have been identified in the risk assessment reviews. This process should also reflect the varying degrees of disruption. For example, it should differentiate flooding in a small area caused by a pipe bursting from flooding that disables the central mainframe, peripherals, and the library. The IS auditor should discuss all the disaster possibilities and recovery options with the concerned systems specialists and users, reach a consensus, and document that consensus.

Developing a Business Continuity Manual

The documentation of the entire business continuity planning process must be contained in a business continuity manual. It should contain complete information about the software and hardware to be safeguarded and who should do what under every type of emergency or disaster condition possible. The process of drafting this manual as well as having various people review the parts they are most concerned with can be helpful. Consulting those who will be responsible for carrying out the recovery process helps reinforce their initial understanding and acceptance of the principles documented in the manual. The manual should define responsibilities of and contain the work and home telephone numbers of all people involved in the recovery process. The recovery plan documentation manual should be in a looseleaf, revisable format, and several copies should be located away from areas vulnerable to a disaster. Many employees will want to keep updated copies of the manual on disk. Widespread and heterogeneous organizations add a dimension of complexity to the job of coordinating business continuity planning throughout the enterprise. Organizations with diverse divisions or computer centers in various locations may opt to have separate manuals for each unit, with at least a common policy.

Many firms sell microcomputer programs that are useful in planning business continuity programs as well as in documenting the facts; the manual produced is a by-product of the planning process. The flowchart in Exhibit 34-1 shows many of the topics that should be covered in the business continuity manual.

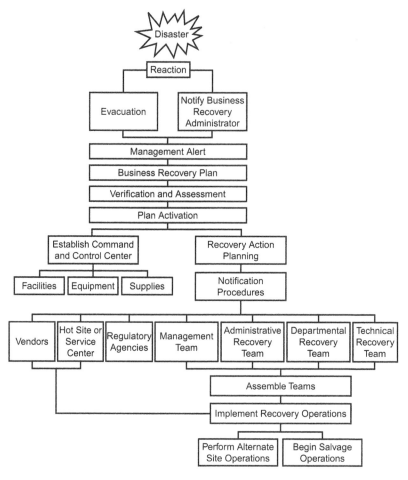

Exhibit 34-1. Flowchart outlining the recovery process.

Providing Training

Training is an important step in the process of developing a recovery plan. Because the instructions for business continuity usually do not have to be followed on a regular basis, continual training is necessary to keep the requirements fresh in the minds of those who must carry out the required actions. The recovery manual contains all the policies, procedures, and instructions to be applied during a disaster and is therefore a helpful aid to training.

Testing the Plan

The business continuity plan cannot be considered complete until it is tested, and it must be tested regularly. The IS auditor should simulate each type of disaster and monitor the compliance of everyone following the established emergency response instructions. In the case of a hot site, the backup data and programs must be used and compared to those from regular operations. These tests invariably uncover oversights and bugs in the recovery system and reveal ways to make it work better.

There are several ways of conducting tests, which can be performed piecemeal or in a group. For example, the various procedures can be simulated, and contingency actions can be discussed or checklists can be used to review whether the recovery procedures are sound or have bottlenecks. The usual way is to take all the steps that are prescribed for the disaster in question, then review the effectiveness of the actions taken. The extreme test, in which the regular operations are actually shut down unannounced and backup facilities and data are used, can be dangerous and is not recommended unless all other tests have not assured management of the plan's reliability.

STEPS FOR MAINTAINING A DISASTER PLAN

Maintaining the business continuity plan is as important as developing it. A plan lying on the shelf with obsolete information and phone numbers can provide only a false sense of security, which could compound an actual disaster. The plan must be thoroughly and regularly updated and frequently tested. The following sections examine the steps required to maintain a business continuity plan.

Reevaluating Vulnerabilities and Needs

Many conditions affect the vulnerability of an organization change. For instance, an acquisition or divestiture, new or modified computer systems, or new research that indicates, for example, that communications systems or building structures are more or less reliable than originally viewed, would all affect the organization's view of its vulnerability. The organization's original assessment of its vulnerabilities is the basis on which its first business continuity plan is founded. The plan must be changed, therefore, to conform to the revised evaluation of these dangers. This reevaluation should be conducted two or three times a year for the first few years, and annually after that.

Keeping Management Interested

In some organizations, senior management may ask the systems group to assure them that they have a sound and updated business continuity plan. It is most often up to the IS auditor to keep senior management aware of the necessity for protective measures and the need for continual action and expenditures to keep them current and effective. IS auditors can do this by making senior management aware of real-life disasters in other organizations and of the organization's own revised vulnerability assessments and the reasons for them.

Keeping the Manual and Plan Current

The manual should contain information as well as policies, procedures, and instructions — that is, everything that everyone needs to know in dealing with disasters. Such information changes because hardware and software item identifications, employees' and vendors' addresses and phone numbers, and vital records should be incorporated as they occur. The looseleaf pages of the manual should be revised and distributed to manual holders, and the changes should be made on the disk copies.

The policy, procedure, instruction, and responsibility revisions are also made as they occur, and they should be reviewed regularly for possible improvements. An efficient time to review revisions is after tests have been made, because they too must be performed periodically and because they often reveal omissions, improved controls and methods, and matters that are not clear.

Providing Continual Training

Because disasters rarely occur, continual business continuity plan training is needed for the procedures and instructions to remain reasonably fresh in the minds of all those who will play a role in the recovery processes. At least some of the training sessions should be scheduled after the testing periods and when revisions to the manual are made.

Performing Frequent Tests and Drills

Hot site vendors report that customers typically do not perform well in their first test and that the problems they have diminish substantially in subsequent trial runs. This observation supports the view that there is value in performing regular tests and drills. Practice is one of the best ways to overcome the weaknesses and limitations of human operators. Repeatedly simulating disasters and their recovery steps is the most effective way to ensure that a real disaster, if it happens, will cause minimal damage and disruption.

RECENT TECHNOLOGICAL DEVELOPMENTS

Some companies use technologies such as electronic vaulting, remote journaling, and database shadowing to move data to backup sites electronically. Although these methods safeguard the information more quickly and eliminate the risks and delays in the traditional delivery method (i.e., by truck), they can be expensive.

In addition, some organizations are wary of putting their vital transaction data in the hands of vendors who handle other customers' data. However, banks, for example, are being pressed by regulators to reactivate their operations rapidly in the event of a disruption, and these new techniques can help make this possible. Several of these new technological developments are discussed in the following sections.

Electronic Vaulting. Electronic vaulting is the batch transmission of data through T1 and T3networks to backup sites. Electronic vaulting permits organizations to back up computer data files by dialing into a storage facility where the data is recorded on disk or tape. Image vaulting, which is the electronic backup of images of documents, is being considered by such organizations as insurance companies.

Remote Journaling. This process remotely records data updates as they occur. A remote online log of updates is maintained, and data can be reconstructed as of the point of failure if a failure occurs, though doing so may take a few hours. One US Army branch stores duplicate log files of critical data at a backup site, and the system is designed to be able to return to regular operations within two hours of a failure.

Database Shadowing. Database shadowing is similar to journaling. The receiving end records interim transactions into the database shortly after the data has been received. In the event of a failure, operations can be resumed within a short period of time.

RECOMMENDED COURSE OF ACTION

The most challenging — and important — actions for an IS auditor to take in achieving a proper business continuity plan are:

- Convincing management of the need for and value of an effective business continuity plan. This entails repeatedly pointing out to them the values of an effective plan and the dangers of a poor plan, so that they will authorize the expenses and time required and play a supportive role.
- Ensuring that the plan covers noncomputer functions. Although it is natural for IS auditors to feel that those other areas are not their responsibility, any sound business continuity plan must include and be coordinated with activities other than information systems.
- Ensuring that the plan is continually updated to reflect operating and organizational modifications, the best and latest technology available, and equipment, software, and personnel changes. It takes persistence and special skill to keep the plan dynamic and current. Regular tests of the protective features of the plan should be conducted.

In addition to the actions already noted, an IS auditor should ask the following questions when devising a business continuity plan strategy:

- Do the defined business continuity planning objectives include the organization as a whole, not just information systems?
- Are the plan goals supported by a thorough risk analysis?
- Do the plan objectives include actions to reduce vulnerabilities and threats?
- Are the plan's goals clearly defined in the manual?
- Have all of the following natural event dangers been considered:
  — Earthquakes?
  — Floods?
  — Tornadoes, hurricanes, or storms?
  — Volcanoes?
- Have other possible causes been adequately weighed, such as:
  — Power outages?
  — Fires?
  — Nuclear disaster?
  — Environmental disaster?
  — Flooding from broken pipes?
  — Human errors and omissions?
  — Aircraft hitting the building?
- Has management been made aware of the legal implications, including:
  — The Foreign Corrupt Practices Act, which allows criminal and civil prosecution for violations?
  — Bank requirements to protect against information systems losses?
  — Possible lawsuits by shareholders and employees for inadequate planning?
- Have all reasonable protective measures been taken to replace damaged equipment and facilities, in order to resume operations?
- Have all reasonable measures been taken to replicate programs, databases, and transaction data so that operations can be resumed within a reasonable time after a disaster?
- Does the disaster plan manual cover all appropriate software, data, equipment, personnel (with their responsibilities and phone numbers listed), policies, procedures, and instructions?
- Is the manual updated as changes are made and at least every six months?
- Are revisions relayed to all people responsible, and do they all have copies of the manual?
- Are key features of the plan tested regularly, at least every three months?
- Are improvements made to the plan as the result of findings and evaluations of the tests?

- Is there a continuing training program that reviews policies and instructions regularly with those responsible, institutes training whenever an employee is given new recovery responsibilities, and checks to ensure that requisite understanding and motivation are achieved?

Notes

1. G.H. Anthes, "Disaster Recovery Takes Broader View," *Computerworld* 24 (September 17, 1990), p. 95.
2. McGladrey & Pullen, *Business Recovery and Planning System* (St. Paul MN, 1991), p. 1D.

Chapter 35

Auditing Contingency and Business Continuity Planning

Fred Gallegos
Karen Sekata

THE CONTINGENCY PLAN OR BUSINESS CONTINUITY PLAN IS AN IMPORTANT TOOL TO BUSINESS. It is a business survival tool to help a business recover in the wake of an event that disrupts normal business operations. Provided the plan is supported by management and staff, updated frequently, and maintained and tested, it offers the chance for the business to survive.

Recent surveys and reports show that disasters can occur in any size business and, frequently, those that are unprepared do not survive to continue. In the recent earthquake that occurred in the San Fernando Valley, 75% of the small businesses did not survive; 50% of the medium-size businesses did not survive. The impact was not only to the business, but the supplier and the customers who relied on that business for its products and sales.

An audit of the Contingency and Business Continuity Plan is a check on the reliability and viability of the Plan to support it when called for. It is a checkpoint for management and staff, to assist them in maintaining a realistic and viable plan.

AUDIT OF BUSINESS CONTINUITY PLANNING STEPS

Each Contingency and Business Continuity Plan should have major steps or processes. Exhibit 35-1 was created to portray what steps an auditor should consider important to a disaster recovery plan. In essence, it is

0-8493-0907-7/00/$0.00+$.50
© 2001 by CRC Press LLC

Exhibit 35-1. Summary of business continuity planning steps.

Source/Step Number	1. DRP	2. Hot/Cold Site	3. System Backup	4. Data Backup	5. BCP Tests/Drills	6. Offsite Storage	7. BCP Committee	8. Telephone Numbers	9. Critical Applications	10. OS/Util/App. Backup	11. Insurance	12. Comm. Plan	13. Documentation	14. Relocation Plan	15. Food and Water	16. Position Backup	17. CPR/First Aid	18. Care for Family	19. Inventory List	20. Mission Statement	21. Manual Procedures	22. Debris Removal
Carpenter 8–10	X	X	X	X		X	X	X	X			X	X						X	X		
A Case Study in Disaster Recovery 24	X						X					X			X		X	X				
Cerullo, McDuffie, and Smith 34–38	X	X	X	X	X	X	X	X	X			X	X	X	X		X					X
Computer Security and Privacy	X	X	X	X		X				X	X		X	X		X					X	
The Computer System Audit 56		X	X	X		X				X	X											
Craig 31					X																	
Disaster Recovery Planning Check-list 6	X	X	X	X	X		X	X	X		X	X				X		X				
Doughty 1–2	X	X	X	X	X	X	X	X	X		X				X		X					
Dwyer, Friedberg, and McKenzie 30–35	X	X	X	X	X	X	X	X	X		X	X			X	X	X					

Source																						
First Steps in Disaster Recovery Prep. 11	X																		X			
Harper 19–20	X	X	X	X		X	X	X		X									X			
Kahan 58–63	X	X	X			X			X													
King 1–8	X	X	X	X		X	X	X		X	X	X	X				X	X			X	X
Krouslis 1–6			X			X		X														
Larson 18	X													X	X							
May 16–24	X	X				X	X					X					X					
Menkus 39	X								X													
Pearce 28–32	X			X	X	X												X				
Patterson 14–16	X	X	X	X		X	X						X	X								
Rehak 14–23	X	X	X			X									X	X						
Rosenthal and Sheiniuk 12–16	X	X	X	X		X	X	X		X	X	X			X	X	X					
Turner 57–61	X	X	X			X		X	X	X												
Watne and Turney 284–288	X	X	X	X	X	X	X		X	X	X	X			X	X	X					
Weber 259–262	X	X	X	X	X	X	X	X	X	X	X	X			X	X						
Count	20	17	16	15	15	14	11	9	9	7	7	7	7	7	5	5	4	4	3	3	1	1
Percent (%)	83	71	67	63	63	58	46	38	38	29	29	29	29	29	21	21	17	16	13	13	4	4

an audit plan. The rows in the table represent the 24 external sources, or references, that were used to obtain the information. The columns represent the steps. Each step in the table is numbered and can be correlated to the numbers and steps listed below:

Number	Step
1.	Written business continuity plan
2.	Hot site/cold site
3.	Full and incremental system backups on a daily and/or weekly basis
4.	Data backed up
5.	Business continuity plan tests and drills
6.	Data and system back-ups stored offsite
7.	Appoint business continuity chairperson and committee
8.	List of emergency telephone numbers
9.	Identification of critical applications
10.	Operating system, utilities, and application files backed up
11.	Insurance
12.	Communication plan
13.	Up-to-date system and operation documentation
14.	Employee relocation plan for alternate work site
15.	Stock food and water
16.	Key personnel positions are backed up
17.	CPR/first aid education
18.	Care for families in an emergency
19.	List of hardware and software
20.	Mission statement for business continuity plan
21.	Manual procedures in place as a backup to automated procedures
22.	Contractual arrangements with clean-up crews to remove debris

The intersection of a row and column, when annotated with an "X," means that the given author or source has discussed the given business continuity planning step in his or her article or book. The "Count" row represents the number of times a particular step has been discussed. The "Percent" row shows the importance of the step. Thus, the higher the percent, the more emphasis the step received in the articles and books. The percent was calculated as follows:

$$\text{Percent} = \frac{\text{Number of occurrences} * 100}{\text{Total Number of Possible Occurrences}}$$

$$= \frac{\text{Number of occurrences} * 100}{24}$$

Business Continuity Planning Steps for a Company

This section defines each of the business continuity planning steps in detail and discusses the current condition one might find at a company.

Written Business Continuity Plan

As stated earlier, a business continuity plan is a plan set up to enable an organization and its computer installation to quickly restore operations and resume business in the event of a disaster. Additionally, since the resources in an installation usually are in a constant state of flux — new applications are being developed, existing systems are being modified, personnel are turning over, and new hardware is being acquired — the plan must be updated on a regular basis. The objective of maintaining the plan in a continued state of readiness is to reduce the likelihood of incorrect decisions being made during the recovery process and to decrease the level of stress that may be placed on the business continuity team members during this process.

Once the plan is developed, members of the organization should be familiar with the plan. If an emergency occurs, it is easy for staff members to execute their roles in the plan. Efforts are not duplicated and all the necessary steps are taken.

An auditor may find that no written business continuity plan exists in the current state. Many recovery procedures have been put into place, but they have not been formally documented.

Mission Statement for Business Continuity Plan

A mission statement and/or objectives should be developed for the disaster recovery plan. These objectives should be realistic, achievable, and economically feasible. These objectives provide direction in preparing the plan and in continually reevaluating the usefulness of the plan.

Again, an auditor may find that the company has not established disaster recovery objectives for the business continuity plan.

Business Continuity Plan Tests and Drills

Disaster simulation drills or tests are used to test the staffing, management, and decision-making of both the computer- and non-computer-related aspects of an organization's business continuity plan. The test reduces the opportunity for miscommunication when the plan is implemented during a real disaster. It also offers management an opportunity to spot weaknesses and improve procedures.

Unfortunately, organizations are often unwilling to carry out a test because of the disruption that occurs to daily operations and the fear that a real disaster may arise as a result of the test procedures. Therefore, a phased approach to testing would be helpful in building up to a full test. The following is a suggested phased approach:

1. Begin testing by using desk checks, inspections, and walkthroughs.
2. Next, a disaster can be simulated at a convenient time (during a slow period in the day). Personnel should be given prior notice of the test, so they are prepared.
3. Finally, simulate a disaster without warning.

Unless a business continuity plan is tested, it seldom remains usable. A practice test of a plan could very well be the difference between the success or the failure of the plan. To quote the old adage about the three things it takes for a business to be successful: "location, location, location. What is needed of a business continuity plan to continue to stay in business is: testing, testing, testing."

If the company under audit does not have a documented disaster recovery plan, then no testing procedures or schedules exist.

Backup Procedures

Adequate backup procedures are some of the most important safeguards against disaster. While backup procedures differ according to the importance of data, its frequency of change, volume, and many other factors, the need for protecting information through backup applies to all sizes and types of computers.

In this area, one may find that the company considers the backup of the VAXs and SUN 690 to be very important. For the VAXs, daily incremental backups occur at 12:15 a.m. and full backups occur weekly from Friday night to Saturday morning. For the SUN 690 system, daily incremental backups occur on Monday, Wednesday, Thursday, and Friday. The full backup occurs weekly on Tuesday morning. However, backup for the PC standalone applications are more lax and uncontrolled. The developer of the PC system is responsible for creating backups, and no procedures are in place as to how and where the backups are stored.

Data Backups

Information is the heart and soul of an organization. Accepting the importance of data backup is the crucial first step in allocating the resources necessary to ensure that data remains accessible, readable, and retrievable. Below, in order of the frequency of their occurrence, are the 12 most common causes of data loss according to Auerbach's newsletter *EDPACS*:

1. The unintentional overwriting of a data file.
2. The failure to backup microcomputer or workstation records on a diskette or magnetic tape because of time pressure or other tasks that appear to take precedence.

3. The crash of a hard drive on a workstation or a network file server, causing not only the loss of information but also damage to or loss of both the operating systems and the bindery of affected network management systems.
4. The malfunction of diskettes or magnetic tapes that prevents them from recording data properly.
5. The inability to locate the diskettes or tapes on which desired data is stored. This usually occurs when material is stored in inappropriately or unmarked boxes or, equally likely, in boxes that were indexed in a fashion that no one in the organization no longer understands.
6. The loss of data because of an unexpected electrical power supply failure.
7. Damage to diskettes or tapes in transit or at a secondary storage site.
8. A computer virus that damages or destroys data files and operating systems.
9. The theft or misuse of data, including its removal or use by unauthorized persons.
10. The degradation over time of the magnetic signal on a diskette or tape.
11. The changing of one or more versions of an operating system or application previously used to create and record data so this data cannot be read without reloading the original software or running routines of varying complexities to convert the data into compatible formats.
12. The destruction of a building or a work area within it by fire, earthquakes, temperature extremes, flood, or other such catastrophes that render diskettes or tapes unreadable or unavailable.

The company, the auditor finds, has excellent backup procedures for the VAXs and SUN 690 data. However, data-specific backup procedures for the PC applications do not exist.

Operating System and Application Program Backups

In addition to backing up data, an organization should also make backup copies of the operating systems, utilities, and application programs. This procedure will eliminate problems with version incompatibility between data and operating systems and/or application programs.

In this area, the audit finds that the company backs up operating system, utility, and application program files for the VAXs and SUN 690 systems. However, specific procedures for the PC applications do not exist.

Offsite Storage

An organization needs an offsite facility to store copies of the disaster recovery plan, data backups, system backups, critical documentation, and procedure manuals. This alternate storage location helps to guarantee that no single disaster can destroy both the primary and backup copies simultaneously. The offsite storage location should permit round-the-clock access to needed backups and documentation. Additionally, a log should be kept that shows updates to the offsite storage location's inventory.

The auditor finds that the company only stores data and system backup tapes at a company-owned Operational Test and Evaluation Center building located one block away from the computer room. The current week's backup tapes are stored in a fireproof case within the computer room or at the desk of the Database Administrator (DBA). After one week, the tapes are moved to the offsite location. The purpose of this procedure is for tape availability. However, no procedures are in place for moving the PC applications and data offsite. Additionally, company personnel do not have a key to the building. After-hours access requires company personnel to contact the company building manager. The auditor finds that this after-hours access procedure has not been tested.

Hot Sites, Cold Sites, and Mutual Contract Agreements

Hot sites and cold sites are business continuity location options that many organizations are establishing to assist them in restoring the IS operations after a disaster occurs. Other organizations cannot afford the cost of a hot site or a cold site, so they are establishing Mutual Contract Agreements with a vendor, distributor, or similar organization. The written agreement must be obtained from the organization or company whose facilities will be used during a disaster. The written contract commands performance and assures appropriate access and service. When establishing an alternate backup location, the following should be considered:

1. The service and support contract should be checked in detail. It is too easy to assume that a contract will cover all contingencies in the event of a disaster.
2. The backup hardware, software, and general configuration should be compatible with the primary computer used for regular processing operations.

The current condition at the company is that no hot site or cold site exists for the information systems. These alternate sites were considered, but the cost was too substantial for the organization. Only the payroll system has established a mutual agreement with another offsite vendor. A mutual agreement contract has been considered for the other systems, but the company is unable to find another location that is capable of supporting the volume of data in a timely manner.

Business Continuity Chairperson and Committee

A chairperson and committee should be assigned to develop a business continuity plan, work with upper management, and educate employees on business continuity procedures. Additionally, these individuals will hold key roles in directing the recovery efforts if the plan is used in an emergency. Therefore, they should be designated by name in the plan. The plan should also have an "Executive Line of Succession," which states who is in charge during the recovery, who is next in line, etc.

Since the company has no business continuity plan, a business continuity chairperson and committee does not exist. Additionally, an "Executive Line of Succession" does not exist. The auditor finds that the employees assume that one of the four key managers will be in charge during and after the disaster, but who and what is their succession?

Communication Plan

Telecommunications service, both data and voice networks, are key components for success in any organization, so it must also play an integral role in a company's business continuity plan. After a disaster, accurate and immediate information is critical; only then can good decisions be made. Therefore, a business continuity plan must consider such scenarios as having a local telephone network sustain damage. In this case, not only voice, but paging, faxing, cellular, and data communication services may be affected. The communication portion of a business continuity plan needs to consider the following:

1. Alternate means of communication such as cellular phones, beepers, two-way radios, and written communication
2. Procedures to let employees know where to meet and who to call for specific instructions
3. Telecommunication backup equipment and/or procedures

The auditor finds that employees have alternate means of communication such as cellular phones and beepers. However, procedures have not been established for their use and cellular telephone numbers have not been provided to employees for official use. Additionally, alternate telecommunication means have been established, such as a T-1 line as a backup for fiber, but these procedures have not been documented.

Emergency Telephone Numbers

An emergency telephone number and address list should be developed to assist personnel in contacting each other in the event of a disaster. The list should include home telephone number, work telephone number, home address, cellular phone number (if available), and beeper number. Additional telephone numbers such as emergency services, vendors, private and public transportation, etc., should be on the list since these companies may be needed to assist with recovery efforts.

Once the list is developed, it should be routinely maintained and two copies of the list should be distributed to each employee: one for work and one for home.

Again, the auditor may find that the company is very good about updating and maintaining its telephone recall list. Each employee is given a list for home as well as a pocket-size card to carry in a wallet. All of the above information appears on the list except for cellular telephone and beeper numbers.

Identification of Critical Applications

A list of priorities to follow in reestablishing the processing of critical or sensitive applications programs should be developed and maintained. The purpose of this priority list is: (1) to establish that all of the organization's application programs were considered relative to the nature and extent of a likely disaster, (2) to assess the time reasonably expected to elapse before operations are restored, (3) to assess the potential loss to the organization if the application program is not restored in a timely fashion, and (4) to determine the point at which normal operations might be interrupted. When prioritizing critical applications, the organization should also consider if manual procedures are available so that totally computer-dependent applications can be processed first.

Since the company has no business continuity plan, a prioritized list of critical applications has not been established. Most personnel who deal with customers would consider the Project Management Report (PMR) and Test Support Plan (TSP) to be critical applications. However, this fact has not been written down and made known to all personnel, as the auditor finds out.

Human Resource Issues

Human Resource issues are some of the most overlooked components in a business continuity plan. Organizations need to remember that people are the most important assets of a company. Do not expect employees to devote themselves to business continuity if they are faced with family or other personal problems as a result of a disaster. Therefore, disaster recovery planning should consider issues and programs for employees such as the ones listed below:

1. Availability of food, water, shelter, tools, etc.
2. Availability of first-aid care
3. Procedures on how employees will ensure the safety of their families
4. Crisis counseling
5. Flexible work hours
6. Salaries procedures during the disaster

The auditor finds that the company has gathered food, water, tools, and first-aid supplies in limited quantities. This is an important first step in caring for employee safety needs. Additionally, the company is very good about working with employees regarding flexible work hours, so it is likely that this policy would be extended during a disaster.

Hardware and Software Inventory

The business continuity plan should include a list of hardware and software that the organization currently uses. Additionally, items such as version numbers and vendor names should be included. This inventory list will assist in bringing up a hot or cold site, establishing a configuration at the "Mutual Agreement Contract" location, and filing an insurance claim.

The auditor finds that the company has information on all their vendors and equipment; however, it has not been compiled into a single, easily accessible inventory list.

CONCLUSION

In a case scenario, several crucial steps that business continuity planning authors have written about in detail on several occasions were presented. The repetition of the same steps by several different authors proves the importance of the subject. These can be used as audit steps to check the validity and reliability of the Contingency and Business Continuity Plan. These steps are crucial in determining where the company or business is in their business continuity planning. Based on this information, the auditor is able to determine the current condition at the company and provide the recommendations for each of the business continuity step findings.

The audit of Contingency and Business Continuity Planning is an important check. The major elements and areas that such a plan should have were validated against recent publications on the subject. In turn, this approach can be used as a checklist to help both the auditor and management assess their plans.

Index

A

Access controls, logical, 190
Accounting procedures, 82
ACD systems, see Automated call-
 distributing systems
Action selection, 70
Actual cash value (ACV), 173
Acute-crisis stage, 70
ACV, see Actual cash value
Administrative services department,
 consulting of in forming
 business continuity steering
 committee, 87
All Risk form, 172, 173
Application
 platform development, 101
 program backups, 379
 software errors, 205
Archival storage, retrieving files from,
 205
Archiving, 343
Area user list, 91
Audit
 participation, in testing, 106
 standards, setting of, 220
Auditing contingency, business
 continuity planning and,
 373–383
 backup procedures, 378
 business continuity chairperson and
 committee, 380–381
 business continuity plan tests and
 drills, 377–378
 communication plan, 381
 data backups, 378–379
 emergency telephone numbers,
 381–382
 hardware and software inventory,
 383

hot sites, cold sites, and mutual
 contract agreements, 380
 human resource issues, 382–383
 identification of critical applications,
 382
 mission statement for business
 continuity plan, 377
 offsite storage, 379–380
 operating system and application
 program backups, 379
 written business continuity plan, 377
Audit resources, use of in IT business
 continuity planning, 349–357
 goal, 349
 main aspects of IS business
 continuity plan, 352–357
 functional and practical scope of
 plan, 355–356
 impact of plan on corporate IS
 assets and business disruption
 limitation, 353–355
 management commitment,
 352–353
 operational effectiveness of
 recovery provisions, 356–357
 overemphasized and misunderstood
 considerations, 350–352
 artificial distinctions, 351
 confusions, 351
 misdirected emphases, 350–351
 underestimations, 351–352
Authority and procedural rules, 54
Automated call-distributing (ACD)
 systems, 219, 277
Automated data importing, 228

B

Backup(s), 341–346
 application program, 379

385

battery, 211
capabilities, 169
encrypted, 156
media management, 343–344
    archiving, 344
    backup, 343–344
media, test of, 346
methodology, 159
needs analysis, 342–343
offsite storage, 344–345
procedures, 84, 205
security, 185, 187
testing of strategy, 345–346
    procedures, 345–346
    testing, 346
vital records, 334
Balance Scorecard, 337
Banking sector case study, 136–137
Battery backups, 211
BCP, see Business continuity plan
BIA, see Business impact analysis
Boundary rules, 54
Boutique vendors, 304
BPI, see Business Process Improvement
Building damage, 105
Business
operations time-sensitive, 45
Process Improvement (BPI), 337, 338
recovery phase, 13
resumption planning, 46, 245
unit
    plans, 102
    recovery planning, 326
    resumption planning, 103
Business continuity
manual, 365
practitioners, 20
responsibility, 110
steering committee, 87
strategy, 111
test, 280
vendors, 163
Business continuity plan (BCP), 6, 11,
    15, 57, 73
business impact assessment element
    of, 115
coordinator, 85, 268
costs of, 8
culture of, 25, 27
developing customized, 131
effectiveness, 324
executive management commitment
    for, 263

foundation for successful, 22
gap analysis, 265
importance of developing, 169
in-house, 291
process initiation, 330
questionnaires, basic information
    required on, 91
restoration plan without, 181
sample outline of, 93–95
sensitivity analysis of, 264
software, 92
team, 30
tests and drills, 377
tools, criteria for selecting, 297
version control, 269
written, 377
Business impact analysis (BIA), 90, 266,
    281
Business impact assessment process,
    115–130
BIA information-gathering
    techniques, 118–119
    electronic media, 119
    group BIA interview sessions or
        exercises, 118
    one-on-one BIA interviews,
        118
BIA interview logistics and
    coordination, 121–122
BIA process description, 116
BIA questionnaire construction,
    119–121
conducting BIA, 122–128
    interpreting and documenting
        results, 125–126
    preparing management
        presentation, 127–128
customizing BIA questionnaire, 119
five-phased approach to BCP,
    115–116
    BCP project scoping and
        planning, 115–116
    business impact assessment, 116
    development of recovery
        strategy, 116
    recovery plan development, 116
    implementation, testing, and
        maintenance, 116
importance of documenting formal
    MTD decision, 117
next steps, 128
use of BIA questionnaires, 117–118
Bus topology, 196

C

Cellular telephone inventory, 232
Central Office, loss of, 252
Chain of command, emergency, 53
Channel Service Unit (CSU), 277
Citizen science, 39
Claims settlement process, 176
CMCC, see Crisis management
    command center
CMT, see Crisis management team
Cold sites, 31, 112, 364, 380
Comdisco Disaster Recovery Services,
    305
Command center
    operation of, 274
    procedures, 104
Communication(s)
    department
        consulting of in forming business
            continuity steering committee,
            87
        representation of on project team,
            80
    hardware, developing inventory of,
        228
    network, changes in, 101
    restoring, 276
    right-of-way, 223
    systems recovery plan, 241
Communications, business recovery
    planning for, 217–226
    assessing impact of loss of service,
        219
    business's reliance on
        communications, 218
    internal disruptions, 225
        infrared scanning, 225
        IS manager's checklist, 225
    isolation from serving facility,
        223–225
    loss of network serving facility,
        222–223
    loss of network switching capability,
        221–222
    preliminary activities in recovery
        planning, 219–221
        defining exposure in executive
            summary, 219
        educating personnel and setting
            audit standards, 220
        identifying threats to voice
            communications, 220–221

implementing network business
    continuity plan, 220
recommended course of action, 226
Communications network support,
    adding of to existing business
    continuity plans, 235–241
  business risk analysis, 235–236
  documenting of plan, 238–241
    recognition, 238
    recovery, 239
    regroup and reassess, 240–241
    response, 239
    restoral, 239
    rest and relax, 240
    return to normal operations,
        239–240
  updating of procedures, 236–238
Communications recovery plan,
    documenting of, 227–233
  components of up-to-date plan,
    230–232
    assigning technical teams, 232
    developing inventory of software,
        231
    equipment room diagrams,
        231–232
    importing components of
        corporatewide plan, 232
    importing information of
        personnel and vendors,
        230–231
  developing inventory of
    communications hardware,
    228
  maintaining accurate inventories,
    228–230
    automated data importing,
        228–230
    manual updating, 230
  real reasons for disaster planning,
    233
  recommended course of action, 233
Company culture, 27
Competitors, 38
Computer
  business continuity centers, 217
  management, 341
  resources, 8
  systems, redundant, 105
  vendors, 212
Consulting services, 246, 293
Consumer Credit Protection Act, 18
Contingency plan(s), 4, 31, 61, 360

documentation, 167
information systems, 102
methodology, 97
program, 98
statutes, 16
trends, 103
true test of, 168
Contingency plans, details overlooked
    in, 161–168
  communications issues, 164–167
    communication with public and
        news media, 165
    customer briefing of contingency
        plan, 166–167
    management notification of
        personnel groups, 164–165
    messenger service, 166
    phone list, 166
    user department management,
        165–166
  general contingency topics, 167–168
    changes made by user
        departments, 167
    participation of user departments
        in contingency tests, 167–168
  people issues, 161–164
    cafeteria facilities, 163
    common business supplies,
        162–163
    company records, 162
    housing of recovery team staff,
        163
    method of supplying cash
        advances, 164
    transportation, 163
    workstation access, 162
  recommended course of action, 168
Contract requirements, 79
Copy machines 71
Core business process continuity
    planning, 332
Core Business Process Recovery Plans,
    335
Corporate contingency planning,
    97–107
  contingency planning methodology,
      97–101
    business risk assessment, 97–99
    recovery strategy development,
        99
    testing and maintenance of plans,
        100–101
    writing recovery plans, 99–100

contingency planning trends,
    103–104
  business unit resumption
      planning, 103–104
  corporate contingency planning
      program, 104
  information systems continuity
      plans, 103
current issues and trends, 104–107
  audit participation in testing, 106
  compliance with corporate
      standards, 105–106
  new technology, 105
  nonstop processing, 105
  reporting findings to senior
      management, 106–107
  types of disasters, 104–105
recommended course of action, 107
regulatory issues, 101–103
  federal and state requirements,
      103
  financial institution requirements,
      101–102
  standards and exchange
      commission requirements, 102
Corporate disasters, 24
Corporate standards, compliance with,
    105
Credit card processing company, 5
Crisis(es)
  definition of, 48
  identifying of, 37–44
    crisis, 40–41
    crisis management, 42
    negative outcome of crisis, 41–42
    organization culture, 42–43
    risk communication, 40
    risk management, 39–40
    risk perception, 38–39
  learning from, 51–55
  myths, 59
  plans, validation of, 55
  rehearsing of, 57–67
    comment, 65
    conducting crisis management
        rehearsals, 63–65
    crisis defined, 59
    crisis management concepts,
        58–59
    crisis management plans, 62
    crisis management team, 63
    crisis myths, 59–61
    risks, 57–58

role of crisis management
rehearsals, 61–62
situation
by-products of, 43
organization in, 60
successful management of, 51
symptoms displayed by individual
faced with, 74
types of, 49
Crisis management, 42, 66
concepts, 58
experts, 49
plan, 46, 55
rehearsals, 61, 63
team (CMT), 45, 54, 63, 111
Crisis management command center
(CMCC), 69–72
acute-crisis stage, 70
considerations, 69–70
post-crisis stage, 71
pre-crisis stage, 70
prepositioning of resources, 72
resources of, 71–72
use of, 70
Crisis management planning, 45–49, 72
difference in development scenarios,
47–49
crisis defined, 48–49
types of crises, 49
perspective, 45–47
difference between crisis
management and business
resumption planning, 46–47
difference in scope, 47
CSU, see Channel Service Unit
Culture, building of for business
continuity planning, 21–33
building business continuity culture,
32
development of business continuity
plan, 24–32
fundamental guidelines for
building culture, 25–27
steps toward building culture,
27–32
issues in defining disaster, 23–24
philosophy of business continuity
planning, 22–23
Customer
communications, 217
confidence, lost, 226, 236
database inquiries, 166
satisfaction, 338

service, 85
lines, 235
restoration of, 354
Cycle testing, 158

D

Damage
assessment, 86, 88, 89
taking photographs of, 177
Damage Assessment and Disaster
Declaration Procedures, 334
Data
backups, 378
centers, physical layout of, 215
communications
breakdown in, 104
networks, 188, 329
entry screens, 297
input, simplified, 300
integrity, 154
storage, 342
Database
Administrator (DBA), 380
-driven tools, 296, 297
shadowing, 368, 369
DBA, see Database Administrator
DDS, see Digital data services
Decision-making, high-quality, 65
Declaration fees, 307
Dehumidification, 179
Department
coordinators team, 88
managers, 29
Depreciation, 173
Desk checking, 258
Desktop computers, 6
Developing and testing, of business
continuity plans, 245–261
comprehensive business recovery
strategies, 246–253
desktop computers and local area
networks, 251
mainframe systems, 247–248
midrange systems, 249
networking, 252–253
wide area networks, 251–252
work group systems, 249–250
development approach, 253–257
defining business requirements,
254–255
developing detailed resumption
plans, 256–257

project planning and
management, 253–254
selecting appropriate recovery
strategies, 255–256
recommended course of action, 261
testing of plan, 257–261
conducting of test, 260–261
matrix approach to testing,
259–260
testing approaches, 258–259
Dial backup, 199, 202
Dial-up procedures, 189
Digital data services (DDS), 201
Digitized data, recoverability of, 150
Directors and officers (D&O), 19
Disaster(s), 41
anticipating possible, 349
assessment, 9
communication with news media
during, 165
companywide definition of, 26
corporate, 24
decision-making team, 86
declaration, initiation of, 312
environmental, 370
identifying potential, 22
issues in defining, 23
management of, 44
nuclear, 370
plan
creating of, 361
steps for maintaining, 367
preparedness process, 145
prevention, 21, 45
recovery
action plan, 148
plan (DRP), 11, 22, 48, 109, 360
process, 8
regional, 248
relocation of IS staff during, 161
repeatedly simulating, 368
scenario, worst-case, 47
simulation, 378
state of readiness of individual
departments, 1100
types of, 104
unknown varieties of, 124
victims of, 76
worst-case, 48
Disaster Recovery Services, Inc., 303
Disk
duplexing configuration, 208
mirroring, 206

Disruption, trauma created by, 73
Distributed environment, 141–159
business recovery planning, 141–145
awareness and discovery,
142–143
mitigation, 144
preparation, 144–145
response and recovery, 145
risk assessment, 143–144
testing, 145
departmental planning, 146–150
apprising management of
mitigation cost, 150
apprising management of risk,
149–150
information technology's role,
146–148
internal and external exposures,
148–149
policies, 150–157
establishing recovery capability,
151
planning for distributed
environment, 151–157
restoring full operational access,
151
testing, 157–158
Diversified Graphics *v.* Ernst &
Whinney, 19
D&O, see Directors and officers
DRP, see Disaster recovery plan

E

Earthquake, 73, 105, 144, 186, 351
Echoplexing, 190
EDP, see Electronic data processing
Electronic Data Interchange, 251
Electronic data processing (EDP), 174,
175
Electronic document management, 342
Electronic funds transfers, 18
Electronic media, 119, 169
Electronic vaulting, 253, 285, 368, 369
Emergency
management team (EMT), 240
operations team, 86, 89
planning, 53
procedures, 99
response plans, 72
telephone numbers, 381
Employee(s)
temporary, 120

work space, recovery period, 320
Empty shell facilities, 112
EMT, see Emergency management team
Encryption
    card, 148
    keys, 183
End-user departments, changes in, 282
Environmental disaster, 370
E&O, see Errors and omissions
Equipment
    racking, 151
    room
        diagrams, 231
        smoking ban in, 238
Error
    -correction drive, 210
    detection codes, 190
    -management scheme, 203
    and omissions (E&O), 20
Evacuation plans, 72
Event table, consequences of, 134
Executive management team, 273
External change, 4

F

Facility reconstruction team, 278
Fact gathering, 70
Fault
    location, 202
    tolerance, 196
        levels of, 206
        vs. redundancy, 154
Fax
    machines, 71
    server, 204
FCPA, see Foreign Corrupt Practices Act
Federal Financial Institutions
        Examination Council (FFIEC), 17, 101
FFIEC, see Federal Financial Institutions
        Examination Council
Field support services, 85
File backup procedures, 205
Finance and accounting department,
        consulting of in forming
        business continuity steering
        committee, 87
Financial data, backup of, 103
Financial impact information,
        tabulation of, 126
Financial institution requirements, 101

Fire, 144, 318
    abatement systems, 151
    suppression systems, 153
Floods, 103, 186
Foreign Corrupt Practices Act (FCPA),
        17, 102, 359, 370
Fraud, 12, 103
Freeze-drying, 179
Full parallel testing, 157
Funds collection and disbursement, 319
Future State definition, 338

G

Gateways, 251
Generators, 212
Glasshouse syndrome, 112
Goal setting, 39, 43
Graphics files, 205

H

Halon fire suppression system, 149
Hard copy media, salvaging, 169
Hardware
    communications, 228
    configuration, 167
    inventory, 227, 229, 383
    /software platforms, 267
    vendors, 303
Help desk, 232
Hewlett-Packard, 304
Hooper Doctrine, 19
Hot site(s), 134, 380
    agreement, 311
    service providers, 155
Hot site vendor, choosing of, 303–315
    factors for choosing hot site vendor, 304–313
    activation, 312
    alternate facilities, 310
    availability, 313
    capacity and growth, 304–305
    communications capabilities, 310
    complementary services, 311
    contract terms, 311–312
    cost, 307–308
    geography, 306–307
    personnel support, 312–313
    recovery center facilities, 309–310
    recovery and experience, 305
    responsiveness and flexibility, 312
    stability and history, 311

technical environment, 308–309
testing capabilities, 305–306
industry overview, 304
recommended course of action, 313–315
types of vendors, 303–304
Hotspot detection, 196
Human behavior, 51
Human resources department, 84
consulting of in forming business continuity steering committee, 87
representation of on project team, 80
Hurricanes, 73, 103, 306

I

IBM Business Recovery Services, 303, 305
Inbound call centers, 235
Incident response plans, 72
Information
backup, planning of, 363
gathering, 39, 43
rules, 54
Information systems (IS), 141, see also IS auditors, enhancement of business continuity planning by; IS business continuity plan, changes affecting; IS business continuity plan, proactive approach to improving,
assets, corporate, 353
department
consulting of in forming business continuity steering committee, 88
representation of on project team, 80
disaster involving, 167
production, factors related to, 285
staff, relocation of during disaster, 161
Information technology (IT), 141, 146
departments, frustration in, 150
facility
access to, 185
loss of, 12
functions, recovery of interruption to, 245
journals, 292
recovery plan, 123
security concerns, 341

systems, larger, more dispersed, 182
Infrared scanning, 225
Infrastructure and Support Services Recovery Plans, 335
Insurance, 308, 376
adjuster, 176
agreements, 79
broker, multinational, 177
carriers, 170, 176
claims, filing of, 82
coverage, 172, 182
requirements, 83
Insurance Services Office (ISO), 174
Internal Revenue Service (IRS), 103
Interview technique, 122
Inventory, classification of, 157
IRS, see Internal Revenue Service
IS, see Information systems
IS auditors, enhancement of business continuity planning by, 359–371
creation of disaster plan, 361–367
assessing vulnerabilities, 361–362
coordinating with non-information systems function recovery, 364
developing business continuity manual, 365
gaining senior management understanding and support, 362–363
planning facilities backup, 363–364
planning software and information backup, 363
planning steps to take when disaster strikes, 365
preventing disasters and minimizing effects, 364–365
providing training, 366
testing of plan, 366–367
using outside support, 362
defining business continuity planning, 360
recent technological developments, 368–369
database shadowing, 369
electronic vaulting, 369
remote journaling, 369
recommended course of action, 369–371
role of IS auditor and others, 360–361

steps for maintaining disaster plan, 367–368
    keeping management interested, 367–368
    keeping manual and plan current, 368
    performing frequent tests and drills, 368
    providing continual training, 368
    reevaluating vulnerabilities and needs, 367
IS business continuity plan, changes affecting, 281–287
    changes affecting recovery needs, 281–283
        changes in IS and end-user departments, 282
        changes in organization, 282–283
        other changes, 283
    changes in recovery techniques, 283–287
        advanced recovery techniques, 285–287
        IS auditing concept, 287
        other factors affecting selection process, 284–285
        why organizations change to advanced techniques, 283–284
IS business continuity plan, proactive approach to improving, 317–322
    issues and recommendations, 317–322
        ceiling tiles, 321
        funds collected and disbursement, 319
        local fire fighter capability, 318
        possible loss of telecommunications central site, 320
        printed forms, 318
        recovery period employee work space, 320
        rubbish removal, 321–322
        telecommunications capabilities, 319
        time delay, 318–319
        utilities at alternate site, 319
        water and moisture removal, 321
        water sprinkler rating, 320–321
    realistic expectations, 322
ISDN
    bandwidth on demand using, 198
    facilities, 200
    telephone service, 5
ISO, see Insurance Services Office
IT, see Information technology

J

Job descriptions, 90
Just-in-case events, 21

K

Key performance indicator (KPI), 264, 266
KPI, see Key performance indicator

L

Labor contracts, 79
LAN, see Local area network
Laser printer, 204
Legal issues, of business continuity planning, 15–20
    categories of applicable statutes, 16–17
    statutory examples, 17–19
        Consumer Credit Protection Act, 18–19
        determining liability, 19
        Federal Financial Institutions Examinations Council, 17–18
        Foreign Corrupt Practices Acy, 17
        insurance as defense, 19–20
Liability
    determining, 19
    statutes, 16
Life/safety statutes, 16
Link failures, 195
Local area network (LAN), 183
    administration, 156, 215, 227
    data
        residing on, 275
        retrieval of, 277
    file server, 6
    growth of, 341
    information recovery, 251
    managers, 205
    modules, 196
    networks, 230
    protection of, 151
    recovery options for, 202
    servers, 104, 134, 204
    /WAN administration, 159

Long-distance access codes, 221
Loss area, 177

M

Magnetic media, restoration of, 178
Magnetic tapes, 188
Mainframe
  infrastructures, glass house, 326
  recovery strategies, 248
  systems, 247
Maintenance and update, of business
    continuity plans, 263–272
  BCP maintenance regime, 263–266
    amendment/update of BCP, 265
    BCP plan ownership, 263–264
    maintenance schedule, 265–266
    sensitivity analysis of BCP,
      264–265
  formulation of change control
    procedures, 266–270
    BCP version control, 269
    corporate and business plans,
      266–268
    monitoring of
      organizational/operational
      changes, 268–269
    testing of BCP changes, 270
  support tools for maintenance of
    BCP, 270–272
Management
  decision-making team, 85
  operations team, 86, 88
Market
  /competitive forces, 58
  share, lost, 236
  shift, sudden, 49
Maximum tolerable downtimes (MTD),
    115, 333
  decision, importance of
    documenting, 117
  realistic, 125
  senior management decisions made
    regarding, 128
Media management, 342
Microfilm readers, 135
Midrange systems, 249
Mirrored servers, 207
Mirroring, remote, 286
Mission statement, 377
Mitigation, 144, 150
Mobile computing, 309
Mobile recovery program, 215

Mobile telephone serving offices
    (MTSOs), 223
Mock-disaster exercise, 100
Mock surprise testing, 258
Modems, 215, 310
Mortgages, 79
MTD, see Maximum tolerable
    downtimes
MTSOs, see Mobile telephone serving
    offices
Multiplexers, 310
Mutual contract agreements, 380

N

National Credit Union Administration
    (NCUA), 17
National Fire Protection Association,
    292
Natural disasters, 3
Natural phenomena, 73
NCUA, see National Credit Union
    Administration
Needs analysis, 342
Negligence, 20
Network(s)
  availability, 197
  cards, 213
  control center, 232
  data communications, 329
  failures, major, 217
  management, 202
  recovery
    plan, 232
    strategies, 154
  reliability, 195
  schematic diagrams, 232
  security, 189
  serving facility, loss of, 222
  software
    defined, 219
    and node definitions, 167
  switching capability, loss of, 221
  virtual private, 286
Network business continuity planning,
    195–216
  generators, 212
  insurance, 215
  links to remote sites, 214
  methods of protection, 198–202
    customer-controlled
      reconfiguration, 200
    DDS dial backup, 201–202

dial backup, 199–200
ISDN facilities, 200–201
tariffed redundancy and
protection, 198–199
multiple WAN ports, 213
network availability, 197–198
network reliability, 195–197
bus topology, 196–197
ring topology, 196
star topology, 195–196
off-site storage, 212
periodic testing, 214
recovery options for LANs, 202–208
levels of fault tolerance, 206–208
recovery and reconfiguration,
202–204
restoral capabilities of LAN
servers, 204–206
redundant arrays of inexpensive
disks, 209–211
RAID level 0, 209
RAID level 1, 209–210
RAID level 2, 210
RAID level 3, 210
RAID level 4, 210
RAID level 5, 210
RAID level 6, 211
risk assessment, 215–216
spare parts pooling, 213
surge suppressors, 212–213
switched digital services, 213
training, 215
uninterruptible power supplies,
211–212
worst-case scenarios, 214–215
News media, communication with
during disaster, 165
Notification directory, 299
Nuclear disaster, 370

O

OCM, see Organizational Change
Management
Office of the Comptroller, 291
Office of Thrift Supervision (OTS), 17
Offsite storage, 155, 212, 343, 379
Open shortest path first (OSPF), 214
Operational impact information,
implications of, 126
Operations department, consulting of in
forming business continuity
steering committee, 88

Options assessment, 70
Organization
changes in, 282
charts, 90, 121
culture, 42
in crisis situation, 60
risk exposure, 52
virtual, 329
Organizational Change Management
(OCM), 336, 339
OSPF, see Open shortest path first
OTS, see Office of Thrift Supervision
Outsourcing, 4, 147
Overlaying systems technology, 121
Overview, of business continuity
planning, 79–95
business continuity planning
software, 92
developing of plan, 80–83
plan elements, 81–83
plan requirements, 80–81
identifying critical resources, 83–84
organizing of project, 84–90
business continuity steering
committee and planning
coordinator, 87–88
damage assessment and post
investigation team, 89
department coordinators team,
88–89
disaster decision-making team,
86–87
emergency operations team, 89
management operations team, 88
reconstruction team, 90
preparing of plan, 90–92
project planning, 79–80
recommend course of action, 92–95

P

Paper documents, restoration of, 178
Paper walk-through, 270
Passwords, 183, 189
PBX rooms, 225
PC, see Personal computer
Performance monitoring, 202
Personal computer (PC), 143
applications, backup procedures for,
379
-based environments, needs of, 215
free-standing, 345
Phone mail system, 164

Physical security, 153
Plan
  maintenance and testing, 83
  proposal, requesting of, 294
  publication and testing, 81, 82
Planning
  budget, 28
  tools, sources of information on, 301
Planning strategies, selecting right
      business continuity, 131–139
  recovery strategy costs, 133–137
    accommodation costs, 135
    equipment, 135
    information technology, 134–135
    IT resources, 135
    logistics, 135
    non-IT resources, 135
    service level agreements, 135
    staffing, 135
    third-party service providers, 135
    vital records, 135
  recovery strategy risks versus costs,
      137–138
  recovery strategy workshop,
      131–133
    assessing risks, 132–133
    recovery strategies, 132
    strategy risks, 132
PMR, see Project Management Report
Policy statement, 32, 99, 352
Position rules, 54
Post-crisis stage, 71
Power
  cuts, 12
  equipment, 71
  failure, 306
  generator activation, 31
Pre-crisis stage, 70
Preference-merging rules, 54
Private Branch eXchange, 230
Private data communications networks,
      188
Process
  improvement and reengineering, 325
  quality, 338
Product tampering, 12
Project
  Management Report (PMR), 382
  planning, 79
  scoping and planning, 115
Property
  insurance, 172, 175
  management, 154

Public-domain information sources,
      246
Public relations, 53, 87
Purchasing department, consulting of in
      forming business continuity
      steering committee, 87
Push back, value of, 125

Q

Quality of Service, 248
Quick hits program, 335

R

RAID, see Redundant Arrays of
      Inexpensive Disks
RAM mass memory, 204
Real estate
  company contact, 162
  department, representation of on
      project team, 80
Real-time testing, 258
Reciprocal agreement, 248
Reconfiguration, 203
Reconstruction team, 86
Recovery
  capability, 124
  center
    facilities, 309
    setting up of, 276
  experience, 305
  managers, 9
  period employee work space, 320
  plan(s)
    approval of, 257
    selecting, 7
  point objective (RPO), 284
  prevention during, 187
  process, flowchart outlining, 366
  progress, team monitoring of, 88
  resource priorities for, 333
  risks, 133
  security during, 188
  strategy(ies), 104
    costs, 133
    department, 99
    developing of, 116
    low-risk, 132
    risks versus costs, 137
    workshop, 131
  team descriptions, 100
  techniques

advanced, 285
changes in, 283
time objective (RTO), 284
Redundant Arrays of Inexpensive Disks
(RAID), 198, 209
Redundant facility, 250
Reengineering, of business continuity
planning process, 323–339
balanced scorecard concept,
337–338
BCP process improvement, 324–328
interdependencies as business
processes, 328
losing track of interdependencies,
326–328
radical changes mandated, 326
shortcomings of traditional
disaster recovery planning
approach, 326
business continuity planning
measurements, 324
concept of BCP value journey,
335–336
moving to BCP process improvement
environment, 330–335
BCP process initiation, 330
business continuity planning
training, 332
business impact assessment, 333
current state assessment and
strategic alignment, 330–332
development of business
continuity planning support
processes, 332
implementation planning, 335
implementation and testing and
maintenance stages, 335
infrastructure and support
services continuity plan
development, 334
master plan consolidation, 334
post recovery transition plan
development, 334
quick hits program, 335
recovery alternative selection,
333
recovery plan development,
333–334
route map profile and high-level
BCP process approach, 330
testing strategy development, 334
need for organizational change
management, 336–337

process approach to business
continuity planning, 328–329
Relocation site, 162
Remote journaling, 368, 369
Remote mirroring, 286
Remote transaction journaling, 285
Rental/lease equipment, 120
Resources
identifying critical, 83
inventory of, 113
prepositioning of, 72
threats to, 10
Restoration component, of business
continuity planning, 169–182
costs for restoration program,
179–180
ensuring provider performs at time
of disaster, 180
getting support for restoration
program, 181
insurance coverage, 172–177
property insurance claims
settlement process, 175–177
property insurance overview,
172–175
next steps to planning for
restoration, 182
restoration plan with BCP plan, 181
selection of restoration service
providers, 171–172
testing of restoration plan, 180–181
understanding of issues, 171
what's included in restoration plan,
177–179
Ring topology, 196
Risk
analyses, 90
assessment, 37, 143, 215, 350
communication, 40, 52, 55
exposure, of organization, 52
identification, 30
management, 6, 39, 87, 110
nature of, 3
perception, 38
-reduction statutes, 16
strategy, 132
theory of managing, 23
Risk, need for business continuity
planning and, 3–10
business continuity, 6–9
commitment, 7–8
costs, 8
planned procedures, 6

planning, 9
nature of risk, 3–4
risk assessment and management,
    4–6
Risk realization, four phases of, 11–13
    business continuity phase, 12
    business recovery phase, 13
    incident and response phase, 12
    precondition phase, 11–12
Rolling BCP testing, 270
Routers, 213
Royal Commissions, 44
RPO, see Recovery point objective
RTO, see Recovery time objective
Rubbish removal, 321

S

Satellite-sharing arrangements, 200
Scope rules, 54
Security
    administration, 361
    department, representation of on
        project team, 80
    during repair and correction, 191
    functions, 184
    software, 189
    standards, 237
    statutes, 16
Server
    fax, 204
    LAN, 104, 134
        file, 6
        restoral capabilities of, 204
    mirrored, 206
    SQL, 204
    unmirrored, 206
Service
    level agreements (SLA), 135, 264
    -oriented company, 218
Simple Network Management Protocol,
    211
Situation evaluation, 70
SLA, see Service level agreements
SLC, see Subscriber loop carrier
Socio-technical phenomena, 41
Software
    backup, planning of, 363
    business continuity planning, 92
    costs, 308
    -defined networks, 219
    errors, application, 205
    failure, 205

glitch, 220
inventory, 383
    developing of, 231
    forms, 227
    licenses, 212
    network, 167
    security, 189
    selection criteria, 271
    user-friendly, 299
Spare parts pooling, 213
SQL servers, 204
Stakeholder(s)
    education program, 29
    identifying of, 28
Standard of care, 18
Star topology, 195
Statutes, categories of, 16
Storage, off-site, 212
Stress inoculation, 59
Subscriber loop carrier (SLC), 224
Sungard Recovery Services, Inc., 303
Supervisory Policy Statements, 18
Surge suppressors, 212
Switched digital services, 213
System replication, 287
Systems and communications security,
        during recovery and repair,
        183–192
    prevention during recovery,
        187–188
    recommended course of action,
        192
    security during backup, 187
    security during recovery, 188–191
        communications security,
            189–190
        logical access controls, 190
        physical access control, 188–189
        special security provisions,
            190–191
        transfer of data, 188
    security during repair and
        correction, 191–192
    security and recovery basics,
        184–187

T

Table-t?omuop exercises, 51
Tape library, 342
Tariffed redundancy, 198
Technical service teams, 275
Technical support requirements, 90

Technology, planning, and development
department, representation of
on project team, 80
Telecommunication(s)
backup equipment, 381
capabilities, 319
central site, loss of, 320
personnel, 239
Telephone(s), 71
lines, downed, 362
outages, 359
PBX, 311
Terrorism, 362
Test(ing)
approaches, 259
capabilities, 305
costs, 308
planning matrix, 259
Support Plan (TSP), 382
Testing, of business continuity plans,
273–280
executive management team,
273–275
activating of EMT, 274
operating command center, 274
refining of test process, 275
facility reconstruction team, 278–280
evaluating and documenting of
test results, 279–280
restoring of damaged facility,
278–279
technical service teams, 275–278
data delivery and restoration, 277
evaluating performance, 277–278
mobilizing of technical service
teams, 276
restoring communications,
276–277
setting up of recovery center, 276
Theft, 144
Third-party service providers, 135
T1 networking multiplexer, 200, 201
Tools and management options,
business continuity, 291–302
consultant option, 293–295
assessing consultant's
relationships with vendors,
295
negotiating cost, 294–295
obtaining qualifications, 294
requesting plan proposal, 294
validating proposed time and cost
estimates, 294

criteria for selecting business
continuity planning tools,
297–300
in-house option, 295–296
sources of information on planning
tools, 301
what planning tools do not provide,
301
word processor-driven tools versus
database-driven tools, 296–297
database-driven tools, 297
word processor-driven tools,
296–297
Tornadoes, 73, 105, 359
Toxic contamination, 306
Transportation and amenities
department, consulting of in
forming business continuity
steering committee, 87
Trauma, 73–76
addressing of in planning process, 75
addressing trauma in planning
process, 75
behavior of personnel, 74–75
effects of, 76
trauma created by disruption,
73–74
Trials and tribulations, of business
continuity planning, 109–114
business continuity responsibility,
110–111
business continuity strategy,
111–113
resourcing, 113
risk management approach, 110
TSP, see Test Support Plan

U

Uninterruptible power supply (UPS), 6,
211
devices, 6
systems, 151
UNIX, 204
Unmirrored servers, 206
UPS, see Uninterruptible power
supply
US Federal Reserve System, 291

V

Value Journey technique, 336
Vanilla plan, 26

VAXs, 378, 379
Vendor
    boutique, 304
    computer, 212
    contracts, 91, 257
    hardware, 303
    hot site vendor, choosing of,
        303–315
Virtual organization, 329
Virtual private network (VPN), 286
Vital records, 135
    backup, 334
    program, 82
Voice communications, 232
    breakdown in, 104
    threats to, 220
Volcanoes, 359
VPN, see Virtual private network
Vulnerability assessments, 90

W

Walk-through exercise, 100
WAN, see Wide area network
Warehouse shrinkage, 255
Warm sites, 110, 364
Water and moisture removal, 321
WATS lines, 219
Wide area network (WAN), 183, 211, 251
    facilities, protection of, 198
    ports, multiple, 213
Word processor-driven tools, 296
Work-around strategies, 43
Work backlogs, management of, 110
Work group
    facility, 252
    recovery, 246, 250
    systems, 249
Worst-case disaster, 48

Milton Keynes UK
Ingram Content Group UK Ltd.
UKHW031125141024
449569UK00006B/427